Jonathon Porritt, Founder Director of Forum for the Future, the UK's leading sustainable development charity, is an eminent writer, broadcaster and commentator on sustainable development, and a leading adviser to business and government.

In July 2000, he was appointed by the Prime Minister as Chairman of the new UK Sustainable Development Commission, the Government's principal source of independent advice across the whole sustainable development agenda. He is also Co-director of The Prince of Wales's Business and the Environment Programme, a member of the Board of the South West Regional Development Agency, and a Non-executive Director of Wessex Water. Porritt was formerly Co-chair of the Green Party (1980–83), Director of Friends of the Earth (1984–90), Chairman of UNED-UK (1993–96), Chairman of Sustainability South West (1999–2001) and a Trustee of WWF-UK (1991–2005). Porritt received a CBE in January 2000 for services to environmental protection.

Praise for *Capitalism as if the World Matters*

'The world is on the brink of a vast and mostly unpleasant change that may mark the end of the present civilization. To renew and rebuild, we need to listen to the voices of the few truly selfless and thoughtful individuals among us, and Jonathon Porritt is one of them. His vision is much more optimistic than mine, which sees the need for a massive retreat from all development, sustainable or otherwise, if we are to avoid another dark age on a torrid and mostly uninhabitable Earth.'
James Lovelock, creator of the GAIA theory

'We need more people like Porritt ... prepared to ... find the best ways to save both the environment *and* the capitalist system'
Professional Investor

'Jonathon Porritt's book could not have come at a more timely and critical moment ... A vital contribution to the most compelling issue of our times.'
Will Hutton, author of *The Writing on the Wall: China and the West in the 21st Century*

'No US authors have matched this book's treatment of the interconnections between the environment, finance and economy, industry and technology, psychology and politics. Porritt depicts chilling vignettes, and decries greed and unbridled materialism without impugning business as a whole ... The book, which closes with persuasive philosophical evocations and tactical guidelines, invites and repays detailed study.'
F. T. Manheim, George Mason University, in *Choice*

'... provocative and always interesting manifesto for a society that will not destroy the conditions for its own survival ... he is vigorously passionate in describing the catastrophic dangers of global warming or the unsustainability of the "growth fetish" in current capitalism.'
Steven Poole, *The Guardian*

'This is a genuinely important book by one of Britain's most eminent environmentalists who is also both a realist and, cautiously, an optimist. On our present course, Porritt argues that we are heading towards global catastrophe, but that there is a way of escape. In a challenging but carefully reasoned analysis, he charts a way forward that promises sustainable prosperity within the framework of the global market economy. It is an urgent "must-read" for policy-makers and business leaders who have the power and influence to determine whether we all sink or swim.'
Jonathan Dimbleby, political commentator and broadcaster

'Trade in those lightweight summertime paperbacks for something with a bit more bite. Jonathon Porritt looks at how capitalism could create a future where wealth and ecological integrity aren't mutually exclusive.'
Book of the Week, *Scotland on Sunday*

'As the distillation of unparalleled experience on the frontline and formidable reading, it is the best account of where we are now and how we might move ahead. Porritt's book is a brave and important working draft for an essential positive alternative.'
Simon Caulkin, *The Observer*

'Too many environmentalists see capitalism as the enemy. Porritt grapples with its reality – a system capable of delivering sustainability and enhancing wellbeing, but only if we think carefully about what form of capitalism we want. This book stimulates that thinking.'
Adair Turner, Chair of the Economic and Social Research Council

'This book is excellent, readable, comprehensive and ultimately quite optimistic. Essential reading for anyone interested in the world, the environment, humanity or the future.'
Warmer Bulletin

'All too often, NGOs have to campaign against commercial activities that cause environmental degradation around the world. Our message about unsustainable lifestyles is increasingly understood, but greater thought leadership among business and governments is needed. In this refreshing observation of capitalism, Porritt positions the opportunities provided by sustainable development brilliantly.'
Robert Napier, former Chief Executive, WWF-UK

'As ex-chair of the Green Party, one-time director of Friends of the Earth, and co-founder and Director of Forum for the Future, Porritt is possibly the best person to write a book such as this. The reader can feel confident that his views are based on a desire to create a sustainable future rather than less laudable reasons ... an important factor when dealing with such a revolutionary book.'
Pauline Thomas, *The Waste Paper*

'This is a very thoughtful and timely book. Many of those working towards a more sustainable future for our planet see capitalism as a big part of the problem. And with good reason. But if capitalism and free markets cannot be bent towards sustainability – towards being part of the solution – then I believe there is no solution. Hence the importance of this book. Read it.'
Lord May, President, The Royal Society

'A message that businesses may find they are surprised to agree with.'
Financial Times

'This book may well challenge any Christian environmentalists that see capitalism as the enemy.'
Methodist Recorder

'Here's a compelling book that should sound the trumpet for a whole new generation of engaged and optimistic young people, establishing once and for all that we still have choices – we don't have to sleepwalk our way into the future.'
David Puttnam, film producer and politician

'In this brilliant and timely book Porritt has thrown down the gauntlet and provided the necessary data and analysis on our collective dilemma.'
David Lorimer, *Scientific and Medical Network Review*

'Porritt has applied a decade of experience with business and government to address the dilemma that, while capitalism is the most effective system for satisfying human needs, that process is putting intolerable strains on our ecology and climate. The book is a lively and penetrating discussion of how we can build on growing business interest in the challenges and opportunities.'
Mark Moody-Stuart, Chairman, Anglo American plc

'a significant contribution to sustainable development literature and it deserves the attention of business and political leaders on both sides of the Atlantic.'
Inspire (e-magazine of The European Bahá'í Business Forum)

'Capitalism, like the Tin Man on the Yellow Brick Road, needs to prove it has a heart. Jonathon Porritt, like the Wizard of Oz, is doing his best to help!'
Tim Smit, Chief Executive, The Eden Project

Capitalism
as if the World Matters

Capitalism
as if the World Matters

Jonathon Porritt

London • Sterling, VA

Revised paperback edition first published by Earthscan in the UK and USA in 2007

Hardback edition first published in 2005

ISBN: 978-1-84407-193-7

Typesetting by JS Typesetting Ltd, Porthcawl, Mid Glamorgan
Printed and bound in the UK by Cromwell Press, Trowbridge
Cover design by Susanne Harris

For a full list of publications please contact:
Earthscan
8–12 Camden High Street
London, NW1 0JH, UK
Tel: +44 (0)20 7387 8558
Fax: +44 (0)20 7387 8998
Email: earthinfo@earthscan.co.uk
Web: www.earthscan.co.uk

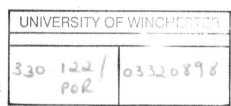
22883 Quicksilver Drive, Sterling, VA 20166-2012, USA

Earthscan publishes in association with the International Institute for
Environment and Development

A catalogue record for this book is available from the British Library

Library of Congress Cataloging-in-Publication Data

Porritt, Jonathon.
Capitalism as if the world matters / Jonathon Porritt. – Rev. paperback ed.
    p. cm.
  Includes index.
  ISBN-13: 978-1-84407-193-7 (pbk.)
  ISBN-10: 1-84407-193-6 (pbk.)
 1. Sustainable development. 2. Capitalism. I. Title.
  HC79.E5P667 2007
  330.12'2–dc22

The paper used for the text pages of this book is
FSC certified. FSC (the Forest Stewardship Council)
is an international network to promote responsible
management of the world's forests.

Mixed Sources
Product group from well-managed
forests and other controlled sources
www.fsc.org Cert no. TT-COC-2082
© 1996 Forest Stewardship Council

for ELEANOR and REBECCA

and for a generation
that depends so much
on our generation
coming to its senses

Contents

PART II – A FRAMEWORK FOR SUSTAINABLE CAPITALISM

Foreword

When my friend Jonathon Porritt asked me to introduce this British book to a largely American audience, I hoped it might build on the foundation of Hawken et al's *Natural Capitalism* (1999). There we laid out a new way of doing business by applying the essence of orthodox capitalism – productive use of and reinvestment in capital – not just to two forms of capital, money and goods, but also to two even more vital ones: people and nature.

Jonathon's important book has not just built on but *expanded* that foundation, synthesizing how to value and revitalize not just four but five or even six kinds of capital (adding social and perhaps spiritual capital to our oversimplified list). Its masterly overview of sustainability, its trenchant critique of environmental politics and its skewering of pathological materialism are all solidly rooted in the moral philosophy of the much-misrepresented Adam Smith.

The book's structure is powerful, its logic clear, its language graceful and its political perspective unapologetic. As well as penetrating insights into their own country, American readers will find here a wealth of valuable British and Continental thought and action that's too little known here.

This book's policy prescriptions reflect the widespread European view that a sound policy framework is indispensable to leading and supporting business. Federal gridlock may rather incline US readers to the view that while government should steer, not row, it usually lags far behind the enormously more dynamic private sector. Working mainly with large firms, co-evolving with civil society, I see extremely fast, accelerating, powerful and exciting shifts, led by business for profit – especially when policy focuses less on proper pricing (helpful though that is) than on 'barrier-busting' so people can respond to price.

Seeking a level of integration rarely attempted, the book's ambitious scope necessarily sacrifices detail for breadth. The challenges posed often do have specific solutions described elsewhere. For example, my own work *Winning the Oil Endgame* (www.oilendgame.com) didn't just claim a solution to the oil problem is valuable and possible, but presented a detailed roadmap for eliminating US oil use by the 2040s. That strategy is now well along in quiet implementation through innovative technologies and competitive strategies; its business logic is proving too compelling to need new national laws, taxes, subsidies or mandates. This makes the peak oil argument irrelevant: nobody can know if it's true, but it doesn't matter, because we should get off oil anyhow, at a cost of one quarter of its current price, just to make money. Similarly, as every practitioner proves daily, climate protection is not costly but profitable, because energy efficiency costs less than the fuel it saves; governments will be the last to know.

Natural Capitalism's analysis of how to wring many times more work from each unit of energy and resources is described by Jonathon as 'hugely optimistic', and the realistic potential is said barely to outpace economic growth. This merits the gentle rebuke that *Natural Capitalism*'s findings are actually proving very conservative. Our recent redesigns of $30 billion worth of facilities in 29 sectors, for example, have consistently found a practical potential for 30–60 per cent energy savings with 2–3-year paybacks in existing facilities, and for 40–90 per cent savings in new ones with nearly always *lower* capital cost. And attentive firms are very profitably cutting their energy intensity by 6–8 per cent per year – several times faster than is needed to stabilize the climate.

Since 1975, even the wasteful US has cut its primary energy consumption per dollar of real GDP by 48 per cent, oil by 54 per cent, directly used natural gas by 64 per cent and water use by slightly more. Yet this just scratches the surface of what's now practical and worthwhile; those savings keep getting ever bigger and cheaper as technologies and design integration improve faster than we apply them.

I therefore feel that efficiency's role in meeting the formidable challenges this book describes has been understated. But that's an empirical question. In a few decades, we'll know whether it was efficiency or other factors – mindful markets, enlightened policies, the grassroots revolution described in Paul Hawken's new book *Blessed Unrest*, a spiritual revival, or others – that ultimately proved decisive. And of course efficiency, though the cheapest, fastest and biggest part of the integrative solution, is only a master key, not the whole toolkit: it can't substitute for many other and complementary methods, any more than technology by itself can triumph without sound policy.

However we get there, Jonathon Porritt has done us all a service by synthesizing a compelling vision of the goals we must steer towards, the main stages of the journey, and how each of us can joyfully bend to our oar. The breadth and incisiveness of his vision oblige us to be grateful, attentive and engaged.

The world does matter. It's all we have. Smarter capitalism can be our most effective tool in making it work, for all, for ever.

Amory B. Lovins
Chairman and Chief Scientist
Rocky Mountain Institute
Snowmass, Colorado
May 2007

Acknowledgements

This book started out as a collaborative enterprise involving a large number of colleagues at Forum for the Future. Having worked hard since our inception in 1996 to operationalize the concept of an economic framework based on five different kinds of capital (natural, human, social, manufactured and financial) through our various partnership schemes, we subsequently felt the need to develop some of the intellectual foundations behind that Framework – a rare example, perhaps, of theory following practice!

That work was done during 2002 and 2003, and particular thanks are due to James Wilsdon for his work on social capital, to Rupert Howes and Brian Pearce for their work on financial capital, to David Bent and David Aeron-Thomas for their work on environmental cost accounting, to Mark Everard and David Cook for their work on manufactured capital, to Martin Wright for his work on security issues and sustainability, and to Peter Price-Thomas and Simon Slater for their work on spiritual capital.

But the real origins of the work go back to discussions between myself and Paul Ekins in the mid-1990s when we were drawing up plans for the organization that would eventually become Forum for the Future. Paul had already done substantial work on the whole question of economic growth and sustainability, and the degree to which the two could be reconciled within a capitalist economy. The idea of using the five different kinds of capital to demonstrate what a genuinely sustainable economy would look like in practice emerged from those discussions, and an internal Forum paper written by Paul in 1997 became the source document for a lot of the work that the Forum has done in this area since then.

I should add that Paul's own book, *Economic Growth and Environmental Sustainability*, has done more to help me get my head around these issues than any other single work.

And there have been many other works over the last couple of years as what started out as a quite self-contained presentation of the Forum's Five Capitals Framework broadened out into an exploration of many other aspects of the economics and politics of sustainability. This book could not have been written without that intellectual feast having been available to me, and I have drawn on it unhesitatingly to lend substance and coherence to my own exploratory journey.

Where I hope I've been able to add something a little different is in the synthesizing of all those different inputs. It is only fair to say, in that context, that for all the guidance I've drawn on from colleagues both within and beyond the Forum, *Capitalism as if the World Matters* is an expression of my own personal views rather than those of Forum for the Future as an organization. It's there that responsibility must lie for any misinterpretations or analytical inadequacies.

FORUM FOR THE FUTURE

Forum for the Future is the UK's leading sustainable development charity. Its mission is to accelerate the change to a sustainable way of life, taking a positive, solutions-oriented approach in everything it does. That mission is shared with partners drawn from business, finance, local authorities, regional bodies and higher education. We communicate what we learn with our partners to a wide network of decision-makers and opinion-formers.

www.forumforthefuture.org.uk

info@forumforthefuture.org.uk

All royalties from the sales of *Capitalism as if the World Matters* are being paid to Forum for the Future to support its ongoing work.

Introduction

The old world is ending, and the new, hesitantly, is emerging. It's a painful process, and it's going to get a lot more painful before it starts getting better. This is not good news for those who believe that the threats to today's dominant model of progress can still be resolved with a few minor economic tweaks and political fixes. But it *is* good news for all those who know that we could be doing something so much more effective in terms of fashioning better lives for the vast majority of people all around the world.

To some, such assertions will sound simply preposterous, given that we've been enjoying the fruits of the triumph of capitalism over communism for little more than twenty years. And the idea of there being some kind of successor to capitalism waiting in the wings is quite understandably dismissed out of hand. But as a citizen of Europe, there's one historical parallel I can't get out of my head. On 11th November 1918, the triumphant allies signed the Armistice with a crushed and humiliated Germany. On 1st September 1939, Hitler invaded Poland, and the world was cast once more into devastating war. The analogy may be somewhat stretching, but twenty years after the collapse of the Berlin Wall, a triumphalist axis of capitalist nations has so profoundly mismanaged and abused its triumph that something much, much worse than the Cold War it brought an end to now looms in our midst.

Hearing that, you may wish to read no further! But this is not just another eco-tract predicting the end of everything we hold dear, if not the end of life on Earth itself. After 35 years banging on about the need for radical change, I'm more optimistic now than I've ever been. There's so much to be hugely hopeful about – technologically, politically, spiritually.

To justify such improbable optimism, I've had to go way back beyond the symptoms of today's disordered world to investigate the root causes of that disorder, and to remind people that capitalism has always been a self-correcting system, capable of startling and seemingly 'unthinkable' shifts at precisely the moment when those shifts are most needed. This investigation has led me to the conclusion that it is indeed still possible for capitalism today to self-correct (or, more accurately, to be corrected) before traumatic collapse.

For all who believe, as I do, that market-based, properly regulated capitalism is still capable of meeting today's daunting challenges, that's our best hope. But this is no easy path. Anything vaguely resembling 'business-as-usual' is no less than a death warrant for the highest ideals of contemporary civilization. And that means we have to dig down a lot deeper than today's superficial, febrile political debates seem inclined to do. Václav Havel, former President of Czechoslovakia and one of the wisest commentators on the lessons to be learned from the collapse of communism, has tirelessly pointed out that 'without a global revolution in the sphere of human consciousness, nothing will change for the better'.

And we will indeed need to engineer tomorrow's world, step by step, with great determination. It won't just happen by chance. The world we live in today is not unplanned; it's the way it is because that's the way earlier political elites wanted it to be. Track back to those extraordinary years after the Second World War where massive entrepreneurial energy was unleashed, particularly in the United States and Europe. In *good faith, without so much as an inkling of today's 'sustainability crunch', the goal was to liberate people the world over (and not just in the rich world) through increased consumption. This 1948 quote from Victor Lebow, one of the most creative retail analysts of that post-war era, will shock people today but was seen then as both visionary and progressive:*

> *Our enormously productive economy demands that we make consumption our way of life, that we convert the buying and use of goods into rituals, that we seek our spiritual satisfaction, our ego satisfaction, in consumption. We need things consumed, burned up, worn out, replaced and discarded at an ever-increasing rate.'*

Sixty years on, this process of 'manufacturing desire' has proved to be massively successful. But two 'unintended consequences' now imperil everything we may aspire to in the future. First, politicians and wealth creators have so successfully risen to Lebow's challenge that the biological foundations of our human civilization are now at risk. Second, that success has enriched so minute a percentage of humankind that even if the world wasn't about to implode physically, it certainly is economically, even in the world's richest countries. For instance, the top 10 per cent of Americans today own 70 per cent of net US wealth, and the top 5 per cent more than everyone else put together. The average CEO in the US today earns in one day what an average worker earns in a year. This is *America* we're talking about, the nation that has made a bigger difference to the world's 'poor and needy', and offered more hope to the world's disenfranchised, than any other country on Earth. Tragically, however, the US today, at this dreadful moment in its eventful history, represents the biggest threat to everything the US once stood for.

Today's lethal cocktail of environmental, social and security issues poses an unprecedented challenge to world leaders. But I'm always slightly startled by the number of my colleagues, in both the US and Europe, who believe it's already too late to pull things back from the brink even if we wanted to. I shall examine the pros and cons of that case, particularly as it relates to climate change, in much more detail at different points in the book. However, in terms of what we would need to do to restore the Earth's basic life-support systems (soils, forests, fresh water, grazing land, biodiversity, fisheries, etc.), this is in fact much more manageable than most people realize, with an asking price that is probably no more than US$100 billion, according to Lester Brown, President of the Earth Policy Institute in Washington.

Does that sound too much? Astonishingly reasonable? What's your benchmark? Perhaps it would help to know that $100 billion is less than 10 per cent of the $1.6 trillion that is reckoned to end up every year in offshore tax havens, beyond the reach of any government, as a result of capital flight, widespread and often endemic corruption, and tax avoidance of every conceivable description (mostly legal). Our world is in fact rich beyond most people's wildest imagination, yet only the tiniest imaginable percentage of that wealth plays any part at all in securing a decent, dignified, sustainable life for the majority of people today.

Capitalism has always had its contradictions, but tax avoidance and 'off-shoring' on this scale warps the very foundations of market capitalism. When people like George Soros and even Zbigniew Brzezinski (a redoubtable neo-conservative who helped shape US foreign policy throughout the 1970s and 80s) begin to warn of a potential implosion in the system as a consequence of today's 'global political awakening around social injustice', then it's probably time to sit up and listen.

There's an interesting correlation here between climate change and poverty. Many scientists today are focused on the possibility of what is called 'non-linear climate change', where the *gradual* build-up of manmade greenhouse gases in the atmosphere leads not to a *gradual* increase in average temperatures, followed by a *gradual* increase in the severity of climate-related events, but rather to a dramatic ('non-linear') step-change in the climate. This hypothesis is underpinned by findings from ice cores in both the Arctic and the Antarctic which show earlier sea level rises of several metres in a single century. About 14,000 years ago, for example, sea levels rose approximately 20 metres over the course of 400 years, or about 1 metre every 20 years.

Far fewer people look to the possibility of 'non-linear social change' as a con-sequence of the very deep-seated, and still gradually worsening, levels of inequity in society. We'll see later that research today shows that nearly 60 per cent of people live in countries where the gap between rich and poor is still getting bigger, not narrowing. As with climate change, the effects of this are often indirect, diffuse, long-term; there's always something more pressing for politicians to deal with, and NIMTO (Not In My Term of Office) mindsets tend to prevail. But we've see many examples of 'non-linear social change' in the past, most recently with the collapse of communism and the Iron Curtain in central Europe in the 1980s, over a remarkably short period of time. So just how unequal will things need to get before political instabilities and other knock-on consequences bring about further non-linear change?

For the best part of ten years, I have been fortunate enough to end up working with a large number of people at senior level in both government and business – through Forum for the Future, the UK Sustainable Development Commission and the Prince of Wales's Business and the Environment Programme – who are increasingly open to seeking answers to those difficult questions. Although it is, of course, possible that the wool is being pulled over my eyes by all of these people all of the time, my overwhelming impression is that more and more of them are now intent upon seriously pushing forward with more sustainable ways of doing their jobs. These are not radical people. They are not activists. They would not dream of looking for change outside the system: if it can't be made to happen inside the system, then for them it just won't work. Given the urgency now required, both the length of time it takes to get the basics sorted and the extraordinary reluctance to take any real risks remain hugely frustrating – but it is still the case that almost all key policy processes continue to move slowly in the right direction.

And that, of course, means that the emerging solutions have to be fashioned within the embrace of capitalism. Like it or not (and the vast majority of people *do*), capitalism is now the only economic show in town. The drive to extend the reach of markets into every aspect of every economy is an irresistible force, and the benefits of today's globalization process are still held by a substantial majority of people to outweigh the costs – however serious those costs may be, as we shall see. The adaptability and inherent strengths of market-based, for-profit economic systems have proved themselves time after time, and there will be few reading this book who are not the direct beneficiaries of those systems.

It's as well to acknowledge both the power and the enduring appeal of capitalism up front. Much of what follows will seek to harness the strengths of that system to the pursuit of sustainable development, while simultaneously challenging our dependence upon *today's* particular model of capitalism. For fear of arriving at a different conclusion, there is a widespread though largely unspoken assumption that there need be no fundamental contradiction between sustainable development and capitalism. That assumption will be rigorously tested in Part I, as will the relationship between most governments' good intentions on sustainable development and the prevailing political and economic framework through which they seek to deliver on those good intentions.

Sustainable development is still a relatively young and unfinished concept, and has had to establish itself over the last 20 years or so at precisely the time when those political philosophies which would have given it more space (social democracy and democratic socialism) have surrendered the field to today's dominant, neo-liberal free market ideology. Organizations and individuals championing sustainable development as a radically different model of progress for humankind have had their work cut out simply trying to mitigate the worst externalities of today's global economy. There has been little time or opportunity to map out more positive visions of what a sustainable world would look like, to stop hammering on and on about the *necessity* of change and start focusing instead upon the *desirability* of change in terms of improved quality of life, greater security, and more fulfilled ways of working and living. We are so preoccupied with avoiding nightmares in the future that we have pretty much given up on offering our dreams of a better world today.

Capitalism as if the World Matters sets out to address that imbalance. It does so on the basis of a new political convergence that I believe is beginning to emerge around the twin concepts of *sustainability* and *wellbeing*. Governments around the world are now struggling to reconcile the legitimate material aspirations of their citizens with the need to protect the natural environment far more effectively than we have been able to do until now. They would, of course, prefer it if there were no such environmental constraints; but the costs of mismanaging our natural capital are now so great as to demand a new and lasting resolution to this long-running dilemma.

At the same time, though even less purposefully, governments are beginning to wake up to the problems of trying to achieve *everything* via the medium of constant economic growth. As we'll see in Chapter 3, growth clearly provides the wherewithal for delivering many of the improvements that people ask of their governments (better public services, security, renewed infrastructure and so on), as well as many of the material benefits that people seek through increased personal wealth and consumption. But it also gives rise to substantial social and environmental costs, and does not appear to be making people any happier or any more contented with their lot in life. So should governments be shifting the focus more towards the promotion of wellbeing and contentment, rather than towards economic growth per se?

The problem is that economies are now so geared towards year-on-year increases in personal consumption (partly in order to keep business growth buoyant and tax revenues flowing) that politicians are extremely reluctant even to question this particular paradigm of progress. At the same time, companies have been equally hostile to the notion that people might actually be better off by consuming *less*, and see any such discourse as a direct attack on the self-evident benefits of free market economics. For many business people over the last fifteen years, this has positioned sustainable development in the wrong psychological boxes – the ones labelled 'regulation and red tape', 'constraint on business', 'increased costs' or 'high risks'. Only during the last few years have we seen the other boxes – labelled 'opportunity', 'innovation', 'increased market share' and 'stronger brands' – opening up in such a way as to provide wealth creators with an entirely different and far more positive proposition. Given the dominant role of business in the world today, this particular mindset transition is critically important: however necessary or desirable something may be, it is unlikely to obtain the necessary traction in today's world unless the business community can be persuaded and inspired to get behind it.

Opportunity is, thus, the third key element in the case made for a rapid transition to a very different variant of capitalism: capitalism as if the world matters.

The politics of sustainability makes change *necessary*: we literally don't have any choice unless we want to see the natural world collapse around us, and with it our dreams of a better world for humankind. The politics of wellbeing makes change *desirable*: we really do have a choice in finding better ways of improving people's lives than those we are currently relying upon. And responding to both those challenges will generate extraordinary opportunities for the wealth creators of the future. When something is both necessary and desirable, and can be pitched to demanding electorates in terms of both *opportunity* and *progress*, then it becomes politically viable – and that's the threshold that I believe we have now, at long last, reached.

PART I

OUR UNSUSTAINABLE WORLD

1

Conflicting Imperatives

INTRODUCTION

Wouldn't it be great if any book dealing with sustainability could open with a resolutely upbeat account of the state of the planet? But that's just not possible – not in this decade, at least. As this chapter confirms, things *are* going from bad to worse, and they'll get worse yet. Despite a growing number of countervailing success stories, almost all of the trends are still heading in the wrong direction.

There is no mystery here: burgeoning human numbers, a spectacularly vibrant, consumption-driven economy, and a continuing inability to accept that there really are natural limits, make for a lethal combination. But no politician can currently gainsay that drive for increased prosperity – offering people more (at almost any cost) – has become the number one political imperative. The resulting impasse poses the greatest challenge we face today: we know that change is necessary, but that doesn't necessarily make it desirable. Nevertheless, this chapter ends with a brief and optimistic account of what it would be like to live in a more sustainable world, just to show how close that already is to most people's idea of a better life.

THE ASSAULT ON NATURE

At the start of the 21st century, our lives are bounded by two very different and *potentially* irreconcilable imperatives. The first is a biological imperative: to learn to live sustainably on this planet. This is an *absolute* imperative in that it is determined by the laws of nature and, hence, is non-negotiable – this side of extinction, it permits no choice. The second is a political imperative: to aspire to improve our material standard of living year on year. This is a *relative* imperative in that it is politically determined, with a number of alternative economic paradigms available to us. These imperatives are therefore very different in both kind and degree.

The need to find some reconciliation between these imperatives has never been more urgent. The world has been completely transformed over the last 60 years, with a combination of rapid population growth and massively increased economic activity (driven by access to relatively cheap sources of coal, oil and gas) exacting a harsh and continuing toll on the physical environment.

It has become fashionable in some quarters to disparage this kind of sweeping assertion. Predominantly right-wing media in the US and the UK have taken to their hearts a succession of dissenting scientists and commentators anxious to reassure people that the environmental and social problems we face today are not nearly as serious as environmental activists and poverty campaigners make out.

Accusations of exaggeration and scaremongering abound. Given that environmentalists started talking in these apocalyptic terms back in the 1970s, how is it that there has been no hint of any terminal breakdown during the last 30 years? The understandable consequence of this barrage of complacency is that many people really don't know who to trust in terms of gauging just how serious things are, especially on issues such as climate change (to which I will return at the end of this chapter) where the ongoing controversies about both the science and the politics are at their fiercest.

Yet, these days, most of the information about the state of the physical environment (and, indeed, about the state of people living in the world's poorest countries) comes from government departments, the United Nations (UN) or other international agencies, and independent academics. Non-governmental organizations (NGOs) are rarely involved in commissioning original research, and concentrate primarily upon disseminating and interpreting the data that comes into the public domain from official sources. With the best will in the world, I find it very difficult to explain how these official sources might have been subverted to falsify information, peddle untruths or generally seek to play games with the general public by exaggerating the seriousness of today's environmental dilemmas. For most environmentalists, this continuing denial on the part of 'contrarians' such as Bjorn Lomborg (2001) is but the last gasp of a 40-year endeavour to make out that all is well with the world, even as our impact upon it grows exponentially year on year.

It may be helpful to briefly review the official position on some of these key environmental problems. In country after country, the data reveals a similar state of affairs: we are continuing to destroy natural habitats of every kind through conversion for human purposes. More than half of the world's original forest area has been lost and one third of what is left will be gone in the next 20 years at current rates of deforestation. A report from the Food and Agriculture Organization (FAO) in March 2007 (FAO, 2007) described the destruction of forests in the developing world as being 'out of control'. Africa lost more than 9 per cent of its trees between 1990 and 2005; the world as a whole lost another 3 per cent of its total forest area. An even larger proportion of original wetlands has been destroyed, and more than one third of the world's coral reefs are either dead or severely damaged. Not surprisingly, this habitat destruction has had a huge impact upon wild species, with various estimates of loss of biodiversity from the World Conservation Union (IUCN) and other international bodies a source of intense concern. This situation has often been exacerbated by the impact of alien species on many indigenous ecosystems, with billions of dollars now being spent across the world on control and eradication programmes.

This litany of bio-devastation has been shouted out so often that it's clear politicians have simply switched off on hearing it. After the relative failure of the 1992 Convention on Biological Diversity, and the near silence that greeted publication of the Millennium Ecosystem Assessment report (MA; see below), perhaps we should be rethinking our entire approach to biodiversity. In July 2006, leading biologists from around the world called for the creation of a new international body for biodiversity to match the impact of the Intergovernmental Panel on Climate Change (IPCC) – for whatever you may think about the IPCC's overall impact, it has compelled governments to take the advice of their scientific institutions far more seriously than they would otherwise have done. And with a 'potentially catastrophic loss of species' now unfolding in front of our eyes, the IPCC's Fourth Assessment Report (IPCC, 2007) couldn't possibly have contained worse news: up to 30 per cent of all plant and animal species are likely to be at increased risk of extinction if global temperatures rise by more than 2°C.

In terms of managed (rather than wild) areas, we have seen little improvement in management techniques over the last two decades. Soil erosion is a chronic problem in many parts of the world, as is salinization, often caused by hugely wasteful and poorly designed irrigation schemes. There are different estimates as to the collective impact of all this upon farmland, but the UN FAO believes that a minimum of 20 per cent of total cultivated acreage is now seriously damaged. Overgrazing of grasslands has resulted in a similar loss of productivity in literally dozens of countries.

More recently, there has also been growing concern about freshwater impacts, both in terms of quantity (with severe water shortages now affecting a large number of countries) and quality, as both rivers and groundwater aquifers are increasingly affected by diffuse pollution of many different kinds. It is true that river quality has often improved substantially in many Organisation for Economic Co-operation and Development (OECD) countries during the last decade through much tighter regulation and a growing reluctance to allow companies to use rivers and streams as their private sewers. But the situation continues to worsen in most developing countries. The same is true with local air quality.

When the will is there, it has occasionally proved possible to get on top of major environmental problems. Quite rightly, the phasing out of gases such as chlorofluorocarbons (CFCs) that were having such a damaging impact upon the protective ozone layer in the upper atmosphere is seen as one of the most effective examples of international diplomacy working to protect the environment and people's health. But even here, we're not exactly out of the woods. There is a thriving black market in banned CFCs, and growing resistance in the US and elsewhere to further measures to phase out other ozone-depleting substances such as methyl bromide. The United Nations Environment Programme (UNEP) still reminds politicians that it is likely to be another 40 years before levels of ozone in the atmosphere are restored to where they were during the 1980s.

One of the biggest problems in all of these areas is that the deterioration is usually incremental, acre by acre, town by town, pollution incident by pollution incident, species by species – and hence all but invisible to people living in the midst of this progressive decline. The position in any one year may not be much worse than in the preceding year, but go back 30 or 40 years and the changes are stark. It is death by a thousand cuts, rather than by some traumatic shock to the system which would be far harder for citizens and politicians to ignore.

Nowhere is this demonstrated more clearly than in the MA released in April 2005 (MA, 2005). This extraordinary study took four years to compile, involving hundreds of scientists all over the world, assessing literally thousands of peer-reviewed papers covering the principal aspects of the relationship between ourselves and the natural world, and bringing those findings together in a single, extremely powerful analysis. Its principal focus is on what are known as 'ecosystem services' – in other words, the benefits that we humans obtain from different ecosystems.

The MA describes 'services' in four categories: 'provisioning services', such as food, water, timber and fibre; 'regulating services', which affect climate, flood control, disease, waste and water quality; 'cultural services', which provide recreational, aesthetic and spiritual benefits; and 'supporting services', such as soil formation, photosynthesis and nutrient cycling. This serves to remind us, however buffered against the impact of environmental damage we may think we are through new technology, that we are still fundamentally dependent upon the constant and reliable flow of ecosystem services to secure our own wellbeing. The MA identifies the essential constituents of human wellbeing as having access to the basic materials for a good life (such as food, shelter and clothing), sound health, good social relations, security, and freedom of choice and action, and its overall conclusions are deeply disconcerting:

- Over the past 50 years, humans have changed ecosystems more rapidly and extensively than in any comparable period of time in human history, primarily in order to meet rapidly growing demands for food, freshwater, timber, fibre and fuel. This has resulted in a substantial and largely irreversible loss in the diversity of life on Earth.
- The changes that have been made to ecosystems have contributed to substantial net gains in human wellbeing and economic development; but these gains have been achieved at growing costs in the form of the degradation of many ecosystem services.
- Approximately 60 per cent (15 out of 24) of the ecosystem services examined are being degraded or used unsustainably, including freshwater, fisheries, air

and water purification, and the regulation of regional and local climate, natural hazards, and pests.

- The full costs of the loss and degradation of these ecosystem services are difficult to measure, but the available evidence demonstrates that they are substantial and growing.
- The harmful effects of this degradation are being borne disproportionately by the poor, are contributing to growing inequities and disparities across groups of people, and are sometimes the principal factor causing poverty and social conflict.
- The degradation of ecosystem services is already a significant barrier to achieving the Millennium Development Goals, and the harmful consequences of this could grow significantly worse during the next 50 years.
- There is established but incomplete evidence that changes being made in ecosystems are increasing the likelihood of *non-linear* changes in ecosystems (including accelerating, abrupt and potentially irreversible changes) that have important consequences for human wellbeing.

Blind optimism in the face of such a litany of continuing destruction and mismanagement is a strange phenomenon. It is premised on the hope that the planet's self-healing capacity remains resilient enough to weather these constant assaults, despite growing evidence of irreversibility in terms of lost productivity and diversity. There is something deeply unhistorical about this cornucopian optimism, as if there wasn't a robust body of evidence available to us – captured authoritatively in Clive Ponting's *A Green History of the World* (1991) and, more recently, in Jared Diamond's *Collapse* (2005) – demonstrating that there really are 'points of no return' when ecosystems are systematically overexploited and abused. A rather more historical perspective would be helpful in all sorts of ways.

Over the last 550 million years, there have been five mass extinctions on planet Earth, the last one just 65 million years ago when the dinosaurs disappeared. For one reason or another (meteor or asteroid impact, dramatic climate change, volcanic or other planetary traumas, or the normal process of speciation and extinction as evolution unfolded), most life-forms that have appeared on planet Earth have turned out to be unsustainable. We are the first species (as far as we know) that is able to reflect upon where we have come from and where we are headed. We are, therefore, able to conceptualize the necessary conditions for our own survival as a species and, in the light of that understanding, so shape our living patterns in order to optimize our survival chances.

It is only in the last few decades that our survival as a species has become an issue. Slowly, painfully, we are coming to realize that there is nothing automatic or guaranteed about our continued existence. If we don't learn to live sustainably within the natural systems and limits that provide the foundation for *all* life-forms, then we will go the same way as every other life-form that failed to adapt to those changing systems and limits. Deep down in our collective psyche, after hundreds of years of industrialization that systematically suppressed a proper understanding of our continuing and total dependency upon the natural world, that atavistic reality is beginning to resurface.

All else depends upon this. If we can't secure our own biophysical survival, then it is game over for every other noble aspiration or venal self-interest that we may entertain. With great respect to those who assert the so-called 'primacy' of key social and economic goals (such as the elimination of poverty or the attainment of universal human rights), it must be said loud and clear that these are *secondary* goals: all else is conditional upon learning to live sustainably within the Earth's systems and limits. Not only is the pursuit of biophysical sustainability non-negotiable; it's preconditional.

Having said that, these are really two sides of the same coin. On the one hand, social sustainability is entirely dependent upon ecological sustainability. As we continue to undermine nature's capacity to provide humans with essential services (such as clean water, a stable climate and so on) and resources (such as food and raw materials), both individuals and nation states will be subjected to growing amounts of pressure. Conflict will grow, and threats to public health and personal safety will increase in the face of ecological degradation.

On the other hand, ecological sustainability is entirely dependent upon social sustainability. With a growing number of people living within social systems that constrain their ability to meet their needs, it becomes increasingly difficult to protect the natural environment. Forests are cleared to make way for land-hungry farmers; grazing lands are overstocked, aquifers depleted, rivers over-fished; and the rest of nature is driven back into ever smaller reserves or natural parks.

Fortunately, all species have a deep survival instinct. Ultimately, they do everything they can to secure their own survival chances. And that is as true of humans as it is of the Siberian tiger or the lowliest of bacteria. We humans have now coined a name for our survival instinct: it's called 'sustainable development', which means, quite simply, living on this planet as if we intended to go on living here forever.

With the publication of Rachel Carson's *Silent Spring* in 1962, it started to dawn on people that in order to generate rising prosperity we have been literally laying waste the planet, tearing down forests, damming rivers, polluting the air, eroding topsoil, warming the atmosphere, depleting fish stocks, and covering more and more land with concrete and tarmac. And as our numbers grow, by an additional 75 million or so a year, the pressures on the planet and its life-support systems (upon which *all* species depend, including ourselves) continue to mount year by year. We can no longer go on ignoring the challenge of biophysical sustainability.

ECONOMIC PROSPERITY

Even as we witness this reality unfolding in front of our eyes, it seems that we have no choice in the rich world but to seek to go on getting richer. On current projections, the global economy will grow from around $60 trillion today to around $240 trillion by 2050. Historians will reflect upon the fact that the current model of progress, premised on year-on-year increases in material prosperity, can only be traced back a couple of centuries; life without any expectation of increased prosperity has, in fact, been the historical norm. And anthropologists might point to the Kalahari Bushmen or other indigenous people as living proof that constant improvements in our material standard of living are not a *necessary* condition of human existence.

Environmentalists argue that the pursuit of increased prosperity is a second-order political aspiration rather than a first-order imperative, and should in no way be set alongside the pursuit of sustainability – a point to which we return later. Exponents of the art of 'voluntary simplicity' (maximizing one's quality of life while minimizing one's dependence upon a wasteful, energy-intensive standard of living) point to the falsehood that increased prosperity automatically leads to a higher quality of life. And adherents of the world's leading religions are able to call upon concepts such as 'right livelihood' or warnings about camels passing through eyes of needles to demonstrate that God and Mammon still inhabit different spheres.

That's all well and good; but the vast majority of people alive today both want to be better off themselves and want their children (if they have them) to be better off than them. This would appear to be as true of citizens in the world's richest nations as of those in the poorest.

There are clearly enormous differences in different people's material aspirations, however. Although there is still serious poverty in almost all OECD countries, what are defined as 'basic human needs' are now largely met in those countries. But as far back as 1930, John Maynard Keynes pointed out that our *absolute* wants (those which we feel regardless of our relative position in society) are limited and finite; it is our *relative* wants (those which we feel in comparison to what others have in society) that are apparently insatiable – and it is these relative wants that keep the wheels of our growth machine spinning merrily away.

This is eloquently summarized in the United Nations Development Programme's (UNDP's) *Human Development Report*, published in September 2005. It describes progress as 'depressingly slow', despite some encouraging signs – an extra 30 million children in school, child deaths cut by 3 million a year, overall life expectancy up by two years, and so on. But more than 460 million people now live in countries with a *lower score* on the Human Development Index (HDI) than in 1990 – an 'unprecedented reversal', as the report puts it.

> *In the midst of an increasingly prosperous global economy, 10.7 million children every year do not live to see their fifth birthday, and more than 1 billion people survive in abject poverty on less than $1 a day. One fifth of humanity live in countries where many people think nothing of spending $2 a day on a cappuccino. Another fifth of humanity survive on less than a dollar a day, and live in countries where children die for want of a simple anti-mosquito bed net.* (UNDP, 2005)

Reaffirming that 'deep-rooted inequality is at the heart of the problem', the report pointedly comments that for every $1 spent on aid in rich countries, $10 is spent on arms and military expenditure. Just the *increase* in defence spending since 2000, if devoted to aid instead, would have been sufficient to reach the UN's target of 0.7 per cent of Gross Domestic Product (GDP) being devoted to international aid. It concludes: 'this development disaster is as avoidable as it is predictable'.

In rich countries and poor countries alike, though with different justifications, it is the pursuit of greater prosperity that drives the political process. Those who claim that many people, deep down, know that increased prosperity won't necessarily make them happier may well be right. But that is not the way they vote. Those who inveigh against today's 'ideological vacuum' (where the pursuit of economic growth has become an all too inadequate surrogate for real politics) may do so with overwhelming justification. But such protestations would appear to count for little across the political scene as a whole.

It was, after all, 35 years ago that two of the world's most eminent economists, William Nordhaus and James Tobin, published a landmark study criticizing the use of Gross National Product (GNP) as the sole indicator of economic progress: '... maximization of GNP is not a proper policy objective. Economists all know that, and yet their everyday use of GNP as the standard measure of economic performance conveys the impression that they are evangelistic worshippers of GNP.' Yet mainstream economists have done next to nothing over those 35 years to challenge the illegitimate ascendancy of GNP, with paralysing consequences for policy-making at every level – as we will see in Chapter 3.

Francis Fukuyama was clearly a little premature when he asserted that the demise of communism heralded 'the end of history'. Nothing lasts forever, and there's little doubt that viable alternatives to capitalism (or, at least, a very different model of capitalism) will emerge over time. The question is 'when' not 'whether', and in which direction. In mapping out the kind of transformation that I believe is now both necessary and desirable, I will be emphasizing the potential of a 'soft landing' for contemporary capitalism, seizing hold of the wealth of opportunity entailed in fashioning genuinely sustainable livelihoods for the 9 billion people with whom we will be sharing this planet by the middle of the century.

Capitalism is a complex, adaptive system, and is clearly capable of profound and rapid shifts. Even those who do not share my views have good reason to be concerned about the durability of this particular model of capitalism. A combination of different factors – the deregulation of cross-border capital flows; the emergence of currency trading on an unprecedented scale in today's 'casino economy'; increased liberalization exerting downward pressure on wages and prices; growing disparities in wealth both within and between countries; extraordinarily high levels of debt in so many countries and particularly in the US; oil trading at around $70 dollars a barrel – makes the maintenance of our current global economy look like an extremely dangerous high-wire act, with the prospects of a vertiginous collapse ever more likely.

Indeed, many of today's most trenchant critics of global capitalism believe that the collapse of capitalism could be upon us far sooner than anyone anticipates, often summoning up the analogy of the dramatic collapse of communism in a manner and at a time that defied all of the prognostications of the world's smartest think-tanks and academics. And the collapse of global capitalism, it is often argued, would usher in more self-reliant, compassionate and sustainable economies, with none of today's frenetic consumerism or aggressive self-interest.

Looking at the state of the world today, this seems an improbable scenario, both in its assumption of a rapid rather than a long-term transition, and in its assumption that such a transition would be benign. Whatever personal or ideological sympathy one may feel for these alternatives, prevailing geopolitical reality would seem to indicate a very different prospect – in which the process of globalization accelerates still further, the phenomenon of mass denial continues as the majority of people in the world today continue to press for improvements in their material standard of living, and 'reform from within' remains the most realistic of all of the political options available.

For anyone concerned about sustainability, such *realpolitik* is extraordinarily challenging on two counts. First, the reconciliation (in part or in whole) of these two imperatives (sustainability and increased prosperity) must therefore be achieved through market-based systems in predominantly capitalist economies. By implication, the more 'market friendly' any proposed reform may be, the greater the likelihood of its adoption. Yet, as we will see, many of the changes that are now required can only be twisted to fit these market disciplines with great difficulty.

Second, it means that measures to achieve reconciliation must win widespread political acceptance within the democratic systems that set the boundaries for those economic markets. They cannot be imposed against the wishes of an electorate; they must be agreed to be either necessary or desirable (and preferably both) given the nature of the challenge we now face. What is more, the public policy measures required to achieve that level of democratic ownership are unlikely to come about through a simple return to the tried and tested precepts of 'top–down' social democracy. As Tom Bentley, former Director of the UK think-tank Demos, says:

The values of individualism, diversity and open exchange, which have been fought for over centuries, have won out in the modern world. They are embodied in the structure of capitalism, which now constitutes the only viable possibility for organizing economies. This combination of forces will not go away: the impulse to personal choice and freedom of expression is more deep-rooted than any specific political project and has a long way to run. It is aided and fuelled by the progress of consumer capitalism, which systematically promotes the idea that the use of individual purchasing power to make lifestyle choices creates fulfilment since such choices are the key engine of capitalism's growth and renewal. (Bentley, 2002)

That puts the highest possible premium on political leadership in an age when such leadership seems more and more elusive. As we will see in Chapter 3, ecological reality is usually ignored if it is identified as any kind of serious barrier to increased material prosperity. Nowhere has this been more evident than in the response of the US to the phenomenon of climate change. Its basic rule of thumb was definitively mapped out by George Bush senior when he arrived at the 1992 Earth Summit in Rio de Janeiro, warning all and sundry that 'the American way of life' was not up for grabs in the negotiations around the United Nations Framework Convention on Climate Change (UNFCCC). The US did, eventually, sign up to the Convention; but that was the last positive thing it has done on the international climate change agenda since that time.

OUR CHANGING CLIMATE

Since the first edition of *Capitalism as if the World Matters* came out in 2005, by far the most dramatic change has been the shift in global opinion on climate change. Indeed, interest in and coverage of climate change is now so widespread that some protagonists of sustainable development as an overarching framework feel that this bigger picture is being eclipsed by an almost exclusive focus on climate change. However, as proxies go, climate change is about as good as it gets in terms of understanding the degree to which today's dominant political and business models are becoming less and less relevant in such a rapidly changing world.

Until now, however, the politics of climate change has been a slow, frustrating process. Serious concern first surfaced in the 1970s, slowly gathering momentum through until the late 1980s, when the debate in the US really took off after three years of extremely severe drought. That led directly to the original UNFCCC, agreed at the Earth Summit in Rio de Janeiro in 1992 and ratified in 1995 by 189 nations – including the US. Those nations all signed up to the goal of 'stabilization of greenhouse gas concentrations in the atmosphere, at levels that would prevent dangerous anthropogenic interference with the climate system'. Since then, no specific limit has been set, and the Americans spent the next ten years trying to prevent the Kyoto Protocol (the first legally binding agreement emerging from the UNFCCC) getting off the ground. Fortunately, they failed in this endeavour, and the Protocol came into force on 16 February 2005.

The hard evidence that our climate is already changing as a consequence of emissions of carbon dioxide (CO_2) and other greenhouse gases had been getting firmer and firmer during that time. Computer models of what *might* happen have come increasingly in line with what *is* happening; even the US Administration now accepts that the 0.6°C warming that has occurred since the middle of the last century is, 'in all probability', the direct consequence of man-made emissions – a huge step forward in terms of the US beginning to acknowledge the scale of the problem.

All around the world, people are witnessing climate change for themselves in terms of extreme weather events or natural phenomena 'out of sync' (for instance, early flowering of trees and plants, or egg-laying in birds); and scientists are tracking in enormous detail the shrinkage of glaciers, the thawing out of the permafrost, the accelerated melting of ice sheets in both the Arctic and the Antarctic, and the late freezing and earlier break-up of ice on rivers and lakes. *High Tide* by Mark Lynas (2004) records the very personal accounts of the impact of changing weather and seasons upon the lives of people in China, the Pacific, Peru, Alaska and elsewhere. Behind the dry scientific data are the real-life stories of people already devastated by a phenomenon too many of us still think of as one of those problems for tomorrow, not today:

> *If there's one message above all that I want people to take from these pages, it's this: that all the impacts described here are just the first whispers of the hurricane of future climate change which is now bearing down on us. Like the canary in the coal mine, those who live closest to the land – the Eskimos in Alaska and the Pacific islanders – have been the first to notice. But they won't be alone for long. As I suspected when I first began to undertake this mission, the first signs are evident to anyone who chooses to look.* (Lynas, 2004).

Courtesy of the IPCC, we now know a lot more about the scale of this 'hurricane of future climate change'. Its Fourth Assessment Report in February 2007 laid it on the line for politicians still prevaricating in the face of residual uncertainty:

- CO_2 levels at their highest for 650,000 years;
- Climate change 'unequivocally' happening;
- 90 per cent certain that it's due to man-made emissions;
- 10–15 years to put in place serious measures to start reducing emissions of CO_2;

- 'Best guess' indicates global temperature will rise by 1.8°C to 4°C by 2100;
- Worst case 'indicates up to 6.4°C';
- Policy responses geared to hold temperature increase below 2°C; and
- Urgent need to agree on global stabilization target for CO_2 and other greenhouse gases.

True enough, 90 per cent isn't 100 per cent, and a small number of dissenting scientists (many of them funded directly or indirectly by US corporations, and by the oil industry in particular) continue to give the impression that the science of climate change is still hotly contested and that no real consensus exists. When the science historian Naomi Oreskes analysed the 928 peer-reviewed papers on climate change published between 1993 and 2003, she came to the very different conclusion that today's consensus is almost universal: 'politicians, economists, journalists and others may have the impression of confusion, disagreement and discord among climate scientists, but that impression is incorrect' (Oreskes, 2004). In *An Inconvenient Truth*, Al Gore (2006) graphically captures the stark disparity between what scientists have concluded and what media commentators make of these conclusions:

> *Number of peer-reviewed articles dealing with climate change*
> *published in scientific journals during the previous 10 years:*   *928*
>
> *Percentage of articles in doubt as to the cause of global warming:* *0%*
>
> *Articles in the US popular press about global warming during*
> *the previous 14 years:*   *636*
>
> *Percentage of articles in doubt as to the cause of global warming: 53%*

A particularly galling example of this hit the news both in the UK and the US when a one-off documentary, *The Great Global Warming Swindle* (Durkin, 2007), paraded a line-up of dodgy scientists peddling one particular theory (that it's increased radiation from the sun that is causing the Earth to warm up, releasing more greenhouse gases in the process) that has been demonstrated time after time to be without any empirical basis whatsoever. The only serious scientist among them, Professor Carl Wunsch, shamefacedly acknowledged that they 'completely misrepresented' him, a trick well known to the writer and presenter of this particular travesty, Martin Durkin, whose earlier environmental programmes have involved such devious misrepresentations that Channel Four was forced to issue grovelling public apologies.

Having been routed scientifically, most contrarians have now shifted their argument to the *economics* of climate change: even if it is happening, and even if it is going to have extremely severe impacts upon humankind in terms of rising sea levels, extreme weather events, disrupted agriculture and so on, the costs of doing anything to mitigate these impacts are deemed by contrarians to be far too onerous. Marshalled by Bjorn Lomborg in Europe, and by a host of right-wing think-tanks in the US (such as the Cato Institute and the Competitive Enterprise Institute), they are succeeding yet again in giving politicians a pretext for delay and half-hearted half-measures.

Even this 'final contrarian redoubt' has now been smoked out by the report from Sir Nicholas Stern, *The Economics of Climate Change*, published in November 2006. In describing climate change as 'the greatest market failure the world has ever seen', this UK Treasury-funded report does for the economics of climate change what the IPCC has done for the science. What Stern seeks to demonstrate above all is 'that there need be no irreconcilable clash between securing increased economic prosperity and addressing the challenge of climate change' (Stern, 2007). The report estimates the cost of action in addressing climate change at around 1 per cent of global GDP every year; 'business as usual' will result in economic damage of between 5 per cent and 20 per cent of global GDP every year, and Stern comments that 'the appropriate estimate is likely to be in the upper part of this range'. In terms of getting one's head around what this actually means, he contrasts that level of damage with disruption on a scale similar to that associated with the two world wars and the economic depression of the first half of the 20th century.

Nonetheless, 1 per cent of GDP is not immaterial. In March 2007, the consulting firm McKinsey published one of the first estimates of the costs entailed in meeting the EU's new target of a 20 per cent reduction in CO_2 emissions by 2020. This was assessed at up to €1.1 trillion (£747 billion). It showed that simple technology (such as energy-saving light bulbs and wind power) will be capable of providing up to 75 per cent of the required reductions in greenhouse gas emissions, and that politicians should concentrate on implementing the most cost-effective environmental measures first, rather than coal-fired power stations with Carbon Capture and Storage (CCS).

No doubt further studies will emerge, both here in Europe and in the US, providing alternative economic projections. But the reality is that things are now moving, all around the world, and the politics of climate change have at long last moved to the very centre of the political stage. It was interesting that in setting the target of a 20 per cent cut in CO_2 emissions (on 1990 levels) by 2020, the 2007 EU Summit also agreed that it would ratchet that up to 30 per cent if other countries (particularly the US, China and India) follow suit. It also determined that 20 per cent of Europe's energy will be required to come from renewable sources by 2020. Bizarrely, however, the category of renewables has been expanded to include nuclear power (primarily to keep France on board), although it's blindingly obvious that the reserves of uranium on which nuclear power depend are no more 'renewable' than reserves of oil or gas.

For all that, different EU countries are bound to take different paths to the same end. Sweden has set the highest ambition level in determining to make itself 'all but fossil-fuel free' by 2020 – it currently relies on fossil fuels for around 35 per cent of its total energy consumption. Sweden's 'green gold' (its huge and well-managed forests) will fill a lot of that gap in terms of biomass and biofuels, but every available technology will be expected to play its part. The UK may lack Sweden's forests, but it too has taken a very strong lead, setting CO_2 reduction targets in a legally-binding framework (at least 26 per cent by 2020 and 60 per cent by 2050, with firm 'milestones' along the way), creating an independent advisory committee to determine appropriate targets in the future, and building in all sorts of 'enabling powers' to ensure that future governments do not have to keep going back to Parliament with primary legislation every time they want to bring in new measures.

Many critics believe that this is the turning point as far as the UK getting its climate change act together in its own backyard is concerned. Hitherto, it has been content to rely on the inspired international leadership of the former Prime Minister Tony Blair, who undoubtedly did more than any other individual to maintain at least some semblance of forward progress with other world leaders. By bringing countries like India and China into the G8 process at the Gleneagles Summit in 2005, he created space for the kind of persistent and less threatening diplomacy that the formal UN-driven negotiations had failed to bring about.

Not that the US took advantage of that space. From the time they went back on their campaign pledge, in 2001, to legislate to control emissions of CO_2, and then pulled out of the Kyoto Protocol shortly after that, President Bush and Vice-President Cheney have remained sunk deep in their denial of the science of climate change, aggressively defending the narrow interests of the US economy, suppressing reports, corrupting advisory bodies and blocking even the most modest of reforms. It is no exaggeration to say that these two figures (supported by the likes of the notorious Senator Inhofe, who describes climate change as 'the greatest hoax ever perpetrated on the American people') have come to represent a quite unique 'axis of evil' regarding climate change. Americans often complain about being 'singled out' for unfair calumny in the climate change 'hall of shame'. They shouldn't – as Joseph Stiglitz explains through these astonishing statistics:

> *The US emits close to 25 per cent of all greenhouse gases. Wyoming, the least populous state, with only 495,700 people, emits more carbon dioxide than 74 developing countries with a combined population of nearly 396 million. The CO_2 emissions of Texas, with a population of 22 million, exceed the combined emissions of 120 developing countries with an aggregate population of over 1.1 billion people.* (Stiglitz, 2006)

Fortunately for the rest of the world, President Bush and Vice-President Cheney have been effectively sidelined since the mid-term elections in 2006. Winning control of both the House of Representatives and the Senate has permitted the Democrats to start undoing six years of neglect. Out went Senator Inhofe as Chair of the most important Committee in the Senate, and in came Barbara Boxer, a redoubtable climate change campaigner. Levels of activity on climate change in both houses are second only to activity on the war in Iraq, with a number of different proposals under consideration to introduce some kind of 'cap-and-trade' scheme for US industry.

In effect, Congress is simply catching up with the rest of America, which selected a very different gear after Hurricane Katrina in October 2005. As Governor of California, Arnie Schwarzenegger took the lead, with an extremely ambitious climate change strategy including mandatory, economy-wide emission reductions. Twenty-three states now have renewable electricity production mandates, and almost as many have adopted greenhouse gas reduction targets, or are in the process of developing their own climate action plans. The eight states in the North East are on the point of introducing an innovative 'cap-and-trade' scheme of their own, and the mayors of almost 400 cities are also on the move in a manner that defies any conventional Republican/Democratic split. Former Vice-President Al Gore has had a huge impact with his Oscar-winning film, *An Inconvenient Truth*, allowing millions of American citizens to get their heads around climate change for the very first time. This has to go down as one of the most influential and effective environmental campaigns ever witnessed in America – even Ralph Nader, who stood for the Green Party against Al Gore in the 2002 Presidential election (and who is held by many to have deprived Gore of the success that would otherwise have been his), is said to be a little bit 'impressed'!

Predictably enough, public opinion in the US is also gradually shifting, despite the fact that until recently mainstream American media had pretty much ignored climate change. However, this is no seismic shift. Throughout 2005, high gas prices were certainly a worry, but little connection was made between concerns about energy security and concerns about climate change. The best efforts of environmentalists to press alarm bells on climate change after Hurricane Katrina (including rallies in more than 30 US cities) quickly faded away as media coverage declined, especially as the 2006 hurricane season turned out to be as benign as 2005's had been traumatic. The simple fact is that Americans remain strikingly less concerned about climate change than their European counterparts: roughly 50 per cent of Americans don't think it's a problem, including 75 per cent of Republicans, and only 40 per cent reckon it's caused by man-made emissions of CO_2 and other greenhouse gases – all of which reinforces the natural caution and conservatism that even the Democrats have shown on climate change until now.

Which makes it all the more encouraging that so many US companies have clearly got the message, led by the likes of Jeff Immelt of General Electric, Lee Scott of Wal-Mart, and Chad Holliday of DuPont, in effect dismissing the Bush Administration's position as scientifically corrupt and increasingly hostile to US economic interests. In January 2007, a powerful consortium of CEOs (from companies like BP, Alcoa, General Electric (GE), DuPont, Caterpillar, Lehman Brothers and Duke Energy) joined forces with the World Resources Institute, Environmental Defense and the Natural Resources Defense Council (NRDC) to call for mandatory reductions in greenhouse gases. The US Climate Action Partnership is clear that voluntary measures will never be sufficient: 'It must be mandatory, so that there is no doubt about the actions required.'

President Bush has of course ignored this, just as he has ignored every other intelligent, constructive proposal during his time in the White House. And he has made it clear that he will veto any cap-and-trade proposals that the legislature brings forward, notwithstanding the minor concession he made at the 2007 G8 Summit in Germany in agreeing to rejoin international discussions to come up with a successor initiative to the Kyoto Protocol by the end of 2008. Such a veto may not matter as much as it once would have, however. As serious campaigning for the 2008 Presidential Election gets under way, it seems more than likely that, whoever is eventually nominated, both parties will go into the election formally supporting some kind of cap-and-trade scheme. And that commitment will have a dramatic effect on the international debate, especially if it brings America back into discussions about what needs to happen after the first Kyoto period comes to an end in 2012. And that should, in turn, change the debate in countries like China and India. The US Administration's intransigence and clear contempt for the rest of the world have allowed developing countries to sit firmly on the sidelines of the Kyoto process. If the one nation that is responsible for more than 25 per cent of global greenhouse emissions, and which clearly has a greater historical legacy than any other, is refusing to make *any* moves to restrict emissions, one can understand why negotiators for China and India have been adamant that they will not budge until America (and the rest of the rich world) has set its own house in order.

But here too things may be changing. Having once declared that it would accept no mandatory reductions in emissions of CO_2 until its citizens have reached an average per capita income of $5,000 – which will not happen for many years, notwithstanding China's dramatic economic growth – China's leaders are beginning to realize that this may not be so smart. Its principal energy-related objective in the latest 5 Year Plan is to reduce energy intensity (the amount of energy required for each unit of economic value) by 20 per cent by 2010. This makes good economic sense, given how disastrously inefficient China is compared with other countries. Such efficiency improvements would simultaneously allow China to slow the growth in emissions of CO_2 – though it has to be said that China is still on track to overtake the US as the world's largest emitter of CO_2 by 2009.

Chinese leaders have also realized that their economy is far more vulnerable to accelerating climate change than most of the OECD countries that caused the problem in the first place. Climate change is already exacerbating problems associated with soil erosion and chronic desertification, and is likely to have a terrible impact on already frighteningly scarce water supplies in key agricultural regions of China. Sea level rises of much less than a metre would have a devastating impact along the whole of the Eastern seaboard, where much of China's economic muscle is located. I shall return to this in more detail in Chapter 6.

This is precisely the picture that the second part of the IPCC's Fourth Assessment Report conjured up in March 2007. As Rajendra Pachauri, Chair of the IPCC, put it: 'The poorest of the poor in the world – and this includes poor people in prosperous societies – are going to be the worst hit. People who are poor are least able to adapt to climate change.' The report says that climate change will cause immediate and unavoidable harm, including less food from farming in some areas (particularly in Africa), more violent storms, more drought and heat waves, and the dwindling of water supplies as mountain glaciers melt.

It seems extraordinary, as one devastating report after another crashes down on politicians' desks, that we should simultaneously be witnessing the largest ever wave of new investment in coal-fired power stations. Coal is the dirtiest and most CO_2 intensive of all the fossil fuels, and has profound impacts on the environment both locally and globally. Yet in the US, after almost 30 years of no new plants coming on line, there are now plans for as many as 150. Coal prices are low and very stable (particularly in comparison to gas), demand is soaring, and companies reckon that if there is to be a 'cap-and-trade scheme' they'd better get their investment in first! This threat was significantly enhanced in March 2007 when the US Supreme Court made a landmark ruling that the Environmental Protection Agency did indeed have the power to treat CO_2 as a 'pollutant' – something that the Agency had always claimed it was not authorized to do.

The picture in China is even worse, with one new coal-fired power station coming on line every ten days. China is already the world's largest coal producer, with 26,000 coal mines employing around 8 million people, and coal accounts for 75 per cent of total electricity generation. It also accounts for 90 per cent of the 25 million tonnes of sulphur dioxide released in China every year, 70 per cent of particulates, 67 per cent of nitrogen oxides and 70 per cent of the 4.7 billion tonnes of CO_2 emissions. Of the $63 billion of damage caused by environmental pollution in 2004 (according to China's State Environmental Protection Agency), 43 per cent is caused by the burning of coal. China has now set ambitious targets for reducing emissions of sulphur dioxide, but it will have its work cut out achieving them as demand for energy continues to soar.

Little wonder there is now so much interest in ways of capturing the CO_2 from coal plants *before* it is released into the atmosphere, and then storing it underground in depleted oil and gas reservoirs or saline aquifers. CCS is suddenly very big business, with increasingly ambitious plans for prototype plants being brought forward in Japan, the US, the UK and elsewhere. Some scientists are very bullish about the technical viability of CCS, claiming that all that is needed to make it work is a proper price for every tonne of CO_2 that is not released into the atmosphere. Others are much more cautious, in both engineering and financial terms, pointing to the very substantial costs involved not just in removing the CO_2 but in taking it from the power station or refinery to the place where it is going to be buried. Al Gore has been particularly critical of CCS, and indeed of all new 'clean coal' technologies: 'It is time to recognize that the phrase "clean coal technology" is devoid of meaning unless it means 'zero carbon emissions' technology.'

In this instance, I think Al Gore may be misled. A lot of coal in China, India, the US and elsewhere is going to get burned over the next 20 years whether we like it or not. I'm no great fan of technological 'fixes', but it seems to me that we have no choice but to find a way of making CCS a success – and a huge success at that. If we can't store away some of the billions of tonnes of CO_2 that will otherwise be released into the atmosphere, then our chances of staying below that 2°C threshold for avoiding 'dangerous climate change' by the end of this century (as reckoned by the IPPC) are zero.

Some scientists believe they are already zero – with or without CCS, or 'clean coal', or huge new investments in solar power, wind power and other renewable technologies, or even massive improvements in energy efficiency. Their view of the IPPC is that it's a hopelessly conservative body and that in having to reflect the consensus among thousands of scientists with widely diverging views it fails to give politicians the true picture. The 2007 Fourth Assessment Report, for instance, contains very little reference to the concerns that many scientists now have about accelerating feedback effects in the way certain natural systems are responding to the warming that we have already caused to happen.

Over the last couple of years, attention has focused in particular on the permafrost in Siberia (where current increases in average temperatures appear to be melting the layer of permafrost under which is trapped billions of tonnes of methane, a greenhouse gas 20 times more powerful than CO_2), or melting sea ice in the Arctic (with less ice, more of the incoming solar radiation is absorbed by the ocean rather than being reflected back into the atmosphere, causing further warming), and on the rainforests of the Amazon starting to dry out, with the very real possibility that over time they will become net emitters of CO_2 rather than a CO_2 sink. And there is even evidence to suggest that more and more CO_2 is being released *all over the world* as average soil temperatures gently rise.

And that's why more and more scientists are now talking not so much of gradual shifts in the climate (more or less in line with the gradual increase in concentrations of CO_2 in the atmosphere), but of abrupt, *non-linear* shifts from one climate state to another. There's plenty of evidence in the historical data culled from ice cores in both the Arctic and Antarctic to demonstrate that this has happened many times before. We just don't know when those feedback loops may kick in, or even whether staying below a 2°C increase by the end of the century really is sufficient to prevent 'runaway' and potentially irreversible climate shifts. After all, a 2°C average rise means increases closer to 5°C or 6°C in the polar regions. If you want to know what this kind of countdown to meltdown looks like, Mark Lynas's new book, *Six Degrees* (2007), spells it out as graphically as you can imagine. To me, it's amazing how unconcerned we still seem to be in the face of this accumulating evidence, with the very real threat, as Jim Lovelock puts it, of 'the world [being] on the brink of a vast and mostly unpleasant change that may mark the end of our present civilization' (Lovelock, 2006).

As the world goes about its 'business as usual' business, climate scientists are wrestling with all of these massively complex variables and potentially devastating consequence. It seems to me, however you interpret all this, that we really are very close now to the ultimate tipping point of all: the point at which the human species loses the ability to command its own destiny in the face of nature's infinitely mightier powers.

But how are we to deal with the psychological implications of all this? I've heard Jim Lovelock speak on a couple of occasions, laying out the central thrust of his *Revenge of Gaia* (2006) that it's basically too late, and that even if we renounced the use of all fossil fuels tomorrow, the level of man-made warming we've already induced would still lead ineluctably to runaway climate change. Sustainable development is therefore a complete fiction; 'sustainable retreat' is all we have to look forward to.

Lovelock is one of my great heroes, despite his zealous and (in my opinion, at least) irrational advocacy of nuclear power – if it really is too late, what difference are a few dozen (or even a few hundred) nuclear reactors going to make? But I'm deeply troubled both by his certainty about the fate that now awaits us, and by the disempowering effect that this has on people struggling to come to terms with something that has been largely invisible to them up until now – that the world really does have non-negotiable limits, that there really are natural laws by which we humans are constrained as much as any other species. The discovery that ours is 'an outlaw civilization' can be deeply disturbing, but nothing like as disturbing as the suggestion that there's nothing we can do to bring ourselves back on the right side of the law.

This is particularly shocking for young people. I shudder to think just how angry young people are going to be when they wake up to the full extent of my generation's negligence. If you subscribe to that uplifting aphorism that 'we do not inherit the Earth from our parents, but borrow it from our children', then we've really screwed up. Having spent the last 20 years or so in outright denial about the declining state of the world, we've now leapt in one fell swoop from denial to despair! Having stolen their future, we are about to steal whatever reasons to be hopeful young people might still have.

And that's precisely why I find Jim Lovelock's disempowering rhetoric so troubling. We cannot afford to lose the anger of young people – indeed, the anger of *any* age-group – as we struggle to set ourselves on a more sustainable path. I just hope that Jim is wrong, and that the views of the vast majority of climate scientists (that we still have between 10 to 15 years to put in place the kind of radical measures that will *not* protect us from an uncomfortable future – that's a dead cert – but *will* protect us from those runaway, irreversible effects that threaten such devastation for humankind) are correct.

BREAKDOWN: BREAKTHROUGH OR COLLAPSE?

One of the biggest problems that we face, and not just with climate change, is the difficulty we have in seeing things as *systems* rather than as discrete elements within those systems. When James Lovelock brought out his ground-breaking book *Gaia: A New Look at Life on Earth* in 1979, one of the principal reasons it met with such a frosty response from the scientific community was his challenge to their self-contained complacency, with all of them working away in their specialist disciplines (geology, biology, climatology, oceanography, atmospheric chemistry and so on), but more or less indifferent to what was happening outside the reduced confines of that particular discipline, let alone thinking in terms of the system as a whole – in this case, the 'whole Earth system', or Gaia.

And that system is massively complex. Even those scientists who feel most confident about today's consensus on climate change are humbled by its complexity. Understanding the conditions that keep that whole Earth system in some kind of dynamic equilibrium is the principal intellectual challenge scientists face today, and all they know for absolute certain is that the system is becoming less and less stable. The threat of non-linear climate change (characterized by rapid and essentially unpredictable shifts from one climate state to another); of ecosystem collapse (as explored above); of synergistic effects where change in one part of the system reacts with change in another part of the system, with wholly unpredictable consequences; of human-induced discontinuities in the system: conceptualizing, let alone managing, this level of complexity is still well beyond our struggling intellectual capabilities.

So it's hardly surprising, when contemplating this complexity (or even when finding every excuse under the sun to avoid contemplating it!), that people come to different conclusions as to the *outcome* of our current interaction with that system. To simplify this in my own mind, I describe it as the Lomborg–Lovelock continuum: at one end of the scale we have the ever-cheerful Bjorn Lomborg, of *Sceptical Environmentalist* fame, full of contempt for the wolf-crying Cassandras of the environment movement, and completely convinced that we have the intellectual and technological resources already available to overcome any and all of these problems if we start to get serious about them without further delay.

At the other, we have James Lovelock himself, whose *Revenge of Gaia* descends into such depths of gloom as to crush even the most redoubtable optimist. Lovelock came to the conclusion some time ago that we have already put sufficient 'warming' into the atmosphere to make it impossible for us to stop certain natural feedback loops dramatically enhancing that relatively small man-made contribution. Sustainable development is therefore an illusion, because even if we stopped emitting all greenhouse gases *tomorrow*, it would make no difference. All that awaits us is a traumatic process of 'sustainable retreat' as nature rebalances by taking us (or, at least, the majority of us) out of the system altogether.

I rebel in the face of both these polarized scenarios – on a very personal basis. With great patience, and for the good of my susceptible environmental soul, I've read pretty much everything that Bjorn Lomborg has written over the last few years, and although I believe he is perfectly sincere in his views (and that these views are cogently and entertainingly presented), there is a partiality about them, a complacency, a deep-down lack of humility that I find seriously off-putting. By contrast, Jim just depresses me. It's true, of course, that I too may be 'in denial' of a different kind, in needing to believe that there is still an equitable, sustainable, compassionate future available for *all* of humankind. How else could I justify the work I do – especially as I'm not sure I'd be very good at 'sustainable retreat', as we hunker down behind a set of increasingly forlorn physical and political barriers to protect what's left of a decent life. What's more, Jim's quite a bit older than I am – and I have two daughters (18 and 15) through whose eyes I look out over the next 50 years. It just can't be too late, I say to myself. It just can't.

So for a long time, I've wavered around between those two polar extremes, seeking some kind of spurious balance between despair in the face of crushing empirical evidence, and optimism in the knowledge of humankind's astonishing problem-solving creativity and adaptability – fashioning in the process an idiosyncratic brand of 'apocalyptic optimism'! But out of that murky confusion, a much clearer sense of exactly where we now are has slowly emerged, an intellectually robust middle-way, tested out in practice through the work we do in Forum for the Future with our partners, and with the hundreds of business people I come into contact with through the Prince of Wales's Business & the Environment Programme.

I've been immensely strengthened in that process through the discovery of Thomas Homer-Dixon's *The Upside of Down* at the end of 2006. This is an extraordinary book, in effect recounting his own journey of self-discovery oscillating between despair and hope in today's world. So though he's not as well-known as either Lovelock or Lomborg, and despite the fact that his name doesn't begin with an 'L', I'm attributing my middle-way on the Lomborg–Lovelock continuum to Homer-Dixon – and I hope all three will forgive me for the outrageous simplifications of their views in Table 1.1 (overleaf)!

Table 1.1 *The Lomborg–Lovelock continuum*

THE WORLD ACCORDING TO:	CURRENT STATE OF PLAY	A TIME OF RADICAL DISCONTINUITIES
BJORN LOMBORG	The natural environment is much more resilient than environmentalists make out; climate change happening, but man-made contribution is small. Best way of protecting environment is for countries to go on getting richer.	Many issues much more pressing than climate change: HIV/Aids, water and sanitation, education, etc. Poverty a major threat to stability, as is corruption and poor governance in Third World.
THOMAS HOMER-DIXON	Cheap fossil fuels underpin a 'fantasy world' of massive population growth and economic development. Environmental stresses are more serious than people realize, with resilience of most ecosystems being systematically eroded away. Unsustainable population growth a major issue. Politicians treating the symptoms, not the causes.	Climate-related 'shocks to the system' start coming fast and furious; real possibility of 'synchronous failure', with lots of things all breaking apart at the same time. An era of 'mega-terrorism' looms unless the West adopts totally different security strategies.
JAMES LOVELOCK	Catastrophe of climate change recognized far too late by politicians, in thrall to the seduction of exponential economic growth and totally false model of progress.	Climate change impacts accelerate dramatically, exacerbating international tension. Global insurance industry collapses; massive economic and social damage follows, with politicians struggling to maintain any kind of order.
	1950–2000	2000–2010

Note: ! = point of irreversibility

THE WINDOW OF OPPORTUNITY	FROM BREAKDOWN TO BREAKTHROUGH OR COLLAPSE	LONG-TERM FUTURE
Technology the answer to all our problems; continued economic growth the best driver for change. Crucial to find more effective ways of distributing wealth and improving conditions for very poor.	Humankind breaks through to better future for all, off the back of technological revolution. High standards of living for all, with impressive narrowing of gap between rich and poor. Climate change remains manageable.	9 billion people living comfortably within planet Earth's natural limits. Environment protected primarily through effective market systems. Human numbers start to decline in line with UN projections.
Still every opportunity for market-based economies to prosper, with dramatically accelerated transition to a low-carbon global economy. Grave doubts about political leadership, especially in US, China and India: denial a major impediment to making faster progress.	**BREAKTHROUGH** Renewable energy technologies substitute for large share of fossil fuels. Western democracies totally redefine meaning of 'security'; massive investments in family planning and restoring exhausted ecosystems.	Slow, often painful recovery. The politics of sufficiency replace politics of excess; global institutions ensure much fairer distribution of wealth and poor. People's quality of life massively improves. Climate stabilizes by around 2075.
	COLLAPSE Synchronous failures overwhelm economic and political systems; mass migration from poor world countries into Europe and America. Average temperature increases by 2.5°C by 2050.	Economic and social collapse deepens as sea level rises by more than 2 metres; political systems implode, communities struggle to survive. Massive loss of life; average temperatures continue to rise.
Belated efforts to put things right, including huge new investments in nuclear power. But many nuclear reactors swept away by rising sea levels. Agriculture collapses in Africa, China and the South of America.	Runaway climate change kicks in; politicians powerless to contain effects of collapsing ecosystems and national economies. Even 'sustainable retreat' becomes an impossible dream.	There is no long-term future for humankind.
2010–2020	2020–2050	2050 →

It's all about complexity, resilience, breakdown and (possibly) renewal. For Homer-Dixon that starts with an intriguing comparison between the Roman Empire and America today:

> Today, just as in the late Roman Empire, deep stresses are rising and system resilience is declining. Just as was true then, the coherence of world order depends critically on the economic, political and military might of a single superpower. The foundation of this might is access to abundant energy. 'More than in any other modern nation', writes the eminent energy specialist Vaclav Smil, 'the United States has acquired its power and influence largely through its extraordinarily high use of energy'. And America survives, as the ancient city of Rome did, on lifelines of energy from distant regions. (Homer-Dixon, 2006)

It may seem a little outlandish to be predicting the imminent demise of the new American imperium; after just 50 years of imposing itself on the rest of the world, that would certainly make it the shortest-lived empire of all time. But on top of all the conventional analysis of why America's days are numbered as an imperial power (the rise and rise of China and India; credibility-defying levels of debt and budget imbalances; two crushing military defeats, first in Vietnam and then in Iraq; corruption and venality throughout the political system; a bullying, unilateral arrogance in its relations with other countries that has turned it from the most admired nation in the world to the most feared and despised), one must then take account of a number of additional sustainability factors: increased dependency on imported oil, a massive 'thermodynamic imbalance' – in terms of the amount of energy it takes America to produce every unit of energy it needs – and a level of wastefulness in both the production and the consumption phases of the economy that beggars belief.

These problems are not unique to America; indeed, it's clear that the booming economies of China and India are going to find their material aspirations even more seriously and more rapidly impacted by the same challenges. As the imperative of producing year-on-year economic growth generates ever greater complexity in the system, with governments ever more forlornly trying to manage increasingly painful trade-offs between people, planet and prosperity, the resilience in those systems is simply being eroded away.

'Resilience' is a key concept here. It represents the capacity of any system, organization or individual to withstand shocks, to resume its original form after any serious perturbation or discontinuity. The more complex a human system is, the less resilient it is. Examples of this already abound: the 1997 collapse of financial markets in Southeast Asia after a minor banking default in Thailand; the total collapse of economic and social support systems in New Orleans after Hurricane Katrina in 2005; the near-panic that swept through the UK economy after a few dozen truckers held the country to ransom in protest against increased fuel taxes in 2000.

This is the principal area of investigation of the Resilience Alliance, an influential group of institutions from all around the world brought together to help decision-makers better understand how to cope with a world characterized more by radical discontinuity than by reassuring predictability. What can we learn from the way natural systems operate? All natural systems go through a growth phase, expanding rapidly, temporarily defying the biophysical boundaries or conditions that constrain them, but must eventually come back within those system conditions. The longer a human system pursues that kind of growth, against all the evidence of the need for constraint and stabilization, the greater its vulnerability to potentially dramatic collapse. Indeed, Homer-Dixon points to the possibility of 'synchronous failure', caused by multiple and synergistic stresses in the system.

So where is the human species in this cycle? You'd have to be Pangloss himself to read through the reports of the IPCC in 2007 and not reckon on imminent massive damage to human societies the world over. Or the reports of the UNEP on biodiversity and ecosystem breakdown. Or the 'limits to growth' analysis covered in the next chapter. Or literally thousands of reports from national, regional and local authorities detailing evidence of chronic air and water pollution, and the build-up of toxins in the environment. We're in for a tough time, come what may – and that's before factoring in any of the equally pressing social and security issues that I will be looking at elsewhere.

So there will be breakdown. Life as we know it today will not carry on undisturbed. Business as usual is not on offer. There will be terrible suffering – over and above that which already afflicts hundreds of millions of people today. It's simply too late to avoid any of that.

But there is a world of difference between *breakdown* and irreversible collapse. If your car (or bike!) breaks down, you can get it fixed. But if it's smashed to pieces, that's it. If life in a village pond breaks down through eutrophication and other forms of pollution, it can be fixed simply by getting rid of the sources of pollution. But if it's been concreted over to make way for a new supermarket, that's it. As Homer-Dixon powerfully points out:

> *All highly adaptive systems go through cycles of breakdown and regeneration. Breakdown is greatly disruptive to parts of the system, but it needn't be catastrophic over all, and it can produce exactly the conditions required for a burst of creativity, reorganization and renewal. This is, in fact, the fundamental challenge humankind faces: we need to allow for breakdown in the natural function of our societies in a way that doesn't produce catastrophic collapse, but instead leads to healthy renewal.* (Homer-Dixon, 2006)

Hence the 'point of irreversibility' in Table 1.1, the point at which changes in our natural systems will worsen whether we want them to or not, and regardless of how purposefully we seek to limit or even eliminate the source of the damage (for instance, CO_2 and other greenhouse gases) at that point. This is hardly an exact science, and I suspect few people will take much comfort from the fact that irreversibility of this kind is not really irreversibility as in 'for ever' – in that life on Earth will, in time, correct any ephemeral imbalances we may have caused and re-establish some kind of pre-human homeostasis. But it does mean irreversible for anything vaguely resembling this particular model of 'human civilization', and possibly for the human species altogether.

Some choice, you might say: painful, often traumatic breakdown on the one hand, or total cataclysmic collapse on the other! Not an easy one to sell, politically speaking. But *everything* depends on exactly how long it takes us to realize that this is now our ineluctable destiny, and that the priceless opportunity we still have to turn that inevitable breakdown into a time of renewal and realistic hope for the future of humankind has to be seized within the next decade or so. And that all depends on where you think the 'point of irreversibility' falls: in the last decade, if you're with Jim Lovelock; not for a long time, if you're with Bjorn Lomborg; at the end of a 10–15 year window of opportunity, if you're with Homer-Dixon – or me, for that matter!

That's why the 'middle-way' I've referred to above bifurcates at that point, at the end of the window of opportunity. By then, we will either have done enough to ensure the breakdown evolves into some kind of *breakthrough* for humankind, or, alternatively, the breakdown will evolve into some kind of collapse simply because we haven't done enough. Erwin Laszlo – whose book *The Chaos Point* provides some interesting insights into the dynamics of this particular transformation – defines the chaos point in the following way:

> *Evolution towards breakdown: the values, worldviews and ethics of a critical mass of people in society are resistant to change, or change too slowly, and the established institutions are too rigid to allow for timely transformation. Inequity and conflict, coupled with an impoverished environment, create unmanageable stresses. The social order degenerates into conflict and violence.*
>
> *Evolution towards breakthrough: the mindset of a critical mass of people evolves in time, shifting the development of society towards a more adaptable mode. As these changes take hold, the improved order – governed by more adaptive values, world views and ethics – establishes itself. The economic, political and ecological dimensions of society stabilise in a non-conflictual and sustainable mode.* (Laszlo, 2006)

The quality of leadership required first to persuade people that this is the choice we now face, and then to enable whole societies to steer their way through to renewal rather than collapse, is in a different league from anything we have available to us today. Those who see part of this picture (Tony Blair, for example, with climate change, or Premier Wen Jiabao with ecosystem collapse in China) are flawed by seeing so little of the rest of the picture. Presidents Bush and Putin, and most leaders today, still don't see any of it. Denial is still the dominant response mechanism today, less so now in terms of denying the evidence itself, but more in terms of denying the implications of that evidence: that the game is up for a model of economic progress that we've all become very dependent on since the 1950s.

The root causes of this kind of persistent denial are investigated in Chapter 12. Suffice it to say, for the time being, that it has kept most people in the world's richest countries almost entirely detached from the physical reality of our continuing dependence upon the natural world, deprived of the information and knowledge that they need to make sense of these conflicting imperatives, and wholly unprepared for the kind of transformation that is now required to secure a sustainable future for humankind.

A GLIMPSE INTO A SUSTAINABLE FUTURE

Nevertheless, as I will keep pointing out, the fact that something is necessary doesn't necessarily make it desirable. And desirability is something that advocates of sustainable development are not very good at. They are often hampered by the fact that the origins of much of what they stand for today were fashioned in the crucible of radical opposition to the established political and economic order back in the 1970s and 1980s. Like all opposition movements, environmental campaigners became better known for what they stood *against* rather than what they stood *for*, and to a certain extent that is still true today. As we will see in the next chapter, sustainable development embraces a far wider range of concerns than environmentalism per se, but it still suffers from the same problem as far as the general public is concerned: we know what you don't want to see happen, and we know that you're broadly in favour of environmental protection and helping the developing world, but what would our lives actually be like if everything suddenly went sustainable?

At one level, it is tempting to say that things probably wouldn't look very different – on the surface, at least. A sustainable society will still need a highly sophisticated infrastructure, and a mix of housing, industry, offices, recreational facilities, farming, open spaces and so on. But construction techniques will be radically different, with energy efficiency and renewables pushed to the absolute maximum. There will still be roads – but fewer of them, and carrying cars that are four or five times as efficient as today's models. People will, indeed, be walking and cycling a lot more than they do today! And there will still be airports – though the numbers of people flying will not increase much as the costs of flying gradually rise to reflect the impacts of aviation upon the environment, and upon climate change in particular.

In terms of the kind of aspirations that most people have today, I very much doubt that these will be very different either. We all want the best possible schools and hospitals, the safest streets, the highest physical quality of life, and the fairest and most effective democratic processes. And we will go on seeking them just as keenly in a sustainable society as we do today. The likelihood that things will, in all probability, be more decentralized, with a lot more going on at the human scale and the community level, won't actually change any of that.

Some of the theoretical thinking behind the idea of a sustainable economy provides the core of Chapters 10 and 11, but some of the basics are not that much different here either: fair prices in properly regulated markets; efficient and reliable public services; a commitment to ensure access to job opportunities and fulfilling work, and so on. No hair-shirt asceticism, but far less frenetic consumerism, less shopping for the sake of shopping, less conspicuous consumption, less waste, less keeping up with the Joneses – with more time, therefore, to do more of the things that people today always claim to regret not having the time to do.

There will also be a lot less international trade. A watchword of sustainable economics is self-reliance – not self-sufficiency, it should be noted, which I believe holds very few attractions. Self-reliance entails combining judicious and necessary trade with other countries with an unapologetic emphasis on each country maintaining security of supply in terms of energy, food and even manufacturing. The idea that today's neo-liberal, no-holds-barred model of globalization will last much longer seems fantastical anyway, as nation after nation feels the pain of China and other low-cost economies making it all but impossible to compete in any serious sense.

In the future, with oil trading at well over $100 dollars a barrel, some of the most absurd anomalies of international trade and travel (food air-freighted many thousands of miles, £10 flights to dozens of destinations, and so on) will have long since disappeared. As part of our efforts to mitigate the worst threats of climate change, it seems increasingly likely that each individual will have his or her own personal carbon allowance, allocated on an annual basis; finding ways of living elegant, low-carbon lives will be both fashionable and profitable. This should usher in the first moment in modern history where cyclists have the edge on the owners of the next generation of gas-guzzling SUVs!

And there is no point beating around the bush on one other thing: people who are better off will almost certainly be paying higher taxes than they do today. Two of the cornerstones of a sustainable economy are increased efficiency (in terms of resources, energy, raw materials, value for money, capital allocation and so on) and increased social justice. No serious definition of the word 'sustainable' could possibly allow for a continuation of the grotesque disparities in wealth that we see today, both within countries and between countries. This is not egalitarianism (at least, not in the market-based model of sustainable capitalism that I will be exploring in this book), but an uncompromising commitment to greater equity and to the elimination of the kind of poverty that still blights the lives of so many hundreds of millions of people.

No amount of enthusiastic visioning processes will make it any easier to reconcile the two conflicting imperatives outlined in this chapter. This will require years of hard practical and ideological graft, and the harsh truth of it is that the majority of protagonists for a 'more sustainable future' are ill-prepared for a journey of that kind. So here, in summary, is the alternative case that I will be laying out over the next 16 chapters:

- It is all but impossible any longer to deny the need for profound change in the face of today's gathering ecological crises. The science upon which that analysis is based is rock solid and more than sufficient to justify far more radical political interventions than are currently occurring.
- The fact that profound change is necessary is obviously not sufficient in itself – the pace of change remains hopelessly inadequate. Conventional environmentalism has so far failed to win over hearts and minds either within the electorate at large or within today's political elites.
- Change will not come by threatening people with yet more ecological doom and gloom. The necessary changes have also to be seen as *desirable* changes: good for people, their health and their quality of life – and not just good for the prospects of future generations. This is a 'here and now' agenda, as well as an agenda for tomorrow.
- This means working with the grain of markets and free choice, not against it. It means embracing capitalism as the only overarching system capable of achieving any kind of reconciliation between ecological sustainability, on the one hand, and the pursuit of prosperity and personal wellbeing on the other.
- That said, today's particular model of capitalism is clearly incapable of delivering this kind of reconciliation, dependent as it is upon the accelerating liquidation of the natural capital upon which we depend and upon worsening divides between the rich and the poor worldwide.
- At its heart, therefore, sustainable development comes right down to one all-important challenge: is it possible to conceptualize and then operationalize an alternative model of capitalism – one that allows for the sustainable management of the different capital assets upon which we rely so that the yield from those different assets sustains us *now*, as well as in the future?
- The case for sustainable development must be reframed if that is to happen. It must be as much about new opportunities for responsible wealth creation as about outlawing irresponsible wealth creation; it must draw upon a core of ideas and values that speaks directly to people's desire for a higher quality of life, emphasizing enlightened self-interest and personal wellbeing of a different kind.
- It is only this combination (sustainable development perceived as answering the unavoidable challenge of living within natural limits, providing unprecedented opportunities for responsible and innovative wealth creators, and offering

people a more equitable and more rewarding way of life) that is likely to provide any serious political alternative to today's economic and political orthodoxy.
- Unless it throws in its lot with this kind of progressive political agenda, conventional environmentalism will continue to decline.
- All things considered, what is the alternative anyway? If not genuinely sustainable development, then what? And if not now, when?

All of these points assume at least a working knowledge of what we mean by sustainable development, which leads us to the next chapter.

REFERENCES

Bentley, T. (2002) 'Letting go: Complexity, individualism and the left', *Renewal*, vol 10
Carson, R. (1962) *Silent Spring*, Houghton Mifflin, Boston, MA
Diamond, J. (2005) *Collapse: How Societies Choose to Fail or Succeed*, Allen Lane, London
Durkin, M. (2007) *The Great Global Warming Swindle*, documentary film, first screened in the UK on Channel 4, 8 March
FAO (2007) *State of the World's Forests 2007*, report, Food and Agriculture Organization of the United Nations, Rome, available at www.fao.org/docrep/009/a0773e/a0773e00.htm
Gore, A. (2006) *An Inconvenient Truth*, Bloomsbury, London (book of the Oscar-winning film of the same name, directed by Davis Guggenheim and starring Al Gore)
Homer-Dixon, T. (2006) *The Upside of Down*, Island Press, Washington, DC
IPCC (Intergovernmental Panel on Climate Change) (2007), *Climate Change 2007*, the Fourth Assessment Report (AR4) of the IPCC, published online in four parts, available from www.ipcc.ch
Laszlo, E. (2006) *The Chaos Point*, Piatkus Books, London
Lomborg, B. (2001) *The Skeptical Environmentalist: Measuring the Real State of the World*, Cambridge University Press, Cambridge, UK
Lovelock, J. (1979) *Gaia: A New Look at Life on Earth*, Oxford University Press, Oxford
Lovelock, J. (2006) *The Revenge of Gaia*, Allen Lane, London
Lynas, M. (2004) *High Tide*, Flamingo, London
Lynas, M. (2007) *Six Degrees*, Fourth Estate, London
MA (2005) *Ecosystems and Human Well-being: Opportunities and Challenges for Business and Industry*, the fourth Millennium Ecosystem Assessment report, available at www.millenniumassessment.org
Oreskes, N. (2004) 'Beyond the ivory tower: The scientific consensus on climate change', *Science*, vol 306, issue 5702, 3 December
Ponting, C. (1991) *A Green History of the World: The Environment and the Collapse of Great Civilizations*, Penguin Books, New York
Stern, N. (2007) *The Economics of Climate Change: The Stern Review*, Cambridge University Press, Cambridge, UK
Stiglitz, J. (2006) *Making Globalization Work*, Allen Lane, London
UNDP (2005) *Human Development Report 2005: International Cooperation at a Crossroads – Aid, Trade and Security in an Unequal World*, United Nations Development Programme, available at http://hdr.undp.org/reports/global/2005

Sustainable Development for Real

INTRODUCTION

It's important to get the definitions out of the way early on – and most people are still very confused as to what sustainable development does or doesn't mean. And is sustainable development the same thing as sustainability? For me, it's the *science of sustainability* that provides the rock-solid foundations upon which the structures of sustainable development are now being raised – still somewhat tentatively and haphazardly, it has to be said. That science takes us back to the core principles of ecological limits, with a brief historical excursion to consider why so many earlier civilizations brought upon themselves their own collapse by ignoring those limits. For most businesses today, however, this remains far too unworldly: here, the language of the triple bottom line (economic, environmental *and* social bottom lines) still prevails, or 'stakeholder strategies', or corporate social responsibility (CSR), all jumbled together in a goulash of jargon and lofty aspiration that somehow still serves to keep physical reality at bay.

DISENTANGLING THE DEFINITIONS

Given that these two concepts of sustainability and sustainable development are very different (although used interchangeably and very confusingly by almost everyone), some brief definitions are necessary.

Sustainability may best be defined as the *capacity for continuance into the long-term future*. Anything that can go on being done on an indefinite basis is sustainable. Anything that cannot go on being done indefinitely is unsustainable. In that respect, sustainability is the end goal, or desired destination, for the human species as much as for any other species.

By contrast, sustainable development is the process by which we move towards sustainability. There have been many attempts to define sustainable development; the most widely used is the definition that first appeared in the Brundtland Report in 1987: 'development that meets the needs of the present without compromising the ability of future generations to meet their own needs' (WCED, 1987). But the limitations of this definition are becoming more and more obvious. Above all, it fails to convey the idea that there are biophysical limits within which society must operate if the natural capital upon which we depend is not to be eroded. The alternative adopted by Forum for the Future – 'sustainable development is a dynamic process which enables all people to realize their potential and to improve their quality of life in ways which simultaneously protect and enhance the Earth's life-support systems' – both affirms sustainable development as a dynamic process and emphasizes the importance of social justice and equity in that it has to be made to work for *all* people. It also makes it clear that achieving sustainable development is not simply about managing the environment more effectively, while people pursue their business as usual. It is a social and economic project as much as an environmental project, with the very positive objective of optimizing human wellbeing.

Sustainable development remains a highly contestable (and contested) concept. It regularly comes under attack on a number of different counts: that it is so vague and indeterminate a concept as to allow almost infinite abuse by politicians and business people who have no real intention of changing their ways any more than they are absolutely required to; that it is a contradiction in terms since it provides no guidance as to how sustainability and development can be made mutually consistent; that it oversimplifies a hugely complex set of interlocking issues; that it inadvertently obscures the truth about impending ecological collapse; and that in its widest definition (embracing social sustainability, equity and justice as much as ecological sustainability) it may even be obstructing the development of sufficiently clear-cut and radical measures to protect the physical environment. Furthermore, there is real concern that sustainable development is an exceptionally difficult bit of jargon, with almost zero sex appeal or political 'street cred'.

Putting to one side that final point (for one really has to ask just how hard politicians beyond today's green parties have made any serious efforts to get to grips with sustainable development), such misgivings need to be urgently addressed. If sustainable development continues to mean all (often mutually exclusive) things to all people, then it cannot possibly carry the intellectual weight required of it at this crucial turning point in human history.

Part of the problem lies in the fact that people have very different views of what is meant by development itself. From the 1960s onwards, the seductive notion of 'development as economic growth' has been dominant, both in terms of the academic literature and the actual policies of Western governments. This carried over into the 1987 Brundtland Report (WCED, 1987), which ended up invalidating much of its own analysis of unsustainable development by calling for substantially higher levels of economic growth throughout the developing world – without for a second questioning what kind of growth would deliver *real* development and what kind of growth actually undermines development by continuing to damage the environment and erode the value of social capital. As the Johannesburg Memo *Fairness in a Fragile World* puts it:

It was politically expedient for everybody, the North, the South and the ex-communist countries, not to question the development-as-growth philosophy. Both the South and the economies in transition could continue to phrase their demands for justice and recognition as demands for unlimited economic growth without making crucial distinctions as to 'what kind of growth', 'for whose benefit', 'growth in which direction'. In this way, the elites in the South and the North could reconcile themselves with the outcome of the 1992 Earth Summit. Indeed, it was an unholy alliance between Southern and Northern governments in favour of development as growth that largely emasculated the spirit of Rio. (Johannesburg Memo, 2002)

It is therefore important to be crystal clear about what development means from a more rigorous sustainable development perspective. Ever since the concept of sustainable development was first used by Dame Barbara Ward (one of the founders of the International Institute for Environment and Development – IIED) and picked up in the 1980 World Conservation Strategy (seven years before the Brundtland Report), development has been seen by many as being as much about health, education, democracy and freedom as it is about increased material prosperity and economic growth. Without ignoring the importance of growth in GDP or personal income, any radical conception of development must go way beyond it.

The most eloquent and powerful articulation of 'development as freedom' rather than development as growth is Amartya Sen's book of the same title, published in 1999. *Development as freedom* puts the removal of lack of freedom as the most important priority facing multilateral bodies and individual nation states across the world:

Development requires the removal of major sources of unfreedom: poverty as well as tyranny, poor economic opportunities as well as systematic social deprivation, neglect of public facilities as well as intolerance or over-activity of repressive states. Despite unprecedented increases in overall opulence, the contemporary world denies elementary freedoms to vast numbers – perhaps even the majority – of people. (Sen, 1999)

Sen describes freedom as the 'primary end of development' – expanding human freedoms including 'elementary capabilities like being able to avoid such deprivations as starvation, under-nourishment, escapable morbidity and premature mortality', as well as the freedoms that are associated with being literate and numerate, enjoying political participation and uncensored speech and so on. He is contemptuous of those who have argued (as some, astonishingly, still do today) that the systematic denial of political freedoms and civil rights is good for rapid economic development.

It is hard to exaggerate the dramatic difference between this kind of approach to development and the so-called Washington Consensus, promoted with such extraordinary ideological fervour over the last few decades by the International Monetary Fund (IMF), the World Bank, the World Trade Organization (WTO) and so on. We are not just talking about different models of development here, but very different models of capitalism.

So, definitions do matter. It may well be true that sustainable development still sounds very 'geeky' as far as most people are concerned, and that it has more than its fair share of potentially alienating jargon, especially from a business perspective. But opting out of rigorous analysis of what sustainable development really means will be much more damaging in the long run.

Many of the notional weaknesses attributed to sustainable development link back to the chronic failure (mostly on the part of its critics) to understand both the differences and the linkages between sustainable development and sustainability. The usefulness of sustainable development depends upon being absolutely clear about what sustainability itself means, principally by reference to the biophysical parameters within which all human activity must be constrained.

So, how do we determine those parameters and then ensure that we stay within them? Contrary to popular opinion (which sees sustainability as something rather fuzzy and hard to pin down), biophysical sustainability is capable of scientific explanation, definition and measurement. It is now well understood that there are basically three sets of *services* provided by the natural world upon which we still totally depend:

1   the provision of *resources* for human activities;
2   the absorption and recycling of wastes caused by those human activities (through a variety of different *sinks*); and
3   the provision of additional ecological *services* (such as climate regulation, pollination and enhancing soil fertility).

It is the desire to ground sustainability in basic science which has led to the development of The Natural Step (TNS) and other science-based initiatives over the last few years. At the heart of TNS lie four key concepts, or 'System Conditions', which collectively define the conditions that must be met for society to be able to live sustainably within the Earth's supporting biosphere (see Table 2.1) It is only by understanding how the world around us works that we can properly understand how we need to manage our human systems so that they do not breach the limits set by the biophysical world.

Jared Diamond's book *Collapse: How Societies Choose to Fail or Succeed* (2005) provides a wealth of historical examples of societies that have breached ecological limits and, subsequently, have collapsed – from the Vikings in Greenland to the Mayans in Central America, from Easter Island to Angkor Wat. His analysis confirms that many of those 'mysterious abandonments' were *partly* triggered by

Table 2.1 *The four System Conditions for a sustainable society*

1 In a sustainable society, nature is not subject to having systematically increasing concentrations of substances extracted from the Earth's crust.	This means substituting certain minerals that are scarce in nature with others that are more abundant, using all mined materials efficiently, and systematically reducing dependence upon fossil fuels.
2 In a sustainable society, nature is not subject to systematically increasing concentrations of substances produced by society.	This means systematically substituting certain persistent and unnatural compounds with ones that are normally abundant or break down more easily in nature, and using all substances produced by society as efficiently as possible.
3 In a sustainable society, nature is not subject to systematically increasing degradation by physical means.	This means drawing resources only from well-managed ecosystems, systematically pursuing the most productive and efficient use of those resources and of land, and exercising caution in modifying nature.
4 And in that society, human needs are met worldwide.	This means using all of our resources efficiently, fairly and responsibly so that the needs of all people, and the future needs of people who are not yet born, stand the best chance of being met.

Source: The Natural Step

people inadvertently undermining the natural systems and resources upon which they depended:

> *Those past collapses tended to follow somewhat similar courses constituting variations on a theme. Population growth forced people to adopt intensified means of agricultural production (such as irrigation, double-cropping or terracing) and to expand farming from the prime lands first chosen on to more marginal land in order to feed the growing number of hungry mouths. Unsustainable practices led to environmental damage, resulting in agriculturally marginal lands having to be abandoned again. Consequences for society included food shortages, starvation, wars among too many people fighting for too few resources, and overthrows of governing elites by disillusioned masses.* (Diamond, 2005)

Of itself, the science of sustainability delivers few answers – merely the secure foundations upon which those answers can be constructed. Sustainability should certainly not be confused with some 'ideal state' where absolutely no damage is done to humans or nature; it simply means that human society can continue to exist because ecosystems are able to go on providing life-sustaining services (such as clean water, soil fertility, climate regulation and so on) and that society is capable of organizing itself so that people have the opportunity to fulfil their needs.

And there is no 'survival guarantee' here either. Imagine, optimistically, that a universal consensus emerges over the next decade regarding what we have to do (economically, politically and technologically) for the whole of humankind to be able to live within those natural limits. Then imagine, even more optimistically, that over the next few decades we actually succeed in reaching that goal. Humankind could, at that very moment, be obliterated from the face of the Earth by some cataclysmic event such as a meteorite impact or see its numbers dramatically cut back in a few thousand years by the inexorable onset of the next ice age. Viewed from a more cosmological perspective, literally *nothing* is truly sustainable inasmuch as the sun itself will, in a few billion years, cease to provide the energy upon which all life depends.

In the short term, however, if sustainability is the *destination* (the point at which we can genuinely claim to be living within those biophysical parameters), then sustainable development is the *process* or *journey* which we must undertake in order to get to that destination. For this reason, sustainable development as a concept remains less scientific, more imprecise and more politically determined. In 1990, Herman Daly put forward four core principles to underpin the sustainable development journey:

1   *Limit the human scale (or economic throughput) to that which is within the Earth's current capacity.*
2   *Ensure that technological progress is efficiency increasing rather than throughput increasing.*
3   *For renewable resources, harvesting rates should not exceed regeneration rates (sustained yield); waste emissions should not exceed the assimilative capacities of the receiving environment.*
4   *Non-renewable resources should be exploited no faster than the rate of creation of renewable substitutes.* (Daly, 1990)

FRAMING SUSTAINABLE DEVELOPMENT

Daly's four core principles have been elaborated upon many times since then. Unfortunately, they have proved to be of only limited use to politicians, given that such principles in themselves still shed little light on the social and economic aspects of sustainable development – and politicians still don't quite accept that the environmental leg of sustainable development's 'three-legged stool' is as important as the social and economic legs.

In 2005, the UK Government sought to address that issue by adopting the following 'framework goal' in the new UK strategy, *Securing the Future*: 'the goal of sustainable development is to enable all people throughout the world to satisfy their basic needs and to enjoy a better quality of life without compromising the quality of life of future generations' (HM Government, 2005).

For the UK Government and the devolved administrations, that goal will be pursued in an integrated way through a sustainable, innovative and productive economy that delivers high levels of employment, and a just society that promotes social inclusion, sustainable communities and personal wellbeing. This will be done in ways that protect and enhance the physical and natural environment, and use resources and energy as efficiently as possible.

This more balanced approach is made even clearer in the way in which the five basic principles underpinning sustainable development (see Figure 2.1) are articulated in the new strategy, reminding people that what we are really striving for through sustainable development is a way of 'living within environmental

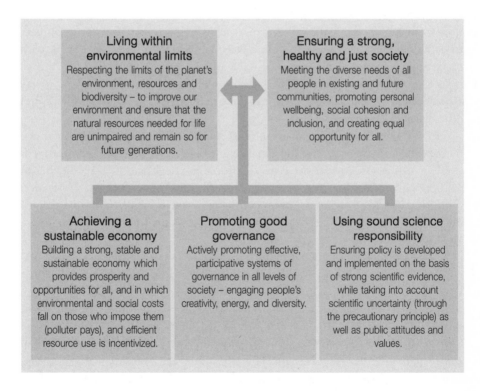

Source: HM Government (2005)

Figure 2.1 *Five principles of sustainable development*

limits' and 'a strong, healthy and just society'. The economy, our systems of governance and the way in which we use science are all *means* to achieving those two overarching *goals*.

It is the equivalent pairing of those two goals (living within environmental limits, and a strong, healthy and just society) that explains why sustainable development has such leverage in political terms. Prior to its arrival on the scene, many conservationists and environmentalists showed little interest or concern in the problems facing humankind, especially in the world's poorer countries. Although it is often strenuously denied by the current leadership of organizations such as the World Wide Fund for Nature (WWF) and Conservation International (CI), there was an unapologetic elitism about those organizations in the past and a much narrower focus on the natural world, with the human element somehow abstracted from it. Indeed, the tendency of some environmental organizations even today – particularly in the US – to try and keep the environment in some depoliticized zone, stripped of human complexity and controversy, may be one of the reasons why the environment movement in its own right has had less political impact than notional levels of public support might indicate.

By the same token, the vast majority of organizations addressing the social agenda (poverty, justice, human rights, health and so on) once had little if any time for thinking about the environment, consigning it to the category of nice-to-do things for the affluent middle classes, while real progressives got on with the serious business of making a better world for humankind. Over the years, strenuous efforts have been made to bring 'the environmental' and 'the social' aspects of sustainable development into more effective organizational forms, but often with little real impact.

That's now changing: cross-sectoral 'coalitions of the willing' are now much more evident. In 2005, for instance, most of the big development and environment charities in the UK (under the aegis of 'Stop Climate Chaos') came together to ratchet up their pressure on government regarding climate change; the motivation for the development organizations in getting involved in such a coalition was now much clearer in that the impact of climate change on the poor is becoming more and more severe.

The common ground between these organizations is unambiguously progress-ive in ideological terms, with an emphasis on justice and redistributive equity as well as on biophysical sustainability. That makes for an interesting and sometimes problematic combination, with the neutral and hopefully 'objective' science of sustainability underpinning the first goal in the UK Government's 2005 strategy ('living within environmental limits'), and the values-driven politics of global justice and progressive governance underpinning the second goal ('a strong, healthy and just society'). As we will see, this combination has led many people of a more conservative ideological persuasion to dismiss sustainable development out of hand, as demonstrated in this thundering quote from a US think-tank called The American Policy Center: 'If you want to keep your guns, your property, your children and your God, then sustainable development is your enemy!'. It may also explain the nervousness that many large companies still feel about it.

Indeed, sustainable development remains a frustratingly elusive and abstract concept as far as many businesses are concerned, a 'wrap around' for more operational business drivers, such as eco-efficiency, business ethics and CSR. The familiar notion of the 'triple bottom line' (with companies demonstrating a growing readiness to attend not just to the economic bottom line but to the environmental and social bottom lines as well) has been seized upon both by business practitioners and commentators as the easiest way of 'grounding' the often stratospheric debate surrounding sustainable development.

Inasmuch as it has been successful in this important but limited purpose, and has enabled some companies to think in a much more integrated way in addressing their environmental and social responsibilities, the triple bottom line has played an important part in the evolution of sustainable development consciousness. But it has clear limitations, particularly with regard to the ways in which each of the respective 'bottom lines' is being interpreted.

The *environmental bottom line* has come to be associated with the practice of environmental management – as in the International Organization for Standardization's ISO 14001 or the EU's Eco-management and Audit Scheme (EMAS) – and with the pursuit of 'eco-efficiency', defined by the World Business Council for Sustainable Development (WBCSD) as:

> the delivery of competitively priced goods and services that satisfy human needs and bring quality of life while progressively reducing ecological impacts and resource intensity throughout the life-cycle to a level at least in line with the Earth's estimated carrying capacity. (WBCSD, 2002)

No problem so far. But if interpreted in a minimalist way (as it almost always is), such an approach fails to shed much light on whether or not a company is moving towards genuine sustainability (as defined by TNS, for instance), and can even discourage scrutiny of much harder questions than 'how' something is produced, such as 'why' it is being produced at all. In that context, it is still surprising to hear people talking about 'environment-friendly landmines' or 'sustainable nuclear power'.

Attention to the *social bottom line* has accelerated a lot of new thinking about CSR, in general helping to reinforce what is referred to by some as the 'stakeholder' model of capitalism, in which the interest of stakeholders beyond the shareholder are given growing prominence. However, in comparison to the environmental bottom line, this is still a relatively new area, and there is considerable confusion regarding different ways of measuring CSR, let alone 'mainstreaming' it into corporate strategies.

Perhaps paradoxically, it is around the interpretation of the *economic bottom line* that the most serious problems have emerged. Given the continuing supremacy of the so-called 'shareholder model' of capitalism (in which a company is seen to have legal or fiduciary obligations only to its shareholders or owners, and to the governments that set the legal boundaries within which it operates), the economic bottom line has come to mean little more than 'business as usual': profits, dividends, return on investments, productivity, growth – in other words, financial performance in the time-honoured sense. Even information about environmental and social expenditures or savings rarely gets included in company accounts or presented in stand-alone environment or corporate responsibility reports.

While it is clearly true that companies need to stay in business to be sustainable, this overall approach (profitable business as usual, plus as much of the green and social 'stuff' that does not conflict with that priority added on) leaves us – and often the companies themselves – in the dark with regard to their overall economic sustainability. Companies can add substantial economic and social value in all sorts of different ways – through their supply chain and procurement policies; through investment in staff training and development; through their employment practices, seeking out best practice beyond that which is mandated through employment law; through their investment and innovation strategies; through the taxes they pay; through their investment in the local economy or community enterprise; and so on. Indirectly, companies also have a substantial impact upon society through their products and the way in which these products are used. But only very rarely will a company even allude to these important economic multipliers, focusing much more narrowly upon what should more accurately be described as its *financial* bottom line.

In January 2005, the *Economist* made its contribution to that dialogue by devoting an entire supplement to CSR. Drawing copiously on the work of David Henderson (2001) – whose *Misguided Virtue* provides perhaps the most elegant attack on CSR today – and on works by Wilfred Beckerman and Elaine Sternberg, the supplement set out to fashion an army of straw men about CSR and then gleefully pulled them to pieces.

As it happens, many people (without sympathy for the ideological positioning of the *Economist*) do indeed have deep reservations about both the intellectual rigour and the practical usefulness of CSR, and I will return to these in Chapter 14. But the *Economist* was not interested in that kind of enquiry. By mischievously confusing CSR with corporate philanthropy, accusing all CSR practitioners as having 'a paranoid fear of capitalism', and falling back on a sequence of heinous misinterpretations of the work of Adam Smith, it failed completely to get to grips with the genuine dilemma of our time: what further interventions by government are necessary to secure a more effective working relationship between the dynamism of a capitalist economy and the discipline of living within the Earth's limits? The *Economist* adamantly adheres to the belief, as an article of revealed truth, that the primary, if not exclusive, objective of business is to maximize profit, and that success in this goal will of itself provide the greatest public good. Hence its reference to Adam Smith's oft-quoted 'nostrum' that 'it is not from the benevolence of the butcher, the brewer or the baker that we expect our dinner, but from their regard to their own interest'. The *Economist* goes on to say: 'This is not the fatal defect of capitalism as CSR advocates appear to believe; it is the very reason capitalism works' (*Economist*, 2005). Markets should therefore be permitted to operate in a strictly amoral way, with individuals empowered to pursue their own self-interest as circumscribed only by the law.

This is disingenuous, if not dishonest. Adam Smith was the author not only of the *Wealth of Nations*, but of the *Theory of the Moral Sentiments*, where he asserts time after time that self-interest has to be pursued by 'people of conscience', informed by their capacity for moral awareness. Without that, the 'invisible hand' of self-interest will not work for the public good. The dominant form of enterprise in Adam Smith's time was the partnership, in which ownership and management were one and the same thing. He supported state intervention to promote fair competition ('people of the same trade seldom meet together [...] but the conversation ends in a conspiracy against the public'), and backed universal, public education. As we will see in Chapter 5, it was the emergence of the limited liability corporation that began to erode the freedom of managers to act with conscience on behalf of the public good – a process which Adam Smith predicted would lead to dangerous consequences. For those keen to advance the benefits of 'moral capitalism' over today's 'brute, amoral capitalism', Adam Smith is undoubtedly their founding father.

Reclaiming the inheritance of Adam Smith may be something of a distraction, but there are good reasons not to be seduced by those who would have us believe that the way capitalism is today is the way it has always been and always should be. As we will see, there are many passionate defenders of capitalism who believe their primary task is to defend traditional capitalism (where the rewards of investing went primarily to those who put up the capital and took the risks) against what some have described as a 'pathological mutation' of capitalism, where an excessive share of the rewards go to corporate managers, speculators, financial intermediaries and those who have no interest whatsoever in the enterprises in which they have invested.

Culture wars in the US

This is becoming an increasingly important battleground in the US, where the combination of aggressive unilateralism in pursuit of a new American imperium, an unprecedentedly radical application of liberal, neo-conservative economic policies, and the mind-boggling (to the average European mind, at least) adherence of large numbers of Americans to various forms of religious fundamentalism poses perhaps the greatest single threat to the prospect of sustainable development gradually becoming the dominant political framework within which today's complex dilemmas should be addressed.

There has never really been anything like this before. In *An Angel Directs the Storm: Apocalyptic Religion and American Empire*, Michael Northcott (2004) provides an insightful critique of the 'deformation of Christianity' being practised by so many adherents of today's fundamentalist churches in the US, and of the naivety of Europeans in not understanding what we are really dealing with in contemporary America, particularly in terms of religious beliefs influencing foreign policy. Opinion polls in the US regularly indicate that at least one quarter of all Americans think they are living 'in the end times', subscribing to a set of pre-millennialist beliefs that cast a dark cloud of fatalism and fanaticism over the US's role in the world today:

> *Pre-millennialists believe they are living in the end time, and it is an era of growing lawlessness and dreadful wars which threaten to extinguish human life on Earth. Only after these events will Christ return to inaugurate a literal 'thousand-year reign of peace', which millennialists believe is predicted by the Book of Revelation. Pre-millennialists also believe that true believers will be 'raptured' or plucked off the planet by God before the Great Tribulation, so that only those 'left behind' will have to face the terrors of the end time – the last great conflagration of Armageddon, or World War III, which will happen as a result of the escalation of crisis in the Middle East.* (Northcott, 2004)

According to a Gallup poll carried out just before the 2004 presidential election, around one third of the US electorate believe that the Bible is *literally* true in every particular. Just under 50 per cent of congressmen are backed – politically and financially – by the religious right. As Bill Moyers, one of the best-known public service broadcasters in the US puts it: 'The delusional is no longer marginal.' Indeed, it is not marginal at all. More than 1600 radio stations and 250 television stations churn this stuff out hour after hour, day after day.

As a distant observer of the US religious scene, I have a very strong sense of mainstream, moderate Christians having first been taken completely by surprise by the ascendancy of fundamentalist views of this kind, and then digging in to re-balance what Christianity is perceived to mean in this troubled world – and in the process to rebalance some of the perceptions of what 'being American' has come to mean to the rest of the world during the Bush Administration. That fight-back has been led in part by moderate evangelicals, in part by progressive Christians representing a multiplicity of different viewpoints, and in part by people of less firmly defined denominational beliefs but still passionately spiritual perspectives.

For many secular progressives, all this seems completely irrelevant, and they will undoubtedly be deeply irritated at my occasional referencing of such religious and spiritual matters. But religion shapes our world today more directly and (in my opinion) more dangerously than at any other time in modern history. Whether people like it or not, this has a massive bearing on whatever prospects we may have for transitioning from a world hell-bent on eco-cidal self-destruction to one in which all 9 billion of us (by 2050) have some reasonable hope of leading dignified, sustainable and satisfying lives. As Michael Lerner points out (in his immensely stimulating *Tikkun Reader*, celebrating 20 years of liberal, left-leaning journalism from both Jewish and interfaith perspectives), to deny the significance of these religious and spiritual challenges just seems immature, and can be immensely frustrating for those seeking a more intelligent riposte to the dominance of right-wing thinking in US politics and religion:

> *The Right gets away with all this because the Left seems completely unable to identify the spiritual crisis as real. Born out of the struggles against feudalism in the 17th and 18th centuries, the Left adopted the emerging scientistic world view that all that was real was that which could be verified through data, or which could be subject to measurement. So the Left has no intellectual tools for understanding the spiritual crisis that the globalization of capital has increasingly made a central reality of the post-modern world. As a result, tens of millions of Americans who are victims of the deprivation of meaning in their lives and of the effects of selfishness and materialism in their families began to respond to a Religious Right that could articulate the pain that they were feeling. While the Left seemed totally tone deaf to the spiritual crisis, and assumed that these Americans were moving to the Right because of sexism, homophobia, racism or just plain stupidity, we had discovered that they were attracted to the Right because it spoke to their well-founded fears about the loss of love and of meaning in daily life.* (Lerner, 2006)

Much of that hunger for some kind of certainty, some fixed and constant point in a turbulent world, has been exacerbated since the attack on the twin towers in New York in September 2001, and by the ensuing war against Iraq. As we know, there is *no* causal connection between those two defining moments in history, although a combination of constant propaganda from the White House and an utterly servile approach from the US media led to an almost inconceivable 70 per cent of US citizens believing that Saddam Hussein *was* involved in the September 11th attacks. Against such a backdrop, the near universal consensus among religious leaders in the US and UK against the war in Iraq (with the exception of the American Southern Baptists) was totally ignored both by George Bush and by Tony Blair. The Bush Administration was quick to equate dissent of this kind as demonstrating a lack of patriotism, and, to their shame, most of the US media again went along with this denial of proper debate.

Worse yet, these events seemed to confirm in George Bush (and, many also believe, in Tony Blair) a feeling that he had been chosen by God to lead his nation at that particular moment in history. The language he has constantly used since then to capture that sense of destiny is resonant with explicitly Christian imagery and phraseology – more so than that of any other President in US history – as he pursues his mission through the war on terror 'to rid the world of evil'. When evil equals Islam, and war equals 'crusade', and Pax Americana equals the unilateral imposition of US military force on those deemed to constitute the greatest threat to this new world order, then many believe that the true fundamentalist purpose of the Bush Administration is fully revealed. As Jim Wallis points out in his admirable *God's Politics*, this melding of theology and foreign policy becomes deeply disturbing:

> *The real theological problem in America today is no longer the religious Right, but the nationalist religion of the Bush Administration, one that confuses the identity of the nation with the church, and God's purposes with the mission of American empire. America's foreign policy is more than pre-emptive, it is theologically presumptuous; not only unilateral, but dangerously Messianic; not just arrogant, but rather bordering on the idolatrous and blasphemous. George Bush's personal faith has prompted a profound self-confidence in his mission to fight 'the axis of evil', his call to be commander and chief in the war against terrorism, and his definition of America's responsibility to 'defend the hopes of all mankind'. This is a dangerous mix of bad foreign policy and bad theology.* (Wallis, 2005)

It's not just in the field of foreign policy that this unique amalgam of neo-liberal economics and fundamentalist Christianity has been felt. The knock-on impacts for the environment in the US have also been extremely serious as the Bush Administration has sought to rewrite and radically dilute the Clean Air Act, the Clean Water Act, the Endangered Species Act and the National Environmental Policy Act – the four pillars of US environment policy. It still wants to open up the Arctic National Wildlife Refuge, and extend both grazing and logging rights on public land. There are still millions of Christian fundamentalists in the US who believe that environmental destruction is not just unimportant, but something to be positively welcomed – even hastened – as a sign of the coming apocalypse. Environmental activists are regularly castigated as both crypto-communists and godless heretics:

> *Why care about the Earth when the droughts, floods, famine and pestilence brought by ecological collapse are signs of the apocalypse foretold in the Bible? Why care about global climate change when you and yours will be rescued in the rapture?* (Moyers, 2005)

This has led to a growing awareness on the part of moderate evangelicals across the US that they have given away far too much of the moral high ground to their more extreme co-religionists, particularly in terms of standing up for God's creation. This rearguard action has been swift and extremely effective. In October 2004, the National Association of Evangelicals adopted an 'evangelical call to civic responsibility', affirming that 'God-given dominion is a sacred responsibility to steward the Earth, and not a licence to abuse the creation of which we are a part.' Two years later, 86 evangelical leaders signed a declaration about climate change ('An evangelical call to action') that was published in the *New York Times*, stimulating a fierce but ultimately very positive debate within key organizations like the National Association of Evangelicals and the Evangelical Environmental Network. In January 2007, building on these initiatives, an extraordinary consultation took place in Georgia where scientific and evangelical leaders met to search for common ground 'to unite to protect creation':

> *We believe that the protection of life on Earth is a profound moral impera-*
> *tive. It addresses without discrimination the interests of all humanity*
> *as well as the value of the non-human world. It requires a new moral*
> *awakening to a compelling demand, clearly articulated in Scripture*
> *and supported by science, that we must steward the natural world in*
> *order to preserve for ourselves and future generations a beautiful, rich*
> *and healthful environment.*
>
> > *We declare that every sector of our nation's leadership – religious,*
> *scientific, business, political and educational – must act now to work*
> *toward the fundamental change in values, lifestyles and public policies*
> *required to address these worsening problems before it is too late. There*
> *is no excuse for further delays. Business as usual cannot continue yet one*
> *more day. We pledge to work together at every level to lead our nation*
> *toward a responsible care for creation, and we call with one voice to our*
> *scientific and evangelical colleagues, and to all others, to join us in these*
> *efforts.* (Center for Health and the Global Environment, with the
> National Association of Evangelicals, 2007)

This is a rare and hugely inspiring declaration, signed by many of America's most eminent scientists as well as leaders of various evangelical organizations. The sole UK signatory was James Jones, the Bishop of Liverpool, who has played a massively influential role working with the evangelical churches in the US to help move them on from a position which he believes is untenable from a theological as well as a scientific perspective. He's one of the very few people in the UK who understands the significance of how this debate is mediated in the US, and its knock-on impact on the rest of the world:

> *in less than eighteen months, Americans will elect a new President and*
> *a new Administration. Already stalls are being set out. Already poli-*
> *ticians are signing up and making a pitch for that evangelical vote*

which secured the Presidency for Mr Bush, but deserted the Republicans in droves at the Congressional Elections in November 2006. I do not think it is an exaggeration to suggest that the redefining of priorities by evangelicals in America could have a decisive effect on the outcome of the election and the future of America, and hence the future of the Earth. (Jones, 2007)

Some Europeans tend to dismiss all of this as yet more bizarre manifestations of a nation dominated by a series of 'culture wars' that go so deep that they seem to be immune to the power of reason. But that seems complacent. The successful advocacy of sustainable development, as articulated in this chapter, depends utterly upon some sense of shared purpose across the world as a whole, including, and especially, the US, as well as upon a wholly rational, evidence-based analysis of the urgent need to change our ways.

Bringing the Americans on board over climate change has proved to be a nightmare, in part because the same body of evidence is being processed in completely different ways on either side of the Atlantic. But the Bush Administration's approach to climate change (explored in more detail in Chapter 12) is just the visible tip of an iceberg of environment-wrecking policies. In *Crimes Against Nature* (2004), Robert Kennedy Jr has provided the most chilling account of the way in which the Bush Administration has set out covertly but systematically to dismantle every single principal building block of his country's environmental legislation. He cites more than 300 major roll-backs in President Bush's first four years in office. Most of these are directly or indirectly connected to financial contributions to the Republican party, with tens of millions of dollars changing hands in a way that makes this particular Administration one of the most shamelessly corrupt governments anywhere in the world.

This assault on the environment has only been possible by subverting the work of the Environmental Protection Agency and every other regulatory body. In case after case, Robert Kennedy Jr itemizes how data have been suppressed, key reports amended to downplay the evidence, and individual scientists harassed and victimized. In February 2004, the Union of Concerned Scientists issued an unprecedented report signed by 60 world-renowned scientists, including 20 Nobel laureates, asserting that the scope and scale of 'the manipulation, suppression and misrepresentation of science by the Bush Administration is unprecedented' (Union of Concerned Scientists, 2004). As Robert Kennedy Jr says:

Science, like theology, reveals transcendent truths about a changing world. The best scientists are moral individuals whose business is to seek the truth. Corruption of this process undermines not just democracy but civilization itself. (Kennedy, 2004)

THE CHALLENGE TO ENVIRONMENTALISM

Over the last few years, there has been an extremely lively debate in the US (under the provocative heading 'the death of environmentalism') about the environment movement's own complicity in the triumph of anti-environmental, neo-conservative politics in America. Many now believe that an excessively techno-cratic, regulation-driven approach to protecting the environment allowed the neo-conservatives to win the battle for people's hearts and minds, appealing unapologetically to their sense of themselves as fair, hard-working, entrepreneurial citizens – oppressed rather than liberated by their environmental protectors. Environmental concerns are usually framed very technically as something to be sorted out by legislators and experts. They are neatly boxed up in discrete self-contained packages: air quality, biological diversity, national parks, toxic waste, climate change and so on. The focus is fixed firmly on the environment as such, without widening the frame to embrace people, their communities or the economy.

Coalitions with other progressive causes are usually seen as too difficult to handle, diluting the environmental message, potentially alienating funders and inviting unnecessary controversy. For instance, why speak out against the war in Iraq or HIV/AIDS or systematized cruelty to animals if these are clearly not 'environmental' issues as such?

All this has led Adam Werbach, a former executive director of the Sierra Club, to the following rather sober conclusion:

> *The signs of environmentalism's death are all around us: we speak in terms of technical policies, not vision and values; we propose 20th-century solutions to 21st-century problems; we are failing to attract young people, the physical embodiment of the future, to our cause; we're failing to attract the disenfranchised, the disempowered, the dispossessed and the disengaged; we treat our mental categories, ourselves and other elements of nature as things; most of all, environmentalism is no longer capable of generating the power it needs to deal with the world's most serious ecological problems.* (Werbach, 2004)

I suspect that most European environmentalists would want to see themselves exempted from such charges. And it is certainly true that they have, to a considerable extent, managed to avoid such constricting demarcation lines. Friends of the Earth continues to campaign with passion on human rights, international trade, governance issues and so on; Greenpeace has steadfastly maintained its work on security issues and nuclear weapons; the WWF has found itself increasingly involved in community-based social and economic initiatives, if only to ensure that its biodiversity work can be more effectively prosecuted.

Sustainable development is more of a lived reality this side of the Atlantic than on the other – even if those organizations still find it difficult to embrace its language and more radical intellectual analysis.

But it's hardly been plain sailing for the European environment movement either. The EU's renewed emphasis on economic growth and competitiveness at almost any cost is having a massively damaging impact upon a number of key environmental issues. People are accustomed to seeing Europe's green parties still winning relatively low percentages in elections (even though those green parties remain by far the most articulate and realistic exponents of what the politics of sustainable development must eventually come to look like).

It is easy to blame the politicians for the usual combination of short-sightedness and poor leadership. Here in the UK, people felt there might be a new dawn after the election of New Labour. But after three years of what looked like real dynamism and promise (confirming the judgement of environmental NGOs, which, with the honourable exception of Friends of the Earth, were positively sycophantic about the new incumbents), the dramatic protests about rising fuel taxes in 2000 took all the wind out of their newly furled green sails. Since then, with the exception of Tony Blair's leadership on climate change and Gordon Brown's leadership on third world debt and social justice, it's been hard graft – 'crabby, uninspiring incrementalism, as if they didn't want anybody to know that they cared about the environment', is how one veteran environmental journalist put it to me recently. Fortunately, that all began to change in 2006 with the arrival of 'the two Davids' – David Miliband, who has injected serious energy and new thinking into his role as Secretary of State for the Environment, making such an impact on the Labour Party, the media and environmental NGOs that he was instantly billed as a future party leader, and David Cameron, leader of the Conservative Party, whose astute decision to focus on green issues has been implemented with considerable skill.

It's impossible to make green politics work in a parliamentary democracy without first-class opposition, and that was entirely lacking before David Cameron's election. Though Labour (and the Liberal Democrats) deny that this has had any impact on them whatsoever, that's simply untrue. With the media suddenly alert to environmental stories, and the general (voting) public much more focused than before, the whole agenda has been ratcheted up several notches. World-weary activists (some of whom – including the author – have been there before during Mrs Thatcher's electrifying but extremely short-lived 'green period' in the late 1980s) are doing their best to persuade themselves that this time it's for real and 'here to stay'.

At the same time, some have already started to question just how effective the UK environment movement has been over the ten years since the current Labour government was first elected. There have been very few out-and-out successes, a huge amount of effort devoted to holding the ground won under preceding Tory governments, and a great string of disappointments and setbacks that certainly were not envisaged when environmentalists so warmly welcomed the Labour victory in 1997. So have we lost the plot? Have we sold out to a government that talks as green as they come, but defaults on almost every occasion to classic 'growth' responses? Even if we aren't necessarily contemplating 'the death of environmentalism' as such, in the UK or in Europe more generally, I would argue that we can now talk with some justification of the *demise* of conventional environmentalism in the face of 20 years of unreconstructed, neo-conservative economic liberalization.

In this regard, the challenge is the same both here and in the US: how to reframe the social and environmental problems we now face in such a way as to win back the progressive ground lost to the conservatives during that time. Conventional environmentalism is demonstrably incapable of rising to that challenge: its appeal is too narrow, too technical, too anti-business, too depressing, often too dowdy, and too 'heard it all before'. Unless environmentalism can reposition itself within the more progressive and radical frame that sustainable development provides – a frame that allows the inevitable (the need for change) to be made desirable – then a continuing decline in influence seems the most likely outcome. That repositioning will inevitably entail a profound shift of mood:

> *Martin Luther King's 'I Have a Dream' speech is famous because it put forward an inspiring, positive vision that carried a critique of the current moment within it. Imagine how history would have turned out had King given an 'I Have a Nightmare' speech instead. In the absence of a bold vision and a reconsideration of the problem, environmental leaders are effectively giving the 'I Have a Nightmare' speech, not just in our press interviews but also in the way we make our proposals. The world's most effective leaders are not issue identified, but rather vision and value identified. These leaders distinguish themselves by inspiring hope against fear, love against injustice and power against powerlessness. A positive, transformative vision doesn't just inspire, it also creates the cognitive space for assumptions to be challenged and new ideas to surface.* (Schellenberger and Norhaus, 2005)

These comments by Michael Schellenberger and Ted Norhaus were made in the context of climate change, and it is interesting to see how rapidly things are now shifting in the US – not just on climate change, but on many other environmental issues. The Democrats' victory in the 2006 mid-term elections has transformed the environmental agenda in both the House of Representatives and the Senate. As soon as the House re-convened in January 2007, it passed a Bill rescinding $15 billion of subsidies and special deals for the oil industry, with a view to re-directing the money into renewable energy schemes. In March 2007, a long-delayed report from the White House admitted that US emissions of greenhouse gases will rise by about 20 per cent between 2000 and 2020, further undermining any residual credibility the White House may have looked for on climate change. Even the President's first positive reference to the importance of climate change in his 2007 State of the Nation address is seen by most impartial observers as a ludicrously belated attempt to acknowledge the changing mood inside the US.

There's now some equally belated soul-searching going on within the US media about its complicity in the anti-environmental, denial-based agenda so ruthlessly exercised by the White House over the last seven years. On several visits to the US, I've been astonished to see how easily the media default to that sad excuse of 'the need for balance', as if all the data so cogently brought together by the Intergovernmental Panel on Climate Change (and even by Al Gore's *An Inconvenient Truth*) should be given no more weight than the mendacious propaganda of the oil industry – whose unbounded cynicism is neatly captured by their latest advertising slogan: 'Carbon dioxide. They call it pollution. We call it life'. They might be right, in that there would certainly be no life without the carbon dioxide in the atmosphere – but that isn't exactly what they mean.

Moreover, it is not just on environmental issues that we need to discover a new kind of innovative and stereotype-busting 'cognitive space'. The neo-conservative elite in Washington is equally reluctant to engage in any serious exploration about the need to transform today's prevailing economic paradigm – the so-called Washington Consensus. Many aspects of today's economic orthodoxy remain as firmly off-limits as ever in terms of any public debate, particularly the notion that progress is best served by the uncomplicated pursuit of ever higher levels of economic growth and personal consumption. This has a huge impact upon the quality of debate about sustainable development, and what it really means in terms of transforming conventional economic policies and practice. There are many in government and business, across the world, who are only too happy to see the concept of sustainable development remain totally detached from the debate about economic growth. But that cannot be.

To engage purposefully in debates about the nature of economic growth and its compatibility/incompatibility with the pursuit of sustainability is surely within the 'manageable universe' of what politicians can and cannot cope with. So why exactly has this become yet another taboo territory, shunned even by those politicians who have fallen off the greasy pole of personal ambition and have nothing to lose in challenging the shibboleths of today's political economy? Is it complacency? Or a lingering belief that this is an impossibly black-and-white area of debate (it's either gung-ho growth at all costs, as we have it today, or zero growth as espoused by fundamentalist greens back in the early 1970s) – even though this is patently not the case? Or an unthinking sense of 'if it ain't broke, don't fix it' – even though the most cursory examination would reveal just how 'broke' our dependency upon conventional GDP-driven economic growth really is? Or a feeling (rarely acknowledged in public) that the rich world can probably get away it with it anyway, just a little bit longer, so long as the poor world isn't allowed to gatecrash the party?

REFERENCES

Center for Health and the Global Environment, with the National Association of Evangelicals (2007) 'An urgent call to action: Scientists and evangelicals unite to protect creation', report of meeting at National Press Club, Washington, DC, January 17, available at www.conservation.org/ImageCache/CIWEB/content/downloads/faith_5 funitecall2action_2epdf/v1/faith_5funitecall2action.pdf

Daly, H. (1990) 'Toward some operational principles of sustainable development', *Ecological Economics*, vol 2

Diamond, J. (2005) *Collapse: How Societies Choose to Fail or Succeed*, Allen Lane, London

Economist (2005) 'The good company: Survey of CSR', *Economist*, 22 January

Henderson, D. (2001) *Misguided Virtue: False Notions of Corporate Social Responsibility*, Institute of Economic Affairs, London

HM Government (2005) *Securing the Future: Delivering UK Sustainable Development Strategy*, TSO, London, available at www.sustainable-development.gov.uk/publications/ uk-strategy/index.htm

Johannesburg Memo (2002) *Fairness in a Fragile World*, Heinrich Böll Foundation, Berlin

Jones, J. (2007) 'Faith and the future of the Earth', St George's Lecture, 1 June

Kennedy, R. (2004) *Crimes Against Nature*, Penguin, London

Lerner, M. (2006) *Tikkun Reader: Twentieth Anniversary*, Rowman and Littlefield, Lanham, MD

Moyers, B. (2005) 'Welcome to Doomsday', *New York Review of Books*, vol 52, no 5

Northcott, M. (2004) *An Angel Directs the Storm: Apocalyptic Religion and American Empire*, I. B. Tauris, London

Schellenberger, M. and Norhaus, T. (2005) 'The death of environmentalism: Global warming politics in a post-environmental world', *Grist Magazine*, www.grist.org

Sen, A. (1999) *Development as Freedom*, Oxford University Press, Oxford

Union of Concerned Scientists (2004) 'Scientific integrity in policy making', report available at www.ucsusa.org/global_environment/rsi/page.cfm?pageID=1642

Wallis, J. (2005) *God's Politics*, Lion Books, Oxford

WBCSD (2002) *Walking the Talk: The Business Case for Sustainable Development*, World Business Council for Sustainable Development, Geneva

WCED (World Commission on Environment and Development) (1987) *Our Common Future*, the Brundtland Report, Oxford University Press, Oxford

Werbach, A. (2004) 'Is environmentalism dead?', speech at The Commonwealth Club, San Francisco, 8 December. Text available at www.grist.org/news/maindish/2005/01/13/ werbach-reprint

3

Re-engaging with Economic Growth

INTRODUCTION

At the heart of contemporary capitalism lies the concept of economic growth. So one can't assess the compatibility of sustainable development and capitalism without first getting to grips with growth. This remains a critical debate, though much less current than it was during the 1970s – perhaps because the laws of thermodynamics have proved such indigestible fare for modern politicians! But today's critique of growth is no anti-growth or zero-growth diatribe: economic growth can still be great, and billions of people all around the world still need a lot more of it. But what *kind* of growth? For *whom*? Within what *limits*? And measured against what kind of *benchmarks*? To shed light on these questions, this chapter considers the so-called 'peak oil debate': how soon will the extraction of oil and gas peak in terms of their contribution to global energy supplies? A lot rests on the answer to this question, given the critical role that access to reliable and relatively cheap oil and gas has played in driving our growth economies over the last 50 years.

THE LIMITS TO GROWTH

Astonishingly, the whole question of sustainability and economic growth has been more or less sidelined over the last couple of decades. The 'limits to growth' debate during the 1970s may well have been somewhat cruder and more polarized than environmentalists would have wanted, but at least it opened up some of the 'killer questions' about economic growth that far too few people are prepared to engage in today. Bald statements like this, from Murray Bookchin, are rarely heard:

> *To speak of 'limits to growth' under a capitalistic market economy is as meaningless as to speak of limits to warfare under a warrior society. Capitalism can no more be 'persuaded' to limit growth than a human being can be 'persuaded' to stop breathing. Attempts to 'green' capitalism, to make it ecological, are doomed by the very nature of the system as a system of endless growth.* (Bookchin, 1980)

In 2005, Jørgen Randers and Dennis Meadows brought out *Limits to Growth: The 30-Year Update*, a new edition of their *Limits to Growth* (the third author of the original work, Donella Meadows, died in 2001). It provides a compelling account of the 'growth and sustainability' conundrum, is as relevant now as it was when first published back in 1972, and is required reading for anyone trying to think these issues through from an integrated, systems perspective. As such, it remains one of the most important contributions to the sustainable development debate that has ever been written.

If that sounds a bit assertive, it may well be because some people still retain a vague folk-memory that the original *Limits to Growth* 'got it all wrong' in predicting the end of life as we know it, was based on faulty computer modelling and was 'seen off' (especially in the US) by a group of growth-fixated economists – the proto-contrarians, as we might see them today. None of these perceptions is accurate. As the *30-Year Update* demonstrates, the many different models that the original work explored have proved to be remarkably robust, and the core analysis about natural limits and the dangers of overshooting these limits is, if anything, more critical now than it was then. It did *not* claim that economic growth leads inevitably to collapse, and it did *not* advocate a zero-growth alternative.

It is the notion of 'overshoot' – meaning, quite simply, to go too far, to cross the line, to go beyond limits without necessarily knowing that this is what one has done – that makes the analysis so powerful. On a finite Earth, physical growth must eventually end. The idea that we can sustain the kind of growth we have seen since 1950 in key areas of economic activity, knowing what we already know about the state of the planet, is simply fantastical. The principal conclusion of the research conducted by Randers and Meadows over a 30-year period is simple:

> *we worry that current policies will produce global overshoot and collapse through ineffective efforts to anticipate and cope with ecological limits. We believe that the human economy is exceeding important limits now, and that this overshoot will intensify greatly over the coming decades.*
> (Randers and Meadows, 2005)

And overshoot can lead to only two outcomes: a crash of some description, or a deliberate, planned turnaround through a series of corrections that will be more or less painful depending upon the timeframe within which they are made.

It is for this reason that any serious analysis of the potential compatibility of sustainability, on the one hand, and capitalism, on the other, must surely address the question of economic growth more systematically than any other. Of all the defining characteristics of post-World War II capitalism, the centrality of economic growth as the overarching policy objective is perhaps the most important. It has driven turnover in the global economy to a staggering $45 trillion per annum, doubling in just 25 years, with the volume of world trade now 12 times what it was in 1945. Hundreds of millions of people's lives have been enriched, often dramatically, in the process.

Yet, as we also know, those dramatic increases in economic activity and material wellbeing have failed to solve many of the world's worst problems (particularly chronic poverty in developing countries) and have created a host of additional problems as a consequence of their environmental and social externalities. That has left some environmentalists arguing that sustainability and the pursuit of economic growth – of any kind – are totally incompatible. But is that really the case?

Going right back to the work of Reverend Thomas Malthus – who examined the impact of population growth in 1798 and reached the conclusion that population growth would naturally check itself in the form of famine, wars and disease – people have always tended to underestimate both the resilience of biophysical systems in accommodating the expansion of the human species, and the sheer genius of the human species in finding new resources, bringing on substitutes for diminishing resources and increasing the efficiency of resource use through market forces. Conventional economics holds that so long as the price of something provides a sufficiently realistic measure of its value, then rising prices for diminishing resources will encourage both greater efficiencies in their use and the development of substitutes. As we will see later in the chapter, this is precisely how most economists address the problem that levels of oil production are likely to peak within the next decade. So what's the problem?

At the heart of the growth conundrum is a misconception so gross that it makes a complete nonsense of the way in which the vast majority of economists and politicians think about economic growth. For them, the global economy is *the* system, within which all else (human society, the planet and all other species) can be subsumed as subsystems. And once the global economy is seen as the overarching, self-contained system, it can then define its own operational boundaries and, theoretically, expand both permanently and exponentially, with constant increases in the throughput of both matter and energy.

Unfortunately, this is as close to biological and thermodynamic illiteracy as it is possible to get. The economy is, in the first instance, a subsystem of human society (the economy may well have appropriated more and more of that broader societal territory, but there is still a lot more to human life than the economic activity we engage in), which is itself, in the second instance, a subsystem of the totality of life on Earth (the biosphere). *And no subsystem can expand beyond the capacity of the total system of which it is a part* (see Figure 3.1).

That may sound so obvious as to insult the reader's intelligence. Yet, despite the re-uttering of it over the years by scores of 'maverick' economists and envi-ronmentalists, it remains steadfastly outside the canon of what passes for con-ventional neo-classical economics, with increasingly disturbing consequences.

It means that the majority of economists (and the politicians whom they advise) still do not appreciate that as an open subsystem of the much larger but

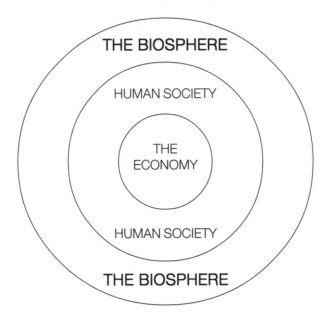

THE BIOSPHERE

HUMAN SOCIETY

THE ECONOMY

HUMAN SOCIETY

THE BIOSPHERE

Source: Forum for the Future

Figure 3.1 *Sustainable systems*

essentially closed ecosystem, it is the physical limits of that ecosystem which will constrain the speed and scale at which the economic subsystem can expand. In the long run, it *cannot* grow beyond the capacity of the surrounding ecosystem to sustain that growth – and the planet (or overarching ecosystem) *cannot* grow. What we have is what we've got. Come what may, therefore, the scale of the economic subsystem will eventually be determined by the overall scale of the ecosystem, by its ability to provide high-grade resources and to absorb low-grade waste, and by the interdependency of all interlocking elements within that ecosystem. As eco-entrepreneur Paul Hawken puts it:

> *Contrary to what many people might believe, the rate and capacity of the Earth to create material quality depends not upon human-driven activities, but upon the sun. Virtually all our human activities remove or consume quality. As ingenious and important as industrial practices are, they also use up quality and order. Nature has the capacity to recycle wastes and reconstitute them into new resources of concentrated material quality. However, its capacity is regulated by sunlight and photosynthesis, not by economic theory or politics. Today's extraction and processing of resources is overwhelming that capacity, while the waste from these processes systematically builds up in our water, air, soil, wildlife – and in ourselves.* (Hawken, 1993)

Trying to buck the laws of thermodynamics is not sensible. The first law of thermodynamics (or conservation law) states quite simply that energy is neither created nor destroyed as it is changed from one form to another (heat, light, motion, etc). The second law of thermodynamics states that the availability of that energy to perform useful work is reduced as it passes through successive transformations. This is sometimes described as the law of entropy – entropy being a measure of the amount of energy no longer capable of further conversions to perform useful work. Entropy within any closed system inevitably increases over time; it is only the fact that our system is open to incoming solar radiation that prevents an inexorable decline into chaos.

These laws lead to two simple but all-important conclusions. First, nothing ever disappears. Every particle of matter in the universe today has been part of the universe since the Big Bang, and will continue to be part of the universe until the end of time. Everything has to go somewhere, and 'stuff' has a way of spreading. And, second, every time energy and matter are converted into another form, their quality is degraded and they become less useful to us. We know all of this from our own daily experience. Natural resources that are extracted or harvested to power our economy must eventually return to nature. Steel eventually rusts, fossil fuels are burned, wood rots, carpets turn to dust – not the other way round. And the value of these resources (and the products in which we incorporate them) is directly related to their *order*, by which we mean the quality or concentration of energy and matter. As that concentration is dispersed, their value drops.

As a result, it is not things or molecules that we are consuming, but the order inherent in them. When we burn a gallon of petrol in an internal combustion engine, we do not really consume those hydrocarbons, but benefit from the work they perform as they are being transformed. When we drink water, we are not only consuming it physically, but also consuming its quality in terms of the concentration of clean molecules. It's that which has value. It is the availability and maintenance of this quality that determines the prosperity of humankind, and if society consumes quality more quickly than it can be reconstituted through biophysical systems, then we are, in effect, becoming poorer, not richer.

The laws of thermodynamics are therefore fundamental to an understanding of our growth dilemma. From Nicolas Georgescu-Roegen in the mid-20th century onwards, alternative economists have sought to persuade mainstream economists that they must link increases in economic growth with increases in entropy. As Paul Ekins puts it:

> *Economic activity increases entropy by depleting resources and producing wastes. Entropy on Earth can only be decreased by importing low entropy resources (solar energy) from outside it. This energy can renew resources and neutralize and recycle waste. To the extent that the human economy is powered by solar energy, it is limited only by the flow of that energy. Growth in physical production and throughput that is not based on solar energy must increase entropy and make environmental*

problems worse, implying an eventual limit to such growth. Gross National Product can free itself from these limits only to the extent that it 'decouples' itself from growth in physical production. Such decoupling has occurred to some extent; but the entropy law decrees that it can never be complete. Optimists believe that the decoupling can be substantial and continuous; pessimists are more sceptical. (Ekins, 2000)

Optimists do, indeed, point to the so-called 'invisible environmental hand', where economic growth can actually help to reduce pollution if it accelerates resource productivity at a faster rate than both resource consumption and population growth. Wilfred Beckerman, for instance, asserts that 'in the longer run, the surest way to improve your environment is to become rich' (Beckerman, 1974). The pessimists promptly point to the 'rebound effect' (whereby any additional 'environmental space' created by increased resource efficiency is immediately offset by additional consumption), and simply invite people to re-examine the irrefutable empirical evidence of continuing and worsening ecological damage.

That situation is further worsened by the fact that we don't just continue to grow, but to grow exponentially. There is a crucial distinction between *linear* growth (when a quantity of something grows by the same amount over each time period, regardless of what is already there), and *exponential* growth (when the increase is not constant, but is proportional to what is already there). It is the difference between 10 per cent on £100 producing £10 per annum year after year, and 10 per cent on £100 producing £10 in year one, £11 in year two (10 per cent of £110), £12.10 in year three (10 per cent of £121), £13.31 in year four and so on. It may not sound much, but as Box 3.1 shows, it has dramatic consequences. And a growth rate of 3 per cent per annum means a doubling of the quantity involved in just 23 years.

As Paul Ekins (2000) points out, this makes it all the more important to distinguish between different kinds of growth:

- *growth in the economy's biophysical throughput (in a world bound by the laws of thermodynamics, indefinite growth of this kind is physically impossible);*
- *growth in the economic value of that throughput (decoupled from the level of biophysical throughput itself); and*
- *growth in economic welfare (which is much harder to calculate and very different from the growth in the economic value of biophysical throughput, although invariably treated as one and the same).*

Growth in economic welfare is what matters most; growth in the economic value of biophysical throughput can, of course, generate precisely that (although it often does not), and can certainly do so without any corresponding growth in biophysical throughput – as we will see in Chapter 10.

BOX 3.1 BEYOND THE LIMITS

The surprising consequences of exponential growth have fascinated people for centuries.

There is an old Persian legend about a clever courtier who presented a beautiful chessboard to his king and requested that the king give him in exchange 1 grain of rice for the first square on the board, 2 grains for the second square, 4 grains for the third, and so forth. The king readily agreed and ordered rice to be brought from his stores. The fourth square on the chessboard required 8 grains, the tenth square took 512 grains, the 15th required 16,384, and 21st square gave the courtier more than 1 million grains of rice. By the 40th square, 1 million million rice grains had to be piled up. The payment could never have continued to the 64th square; it would have taken more rice than there was in the whole world.

A French riddle for children illustrates another aspect of exponential growth – the apparent suddenness with which an exponentially growing quantity approaches a fixed limit:

> *Suppose you own a pond on which a water lily is growing. The lily plant doubles in size each day. If the plant were allowed to grow unchecked, it would completely cover the pond in 30 days, choking off the other forms of life in the water. For a long time the lily plant seems small, so you decide not to worry about it until it covers half the pond. On what day will that be? On the 29th day. You have just one day to act to save your pond.*

Source: Meadows et al (1992)

RAISING THE HAPPINESS STAKES

The truth of the matter is that economic growth, like the process of globalization, has become fixed in people's minds as a given – indeed, 'a force beyond human control'. As Clive Hamilton's (2003) wonderfully provocative *Growth Fetish* makes clear, governments of all persuasions are now mesmerized by economic growth. Not only has it become synonymous with the notion of progress itself, but 'citizens' have gradually been transmuted into 'consumers', so that all human desire and aspiration can be rendered in terms of the products and services that they can choose to consume.

Hamilton quotes extensively from a fascinating piece of research (*Yearning for Balance*) commissioned in 1995 by the Merck Family Fund to survey the attitudes of US consumers. Some unambiguous conclusions emerged, with the vast majority of respondents desperate to achieve a better balance between the material and non-material sides of their lives. 'They believe materialism, greed and selfishness increasingly dominate American life, crowding out a more meaningful set of values centred on family, responsibility and community' (Hamilton, 2003).

Eighty per cent believed that they consume far more than they need to, while recognizing that this lust for material things lies at the root of crime, family breakdown, drug addiction and so on:

> *They can see that materialism is corroding society in themselves, but they are too fearful to change their behaviour in any significant way. They are wedded to 'financial security', even though they understand that non material aspirations are the ones that will give them contented lives.* (Hamilton, 2003)

This goes right to the heart of today's growth dilemma. Politicians' near obsessive pursuit of increased growth, year after year, regardless of increasingly negative consequences, might be justifiable (albeit in a somewhat morally defective way) if people were genuinely getting happier – if all that planet-trashing, consumptive economic activity resulted in more and more people feeling more and more content with their lot every year. But this is absolutely not happening. Surveys of national wellbeing and satisfaction levels show that when a nation moves from developing to developed status, there is, at first, a significant increase in wellbeing. But once nations reach the level where most or all of their citizens' basic needs are being met, increases in relative affluence beyond that point do not make much of a difference.

In *The Loss of Happiness in Market Democracies*, Robert Lane (2000) describes this as 'the waning power of income to yield that ephemeral good utility', and castigates both academics and politicians for being in thrall to the 'economistic fallacy' that, beyond poverty or basic subsistence levels, higher incomes will automatically increase levels of subjective wellbeing.

The relationship between economic growth and people's quality of life (or 'life satisfaction') has been picked up by senior government advisers in the UK. In a paper published by the Cabinet Office's Strategy Unit in December 2002 ('Life satisfaction: The state of knowledge and implications for government'), Nick Donovan and David Halpern highlight the basic problem contained in the life satisfaction data from the Eurobarometer survey (see Figures 3.2 and 3.3). And there are plenty of surveys and opinion polls that bear this out. As part of its 'Happiness Formula' programmes in 2006, the BBC conducted an on-line poll to assess the nation's happiness. Key findings included feedback that 'Britain today is less happy than in the 1950s – despite that fact that we are three times richer'. The proportion of people saying they are 'very happy' has fallen from 52 per cent in 1957 to just 36 per cent today. Furthermore, the poll asked 'whether the Government's prime objective should be the "greatest happiness" or the "greatest wealth" of the nation'. A remarkable 81 per cent wanted happiness as the goal. Only 13 per cent wanted wealth.

All opinion polls of this sort should of course be treated with caution. The Ipsos MORI 'International Social Trends Monitor', carried out at almost exactly

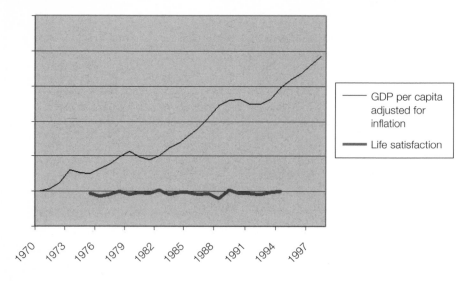

Source: adapted from Donovan and Halpern (2002)

Figure 3.2 *Life satisfaction*

the same time, showed the UK as the *most* optimistic of the large European countries in terms of our satisfaction with life in general. Nearly 90 per cent of us declared that we were either very or fairly satisfied with the life we lead, and nearly half of us think that life will apparently get better over the next 12 months. Italy and Germany turned out to be the least optimistic of the large European countries, with France and Spain in between.

I suspect most people would see this as something of an anomalous set of conclusions. In *Affluenza*, Oliver James (2007) reviews a vast body of sociological data from different countries relating to levels of contentment and wellbeing, and the overwhelming weight of evidence points to the highest levels of dissatisfaction and 'emotional distress' in countries like the US and the UK. For James, that's quite simply because there are more people in the US and UK suffering from the 'Affluenza virus' – defined as 'a set of values which increase our vulnerability to emotional distress, and which entail placing a high value on acquiring money and possessions, looking good in the eyes of others, and wanting to be famous'. His compelling analysis sets out to demonstrate that the kind of capitalism driven forward so aggressively by the US and UK since the 1970s is the principal cause of today's epidemic of Affluenza virus, accounting for much of the increase in emotional distress during that time:

> To fill the emptiness and loneliness, and to replace our need for authentic,
> intimate relationships, we resort to the consumption that is essential for

economic growth and profits. The more anxious or depressed we are, the more we must consume, and the more we consume, the more disturbed we become. Consumption holds out the false promise that an internal lack can be fixed by an external means. Compensation for personal misery is why people with the Virus are at the greater risk of substance abuse (alcohol, illegal drugs), but more importantly, of the legal 'aholias', shopaholia ('till we drop'), workaholia, sex and other compulsions of mass consumption. We medicate our misery through buying things; its purveyors have never pretended otherwise. (James, 2007)

What gives this analysis extra bite is the linkage between declining levels of contentment and inequality: the greater the inequality of income distribution within a developed country, the higher the levels of dissatisfaction and alienation – with the interesting exception of Singapore! As the study reveals, 'prevalence of emotional distress' is at least twice as high in English-speaking OECD countries (the US, the UK, Australia, New Zealand and Canada) as in other OECD countries (Europe, Japan and so on). America is, by some margin, the most emotionally distressed of all nations: 'put crudely, the more like America a society becomes, the higher its rate of emotional distress'.

All this just confirms a strong historical trend. As Fred Hirsch (1977) so eloquently demonstrated more than 25 years ago in his ground-breaking *Social*

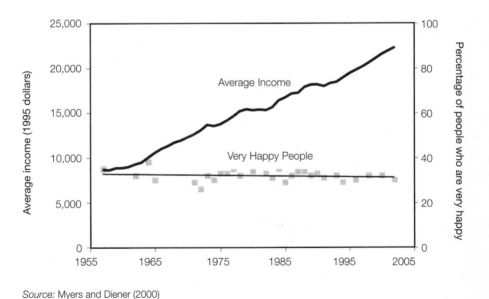

Source: Myers and Diener (2000)

Figure 3.3 *Average income and happiness in the US, 1957–2002*

Limits to Growth, contentment is not a matter of *absolute* wealth but *relative* wealth. The steady rise in individualistic materialism since World War II has made us all far more preoccupied with status and wealth relative to others. This is sometimes described as the 'Mr Toad syndrome'. In Kenneth Grahame's *Wind in the Willows* (1908), Mr Toad was quite happy with his narrow boat until he set eyes on a passing horse-drawn caravan, and quite happy with his caravan until he saw a car. These days, of course, one car leads inevitably to another (bigger, faster, snazzier) car. As Richard Easterlin (2001) puts it: 'Even though rising income means people can have more goods, the favourable effect of this on welfare is erased by the fact that people want more as they progress.' He refers to this effect as 'the hedonic treadmill' as our desire for more constantly outstrips what we already have.

Not unreasonably, critics of our consumer culture have questioned the degree to which this sense of 'relative dissatisfaction' is, in fact, created (or at least inflated) by the advertising and marketing strategies of those who stand to benefit most from persuading people that they are not quite as happy as they could be – and would be if they bought x or y. The power of marketing to create demand is, of course, hotly contested – ever since Vance Packard's astonishing exposé of the advertising industry, *The Hidden Persuaders*, back in 1957, academics and industry insiders have argued the toss on just how explicit 'the creation of dissatisfaction' has been in shaping today's consumer-driven capitalism. But any parent who's had to watch Saturday morning television with their young children will be deeply unimpressed by the marketing industry's expressions of innocence in this regard. George Monbiot invites us to come to what he sees as an obvious conclusion:

> *Plenty of evidence suggests that as we become richer, we become less content with ourselves. It is incorrect to say that necessity is the mother of invention. In the rich world, invention is the mother of necessity. When people already possess all the goods and services they need, growth can be stimulated only by discovering new needs. Advertising creates gaps in our lives in order to fill them. We buy the products, but the gaps remain.* (Monbiot, 2002)

Ever since the ground-breaking work of Abraham Maslow identifying the 'hierarchy of needs' that people seek to meet, psychologists and alternative economists have set out to demonstrate that far from there being any automatic increase in wellbeing for every increase in levels of consumption, much of our current consumption is turning out to be a very inadequate surrogate for meeting human needs in a more satisfying, durable way. But it may still be playing a very important macro-economic function, as Clive Hamilton points out:

> *Modern consumer capitalism will flourish as long as what people desire outpaces what they have. It is thus vital to the reproduction of the system that individuals are constantly made to feel dissatisfied with what they*

have. The irony of this should not be missed: while economic growth is said to be the process whereby people's wants are satisfied so that they become happier – and economics is defined as the study of how scarce resources are best used to maximize welfare – in reality, economic growth can be sustained only as long as people remain discontented. Economic growth does not create happiness: unhappiness sustains economic growth. Thus, discontent must be continually fomented if modern consumer capitalism is to survive. This explains the indispensable role of the advertising industry. (Hamilton, 2003)

Worse yet, beyond these relatively manageable levels of dissatisfaction, there is a growing body of evidence which shows that things are actually getting worse in terms of mental wellbeing. There is a growing consensus among psychiatric researchers that rates of depression, for instance, have been on the increase since the 1950s, especially among the young.

Oliver James's hugely revealing *Britain on the Couch* (1998) also points out that suicide rates have increased markedly since 1950, as have levels of violence against the person, alcoholism, drug addiction and substance abuse – all part and parcel of a clear increase in mental illness generally. According to the World Health Organization (WHO), mental health problems are fast becoming the number one health issue of the 21st century, with one in ten people suffering at any point in time, and one in four suffering at some point in their lives. Anthony Stevens and John Price make the necessary connection:

It seems likely that the various neuroses, psychopathologies, drug dependencies, the occurrence of child and spouse abuse, to say nothing of the ever rising crime statistics, are not unconnected with Western society's inability to satisfy the archetypal needs of our kind. The number of people in whom these basic needs are not met is large and growing, as indeed are the psychiatric problems which they represent. (Stevens and Price, 1996)

It is strange how little political salience this seems to have. As a quality-of-life issue, it's difficult to imagine a bigger set of cumulative problems. In 2002, the Institute for Optimum Nutrition surveyed around 22,000 UK citizens, most living in towns and cities, and most below the age of 30. They found that:

- *76 per cent of people are regularly tired;*
- *58 per cent suffer from mood swings;*
- *52 per cent feel apathetic and unmotivated;*
- *50 per cent suffer from anxiety;*
- *47 per cent have difficulty sleeping;*
- *43 per cent have poor memories or struggle to concentrate; and*

- *42 per cent suffer from depression.* (Institute of Optimum Nutrition, 2002)

One of the few organizations to address this head-on here in the UK is Compass, perhaps the most eloquent and thoughtful of those organizations on the Centre Left seeking to remind us just what progressive politics might look like. It believes the UK is in the grip of an extremely serious 'social recession', with New Labour obsessively preoccupied with the crass ephemera of consumerism and celebrity, and all but incapable of addressing deeper equity concerns, especially as they relate to the young and the old. In February 2007, this critique was powerfully reinforced by a report from UNICEF comparing the wellbeing of children and adolescents in 21 developed countries (UNICEF, 2007). The survey was based on data gathered together in six main areas: financial wellbeing; health and safety; educational wellbeing; family and peer relationships; social behaviour and risk; and own perception of wellbeing. The Netherlands, Sweden, Denmark and Finland topped the league; the US and the UK came right at the bottom. Al Aynsley-Green, the Children's Commissioner for England, commented as follows:

> *These children represent the future of our country, and from the findings of this report, they are in poor health, unable to maintain loving and successful relationships, feel unsafe and insecure, have low aspirations, and put themselves at risk. There is a crisis at the heart of our society, and we must not continue to ignore the impact of our attitudes towards children and young people, and the effect that this has on their wellbeing.* (Aynsley-Green, 2007)

Behind these high-level abstractions stands a wealth of more detailed evidence. In November 2002, a report from the Joseph Rowntree Foundation compared 10,000 people born in 1958 with 10,000 born in 1970. While in their mid-20s, both groups were questioned about their mental health. Among the post-World War II generation, just 7 per cent of those questioned had a tendency to non-clinical depression; among those born in 1970, the figure had doubled to 14 per cent. In June 2006, a report from the British Medical Association indicated that nearly 10 per cent of 5 to 16 year olds suffer from psychological problems that are 'persistent, severe, and affect functioning on a day-to-day basis'. Roughly a million children under the age of 18 would benefit from specialist services. Even though our Government has had some success in reducing levels of child poverty, this does not seem to be translating through into any clear reduction in emotional distress in childhood.

Sue Palmer's powerful book *Toxic Childhood* (2006) highlights a wide range of changes in the lives of children that are contributing to this phenomenon: a massive reduction in the time children spend interacting with the significant adults in their lives, with parental love measured in presents rather than presence;

the 'atomization' of family life, with family members splintering off into different rooms of the home; dramatic changes in children's play habits, with many children now incarcerated in the home for fear of traffic, bullying, 'stranger-danger' and a host of additional perceived 'risks'; and junk food, sedentary life-styles, screen-based lives and constant exposure to a 'marketing maelstrom' as companies strive to recruit children to their brands as young as possible. This is an extract from a letter in the UK *Daily Telegraph* that I co-signed back in September 2006:

> *Children need what developing human beings have always needed, including real food (as opposed to processed junk), real play (as opposed to sedentary, screen-based entertainment), first-hand experience of the world they live in, and regular interaction with the real-life, significant adults in their lives. They also need time. In a fast-moving, hyper-competitive country, today's children are expected to cope with an ever-earlier start to formal schoolwork, and an overly academic test-driven primary curriculum. They are pushed by market forces to act and dress like mini-adults, and exposed via the electronic media to material that would have been considered unsuitable for children even in the very recent past.* (Greenfield et al, 2006)

It's hard to say which of these commercializing factors is having the worst influence. As a deep sceptic about the apparently wondrous benefits of modern information and communications technologies, I find myself increasingly concerned about the degree to which internet-based *virtual* networks are taking over from real *physical* communities. It's not so much a global, internet-enabled village that I see people participating in, as yet another shopping mall, one which offers much less genuine human contact and far more violence, pornography, paedophilia and every expression of human depravity one can imagine. Children who used to play with other children now play by themselves on home consoles or the computer – a perfect representation of a society progressively decoupling itself from the warmth and constancy of face-to-face interaction. Much of today's new technology leads, remorselessly, to increased isolation – and the fact that anyone who points out as much is instantly dismissed as a neo-Luddite elitist ensures that there is little debate about this hugely influential social trend.

In America, surveys show that media and technology consumption is the number 1 life activity. A recent study by the Office for National Statistics revealed that the average UK citizen is spending more time watching television and using the internet than sleeping. The average young child in the UK watches up to 4½ hours of television a day, with a typical 11 to 15 year old in front of a TV or computer an astonishing 7½ hours a day – the majority of children in the UK now have a TV in their own bedroom. In April 2007, Dr Aric Sigman challenged claims by the BBC and other TV producers that TV viewing at that age is primarily 'educational' by helping children get interested in the outside world ('the world around them is what gets them interested in the outside world') and launched a campaign for MPs to seek to ration exposure to TV, with zero viewing for children under three, 30 minutes a day for 3 to 7 years old, and one hour a day for 7 to 12 year olds.

People might consider this to be less unrealistic if they understood better the links between TV viewing and violence. By the time the average US schoolchild leaves elementary school, he or she will have witnessed more than 8,000 murders and more than 100,000 other acts of serious violence on television. And this immersion in violence starts young: every hour of children's television shows between 20 and 25 aggressive acts. Researchers working with Jeffrey Johnson at Columbia University in New York, who followed more than 700 families over 17 years, showed a strong association between the amount of television watched during childhood and early adolescence and the likelihood of behaving aggressively and violently towards others – regardless of any other factors such as family background, neighbourhood, education and so on.

Amazingly, the cumulative impact of all this on children's minds is still strenuously denied by 'the entertainment industry', who continue to suggest that there is still a lot of evidence to demonstrate that such violence is having no effect whatsoever. That view is flatly contradicted by the vast majority of researchers in this area, as the *New Scientist* pointed out in a hard-hitting editorial after the tragic shootings at Virginia Tech University in April 2007:

> *Researchers see a clear link between media consumption and aggression, and also mounting evidence for an increased risk of attentional, behavioural and educational problems with extended exposure to TV and computer games. They have been in little doubt for around half a century, and over that time, scientific confidence in the detrimental effects of media violence has only increased. The issue is no longer whether there is an effect, but what it means to each one of us, and how much we care. The effects are subtle, and it will remain impossible to pin any specific act – such as the horrific shootings at Virginia Tech University – to a single media experience.* (*New Scientist*, 2007)

Against such a massively powerful (and, in my opinion, massively damaging) societal backdrop, particularly in the UK and the US, those who are now urging a shift away from the politics of economic growth to the politics of wellbeing are really up against it – in part because it is naïve to expect a dispassionate coverage of such controversial issues from the self-same media whose parent companies are invariably making a ton of money peddling this barrage of violence. When David Cameron, as newly-elected leader of the Conservative Party, dipped his toe into these waters in 2006, the UK print media started an orgy of virulent and contemptuous coverage. How could any 'serious' politician even begin to suggest that there might be a more direct and effective route to securing improved wellbeing for the majority of people than generating economic growth in such a way that it can't help but destroy the very foundations of human happiness?

This kind of unscientific, knee-jerk denial is very similar to the denial that once held sway about climate change. The *fact* that persevering with this particular model of economic growth is leading *directly* to increased social problems, and ever-worsening levels of personal dissatisfaction and emotional distress, is another 'inconvenient truth' that politicians can barely bring themselves to acknowledge. Yet the facts won't go away. One in six people here in the UK suffers depression or some kind of chronic anxiety disorder – not the 'worried well', but people with severe mental difficulties. Some 40 per cent of people claiming disability allowance here in the UK do so because of mental illness.

Yet we actually spend relatively little on mental health. In the US, only 7 per cent of health expenditures are targeted at mental illness, and in the UK only 13 per cent, with just 2 per cent going to treat depression and anxiety.

In the UK, only one in five patients suffering from depression is treated by a specialist psychiatrist. Most are simply put on drugs by their GP. Nevertheless, it has been calculated that stress-related illness alone costs the UK around £7 billion a year, a figure which has led Richard Layard (2005) to propose to the Treasury that it should set aside around £600 million a year to appoint thousands of Cognitive Behaviour Therapists. According to the National Institute for Health and Clinical Excellence, just £750 for 16 one-hour sessions would be by far the most effective intervention available for the majority of patients.

Ironically, from a straight growth-driven, GDP-measured perspective, such astonishing levels of emotional distress may not be a huge problem. The economy, after all, continues to prosper. The more we spend on the National Health Service, the bigger our GNP. The more people spend making themselves ill, fat, unhappy and unhealthy in the first place, the more they can then spend trying to make themselves thin, happy and healthy all over again – all of which keeps the wheels of the economy whirring merrily away, even if it is rather difficult to see what this has to do with real progress. Writing in the *RSA Journal* in December 2002, Richard Reeves put it like this:

> *In the last couple of decades, the very idea of progress has lost its mooring. The principal means through which Western societies have advanced throughout modern history – economic growth – is faltering: richer no longer means better. We have lost the philosophical comfort of the Cold War, which at least provided a clear picture of what we were not. And science and technology now often appear as handmaidens to scary futures full of cloned people with microchips in their eyelids, rather than offering escape routes from disease and want. If we measure our progress in terms of our happiness or evaluation of our own wellbeing, we have not advanced for half a century.* (Reeves, 2002)

Much of this research is brought together in Richard Layard's (2005) book *Happiness*. Defining happiness quite simply as 'feeling good', he asks why it is that governments all around the world (with the odd exception such as Bhutan, with its emphasis on Gross Domestic Happiness) more or less refuse to engage in the politics of happiness, to explore the disconnections outlined above, or to address them *explicitly* through different policy interventions. Taking as his mentor the redoubtable 18th-century philosopher Jeremy Bentham ('Create all the happiness you are able to create; remove all the misery you are able to remove'), he goes on to explain the 'greatest happiness' principle: the right action is the one that produces the greatest happiness, and a law is a good law if it increases the happiness of citizens and decreases their misery. He also offers his readers an elegant ten-point exposition as to why happiness matters so much (inadequately summarized here in my words rather than his):

1 Happiness is an *objective* dimension of all our experiences and it can be measured.
2 Human beings are programmed to seek happiness.
3 It should therefore be self-evident that the best society will be the happiest society rather than the richest society.
4 Our society is not likely to become happier unless people explicitly agree that this is what they want to happen.
5 Human beings are deeply social beings; as such, we want to be able to trust each other. Happiness is profoundly affected by levels of trust.
6 Human beings are also very status conscious and are deeply attached to the status quo – they hate loss of any kind.
7 However, extra income increases happiness less and less as people get richer.
8 Human beings are also very adaptable; just because consumption is addictive now does not mean it always will be.
9 Happiness depends upon your inner life as much as upon your outer circumstances.
10 Public policy can more easily remove misery than augment happiness itself.

What makes all of this so interesting is that Professor Layard is an extremely eminent economist, best known for his work on employment issues and inequality. As such, he knows better than most that this is almost taboo territory for orthodox economists, whose focus is predominantly on people's purchasing power rather than on how happy they are. He has come to the conclusion that the economic model of human nature (which dominates contemporary politics) is far too limited – 'it has to be combined with knowledge from the other social sciences'.

And that is precisely where the distinction between economic growth and sustainable development becomes so crucial. As Herman Daly (1996) and others have argued, economic growth is all about *quantitative expansion*, the notionally 'limitless transformation of natural capital into man-made capital'. Sustainable development is about *qualitative improvement*, permitting increased economic activity only in so far as it does not exceed the capacity of the ecosystem. In pursuit of economic growth, conventional economists almost exclusively put the emphasis on the non-physical parameters of the economy (income, choice, distribution, productivity and so on) and expect the physical variables to be 'adjusted' accordingly. In pursuit of sustainable development, economists must, in future, put the emphasis on the physical parameters (such as resources and the laws of thermodynamics) and accept that the non-physical variables must be adjusted accordingly. Set the physical laws of nature against the vagaries of neo-classical economics and there can only be one winner – and it won't be humankind.

Deep down, more and more economists accept that growth and development are not the same thing, and that there is something here that they just can't go on ignoring. But it is proving hard to give up the old ways:

> *The concept of limits to growth threatens vested interests in power structures; even worse, it threatens value structures in which lives have been invested. Abandonment of belief in perpetual motion was a major step towards recognition of the true human condition. It is significant that mainstream economists never abandoned the belief, and do not accept the relevance to the economic process of the second law of thermodynamics; their position as high priests of the market economy would become untenable did they do so.* (Cook, 1982)

Instead, those 'high priests' of the economics profession keep coming up with all sorts of Houdini-like tricks to escape the laws of nature. We're told that human ingenuity in substituting man-made capital for natural capital will keep pushing those limits away – ignoring the fact (as we will see in Part II) that man-made capital and natural capital are *not* always direct substitutes. Beyond that, we are told that the 'dematerialization' of the economy will indefinitely defer the day of reckoning. Crucial though these responses are (in terms of dramatically reduced biophysical throughput of energy and matter), they do not constitute a panacea for those problems. As Herman Daly (1996) says, 'We can surely eat lower on the food chain, but we cannot eat recipes.'

What makes this so hard to address is that our single most important indicator of economic prosperity (namely GNP) obscures the reality of what is actually happening. The standard, aggregated index of GNP is used to capture the sum of all marketed exchanges and government expenditures, and therefore measures the increase in the economic value of overall production – but *not* decoupled from levels of biophysical throughput that generate that increased economic value. So as we eat up our 'natural capital' or degrade the ecosystem's capacity to renew the kind of natural services upon which we depend, we persist in counting all that destructive economic activity as current (benign) income. At the same time, we also count in many so-called 'defensive expenditures', caused by having to deal with some of the externalities of economic growth, be they environmental (such as environmental protection and restoration, and damage compensation) or social (such as car accidents, poor health and rising crime).

As we will see later in Chapter 13, there *are* alternative ways of measuring economic activity, but they are paid only lip service by politicians and are ignored by most mainstream economists. That represents just one facet of the institutionalized denial about the limits to growth that has been going on for decades. As mentioned earlier, this debate almost ground to a halt during the late 1970s, when politicians took stock of the consequences to them and their parties if they could no longer fall back on the tried and tested certainties of economic growth. Since then, people have become so accustomed to the notion that 'economic growth solves all' (albeit on the patently inadequate grounds that a bigger overall 'economic cake' means there is more to spread around, or at least more crumbs to trickle down) that to disabuse them of the thermodynamic impossibility of this would exact a heavy political price. Better by far to subscribe to the physically impossible (that biophysical throughput can keep on growing indefinitely) than face the political impossibility of persuading electorates to reduce their expectations.

The latest pernicious attempt to obscure that fundamental reality lies in the self-evident oxymoron of 'sustainable growth' – assuming that we are talking about conventionally determined growth (as above) rather than (to put it somewhat laboriously) growth in levels of welfare derived from growth in economic value decoupled from biophysical throughput!

THE END OF CHEAP OIL

The self-inflicted blindness of contemporary capitalism to the laws of thermodynamics is the first and most problematic barrier to reconciling capitalism and sustainability. It is by no means the only barrier.

However one reacts to the explosion in economic activity and material prosperity over the last 60 years or so, there is no denying that it has been fuelled predominantly by access to cheap oil and gas. Without that massive and exhilarating infusion of plentiful hydrocarbons, our world today would look *very* different.

These are, by definition, non-renewable resources. They will, inevitably, start running out at some stage in the future. At that point, our lives will change dramatically. Even if we are successful in preparing ourselves for the transition from an oil-rich world to a world largely without oil, the disruptions will still be dramatic and potentially disastrous.

This debate has only just started to warm up again. There is an inevitable sense among politicians of a certain age that they have 'been there and done that'. Most lived through the oil shocks of the 1970s and were exposed to a turbulent debate about the possibility of oil running out in their own lifetime. But just like the debate about economic growth itself, those concerns soon sputtered out. Jimmy Carter's enthusiastic but often ill-directed attempts to get the American people to understand the consequences of their gas-guzzling lifestyles (during which he famously described energy conservation as the 'moral equivalent of war') were swept away by the election of Ronald Reagan in 1980. Right-wing commentators and economists seized the moment to lambaste the doom-and-gloom merchants who had predicted the all-but-instant drying-up of oil supplies, and the high ground occupied by environmentalists concerned about the physical limits to growth was systematically cut away from beneath them.

Looking back over those 30 years, it is clear that this lost opportunity (to set humankind on a more sustainable energy path) represents the single biggest setback for the environment movement during that time. Instead of shifting both public and private sector investments into energy efficiency, renewable technologies and less energy-intensive infrastructure, we have burned our way through billions of barrels of oil with no thought for the future and no thought for the environmental consequences.

Encouragingly, it would appear that this is now beginning to change. The debate about the availability of oil has suddenly livened up again. In March 1998, *Scientific American* published a ground-breaking article by Colin Campbell and Jean Laherrere under the provocative title of 'The end of cheap oil?'. Five years on, Richard Heinberg (*The Party's Over: Oil, War and the Fate of Industrial Societies*, 2003) set out to review all of the conflicting voices commenting on just how long the oil era will last. We know when this 'historic interval' started (with the very first commercial oil well being drilled in Pennsylvania in 1859); but when will it end? The key date for assessing this is the point at which *global* oil production peaks: US production peaked in 1970; UK production peaked in 2000/2001; Saudi Arabian oil is not due to peak until after 2015. But when is the 'big roll-over' likely to come for the world as a whole?

This is no easy calculation, with huge controversy around every aspect of the debate – the size of 'ultimately recoverable reserves'; the growing significance of different extraction techniques; the influence of the price mechanism; the fact that no one really knows how much oil is left in Saudi Arabia's oil fields; the impact of war and security issues, and so on. Geologists involved in the debate tend to incline towards an earlier date (perhaps as soon as 2008), principally on the basis that overall discoveries of oil peaked in the 1960s, with just one new barrel of oil being discovered today for every four that are consumed; economists incline towards a later date (2015/2020), on the basis that there has always been more in the ground than the experts have historically predicted and that extraction techniques just go on getting better and better. Lord Browne, former Chief Executive of BP, was for ever reassuring people that there would be no supply problems until around 2030.

The case for the 'early toppers' (those arguing that we're on the verge of that 'tipping point' right now) has until recently been drowned out by the sheer weight

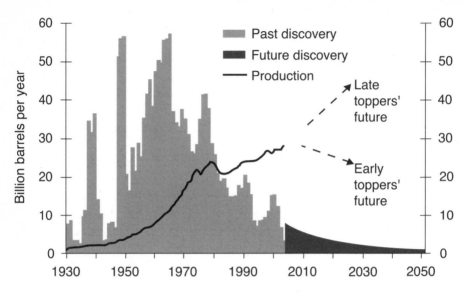

Source: Leggett (2005), p63

Figure 3.4 *Past and future global oil discovery and production*

of institutions and industry voices lining up behind the 'late toppers' scenario. In *Half Gone*, Jeremy Leggett (2005) systematically works his way through every single one of the more bullish assumptions that lie behind the oil companies' estimates. Perhaps the most shocking revelation for those not familiar with this running controversy is just how difficult the oil companies are now finding it to make *any* significant new discoveries. As Leggett points out, the last year in which we discovered more oil than we consumed was back in 1980, as Figure 3.4 demonstrates with compelling clarity.

Global production peaking is not, of course, the same thing as oil running out. Huge amounts of oil will still be pumped after that point – *but on an inexorably declining basis*. Politicians just seem to be drifting into this hugely challenging new world without so much as a passing recognition of the fact that oil production could be down by as much as 75 per cent within just 30 years. As Colin Campbell (2005) points out in a new collection of articles about the peak oil debate, *The Final Energy Crisis*, we are planning to undertake this transition 'without sight of a substitute energy that comes close to matching the utility, convenience and low cost of oil and gas'.

But is it right to be pressing the panic button at this stage? Long before we see that drop in production of 75 per cent, the price mechanism will, indeed, kick in, and rising prices will extend the period of time that oil remains available for various uses in society – if the worsening consequences of climate change have not already compelled politicians to force all users of hydrocarbon fuels to internalize more of the costs of their use. Many commentators believe not only that these market mechanisms provide the best antidote to today's 'peak oil Cassandras', but that the 'managed volatility' in oil prices provides proof positive that the system is working quite adequately.

In 2005, however, many analysts began to see things rather differently. Prices bumped up against $70 dollars a barrel, and stayed obstinately above the $50 dollar threshold. Goldman Sachs published a report predicting that oil would move to $100 a barrel in a much shorter period of time than anyone was counting on. The debate in the US became much more engaged, with a number of heavyweight commentators castigating the inertia of the Bush Administration in refusing to do anything to reduce US oil consumption. US motorists suddenly found themselves paying a whole lot more for their petrol, and began to wonder why the big US car companies (particularly Ford and General Motors) seemed to have so little to offer them by way of fuel-efficient cars. In 2006, it got even worse as oil prices hit a new high of $79 a barrel. And they're gone that high again in 2007.

Even those who had spent years rubbishing the exponents of the 'peak oil' hypothesis began to acknowledge that something momentous – and really rather scary – was going on.

THE PEAK OIL/CLIMATE CHANGE INTERFACE

The interplay between climate change on the one hand, and 'peak oil' on the other, is having a significant impact on all oil companies, but on Shell in particular. Along with all the other oil majors, it has acknowledged that it's getting harder and harder to secure access to new sources of 'easy (or conventional) oil' to make up for the amount it depletes every year. After the damaging scandal regarding mis-reporting of reserves with the Securities and Exchange Commission (SEC) in the US in 2004, Shell is more in the hot seat on this issue than any other company – even though they are *all* facing exactly the same dilemmas.

Shell's response to those dilemmas is fascinating – and indisputably high risk. It has decided to pursue a strategy based on so-called 'unconventional hydrocarbons' to replace the easy stuff – in essence, massively to expand its operations in Canada to exploit the huge reserves of tar sands in Athabasca, and to start getting serious about the equally vast deposits of oil shale in the US Rockies. The fact that the SEC currently refuses to treat these assets as proper reserves (on the grounds that they both involve mining operations rather than conventional 'extraction') is neither here nor there. Shell is clearly right in assuming that shareholders will see them for what they are: potentially *vast* substitute supplies to make up for the ever-diminishing easy stuff. Better yet, they both happen to be located in North America, where *the* key issue right now is *energy security*: how to make the citizens of the US and Canada much less dependent on imports either from the Middle East or from Venezuala.

So far, so good – even if production costs are much higher than for conventional oil. But there's a snag – a huge snag. Barrel for barrel, the raw material delivered to the refinery from the tar sands in Athabasca causes the emissions of at least twice as much CO_2 as conventional oil – four times as much according to NGOs. As regards the oil shale in Colorado, detailed estimates as to the carbon intensity of each barrel of oil equivalent delivered to the refinery are not available. But when they do become available, it is suggested that they will be pretty horrendous, primarily because the chosen technology (essentially 'cooking' the shale oil in situ, underground, before it is extracted, having first contained it within a 'frozen firewall' to suck all the water out of it) is so massively energy-intensive in its own right that there's simply no way the carbon balances can be made to stack up. Especially as the source of energy for this process is likely to be coal!

Though one can see *exactly* why Shell is going down this route, the 'reserves versus CO_2' dilemma couldn't be more painful. As far as shareholders are concerned, Shell is basically asking them to go along with four separate high-level judgements:

1   That the price of oil will remain high enough (in this case, above $50 a barrel) to justify the additional costs involved in exploiting those unconventional sources. As I see it, that's a sound bet!

2   That Carbon Capture and Storage (CCS) technologies will deliver the goods in terms of 'best value' carbon capture processes at the refinery and highly cost-effective ways of storing it underground. As I see it, the jury's out on this, although I'm a lot more sympathetic to CCS than most environmentalists, as I will explain in Chapter 10. But there's simply not enough data to hand, either on the 'capture' end of things or on 'storage'. By all accounts, none of the current cost projections that have been carried out to date give a figure of less than $40 for every tonne of CO_2 captured and stored.

3   That the cost of CO_2 will remain 'manageable'. As Shell planners carry out their forward calculations for new investments in both Athabasca and the Rockies, they have to factor in a notional or 'shadow' price for each tonne of CO_2 emitted to deliver each barrel of oil equivalent, given that there's currently no actual carbon trading scheme in the US. As I see it, these investments *may* make sense at $5 or even $10 for a tonne of CO_2, but at anything above $100 (which is where the Stern report (Stern, 2007) indicates a realistic price should settle in the medium term), that looks pretty questionable. From an investors' perspective, can you justify pumping in hundreds of millions (probably billions) of dollars when you can't calculate in advance one of the most critical cost elements?

4   That climate change won't 'go ballistic' over the next 10–20 years, which means that average temperatures and sea levels will *gradually* rise in line with *gradual* increases in the atmosphere of concentrations of CO_2 and other greenhouse gases, rather than trigger dramatic, non-linear shifts in the climate in ways that we can't even begin to imagine. As I see this one, I hope they're right, but I rather doubt the quality of the data on which they're making the call.

These dilemmas are not actually all that different for the other oil companies – it's just they've had less of a run-in with the authorities on declared reserves. But they all face their own Scylla and Charybdis look-alikes: on the one hand, investors expect increased (and ever more efficient) production to underpin increased dividends – and that means getting out there and finding the stuff to produce, even if it's in dodgy countries or of dodgy quality from an energy/carbon intensity perspective; on the other, growing concerns about climate change (even in America) mean that even the oil majors are having to start thinking about a dramatically different measure of corporate success: how much CO_2 have you caused to be emitted to deliver the same amount of economic value (measured either by turnover or profit)? It won't be long before 'CO_2 intensity' becomes as important an indicator to investors as any of the conventional financial indicators. Imagine a world in which carbon is trading at $100 a tonne; even with oil selling at $100 a barrel, which it shortly will be, whichever oil company has the highest CO_2 intensity ratio will surely be the first of them to go to the wall.

Which is why investors are beginning to track another current indicator – one which provides important information as to future CO_2 intensity – and that is the percentage of total invested capital going into renewable energy. Oil companies have always had something of a dilemma with renewables, not least because the return on investment (feeding into dividends for shareholders) has historically been derisory when compared to returns on investment in conventional, hydrocarbon-based assets. Renewables have always looked a bit like the charitable also-rans as far as the oil majors are concerned, and at least ExxonMobil has the honesty to proclaim its contempt for renewables publicly rather than in private.

But these investment conditions are rapidly changing. Inspired perhaps by decisions like General Electric's (GE) to set up Ecomagination as a new business within the GE empire, BP created a new division in 2006, called Alternative Energy. The total sum of capital currently to be invested is around $8 billion, though that reduces to around $6 million once you subtract investments in gas-fired power generation – which can just about be described as 'alternative' for BP, but certainly not as 'renewable'. The lion's share of the remaining $6 billion will go on wind (predominantly in the US in the first instance), then solar, then hydrogen. BP's pilot Carbon Capture and Storage projects are also included here. All in all, that level of investment is probably around 4.5 per cent of BP's total annual capital investment, although it's exceptionally difficult to make that judgement as *all* the oil companies are extremely coy in declaring exactly what proportion of investment is going where. What's more, it's still 'small beer' in real terms, even though it's certainly more than is being invested by any of its competitors.

Shell itself has by no means given up on its own renewables portfolio. Chief Executive Jeroen van der Veer has steadfastly maintained that it will keep an active interest in wind power (where its current investments amount to around 500MW, with a modest amount in development, including a one-third stake in the massive London Array offshore project), solar power (where it's switched out of silicon-based photovoltaics (PVs) into thin-film technologies) and biofuels (with a number of joint ventures in Canada and Germany).

Shell's plan is to go with just one of these in due course, and recent decisions in 2007 indicate it may well be the biofuels business. In 2007, Shell announced a new investment in its joint venture with Choren Industries, a German company specializing in what are called 'second generation' biofuels. Choren has pioneered a gasification process that converts certain kinds of biomass into diesel. A new plant is to be constructed in Freiburg at a cost of several hundred million dollars, and Shell has another joint venture with a Canadian company called Iogen, which is successfully converting cellulosic wastes into ethanol. BP is also very interested in these second generation opportunities, with a joint venture with British Sugar designed to produce bio-butanol (a much denser and therefore more economically viable bio-substitute than ethanol), and substantial interests in a plant called 'jatropha' in Africa, which promises much for the future. It's important to emphasize that the interest here is very much on 'second generation' biofuels. The reality is that 'first generation' biofuels (growing crops such as corn, wheat, palm oil, soya, rapeseed, sugar beet and so on) are for the most part likely to prove highly problematic from a sustainability perspective – which may well explain why the oil companies are very cautious about any involvement in first generation biofuels, except in countries like Brazil where the sustainability benefits of producing ethanol from sugarcane are well established.

How can this be? After all, it was little more than five years ago that Greenpeace itself was advocating the wholesale substitution of biofuels for hydrocarbon-based fuels, on the grounds that biofuels would be (more or less) 'carbon-neutral', in that the CO_2 they release on combustion would be no more than the CO_2 'sequestered' as the crops are growing. But that simplistic analysis has proved to be highly suspect, and with the sole exception of sugarcane in tropical countries, the business of converting different crops into ethanol has thrown up an ever more daunting array of sustainability problems. Put at its simplest, we're back to the same old business of calculating carbon balances: when you look at the CO_2 intensity of the production cycle for these crops (in terms of fertilizers, pesticides, drilling, harvesting, transporting, processing and so on), there's often not that much difference between a conventional barrel of oil equivalent and a bio-barrel.

Which makes what is happening in America something of a scandal. Corn-based ethanol is currently all the rage for US farmers permanently on the look out for the next dip into the subsidy-drenched pork barrel of US agriculture. President Bush clearly doesn't get climate change, and is never likely to, but he does get energy security (reducing US dependence on imports of oil from the Middle East or ideologically-suspect nations like Venezuela), and he does get the business of securing votes for the next election. So ethanol it is, as confirmed in his 2007 State of the Nation Address, in the form of the direct conversion of millions of tonnes of corn (or maize as we Europeans know it) into ethanol as a direct bio-substitute for petrol or diesel.

The consequences of this are already pretty startling. According to Lester Brown (President of the Earth Policy Institute in Washington and a veteran commentator on global agricultural issues), at least 41 million tonnes of the US corn harvest were diverted into the fuel chain rather than the food chain in 2005, and that will rapidly grow to around 120 million tonnes. He bases this calculation not so much on the President's over-excited rhetoric (to expand ethanol production five-fold by 2017, supplying nearly a quarter of the nation's transportation fuels) as on the number of new ethanol distilleries that are currently being constructed to take advantage of this massive bio-windfall:

> *The pace of groundbreakings for new ethanol distilleries is accelerating. Between November 2005 and June 2006, ground was broken for one new platform every 9 days. From July 2006 to September 2006, construction starts increased to one every 5 days. In October, it was one every 3 days. To calculate the amount of corn that will be going into ethanol, we start with the 41 million tonnes of the 2005 crop, and add to that 39 million tonnes for the new construction starts – a total of 80 million tonnes of corn. We could then see even more construction starts in the next 12 months. If so, these distilleries could easily absorb an additional 40 million tonnes of corn.* (Brown, 2006)

Europe is going down the same path, though somewhat more sedately. From 2008, all suppliers of petrol and diesel in the UK, for instance, will have to ensure that 2.5 per cent of the fuels they sell are biofuels. If they can't, they will have to pay a penalty of 15p a litre. The percentage rises to 5.75 per cent by 2010, and, following the decision taken at the EU Summit in February 2007, to 10 per cent by 2020. European farmers will of course respond enthusiastically to such market-transforming measures, and even critics of the biofuels revolution acknowledge that there's no reason why Europe shouldn't use some of its land (particularly the land that has been set aside over the last ten years or so) for biofuels. But there are serious limitations: carbon savings are small (indeed often near zero), and biofuels are costly, meaning that governments have to cut the duty on both bio-ethanol and biodiesel to keep it attractive to consumers. That pretty much guarantees there will be competition between land use for fuel and land use for food, as George Monbiot has been pointing out for some time:

> *Road transport in the UK consumes 37.5 million tonnes of petroleum*
> *products a year. The most productive oil crop that can be grown in this*
> *country is rape. The average yield is 3–3.5 tonnes per hectare. One*
> *tonne of rapeseed produces 415 kilograms of biodiesel. So every hectare*
> *of arable land could provide 1.45 tonnes of transport fuel. To run our*
> *cars and buses and lorries on biodiesel, in other words, would require*
> *25.9 million hectares. There are 5.7 million hectares in the UK. Even*
> *the EU's more modest target of 10 per cent by 2020 would consume*
> *almost all our crop land.* (Monbiot, 2004)

So it's clear that these targets cannot possibly be met without massive imports of palm oil from Indonesia and Malaysia, or other bio-crops from other countries. This is a nightmare in the making. In Indonesia, huge amounts of rainforest are being converted into palm forests to meet this demand, with the United Nations Environment Programme (UNEP) now predicting that 98 per cent of Indonesia's rainforests (with all its wonderful flora and fauna) will be gone by 2022. Things are not quite so bad in Malaysia, where the government has introduced strict laws to protect permanent rainforest and a 'zero burning' policy where land is being cleared for new plantations. Even so, nearly 0.7 per cent of the Malaysian rainforest is being cut down every year, partly to create new palm oil plantations – and the best efforts of those companies and NGOs who have set up the Roundtable on Sustainable Palm Oil (RSPO) are becoming increasingly urgent. An industry-wide certification scheme would have some impact in eliminating the worst excesses and rewarding the more responsible of producers.

Overall, however, it's a pretty grim picture. Yet again, politicians have hurled themselves headlong into what must have looked like a very convenient 'techno-fix': if emissions from burning fossil fuels and cars are the problem, source the fuel from nature on a carbon-neutral basis. Little thought, from any kind of systems perspective, was given to the *real* carbon balances involved once the intensive production systems have been taken into account, let alone to the knock-on impact on other countries rushing to meet demand for this new 'green gold'. A 2007 report by the Dutch consultancy Delft Hydraulics shows that as the rainforests are burned down to make way for palm oil in Indonesia, huge amounts of CO_2 are being released both from the forest itself and from the peaty soils beneath them. This report has shown that every tonne of palm oil causes 33 tonnes of CO_2 to be released into the atmosphere – that's ten times as much as would be released by the equivalent amount of petrol or diesel!

Politicians will no doubt describe this disaster as an 'unintended consequence'. It's no such thing. It could have been anticipated had a proper systems perspective been brought to bear on a market transformation of this kind. A genuinely joined-up analysis would also have revealed some of the 'unintended' socio-economic consequences of the rush to biofuels as the competition between land being used for fuel and land being used for food intensifies. In the US, the price of corn has already doubled, with dramatic impacts on Mexico (which imports a huge amount of corn from the US), where food riots are already becoming more frequent. The US is responsible for 70 per cent of global corn exports. Stockpiles of both corn and wheat are down to their lowest levels for more than 30 years – in six of the past seven years, world grain production has not matched demand. Little wonder that corn and wheat futures are both trading at ten-year highs.

It's difficult to predict where this will all end up. As prices rise, it may make sense for farmers to transfer back into production for food rather than production for fuel, despite the subsidy for ethanol conversion. This would mean that billions of dollars of new investment in ethanol distilleries would have to be mothballed. The first generation 'biofuel bubble' could have come and gone within a decade, enabling second generation biofuels to fill some of that space. The feedstocks for these fuels are not food crops as such, but rather agricultural and forestry waste, or straw and switchgrass. Some of these will still compete for land, but not as directly as the first generation biofuels, and there's every reason to anticipate substantial sustainability benefits arising from these second generation breakthroughs.

That's as close to a 'soft landing' as we're likely to get from first generation biofuels. A much grimmer scenario brings together a combination of potential factors: an accelerated conversion of both wheat and corn in the US for biofuels, leading to a complete collapse in global stockpiles; a huge surge in demand in countries like China as their new-found prosperity leads to an ever more meat-intensive diet; a climate-induced 'natural disaster' in one of the world's main grain-producing countries, causing net exports to plummet; and prices soaring over a 2–3 year period, dramatically raising the cost of food throughout the world, and making it impossible for some of the world's poorest countries to get their hands on any supplies at all, either through aid programmes or subsidized imports. Famine stalks the land all over again, as the UN Millennium Development Goal of halving the number of people suffering from hunger by 2015 perishes in the biofuel bonanza – bearing in mind that at least 850 million people are already chronically hungry or malnourished.

Just another self-indulgent, fantasy apocalypse? Possibly. You'd certainly think so talking to government officials in Europe, the US or India, where any talk about 'food security' is thought to be embarrassingly 'retro' – as if they hadn't seen off all that neo-Malthusian nonsense back in the 1970s. This strikes me as startlingly complacent. Food systems today – all the way through from energy-intensive production systems to global supply chains and centralized distribution systems – are hugely dependent on oil. Indeed, the almost total dependence of modern agriculture on oil is just accepted as a given – as something that can be relied on indefinitely into the future. But governments know that the 'peak oil moment' cannot be far away, and from that point on, prices will do what they always do in a market where demand exceeds supply.

At that point, the massive inefficiencies in our current production systems (with roughly 10 calories of fossil fuel energy consumed for every calorie of food energy produced) will become painfully exposed. Prices of synthetic fertilizers and chemicals will rise steeply (nitrogen fertilizers have already doubled in price since 2003), as will the cost of all plastic packaging in the food chain. Countries that import a high percentage of their food (with around a third of the food we eat imported into the UK, we have one of the lowest self-sufficiency ratios in the EU) will be vulnerable to soaring transport costs.

Politicians love to look at issues in isolation, and are not good at systems-based, multi-factoral analysis. But just put together competition for land (food versus fuel), rising oil and energy prices as energy demand exceeds supply, as well as the possibility of dramatic impacts on food production as a result of climate change, both locally and globally, and one is looking at a potential 'synchronous failure' that leaves no room whatsoever for complacency.

It's only in China that food security is still seen as a huge political priority, with memories of the terrible famines that struck China in the 20th century still very live. Indeed, one of the reasons why Chinese politicians are now so focused on climate change is because of its potential impact on agricultural productivity. Grain harvests in China have already suffered a severe decline (down 9 per cent between 1998 and 2005). We're right back to that good old ecological adage that you can't get a quart out of a pint pot. Natural systems have limits; you can temporarily squeeze more out of those systems through more intensive production, but not for long, and not without a price to be paid in the longer term. And you can shift pressure off one system on to another, but not for long and not without a price to be paid in the longer term. As we import more and more biofuels into the UK, for instance, *our* CO_2 balance sheet will look just a little bit better as those fuels displace a small amount of hydrocarbon-based fuels. And politicians will no doubt enjoy the plaudits they get. But the global balance sheet has just got a great deal worse.

So if it's not biofuels (or not biofuels in their current state), does the answer lie with nuclear power? With the threat of climate change becoming more and more fixed in politicians' minds, a new pro-nuclear bandwagon would seem to be gathering pace. But unless things change significantly over the next few years (for instance, through new reactor designs), the problems with nuclear power remain substantial in terms of excessive costs, disposal of nuclear waste, decommissioning and so on. Two further issues now loom very large indeed: opportunity costs (there is only going to be so much capital available for investments in new generation and infrastructure) and security.

The fact that one of the hijacked planes in the 11 September 2001 terrorist outrage was, by all accounts, headed for a nuclear reactor before it crashed has heightened concerns about the vulnerability of nuclear facilities in such an insecure world. For very understandable reasons, governments are keen to ensure that this is not widely debated in the media or beyond; but for those charged with securing these facilities against potential terrorist attacks, this remains a major concern.

It would of course be possible to devote an entire chapter to the pros and cons of nuclear power in a growth-bound world rapidly shrinking because of diminishing supplies of 'easy' fossil fuels and diminishing global 'sinks' to absorb the CO_2 and other greenhouse gases we are emitting. For those who are interested in my views on this, please check out the UK Sustainable Development Commission's website (www.sd-commission.org.uk), where you will find a personally authored report from March 2006, 'Is nuclear the answer?'. The short answer is 'No'; certainly not for the UK, and probably not for most other nations. Given costs, investment uncertainties, waste management challenges, proliferation issues and *serious* security concerns, it is my belief that nuclear power will never play a significant role in the energy economy of the future.

The worst scenario for potential investors in nuclear power is that the whole nuclear myth blows apart (quite literally) as a result of a terrorist outrage involving some 'home-made dirty nuclear bomb'. Even quite small amounts of highly-enriched uranium would be sufficient to sterilize an entire city centre, and there are still large amounts of the stuff stored in insecure facilities in the former Soviet Union. In January 2007, the FBI confirmed that a small amount of 90 per cent enriched uranium had indeed been seized by authorities in Georgia who had set up a 'sting operation' to trap a Russian businessman offering to sell up to 3 kilos (enough to make a small bomb) to a group posing as radical Islamists. Little wonder that a growing number of security experts are becoming more and more worried about the threat of this kind of 'mega-terrorism'.

That leaves the renewables – wind, solar power, hydroelectricity, tidal and wave power, biomass and biofuels, as well as the use of hydrogen *if* the hydrogen can be produced using renewable energy. As we will see in Chapter 10, these undoubtedly offer by far the 'best bet' from a true sustainability perspective, and it is critical that politicians the world over stop flirting with renewables as 'an interesting little niche' and start investing in them as if our very future depended upon them – which, indeed, it does.

But even renewables have their built-in limits – in terms of availability, intermittency, net energy returns, reliability and so on. They will *not* substitute – like for like – for oil and gas in all circumstances.

This is a very challenging prospect for politicians of any persuasion as they seek to keep growing their economies. It means that every facet of our lives will change – and, as we have seen, that change will be upon us in the not too distant future. What is remarkable is the failure of politicians to start planning in any way for this *inevitable* transition, or even to start preparing their electorates for its inevitability.

There are, of course, all sorts of 'good' reasons for this: the fact that 2015 sounds like another era in political terms; that the credibility of those who first raised this conundrum back in the 1970s took a knock when the wheels didn't instantly drop off our industrial juggernaut; that the current US Administration is violently opposed to any such debate being opened up, as seen in a typical comment from US Vice President Dick Cheney that 'energy conservation may be a sign of personal virtue, but it is not a sufficient basis for a sound, comprehensive energy policy'; and so on. But the principal reason, I suspect, is that the end of cheap oil means the end of easy economic growth, and the end of that whole 'historic interlude' in which cheap oil fuelled fast growth, high living standards and the kind of 'live for today, live for yourself' lifestyles that have now become so destructive. This will be a crunch point for politicians in every party in every country. Conventional economic growth and cheap oil have marched hand in hand for the best part of 60 years; within just a few years, it will become increasingly apparent that both are on their last legs.

REFERENCES

Aynsley-Green, A. (2007) quoted in the *Guardian*, 14 February

Beckerman, W. (1974) *In Defence of Economic Growth*, Jonathan Cape, London

Bookchin, M. (1980) *Toward an Ecological Society*, Black Rose Books, Montreal, Canada

Brown, L. (2006) 'Grain drain', *Guardian*, 29 November

Campbell, C. (2005) 'The assessment and importance of oil depletion' in A. McKillop (ed) *The Final Energy Crisis*, Pluto Press, London

Campbell, C. and Laherrere, J. (1998) 'The end of cheap oil?', *Scientific American*, June

Cook, E. (1982) 'The consumer as creator: A criticism of faith in limitless ingenuity', *Energy Exploration and Exploitation*, vol 1, no 3

Daly, H. (1996) *Beyond Growth*, Beacon Press, Boston, MA

Donovan, N. and Halpern, D. (2002) 'Life satisfaction: The state of knowledge and implications for government', Cabinet Office, HMG, London

Easterlin, R. (2001) 'Income and happiness: Towards a unified theory', *Economic Journal*, no 111

Ekins, P. (2000) *Economic Growth and Environmental Sustainability*, Routledge, London

Grahame, K. (1908) *The Wind in the Willows*, Methuen, London

Greenfield, S. and co-signatories (2006) 'Modern life leads to more depression among children', letter, *Daily Telegraph*, 12 September

Hamilton, C. (2003) *Growth Fetish*, Allen and Unwin, Sydney

Hawken, P. (1993) *The Ecology of Commerce*, Weidenfield and Nicholson, London

Heinberg, R. (2003) *The Party's Over: Oil, War and the Fate of Industrial Societies*, Clairview, Forest Row, UK

Hirsch, F. (1977) *Social Limits to Growth*, Routledge and Kegan Paul, London

Institute for Optimum Nutrition (2002) 'Nutrition and public health', Institute for Optimum Nutrition, London

James, O. (1998) *Britain on the Couch*, Arrow Books, London

James, O. (2007) *Affluenza*, Vermilion, London

Lane, R. (2000) *The Loss of Happiness in Market Democracies*, Yale University Press, New Haven, CT

Layard, R. (2005) *Happiness*, Allen Lane, London

Leggett, J. (2005) *Half Gone*, Portobello Books, London

Meadows, D., Meadows, D. and Randers, J. (1992) *Beyond the Limits*, Earthscan, London

Monbiot, G. (2002) 'What do we really want?', *Guardian*, 27 August

Monbiot, G. (2004) 'Fuel for nought', *Guardian*, 23 November

Myers, D. and Diener, E. (2000) 'The American paradox: Spiritual hunger in an age of plenty', *Scientific American*, May

New Scientist (2007) 'In denial', editorial, *New Scientist*, 21 April

Packard, V. (1957) *The Hidden Persuaders*, David McKay, New York

Palmer, S. (2006) *Toxic Childhood*, Orion, London

Randers, J. and Meadows, D. (2005) *Limits to Growth: The 30-Year Update*, Earthscan, London

Reeves, R. (2002) 'The sun sets on the enlightenment', *RSA Journal*, December

Stern, N. (2007) *The Economics of Climate Change: The Stern Review*, Cambridge University Press, Cambridge

Stevens, A. and Price, J. (1996) *Evolutionary Psychiatry*, Routledge, London

UNICEF (2007) *Child Poverty in Perspective: An Overview of Child Well-Being in Rich Countries*, Innocenti Report Card no 7, UNICEF (United Nations Children's Fund) Innocenti Research Centre, Florence, Italy, available at http://image.guardian.co.uk/sys-files/Society/documents/2007/02/14/UNchildwellbeing.pdf

4

Unsustainable Capitalism?

INTRODUCTION

Today's optimists are convinced that free markets provide by far the most powerful tool at our disposal in terms of fashioning a sustainable economy. Today's pessimists see free markets (*as they operate today*) as deeply implicated in everything that is unsustainable about today's economy. But the free market (which often isn't free at all) is just one of the defining features of capitalist economies: we must also take into account the pursuit of profit, trade, competitiveness, private property and so on. This chapter takes a whirlwind tour through some of these fundamental characteristics of capitalism to assess whether there is any kind of unavoidable incompatibility in terms of achieving a sustainable society, or whether it is more a question of taming and modifying this particular manifestation of capitalism – variously described by people as 'brute capitalism', 'killer capitalism', 'crony capitalism', 'neo-liberal capitalism' and so on. No easy answers emerge; but this chapter presents enough of a feel for some kind of theoretical compatibility to warrant further investigation in Parts II and III.

CAPITALISM AND SUSTAINABILITY

In mainstream political and business discussions about sustainable development, the key question (are capitalism and sustainability mutually exclusive?) goes largely unasked. In fact, it seems to be almost unaskable. Ours is a capitalist world, with businesses (large and small) creating wealth within the embrace of a capitalist system, and with politicians dedicated to managing those capitalist systems to ensure economic stability and to maximize economic wellbeing. If sustainability as a goal cannot be attained within that broad macro-economic framework, then it is not a goal to which contemporary politicians or business people will want to commit themselves. In those circumstances, the fact that, in the long term, sustainability is a non-negotiable imperative (the only alternative being unsustainability or, in biological terms, extinction) is a truth that will continue to be set aside or actively denied for as long as possible, even by the 'progressive' Left and Centre parties in the UK and by the Democrats in the US.

But it is a question that *must* be asked. If, as a politically active environmentalist or campaigner for social justice, one's answer to the question is that they are, indeed, mutually exclusive (that capitalism, in whichever manifestation, is in its very essence *inherently* unsustainable), then one's only morally consistent response is to devote one's political activities to the overthrow of capitalism. If one's answer is that they are entirely compatible (that there are no structural, inherent characteristics within a capitalist system that would make sustainability an un-attainable goal), then it is morally consistent to pursue sustainable development (as the path that leads to that goal) within and through that capitalist system. And if one's answer is that they are only compatible under certain conditions (it isn't capitalism per se that is at issue here, but which particular model of capitalism), then the transformation of those aspects of contemporary capitalism that are incompatible with the attainment of sustainability becomes both a moral and a political precondition of being an effective environmentalist or campaigner for social justice.

From a conventional green perspective, such an enquiry is not uncontroversial. Historically, greens have always veered more to the left than to the right, sometimes explicitly (as with the green parties around the world and various green–red coalitions), and sometimes implicitly (as with those organizations such as Friends of the Earth and Greenpeace who claim strict party-political neutrality, but whose core political sympathies are there for all to see). Over the years, as the range of policy instruments available to governments broadened out to include a much wider variety of market-based mechanisms (taxes, trading schemes, incentives and so on), some greens have adapted with enthusiasm, while others remain suspicious. 'Supping with the devils of capitalism' is a charge that has been brought against all sorts of green activists – including the author of this particular text. The divide still runs deep, as Marcel Wissenburg explains:

> One of the odd aspects of the green critique of economic liberalism is that some see it as the source of most environmental evil, whereas others believe that it is the solution. 'Leftish' greens argue that private ownership and free market conditions, in general, or capitalism and the perpetual quest for economic growth, in particular, are at least barriers for a greener society, often the cause of environmental degradation and according to some even the main cause. On the right, especially in libertarian circles, it is state interference that prevents the free market from developing into a green market. If property and use rights were better defined, individuals would be enabled to defend their rights against polluters and exploiters of nature – and the mechanism of the free market would ensure that no more nor less natural capital than necessary was used for consumption. (Wissenburg, 1998)

The majority of green philosophers and political academics remain convinced that a sustainable society would necessarily be closer to a socialist society than to a liberal, capitalist society. Some of the 'drivers' of capitalism (growth for growth's sake, accumulation, red-in-tooth-and-claw competitiveness, fierce individualism and so on) are seen as major if not irreducible barriers to achieving a sustainable society. Few attempts have been made to interrogate this core assumption, perhaps the most comprehensive of which is Wissenburg's own 'green liberalism'.

After a painstaking comparison between the key tenets of political liberalism and the multifarious 'schools of thought' that make up the global green movement, Wissenburg (1998) identifies a number of significant conflicts between sustainability and liberalism, particularly around the issues of private property and consumption. However, he emerges from his investigations persuaded that there is no *fundamental* incompatibility between the pursuit of sustainability and political liberalism – a modest but reassuring conclusion to set against a growing number of less well-informed commentators who default so predictably to the canard that a truly sustainable society would have to be a sub-fascist society given the need to constrain human nature and dictate human behaviour. However, faced with a clash between constantly growing wants and needs, on the one hand, and limited natural resources and systems, on the other, Wissenburg reveals the limitations of the liberal position: 'People's needs – for company, children, food, technology, travel and trinkets – are private affairs; control, if possible at all, is impermissible.'

Impermissible! In which case, there is little between where we are now and the ecological abyss that necessarily awaits us if 9 billion people are 'permitted' to acquire trinkets, get obese, travel the world, and own several cars along the lines of the Californian model.

In that context, one thing can be stated with reasonable certainty at this point: capitalism *as we know it today* would, indeed, appear to be incompatible with anything even vaguely resembling sustainability. The continuing (and seemingly inexorable) liquidation of our natural capital throughout the global economy provides ample evidence on this score. And contemporary capitalism's growing social externalities (in terms of widening disparities in wealth, continuing economic exploitation, and the adamantine reality of more than 2 billion people still living on less than $2 a day) compound that physical evidence many times over.

To make such a categorical assertion should not automatically mark one down as an out-and-out anti-capitalist. Indeed, there are many critics of contemporary capitalism whose criticism stems precisely from their strongly held belief that capitalism remains the best and *only* ideological option for enhancing the wellbeing of humankind – but that the flaws in its current form are starting to obscure that reality from less sympathetic critics. As George Soros has said on a number of occasions:

Although I have made a fortune in the financial markets, I now fear that the untrammelled intensification of laissez-faire capitalism and the spread of market values into all areas of life are endangering our open democratic society. The main enemy of the open society, I believe, is no longer the communist but the capitalist threat. (Soros, 1997)

Inevitably, different people will have different opinions both about the fundamental characteristics of capitalism (those characteristics that are generic in all manifestations of capitalism) and about those characteristics that are 'inherently unsustainable' – and those that are capable of correction. A constant flow of comparative data from different countries shows that alternative models of capitalism will generate very different outcomes on key economic and social concerns. For instance, a major international study on social mobility commissioned by the Sutton Trust from the London School of Economics (LSE) in 2005 demonstrated extreme divergences in performance between the UK and the US, on the one hand, and Germany, Canada and the Scandinavian countries, on the other. Social mobility is a critical indicator of how well any country is managing inequity, holding out the promise that it is possible (through 'equality of opportunity' interventions and targeted education investments for the most disadvantaged) for even the poorest to break out of poverty and secure reasonable material prosperity later in life.

The results of this study showed that social mobility in the UK and the US (both of which advocate and practise a much more neo-liberal, free market version of capitalism than all of the other countries in the study) is much lower – and in the case of the UK, still declining even after eight years of a Labour government and huge new investments in education. The situation in the US is even more extreme: a child born into a poor family has a 1 per cent chance of growing up to become one of the richest 5 per cent, while a child born into a wealthy family has a 22 per cent chance. American citizens, however, don't see it like this, with surveys regularly showing more than 75 per cent of Americans believing that all it takes to become rich is hard work.

Prima facie, whatever the evidence may be about social mobility, there is clearly a very strong case for arguing that since market-based economies provide the only economic system that can live side by side with democracy, and that democracy is a necessary precondition of human sustainability, then a sustainable economy must, by definition, be a market-based economy. That is not the same thing as saying that capitalism is the *only* economic system with the potential to deliver a sustainable society in the future, but no attempt is made here to explore the feasibility of non-capitalist economies: this is a pragmatic exploration of the viability of *capitalism* when it comes to delivering sustainability, not of any other system.

Nevertheless, it is interesting to note just how little enthusiasm there is today for any hankering after some kind of communist alternative. With the predictable exception of a few remnant green parties in former Eastern European countries, it is now almost universally acknowledged that communism and sustainability are far more incompatible as ideological bedfellows than capitalism and sustainability. It's now nearly 15 years since Murray Feshbach and Alfred Friendly (1992) published their devastating *Ecocide in the USSR: Health and Nature Under Siege*; but all the evidence that has emerged since then has confirmed both the scale and the severity of the damage done under communism to every facet of the environment in Russia and its allies.

The resulting legacy, both in human and financial terms, is truly staggering, and explains why even the harshest critics of today's global capitalism demonstrate zero interest in any communist alternative. In their *Green Alternatives to Globalisation*, for instance, Michael Woodin and Caroline Lucas (2004) look primarily to the *scale* of any market-based economy, pinning their hopes on a wholesale process of 'localization' rather than on any return to nationalization or central planning, or command-and-control socialism, let alone communism.

I will return to the whole question of scale; but it is first necessary to review some of the defining characteristics of a capitalist system in order to test for any fundamental incompatibilities between capitalism and the attainment of a genuinely sustainable economy: markets, profits, private property and free trade.

Markets

Markets existed long before the emergence of capitalism, and even today can (and do) exist without capitalism. But the opposite is not true: capitalism cannot exist without the marketplace as the principal mechanism for the exchange of goods and services. It is almost universally agreed that markets (though never completely 'free' in the true sense of the word) provide the most effective mechanism for the allocation of resources. It may, indeed, be true that 'markets were never meant to achieve community or integrity, beauty or justice, sustainability or sacredness' (von Weizsacker et al, 1997), but there seems no reason to suppose that properly regulated markets, operating within a genuinely sustainable macro-economic framework, will not continue to be the most effective (and sustainable) mechanism for the allocation of resources. It is also well understood that competition within properly regulated markets is one of the few things that prevents the drift to monopoly which characterizes all capitalist economies.

If one accepts, for instance, that one of the most important characteristics of a genuinely sustainable economy is to squeeze the maximum utility out of the lowest possible throughput of energy and raw materials, then serious thought has to be given to the embedding of 'more-from-less' practices in every facet of the market economy. For all sorts of reasons, it is apparent that command and control regulation cannot achieve that outcome on its own; once an efficiency standard has been mandated, there is no economic incentive to go beyond it, eliminating the possibility of continuous efficiency improvements. But with prices set in such a way as to reflect the *true* cost of the use of energy and resources, competition between producers on a so-called level playing field is not just compatible with the pursuit of sustainability, but a necessary aspect of it. As we will see later on, this is clearly an instance where some of the tools and disciplines of capitalism offer enormous benefits to politicians seeking the right mix of instruments to help transform corporate and personal behaviour.

But 'the market', as a social institution, has taken on an iconic role given its centrality to the neo-liberal revolution over the last 25 years. The market has been promoted not just as an efficient mechanism of exchange and resource allocation, but as an ideological weapon against state socialism and the self-evident horrors of centralized command and control. The idea of the market as the most effective way to reconcile the growing diversity and complexity of human preferences has retained its extraordinary political cachet in capitalist economies long after the wilder extremes of Thatcher/Reagan neo-liberalism are beginning to recede. That still begs all sorts of questions about what we mean by 'properly regulated markets' to secure some kind of 'social purpose': regulated by whom, at what scale of activity, using what mechanisms, and to achieve what sort of social and economic outcomes? But those are *secondary* issues. In and of itself, transacting the exchange of goods and services through a market is *not* the problem as far as the pursuit of sustainability is concerned – as evidenced in practice by the emergence of all sorts of new market-based solutions to today's sustainability crisis, all the way from proposals for a global market for trading carbon through to local schemes, such as farmers' markets and even Local Exchange and Trading Schemes (LETS), which depend both upon market principles and the principles of mutuality and cooperation.

This kind of broad approach features increasingly even in the work of anti-globalization campaigners. Writing in the *Guardian* in April 2001, the environmental campaigner George Monbiot expanded upon the idea that market freedom would become an increasingly important part of the pursuit of sustainability, but only on certain conditions:

> *A genuine free market is surely one which is free for everyone, rather than one in which the powerful are free to squeeze economic life out of everyone else. The prerequisite of freedom, in other words, is effective regulation. This means that in some respects the state will have to become not weaker – as both the anarchists and the neo-liberals insist – but stronger. It must be empowered to force both producers and consumers to carry their own costs, rather than dumping them on to other people or the environment. It must be allowed to distinguish between the protection of workers, consumers and the ecosystem, and trade protectionism. Agreements such as those set by the World Trade Organization, in other words, must be reversed. Rather than setting only maximum standards for the defence of people and the environment,*

they should set minimum standards to which multinational companies must subscribe before they are licensed to trade. (Monbiot, 2001)

Profits

The very purpose of wealth creation in capitalist economies is to generate profits. Production for profit, as opposed to production for human needs, was perhaps the simplest of the old ideological divides between capitalism and communism. Some socialists and radical greens continue to argue that it is 'the profit motive' (the pursuit of profit as the single most important objective in any economic exchange) which still lies at the heart of capitalism's inherently destructive tendencies; many mainstream environmental and community development organizations remain wary of the whole concept of profitability, though less so today than during the 1970s and 1980s. As we saw in Chapter 3, it is the urge to maximize profits that causes some companies to cut corners if they can get away with it and to externalize as high a proportion of their costs as they are legally permitted to do. In *The Corporation*, Joel Bakan (2004) describes the modern corporation as 'an externalizing machine'. Because of its legal status and fiduciary duties to shareholders, it is literally duty bound to maximize profit for those shareholders as long as it stays within the law:

> *The corporation can neither recognize nor act upon moral reasons to refrain from harming others. Nothing in its legal makeup limits what it can do to others in pursuit of its selfish ends, and it is compelled to cause harm where the benefits of doing so outweigh the costs. Only pragmatic concern for its own interests in the laws of the land constrain the corporation's predatory instincts, and often that is not enough to stop it from destroying lives, damaging communities and endangering the planet as a whole. These tend to be viewed as inevitable and acceptable consequences of corporate activity – 'externalities' in the coolly technical jargon of economics.* (Bakan, 2004)

Only governments can systematically force companies to internalize these externalities through proper regulation or through company law. Within a corporate governance framework geared more to sustainability and equity, the concept of *sustainable profitability* should therefore be viable – and perhaps even a necessary condition of making the transition to a sustainable economy as efficiently and painlessly as possible. Excelling in the pursuit of legitimate profitability while simultaneously making continuous progress towards genuine sustainability will become an increasingly important test of real business leadership.

As we will see, however, governments are less and less inclined to introduce, let alone to enforce, new regulations that are invariably opposed by business and their trade associations. Governments in the rich world are not so much the ring holders between civil society, on the one hand, and corporations intent on making other people pay their bills, on the other; more and more, government and business seem to be working as partners, especially as governments around the world follow in the footsteps of the UK and the US in opening up more and more of the public sector to privatization and market forces.

Even more problematic is the whole question of *accumulation*, with critics of capitalism arguing that its principal purpose is not just to generate profits, but to generate profits with a view to accumulating capital – as much of it as possible, accumulated as fast as possible. No one expressed this more eloquently or authoritatively than Murray Bookchin, one of the most radical of all the ecologists who have inspired the US environment movement over the last 40 years:

> *Capitalism not only validates pre-capitalist notions of the domination of nature – it turns plunder of nature into society's law of life. To quibble with this kind of system about its values, to frighten it with visions about the consequences of growth, is to quarrel with its very metabolism. One might more easily persuade a green plant to desist from photosynthesis than to ask the bourgeois economy to desist from capital accumulation.* (Bookchin, 1980)

Profitability has quite simply become the key measure of corporate success in a capitalist system, ensuring frequent and rapid shifts in the productive base of any economy. This process of 'creative destruction' ensures the reallocation of capital and other resources from the less productive to the more productive, however painful such reallocations may be at both the micro and the macro level. And it is those profits that provide the dividends upon which the lives of hundreds of millions of people now depend in terms of their pensions and other investments.

However, it is particularly difficult to make dispassionate judgements about the negative and positive aspects of the pursuit of profit at this particular point in the swing of capitalism's pendulum. We have just come through what must have been one of the most spectacularly debauched periods of unfettered profit maximization since the 19th century, culminating in a sequence of corporate scandals and collapses that has undoubtedly contributed to the pendulum starting to swing back again from its outer neo-liberal extreme.

This wasn't just a case of the odd rotten apple in the barrel. A report published in 2002 by the US NGO United for a Fair Economy looked at the finances of 23 large US companies under investigation for accounting irregularities. Between 1999 and 2001, the CEOs of those companies (including household names such as AOL Time Warner, Bristol Myers Squibb, Enron, Halliburton, Kay-Mart, Lucent Technologies, Tyco, WorldCom and Xerox) took home $1.4 billion between them – at a time when shares in those companies lost $530 billion

– roughly 70 per cent of their value. During that time, they earned an average $62 million each, in comparison to CEOs in companies not under investigation earning an average of $36 million.

For many people, this represents the acme of personal greed and corporate fat-cattery; but it is part of a much wider and more pervasive malaise. Over the last five years, board directors in the UK's biggest companies received an average 21 per cent rise, nearly seven times as much as average earnings. There's a lot of high-flown rhetoric from politicians and business leaders about the need to protect our competitive position in the global economy, but in reality there can be no conceivable justification for such disproportionate self-advancement. Many business leaders still fail to understand the damage this does to the reputation of the business community as a whole – and, indeed, to the legitimacy of the capitalist system that permits such behaviour. Big share options and other benefits incorporated within pay packages create an utterly perverse incentive for company directors to prioritize short-term profit maximization and share-price inflation over any sense of their company's (and investors') longer-term interests.

Defenders of such an astonishingly powerful accumulative capacity point out that none of this *necessarily* impacts negatively upon those on low incomes in the UK or, in terms of the global economy, upon the world's poorest people. All of that money still has to go somewhere, whether it's in terms of consumption, philanthropy, investment or anything else. There is, therefore, an unavoidable trickle-down effect, regardless of the scale of accumulated wealth. Markets for consumption and investment simply recycle the proceeds. However, it seems impossible to argue that the world is a better place for the concentration of wealth in the hands of so few; by implication, therefore, 'sustainable capitalism' would necessarily need to find ways of limiting the concentration of wealth.

Private property

Not surprisingly, one can find every shade of political opinion about the rights and wrongs of private property within the green movement. Deep ecologists assert that the land belongs to no one and that it is absurd for humans to assume that they have any rights in that respect – either individual or collective. Socialist greens continue (somewhat romantically, it has to be said) to talk up the advantage of collective ownership, while those of a more liberal persuasion see private property rights as all but God-given and a non-negotiable tenet of any effectively functioning market economy.

The traditional justification of the right to own land and other property goes all the way back to the philosopher John Locke (1632–1704) and the prevailing assumption of his time that resources would remain so abundant that one person's private ownership would not constrain anyone else from achieving the same benefits of ownership in due course. The world has got to be a much fuller place since those days! If resources are in short supply rather than abundant, and if they are therefore 'rationed' via the price mechanism, as they are in today's world, then some people will necessarily go without.

But the question for consideration here is a rather different one: is there any fundamental incompatibility between the right to own private property and the pursuit of sustainability? Subject to the same kind of caveats expressed in the preceding section, 'Profits', about the accumulation and concentration of wealth, the *principle* of private ownership itself could surely be managed in such a way as to underpin a genuinely sustainable society. Indeed, there are some critics of contemporary capitalism, such as Jeff Gates, who argue strongly for the rapid extension of private property as one of the most effective ways of combating rather than reinforcing institutionalized inequity: 'With the proper policy environment, humanized ownership of property could do much to advance sustainability across an array of inescapably interdependent domains: economic, social and environmental' (Gates, 1998). From a very different Southern perspective, Hernando de Soto, a passionate advocate for 'capitalizing the poor', has suggested that governments should grant legal title to squatters over their currently illegal huts and shacks. Give them access to capital and to credit, and their prospects for improving their lives will improve dramatically.

Going even further than that, there are many who now believe that the extension of private property rights to those parts of the global commons that are either not managed at all (for example, the atmosphere) or inadequately managed on our behalf by governments or international agencies (such as ocean fisheries) will greatly benefit the pursuit of sustainability. I quote as an extreme but interesting example of this approach an extract from an article in *Nature* by Graciela Chichilnisky and Geoffrey Heal:

> *The environment's services are, without doubt, valuable. The air we breathe, the water we drink and the food we eat are all available only because of services provided by the environment. How can we transform these values into income while conserving resources? We have to 'securitize' (sell shares in the return from) 'natural capital' and environmental goods and services, and enrol market forces in their conservation. This means assigning to corporations – possibly by public–private corporate partnerships – the obligation to manage and conserve natural capital in exchange for the right to the benefits from selling the services provided. Privatizing natural capital and ecosystem services is a vital step as it enlists self-interest and the profit motive in the cause of the environment. Regulation can thus be confined to the more difficult cases.* (Chichilnisky and Heal, 1998)

Such free market zeal is unlikely to win many adherents, not least because it represents a chauvinistic Western point of view that totally ignores countless examples in the rest of the world of extremely successful *common* ownership of common resources. While Garrett Hardin's (1968) much-quoted story of 'The tragedy of the commons' might well apply to the appalling mismanagement of shared resources in the rich world, it does great disservice to all those elsewhere in the world sustaining highly effective systems of resource management and environmental protection without the support of private property or commoditized natural resources. Nonetheless, the notion of 'securitizing natural capital' is a powerful one (see Chapter 7).

Free trade

From the writings of David Ricardo at the start of the 19th century onwards, trade between nations has been considered an essential aspect of capitalism. Economic growth and free trade remain the two driving forces behind the spread of capitalism to every corner of the Earth, and 'opening markets to the benefit of free trade' is still the central ideological tenet of key institutions such as the International Monetary Fund (IMF) and the World Trade Organization (WTO).

Over the last few years the automatic acceptance of the benefits of free trade has been subjected to ever greater scrutiny. Critics have gone back to the work of David Ricardo to remind latter-day free trade apostles that the principle of comparative advantage (enabling capital to be allocated to those areas of enterprise in which a country has natural or acquired advantages in comparison to its trading partners) was premised on the assumption that capital (as well as labour) stayed at home – only the goods were traded internationally.

The mobility of capital changes all that. With capital now more mobile internationally than goods themselves, it is perfectly feasible (and from one perspective, perfectly reasonable) for transnational corporations to capitalize on cheap labour, cheap resources and lower environmental and social standards anywhere in the world that they can find them. In areas of economic production that are not geographically bounded, capital now tends to flow to countries with an 'absolute' advantage in these areas, leading to a standards-lowering competition between nations.

From a sustainability perspective, this is becoming more and more problematic. As we have seen, one fundamental element in moving towards more sustainable economies is the internalization of costs that have historically been 'externalized' on to the environment, other people, future generations and so on. From the earliest social reforms during the 19th century through to the introduction of a raft of environmental measures during the last two decades of the 20th century, legal and fiscal mechanisms have been used to ensure that the price consumers pay for any product or service more accurately reflects the real costs in bringing it to market. 'Footloose capital' can avoid the internalization of those costs by relocating to countries with lower standards; for lack of compensatory tariffs levied on goods at the point of entry into countries with higher standards, competition in the global economy often rewards continuing and perverse cost externalization. I will return to this theme in more detail in the next chapter.

The implications of this are becoming increasingly problematic as nations wrestle with appropriate policy responses to climate change. Not only are countries like the US, China and India still playing a hugely destructive 'spoiler' role (having spent the best part of 2007 trying to dilute and neutralize the scientific consensus established through the Intergovernmental Panel on Climate Change), but by doing absolutely nothing to reduce emissions of greenhouse gas in their own economies they gain a competitive advantage over all those countries (particularly the EU) that *are* doing something. In *Making Globalization Work*, Joseph Stiglitz (2006) presents some splendidly robust ideas on this score, advocating a global carbon tax as an immeasurably simpler and ultimately more effective policy instrument than the complex trading schemes that are being pushed in the EU, parts of the US and, ultimately, the world:

> *Any system, whether of targets or taxes, will require enforcement – including action against countries that refuse to cooperate. Global warming is too important to rely on any country's good will. If the US continues to refuse to reduce its emissions, trade sanctions should be imposed. Europe must use the foundations of the international trade law we have created to force any recalcitrant country, any rogue state, to behave responsibly. Europe has to be willing to use the enormous power of economic globalization to address the world's most important global environmental problem.* (Stiglitz, 2006)

Stiglitz goes on to suggest that, under WTO rules, Europe and other countries which are being disadvantaged by the 'indirect subsidy' going to US businesses should impose countervailing duties on imports from the US. If economists were able to agree on an appropriate price for every tonne of CO_2 emitted, then it would be relatively simple to calculate the unfair competitive advantage exporting countries were gaining by not imposing a charge on emissions, then assess average CO_2 intensity for every million dollars' worth of exports (a crude but effective measure), and then levy the equivalent as a non-tariff barrier for every million dollars' worth of imported goods. Simple – but I fear unacceptable in the eyes of the WTO, and most critics (although not Jospeh Stiglitz himself) believe that the WTO would rather see the planet fry than do anything to impede 'free' trade or the free movement of capital.

It is worth remembering, however, that this idea of mobile capital (and un-regulated currencies) is still a very new phenomenon – and, in reality, one that is still being put to the test. In his *General Theory of Employment, Interests and Money*, John Maynard Keynes (1936) expressed an opinion that is highly unfashionable today, but to which many exponents of the 'new economics' keep returning as they contemplate the consequences of footloose capital:

> *I would sympathize with those who would minimize rather than those who would maximize economic entanglements between nations. Ideas,*

knowledge, art, hospitality, travel – these are the things that should of their nature be international. But let goods be home spun wherever it is reasonable and conveniently possible, and above all let finance be primarily national. (Keynes, 1936)

SCALE

Small is Beautiful (the title of Fritz Schumacher's best-known book, written in 1973) remains one of the most resonant catchphrases ever thrown up by any green author. It appeals at a deep instinctive level to those keen to keep relationships personal and direct, to retain the closest possible ties of neighbourhood and community, to keep supply chains short, and generally to ensure that things are kept as simple and manageable as possible.

This is not the place to reprise what has been a fiercely controversial debate within the green movement over the last three decades. The proper balance, from a sustainability perspective, in terms of what is best done locally, regionally, nationally, internationally and globally is an extremely complex one. For some, it is almost an article of faith that the more local something is, the more sustainable it is likely to be; pragmatists tend to take a 'horses for courses' approach, looking at the usual trade-offs between environmental, social and economic benefits from things done at different scales. The underlying concern, which permeates the whole of this chapter, is whether there is some dynamic at the heart of capitalism which distorts that kind of balanced approach, which mandates 'getting bigger' as a condition of getting richer, and which unavoidably crushes human scale, diverse cultures and local differentiation.

At the global level, without the kind of systems understanding referred to in Chapter 3, contemporary capitalism has no self-correcting mechanisms when it comes to gauging how big the economy should be, relative both to society and to the biosphere. Bigger is seen quite simply as better and always has been. The world now produces in less than two weeks the equivalent of the entire physical output of the year 1900; total throughput in the global economy doubles every 25 to 30 years. So even though the combination of huge population growth and exploding economies has turned an all but empty world into an all but full world in little more than a couple of centuries, unfettered expansionism is still the name of the game.

One of the best indices of human scale in relation to the biosphere is the percentage of the total product of photosynthesis now appropriated by humankind as the dominant species. Back in 1986, Peter Vitousek and colleagues calculated that 40 per cent of net terrestrial photosynthesis (the total amount of solar energy used by plants, trees, grasses and so on, less the energy used in their own growth and reproduction) was already being appropriated by human beings. If a doubling of the global economy simultaneously entails a doubling in our appropriation of net terrestrial photosynthesis, this would leave just 20 per cent for all other organisms. And since we now know that we cannot survive without the many services nature provides for free, the issue of relative scale is far from academic. Herman Daly has argued:

> *Our manifest inability to centrally plan economies should inspire more humility among the planetary managers who would centrally plan the ecosystem. Humility should argue for the strategy of minimizing the need for planetary management by keeping the human scale sufficiently low so as not to disrupt the automatic functioning of our life-support systems, thereby forcing them into the domain of human management. Those who want to take advantage of the 'invisible hand' of self-managing ecosystems have to recognize that the invisible hand of the market, while wonderful for allocation, is unable to set limits to the scale to the macro economy.* (Daly, 1996)

But what exactly does 'a sufficiently low human scale' look like? Although globalization as a phenomenon is now widely discussed, with literally hundreds of books exploring its every aspect, one hears very little by comparison of the phenomenon of localization. Most mainstream economists, business people and even political parties (despite all their cringe-worthy lip-service to decentralization) are contemptuous of the idea of 'local solutions to global problems'. A rich tradition of green authors and thinkers has therefore largely been set aside as unworldly and impractical – to the great detriment of contemporary political debate. I shall revisit this in Chapter 16.

And at the heart of the issue of scale lurks the vexed issues of population growth. Cut it which way you will, growing populations necessitate growing economies to provide more food, more houses, more services, more teachers, more doctors and more jobs. Growth-bound economists and politically correct environmentalists conspire to keep the issue of population off the agenda, obscuring the incontrovertible reality that every extra human being makes it just a little bit harder to find ways of living within the Earth's limited carrying capacity. It would, however, seem unreasonable to lay the blame for this uniquely at the door of capitalism. Religion, ignorance, prejudice and political cowardice have at least as much to answer for, and I shall return to this critical sustainability challenge in Chapter 5.

WANTS AND NEEDS

In the erstwhile ideological battle between capitalism and communism, few issues were as stoutly delineated as the question of production for the market versus production for human needs. Although relations between green activists and socialists have often been extremely fractious, the espousal of a steady-state economy by green parties during the 1970s gave some succour to socialists, who believed that it would permit a clear hierarchy of production: satisfy all reasonable consumption needs first, and then aim at a 'replacement level' for future production, entirely eliminating any need for capital accumulation. These days, however, the concept of 'production for human needs' would seem to have little currency in the debate about sustainability, and even less in discussions about contemporary capitalism. In those countries where basic needs are met – and this would apply to most people in Organisation for Economic Co-operation and Development countries – it is seen as the natural by-product of rising economic prosperity. When they are not met (as applies to more than half of humanity), an enduring faith in the promise of trickle-down economics somehow continues to divert attention from the thorny question of whether they will *ever* be met in today's global economy. Rather than trickling down, many of the benefits of the global economy as it is structured today continue to gush upwards. The United Nations Development Programme's annual *Human Development Report* continues to offer the most sobering assessment of today's trend: 'Development that perpetuates today's inequalities is neither sustainable nor worth sustaining' (UNDP, 2003).

But is this really as simple, as morally clear-cut, as the 'case against' would seem to indicate? Markets are, indeed, amoral; but governments can (and constantly do) intervene to buttress amoral markets with fiscal and regulatory measures that at any one time may be said to embody a nation's moral precepts – a sense of what is 'owed' to each citizen and what each citizen owes the state. And there is no shortage of eloquent prescriptions regarding how the system could be made to work both more equitably and effectively, all the way from the urbane, market-friendly blueprints of people such as Jean-François Rischard (the World Bank's Vice-President for Europe) in *High Noon* (Rischard, 2003) through to uncompromising, NGO-based manifestos that would dramatically rearrange the balance of power between civil society and big business.

Is it right, anyway, to bemoan the fact that capital allocation is not geared to meeting needs, but rather to maximizing rates of return? Would any other generic approach produce the kind of efficiencies in capital allocation that ensure the best use of a scarce resource? Isn't sub-optimal capital allocation as much a threat to sustainability as sub-optimal resource utilization? Contemporary proponents of ecological sustainability and social justice would seem to be drawing few historical lessons from the grotesquely inefficient, polluting and corrupt economies of the former Soviet bloc countries. Rather than seeking to achieve those fundamental social and environmental outcomes upon which sustainability depends through sub-optimal allocation of capital, the trick surely is to ensure that 'optimality' is redefined in order to encompass those fundamental social and environmental concerns?

There is of course a much deeper issue here about what we mean by 'wants and needs'. The ubiquitous Brundtland Report (WCED, 1987) definition of sustainable development ('development that meets the *needs* of the present without compromising the ability of future generations to meet their own *needs*' [emphasis mine]) has little to offer by way of actually defining those 'needs'. And although it's abundantly clear that there are still untold unmet needs in many poor countries (as summarized in the Millennium Development Goals on page 223), it's by no means clear that much of the economic activity driving the economies of the rich world any longer has much to do with meeting needs. However, as people get richer, their 'wants' become 'needs', part of the *minimum* material entitlement that the average citizen may now reasonably aspire to, with as little delay as possible in securing it and at the lowest possible cost.

This is where we come back to the 'hedonic treadmill', the great driving force of modern capitalism, with governments compelled to condone and even exhort ever higher levels of consumption in order to keep their tax revenues flowing, with businesses able to deploy ever more sophisticated marketing to reinforce a sense of permanent dissatisfaction on the part of individual consumers, and consumers themselves (for lack of any evidence to the contrary, let alone any serious Plan B) seemingly persuaded that consumption as a proxy for living is probably the best thing on offer. Even though it leaves them no happier or more fulfilled, even as levels of personal consumption move remorselessly upwards. And as we saw in Chapter 3, that drive for individual material gain ultimately threatens wellbeing as it leaves no room for the things in life on which mental health finally depends – productive social and family relationships, rewarding work, a sense of belonging and community.

This, in essence, is the triumph of modern capitalism: seducing at least two generations of politicians and power-brokers that increased GDP and increased per capita consumption are the *only* routes to meeting people's needs. Yet all the psychological and sociological evidence tells us that this strategy is doomed to failure, with the vast majority of people's *real* needs (especially in the developed world) remaining largely unmet despite constant increases in economic growth. The great Chilean economist, Manfred Max-Neef, was one of the first to highlight the utter folly of this approach, eloquently demonstrating that fundamental human needs (which he identified as subsistence, protection, affection, understanding, participation, creative expression, identity, freedom and (perhaps with the custom of the siesta in mind!) idleness, can only be satisfied in very small measure by the purchase of products and increased consumption. Hence his concept of 'pseudo-satisfiers' in the shape of any activity that generates a false and usually short-lived sense of satisfaction for a given need. As the need stays unmet, the appetite for further pseudo-satisfiers intensifies.

The systematized disconnection between capitalist wealth creation and the meeting of fundamental (and universal) human needs is one of the most complex challenges that advocates of sustainable capitalism face today. Is it going to be possible to secure a constant and sufficient flow of wealth in seeking to satisfy those *real* needs head-on, rather than in seeking (misguidedly if not dishonestly) to meet them indirectly via increased consumption of every kind at any cost? In

Affluenza, Oliver James suggests that we already have a perfectly viable model of this kind of capitalism in the country of Denmark, which scores very highly in all key indices of wellbeing:

> *When happiness or life satisfaction is rated, Denmark consistently comes out as one of the best countries in the world. Indeed, it is one of the very few developed nations in which these ratings have increased since 1950, rather than remaining the same or dropping. The gap between rich and poor is almost implausibly small by the standards of the English-speaking world. Because being richer than the other guy is very actively discouraged by the tax system and the culture, it is not a source of status – and status cannot be bought by conspicuous consumer goods.*
> (James, 2007)

But as Oliver James points out, all this comes at a price, with much higher levels of taxation strategically deployed to provide probably the best day care and educational systems in the world, and to nurture human relationships at every level in society. Significantly, however, Denmark remains an exceptionally successful and competitive small nation economy, not just staying afloat in today's global economy, but positively thriving.

COMPETITION

Within any capitalist system, to be 'uncompetitive' at either the company level or at nation-state level is to fail. It is a simple as that. Competition for customers, competition for capital, competition for talent, and competition for reputation and brand value: it is competitiveness that sorts out the capitalist sheep from the capitalist goats. Competition has become both dominant and deeply divisive, as pointed out by Tony Stebbing and Gordon Heath:

> *Competition makes economies inherently unstable and leads to the extinction of businesses through dominance and monopoly. The widespread belief that the competitive process must permeate every aspect of life is damaging the global environment since the pace of economic activity exceeds its capacity to assimilate polluting consequences. Competition drives the rate of economic activity towards the maximum energy and resource use. It is unsustainable because there are no intrinsic controls upon the pace of economic activity.* (Stebbing and Heath, 2003)

However, as we have already seen, competition itself need not necessarily pose such a dilemma. In terms of the efficient use of both resources and capital, the challenge to eke out maximum economic value for every unit of energy and raw materials is as critical to sustainability as it should be to commercial success. The problem is not competition per se, but the incorrect valuation of resources and inadequate levels of regulation to create a level playing field conducive to sustainability.

This is probably a judgement that most people would arrive at instinctively anyway. Populist interpretations of evolution, from Herbert Spencer and Thomas Huxley onwards, have accustomed people to the idea of nature being 'red in tooth and claw', with all life-forms engaged in endless titanic struggles to ensure 'the survival of the fittest'. So what could be more 'natural' than the history of humankind (both before and after the Industrial Revolution) being cast in the same metaphorical framework? This rationale of social Darwinism has been taken up with unbounded enthusiasm by the politicians and academic economists most centrally involved in the neo-liberal revolution of the last 25 years. When all else fails, it has provided at least some flimsy justification for patterns of irresponsible and uncaring corporate and political behaviour that prioritize competition over everything else, characterized by folksy phrases along the lines of 'It's a jungle out there', 'It's a dog-eat-dog world', 'Let the devil take the hindmost', and so on.

So it often comes as a bit of a blow to them when this interpretation of evolution is revealed as a complete fabrication, a socio-political distortion that tells us much more about Britain during the mid-19th century than about the evolution of life on Earth. What we now know is that individual organisms in a mature ecosystem go to great lengths to avoid competition by specialization or by developing their own differentiated niches. Resources are often shared with frugal efficiency. Territorial animals actually avoid fighting if at all possible, relying upon complex behaviours and rituals that stop short of actual conflict. This has all been formalized by ecologists in what is known as the 'competitive exclusion principle': the occupant of any niche excludes all others by virtue of specialization, and therefore avoids competition and possible extinction.

Beyond that, the work of scientists such as Lynn Margulis and Janine Benyus has revealed fascinating patterns of mutual interdependence and elegant symbiosis. The great biologist Lewis Thomas is quoted as saying:

> *The urge to form partnerships, to link up in collaborative arrangements, is perhaps the oldest, strongest and most fundamental force in Nature. There are no solitary, free-living creatures; every form of life is dependent on other forms.* (Thomas, 1980)

This mismatch between how evolution really works and how the majority of people have come to think it works has assumed ever greater significance in the minds of those trying to understand how it is that we permit market economics to destroy so much of what we hold dear. Just before her death in 2001, the renowned environmental activist Donella Meadows wrote a powerful article showing how today's economic 'laws' clash fundamentally with the laws of the planet. Competition is top of that list of clashes:

> *Economics says: compete. Only by pitting yourself against a worthy opponent will you perform efficiently. The reward for successful competition will be growth. The Earth says: compete, yes, but keep your competition in bounds. Don't annihilate. Take only what you need. Leave your competitor enough to live. Wherever possible, don't compete, cooperate. Pollinate each other, create shelter for each other, build firm structures that lift smaller species up to the light. Pass around the nutrients, share the territory. Some kinds of excellence rise out of competition; other kinds rise out of cooperation. You're not in a war, you're in a community.* (Meadows, 2001)

There is, of course, a big difference between how nature does it and how we humans choose to do it: we are able to bring *moral purpose* to bear on the issue. Neo-liberals would have us believe that markets are morally neutral, and that competition within those markets exempts policy-makers from having to choose between different approaches or to make any moral judgements. This moral relativism is now being challenged, however, not just through the predictable swing of capitalism's pendulum away from the excesses of neo-liberalism, but by our increasingly sophisticated understanding of the balance between competition and collaboration in nature. In that regard, one can derive a fair amount of gentle amusement by reminding free market fundamentalists of the etymology of competition, derived as it is from the Latin *competare*, meaning 'to strive together'.

INEQUALITY

Leading on from that, there's the equally vexed question of whether *inequality* is an inherent and inevitable element in *any* capitalist system. The answer to this must surely be 'yes'. Even with a better balance between competition and collaboration, the dynamism of capitalism depends upon 'winners' making better use of capital and resources than their competitors; and where there are winners, there will inevitably be losers.

Any system that stops short of outright egalitarianism must, by definition, permit the existence of some inequality. Post-war capitalist meritocracies have relied upon varying combinations of the same basic elements to manage that inequality: equality of opportunity (in theory, if rarely in practice); fiscal redistribution to iron out extreme disparities in income and wealth; and a welfare 'net' to catch those who fall through the system. It has worked a great deal better in some countries than in others. As shown in the report from the Real World Coalition, *From Here to Sustainability* (Christie and Warburton, 2001), neither the US nor the UK have yet come close to reconciling the astonishing dynamism of entrepreneurial capitalism with the meeting of basic human needs or social justice. Elsewhere in Europe, particularly in the Scandinavian and Benelux countries, this would appear to be a rather less elusive combination than in the US or the UK. And there is clear evidence, for those who want to see it, that capitalist economies *can* be managed in such a way as to maximize equality of opportunity and to minimize persistent cycles of deprivation and inequality.

The perpetuation of extreme disparities in wealth is becoming increasingly disturbing even for the most zealous defenders of our contemporary model of capitalism. It looks 'inherently unsustainable' for all sorts of pragmatic reasons: just how long do you suppose people will put up with this level of transparent injustice? But social justice has been of little concern to those intent on driving a particular model of US-led globalization, which in country after country has indisputably worsened levels of inequality. This is partly to do with the insupportable levels of debt that many developing countries have accumulated (the cost of servicing that $2.5 trillion worth of debt is around $375 billion a year – more than all developing world spending on education and health combined, and 20 times what they receive annually in terms of foreign aid), and partly to do with the enforced development model that has enriched tiny but hugely powerful elites in most poor countries. The top 1 per cent of households in developing countries account for anywhere between 70 per cent and 90 per cent of all private wealth in those countries.

For most people, these shocking phenomena are still seen as 'unfortunate side effects', the dark side of a process of development and investment in some of the world's poorest countries that they imagine to be largely benign. A growing number of commentators are keen to dispel that illusion, and some have gone so far as to argue that today's inequality is a direct consequence of the way in which the global economy has gradually become a tool of US foreign policy and its hegemonistic intentions. John Perkins, a former 'economic hit man' for American big business, likens their impact upon the world's poor to that of the slave traders:

> *The old-fashioned slave trader told himself that he was dealing with a species that was not entirely human, and that he was offering them the opportunity to become Christianized. He also understood that slaves were fundamental to the survival of his own society, that they were the foundation of his economy. The modern slave trader assures himself (or herself) that the desperate people are better off earning $1 dollar a day than no dollars at all, and that they are receiving the opportunity to become integrated into the larger world community. She also understands that these desperate people are fundamental to*

the survival of her company, that they are the foundation for her own lifestyle. She never stops to think about the larger implications of what she, her lifestyle and the economic system behind them are doing to the world – or of how they may ultimately impact upon her children's future. (Perkins, 2004)

The US itself remains the richest nation on Earth, but also one of the most unequal. The percentage of children living in poverty in the US is the highest in the developed world – one in six. The numbers of so-called 'working poor' (people who work full time without being able to support a family in decent health) have been increasing steadily over the last decade. Household debt as a percentage of income rose from 58 per cent to 85 per cent between 1973 and 1998. Average weekly wages in 1998 were 12 per cent below those for 1973 – and it has got worse since then. The top 1 per cent of Americans now earn more than the bottom 95 per cent (up from 90 per cent just a year earlier). While there are now more than 200 American billionaires, one in seven American adults is functionally illiterate. And while Americans remain more tolerant of this extraordinary economic failure, on the grounds that social mobility in the US is theoretically high enough to ensure that everyone has as good a chance as anyone else to reach those material heights, that is simply no longer true: the chance of American workers in the bottom 20 per cent of the economy moving to the top 60 per cent is less than in any other developed country.

I am indebted to Margaret Legum (2002) for many of those statistics – extracted from her inspiring exposition of what today's alternative economics looks like, *It Doesn't Have to Be Like This*. She also draws a telling comparison between the US economy (still vaunted in most media as the world's most dynamic economy) and the Japanese economy, which is endlessly marked down as 'stagnant' or 'failing'. In fact, the Japanese economy is not only the most egalitarian of all developed countries, it is still among the most successful:

> *The Japanese have high incomes, more savings, longer lives and better health than Americans. And they work less hard to achieve it. The Japanese also pay lower taxes – less than 12 per cent of their incomes compared to more than 16 per cent. And they get more services. Healthcare is virtually free. More Japanese take overseas holidays than Americans. And they still manage to save money. While American workers spent more than they earned in 2000, the average Japanese family put away 13 per cent of its pay cheque in savings. [...] Every Japanese household has a colour television, nine in ten have a microwave oven, 85 per cent have a car, 40 per cent a computer and 39 per cent a set of golf clubs. The rate of heart attacks is one third of that in the US; the divorce rate is half the American, the crime rate one third and the homicide rate one sixth. Proportionately, more Japanese 18-year olds go*

to college than do Americans. Japanese read twice as many books per capita as Americans. There are hardly any homeless Japanese, compared with 700,000 American. (Legum, 2002)

INHERENT UNSUSTAINABILITY?

The *realpolitik* of all this is clear. Sustainability (at the species level) is a non-negotiable imperative for humankind. Allowing for some increasingly rare exceptions such as Cuba and North Korea, and while observing with some gratification the intense discomfiture of the Bush Administration in the face of Hugo Chavez's '21st Century Socialism' in Venezuela and its knock-on effects throughout South America, the truth of it is that capitalism, in one form or another, is likely to provide the all-encompassing ideological framework for the foreseeable future – as Tom Bentley says:

> *The values of individualism, diversity and open exchange, which have been fought over for centuries, have won out in the modern world. They are embodied in the structure of capitalism, which now constitutes the only viable possibility for organizing economies.* (Bentley, 2002)

Logically, whether we like it or not, sustainability is therefore going to have to be delivered within that all-encompassing capitalist framework. We don't have time to wait for any big-picture ideological successor.

Clearly, each of the different fundamental characteristics of capitalism covered above requires a great deal more analysis from a sustainability-driven perspective before any definitive judgement can be made about the compatibility of capitalism and sustainability. Is there some 'accommodation' that would permit the pursuit of genuine sustainability through a different model of capitalism than that which we have today? Indeed, is there *any* model of capitalism that can accommodate the non-negotiable imperative of achieving biophysical sustainability and the increasingly pressing concerns of global equity and social justice?

This chapter does not pretend to be able to answer that question in one fell swoop; all it seeks to do at this stage is to frame the question and open it up for discussion within the sustainability community. At the very least, based on this kind of analysis, it should be possible to set some of the principal dysfunctionalities of contemporary capitalism against some of the minimum conditions necessary for achieving a sustainable economy – and then explore the political, economic and fiscal reforms that would be required to bridge the gap between the two.

To a certain extent, that is what has been happening when comparisons are made between different models of capitalism, starting with Christopher Hampden-Turner and Fons Trompenaars' (1993) magisterial analysis of *The Seven Cultures of Capitalism* through to Will Hutton's (1995) *The State We're In,* and more recent comparisons between stakeholder capitalism and shareholder capitalism. The collapse of Enron and a string of high-level corporate scandals over the last few years have encouraged a far more rigorous scrutiny of today's capitalist paradigm than was available during the 1980s or 1990s. But the 'success criteria' that underpin these comparisons rarely take any proper account of the non-negotiable imperative of securing critical natural capital, and even tend to play down the importance of protecting and building new social capital.

Beyond that kind of economic analysis, it would then be necessary to explore some of the deeper moral and philosophical concerns that many people believe to be at least as important in scrutinizing the 'disconnect' between capitalism and sustainability. Beyond questions about the *feasibility* of continuous economic growth within a capitalist system are questions about its *desirability*.

At a more abstract level, for instance, it is worth bearing in mind that in all variations of capitalism, *money* is the common denominator and the measure of value. Price regulates supply and demand, and is the principal source of information for consumers. For something to have value in such a system, it needs to have a price. Effective markets depend upon the transparent use of the price mechanism. Yet, in giving everything a money value, are we not undermining our capacity to judge what is truly valuable? This continues to raise enormous difficulties for those seeking to protect the environment within decision-making processes (such as planning, development appraisals and cost–benefit analysis) where the choice is often between trying to give that aspect of the environment one is seeking to protect a *monetary* value, however spuriously determined and philosophically corrosive such a valuation might be, or seeing it trashed as 'having no value whatsoever'. The pressure to transmute every aspect of the environment into a commodity that can then be bought and sold like any other commodity is often overwhelming. This would seem to indicate that no capitalist system is likely to value nature properly unless it is framed by a set of deeper, wiser precepts and spiritual values, where the value of something is not exclusively determined by its price.

More than 25 years ago, writers such as E. J. Mishan and Fred Hirsch sought to highlight the less tangible social and moral costs of economic growth, pointing out that when the 18th-century Scottish moral philosopher Adam Smith first started writing about the invisible hand of competition, people could be trusted not to harm the community in pursuing their self-interest – simply because of built-in restraint derived from morality, religion, custom and education. But that is clearly no longer the case in a more secular and relativistic modern world. More recently, Herman Daly has taken this analysis one step further:

> *The forces propelling economic growth are simultaneously eroding the moral foundation of the very social order which gives purpose and direction to that growth. On the demand side of the market, the glorification of self-interest and the pursuit of 'infinite wants' leads to*

a weakening of moral distinctions between luxury and necessity. Moral limits constraining demand for junk are inconvenient in a growth economy because growth increases when junk sells. So the growth economy fosters the erosion of the values upon which it depends, such as honesty, sobriety, trust, etc. On the supply side, the 'infinite' power of science-based technology is thought to be capable of overcoming all biophysical limits. But even if this erroneous proposition were true, the very world view of scientism leads to the debunking of any notion of transcendental value and to undercutting the moral basis of the social cohesion presupposed by market society. (Daly, 1996)

It is this combination of questionable feasibility and doubtful moral desirability that continues to prompt campaigners to predict the demise of capitalism itself. Though such apocalyptic predictions and questions are usually dismissed out of hand by mainstream political parties, the more far-sighted among them are much more nervous than they let on about the increasingly visible 'fault lines' in the system.

REFERENCES

Bakan, J. (2004) *The Corporation*, Constable, London

Bentley, T. (2002) 'Letting go: Complexity, individualism and the left', *Renewal*, vol 10

Bookchin, M. (1980) *Toward an Ecological Society*, Black Rose Books, Montreal, Canada

Chichilnisky, G. and Heal, G. (1998) 'Economic returns from the biosphere', *Nature*, vol 391, February

Christie, I. and Warburton, D. (2001) *From Here to Sustainability*, Real World Coalition/ Earthscan, London

Daly, H. (1996) *Beyond Growth*, Beacon Press, Boston, MA

Feshbach, M. and Friendly, A. (1992) *Ecocide in the USSR: Health and Nature Under Siege*, Aurum Press, London

Gates, J. (1998) *The Ownership Solution*, Penguin, London

Hampden-Turner, C. and Trompenaars, F. (1993) *The Seven Cultures of Capitalism*, Piatkus, London

Hardin. G. (1968) 'The tragedy of the commons', *Science*, vol 162, pp1243–1248

Hutton, W. (1995) *The State We're In*, Vintage, London

James, O. (2007) *Affluenza*, Vermilion, London

Keynes, J. M. (1936) *The General Theory of Employment, Interest and Money*, Harcourt Brace, New York

Legum, M. (2002) *It Doesn't Have to Be Like This*, Wild Goose Publications, Glasgow, UK

LSE (2005) *International Perspectives on Social Mobility*, London School of Economics, London

Meadows, D. (2001) 'Economic laws clash with planet's', *Earthlight Magazine*, spring

Monbiot, G. (2001) 'Turn the screw', *Guardian*, 24 April

Perkins, J. (2004) *Confessions of an Economic Hit Man*, Berrett-Koehler, San Francisco, CA

Rischard, J.-F. (2003) *High Noon: 20 Global Problems, 20 Years to Solve Them*, Basic Books, New York

Schumacher, E. F. (1973) *Small is Beautiful*, Abacus, London

Soros, G. (1997) 'The capitalist threat', *Atlantic Monthly*, vol 279, no 2, pp 45–58

Stebbing, T. and Heath, G. (2003) 'Competition and the struggle for existence', unpublished article

Stiglitz, J. (2006) *Making Globalization Work*, Allen Lane, London

Thomas, L. (1980) 'On the uncertainty of science', *Phi Beta Kappa Key Reporter*, vol 6, no 1

UNDP (2003) *Human Development Report 2003*, United Nations Development Programme, available at http://hdr.undp.org/reports/global/2003

von Weizsacker, E., Lovins, A. and Lovins, H. (1997) *Factor Four*, Earthscan, London

WCED (World Commission on Environment and Development) (1987) *Our Common Future*, the Brundtland Report, Oxford University Press, Oxford

Wissenburg, M. (1998) *Green Liberalism*, UCL Press, London

Woodin, M. and Lucas, C. (2004) *Green Alternatives to Globalisation*, Pluto Press, London

Through the Global Looking Glass

INTRODUCTION

If it is not capitalism per se causing the problem, is it globalization? Or, at least, the kind of globalization that is extending the influence of free markets and multinational companies into every corner of every country, even where it is not wanted? It turns out, on further investigation, that even the so-called 'anti-globalization movement' is passionate about what they see as the right kind of globalization. These are hotly contested ideological positions; even those archetypal motherhood-and-apple-pie notions of 'freedom' and 'democracy' have been conscripted into the war of words around the war on terrorism. Both *public* institutions – with organizations such as the World Bank and the International Monetary Fund (IMF) representing a 30-year-old Washington Consensus – and *private-sector* multinationals are increasingly under the cosh for accelerating environmental damage and making the lives of the poor even worse – charges which are strenuously denied by both political and business leaders. But does 'sustainable capitalism' mean an end of the huge global companies that have become so powerful over the last 20 years? Or can they, too, be 're-engineered'? Could they really become a genuine 'force for good', as well as a continuing engine of profit generation?

DEMOCRACY AND GLOBALIZATION

Each and every one of the essential characteristics of capitalism considered in the previous chapters has taken on an additional dimension through the pheno-menon of globalization. As international trade and foreign direct investment have multiplied, and more and more business is transacted on a global basis, globalization is alternately eulogized as the solution to the world's problems (and poverty alleviation, in particular) and then demonized as the principal accelerator of all things unsustainable under capitalism. As with capitalism, many people believe it's the particular model of globalization that dominates the world economy that is causing the problems. As Naomi Klein says, commenting on the so-called 'anti-globalization' movement:

If this new movement is 'anti' anything, it is anti-corporate, opposing the logic that what is good for business – less regulation, more mobility, more access – will trickle down into good news for everybody else. By focusing on global corporations and their impact around the world, this activist network is fast becoming the most internationally minded, globally linked movement ever seen. When protesters shout about the evils of globalization, most are not calling for a return to narrow nationalism, but for the borders of globalization to be expanded, for trade to be linked to labour rights, environmental protection and democracy. This network is as global as capitalism itself. (Klein, 2002)

The designation of the seemingly inchoate array of concerned organizations and individuals campaigning against poverty, developing world debt, abuses of human rights, corruption, environmental degradation, privatization of the public commons and the unaccountability of multinationals (to name but the most prominent of concerns) as an 'anti-globalization movement' is profoundly misguided. There may well be a very small number of campaigners for whom the only solution to today's converging crises is, indeed, a rapid regression to autarchic, self-sufficient communities; but they are utterly unrepresentative of the vast majority of those campaigning against today's corporate globalization. They are indisputably *anti-corporate* and a rather smaller number are *anti-capitalist*; but all would acknowledge that the world is by and large a better place for improved global communications, the internet and improved understanding between nations, and that global problems demand global solutions mediated through accountable global initiatives and institutions.

Beyond that, it's not even correct any longer to argue that this is an exclusively negative movement, eloquent in its denunciation of literally countless abuses of people and planet, but incapable of coming to any kind of agreement as to what it actually stands for – although it *is* true that this is emphatically not a homogenized, unified movement. Phoney consensus is discouraged (at gatherings such as the World Social Forum), and vibrant diversity and divergence are positively promoted. But the extent of the common ground upon which they *all* stand is becoming clearer and clearer: increased decentralization of power; global and national regulation of large corporations; community-based and local enterprise as a complement to international trade; and a passionate belief in development as freedom rather than development as growth, reverting back to Amartya Sen's (1999) core philosophy.

For all the confusion, it is actually the defence of democracy and freedom that lies at the heart of the 'anti-globalization' movement, just as the evangelists of increased liberalization claim that it is the defence of democracy and freedom that drives their own passion for free markets and global trade. The neo-liberal rhetoric has always been very strong on the 'democracy through trade' argument, based upon the assumption that free markets create free peoples. As George Bush himself puts it: 'People who operate in open economies eventually demand more open societies.' There is no denying that US neo-liberals are sincere in their belief that today's pattern of globalization fosters democracy. Such a belief is usually premised on the apparently reasonable extrapolation that since market-based economies are an essential feature of democratic societies, then the bigger those markets are, the more 'open' they are likely to be, and the more global they are, then the greater will be the reinforcement of pro-democratic processes and institutions.

Since 11 September 2001, that has become an even more dogmatic element in the promotion of corporate globalization; it's now all part of the 'for us or against us' logic that the US first imposed on the rest of the world to secure agreement for what was clearly an illegal, immoral and wholly unnecessary war against Iraq. The war against terrorism is therefore being waged as much through the imposed will of the World Trade Organization (WTO) as through the military might of the US, and those who stand opposed to that particular model of globalization must, in the twisted logic of the Bush Administration, be supporters of Al-Qa'eda and apologists for global terror.

There is a strong religious undertone to this analysis: free trade and democracy traditionally thrive in countries buttressed by Christian values and practice; Islamic countries are traditionally undemocratic, often oppressive and remain reluctant to throw in their lot with today's US-dominated global economy. Free trade has therefore been conscripted into a latter-day crusade to open up those closed nations and 'liberate' their people – just as is now being attempted in Afghanistan and Iraq. It is true that the political regimes in some Islamic countries are, indeed, abhorrent – illiberal, anti-women, corrupt, oppressive and usually hostile to any extension of civil rights or political freedoms. The democratization of those countries cannot come too soon. But the idea that the only route to democratization is via the imposition of corporate-led, US-driven globalization is perverse – and extraordinarily dangerous from the perspective of future world peace.

Roger Scruton's *The West and the Rest: Globalization and the Terrorist Threat* (2002) provides some deeply disturbing insights into the potential consequences of this geopolitical stand-off. He argues that Islam and the West have completely diverging views on citizenship, community, law and the role of religion in the lives of both citizens and states. From that perspective, the forward momentum of Western, corporate-led globalization is highly threatening to Islamic values, culture and morality, and the insensitivity of the West to this perceived threat is much resented.

For Scruton, there is additional resonance here in that he personally is persuaded that the Western values which underpin globalization (selfish individualism, moral relativism, progress through increased consumption and materialism, the dominance of individual rights over reciprocal responsibilities, and so on) are, indeed, inimical to the betterment of society and community the world over. While he abominates bin Laden (and the betrayal of the teachings of Islam that bin Laden is responsible for), he can't help but sympathize with the Islamists' horror of the decadence and the corruption at the heart of Western globalization.

The logic of Scruton's thinking leads to one grim conclusion: if we persist with this imposed monolithic pattern of globalization, then a 'clash of civilizations' is all but unavoidable.

The combination of the extreme economic neo-liberalism of the current US Administration and the kind of warped millenarian beliefs referred to in Chapter 2 is having a marked impact both upon social cohesion inside the US itself and upon the diminishing opportunities for improved global security. It is clear that although the US constitution still declares that all people in the US are 'created equal', that is not the view of the religious right, who see the world clearly divided by God into the righteous and the wicked. Ideologically speaking, the US Administration would appear to be perfectly comfortable with the extreme inequalities and social divisions both within America itself and between rich and poor nations. Michael Northcott (2004) describes this as 'a tragic example of the capacity of perverted religion and secular ideology to distort human lives and relationships and destroy communities', and comments somewhat despairingly upon the malign synergies between neo-conservative economics and pre-millennial fundamentalism:

> For the pre-millennialist, righteous individuals will be mysteriously and suddenly plucked from their beds or workplaces by the divine hand, and so secured from the coming conflagration of Armageddon at the rapture. For the free marketeer, individuals will be redeemed by the invisible hand of market forces. In neither case can collective action decisively affect their fate. It is in the light of the dual effects of these two kinds of fatalism that the increasingly brutal as well as self-interested assertion of American imperial power on every continent in the last few years can be better understood. The US corporate elite increasingly see themselves as engaged in a planetary war for the maintenance of their own prosperity and way of life, and for the directing of all human history to American ends. (Northcott, 2004)

Confronting the Washington Consensus

Nowhere is this sense of America seeking to direct human history to its own ends clearer than in the operations of the principal economic institutions working at a global level: the IMF, the World Bank and the WTO. It is a constant refrain of campaigners today that the so-called Washington Consensus is an enemy not a friend of democracy. Historically, as has now been documented in massive detail, the IMF's Structural Adjustment Programmes (SAPs) have compelled many governments over the last 20 years to set aside their own social and economic priorities and accept the IMF's conditions. As former chief economist to the World Bank, Joseph Stiglitz, says:

> *In theory, the IMF supports democratic institutions in the nations it assists. In practice, it undermines the democratic process by imposing its own policies.* (Stiglitz, 2002)

Both the World Bank and the IMF now intrude ever more deeply into the affairs of sovereign states in ways that go far beyond their original mandates and terms of reference. The IMF's reviled SAPs have now been replaced with poverty reduction strategies; but many campaigners have yet to be persuaded that much has changed in practice.

The World Bank likes to make out that it is now the much friendlier face of those bodies promoting the Washington Consensus. Under the leadership of James Wolfensohn, it tried to recast itself as a global poverty elimination campaign, but with very mixed results. It is reckoned to have paid out $3 to Western companies (to help delivery in the developing world) for every $1 received as aid in developing countries. All too often, it has advanced loans to some of the poorest countries in the world for wholly inappropriate mega-projects or to develop export-driven manufacturing or cash-cropping. The fiasco over coffee (in which country after country has been encouraged to make huge new investments in coffee for export, leading to glutted markets and collapsing prices) is a direct consequence of the World Bank's obsession with export-led development. These interventions have often led to severe environmental damage, continued displacement of people in rural areas and the proliferation of dead-end sweatshop jobs. Many Western companies have benefited substantially; but the results for the developing world have often been extraordinarily disappointing.

National governments fare no better at the hands of the WTO. National ownership of key public services is increasingly interpreted as discrimination against foreign companies; democratic decisions (such as that taken by the EU to ban the import of US beef reared with the help of growth hormones) are fiercely contested and serve as the pretext for yet another trade war; governments may no longer defend higher environmental or social standards if these are seen to represent a non-tariff barrier to trade. At the disastrous WTO meeting in Cancun, Mexico, in 2003, developing countries finally decided that it was time to draw that proverbial line in the sand, after literally decades of hypocritical rhetoric from the rich countries about the importance of opening markets and getting rid of subsidies, and decades doing next to nothing about it in their own backyards. As a result, the meeting fell apart in utter disarray. Since then, a rancorous stalemate has dominated proceedings, and it is now hard to see how the WTO is going to be able to transform itself sufficiently so as to become part of a sustainable solution to today's social and economic problems, even if it does cobble together some kind of compromise as part of the Doha Round of Trade Negotiations before the end of 2007. Outside of the global institutions themselves, some of the world's largest multinational companies unscrupulously use their bargaining power as foreign direct investors to secure exemptions from planning laws, 'special deals' and high-level agreements in which the wishes of local people (or even of the electorate as a whole) are routinely set aside in the interests of a greater economic good. Self-regulation is their demand, and they have secured astonishingly favourable trading conditions as a result. Percy Barnevik, a former CEO of the multinational ABB, defined globalization as 'the freedom for my group to invest where it pleases, when it pleases, in order to produce what it wants by getting supplies and selling wherever it wants, supporting as few constraints as possible regarding workers' right and social conventions'. In the face of all that, as Naomi Klein argues, it seems a bit rich that trade through the global economy is suddenly seen as the great deliverer of freedom and democracy:

> What I dislike most about the trickle-down democracy argument is the dishonour it pays to all the people who fought, and fight still, for genuine democratic change in their countries, whether for the right to vote, or to have access to land, or to form trade unions. Democracy isn't the work of the markets and the invisible hand; it is the work of real hands. It is often stated, for instance, that the North American Free Trade Agreement is bringing democracy to Mexico. In fact, workers, students, indigenous groups and radical intellectuals are the ones slowly forcing democratic reforms on Mexico's intransigent elite. NAFTA, by widening the gap between rich and poor, makes their struggle more militant and more difficult to stop. (Klein, 2002)

Economists have estimated that reducing the worst remaining trade barriers could lead to huge income gains for developing countries – in excess of $100 billion a year. That could be as much as three times the total amount of official development assistance on offer. However, it is becoming increasingly obvious that trade liberalization isn't necessarily delivering against its own economic objectives. It is clearly working well in terms of opening up the world to the already rich and powerful, but has failed time after time to provide equal access for poorer countries to the rich world. The United Nations Conference on Trade and Development (UNCTAD) has found that the rapid and extensive trade liberalization undertaken by the poorest countries during the 1990s failed to benefit the poor. In fact, it was associated with rising poverty, with the countries worst affected being those that had liberalized most.

This takes us promptly back to Amartya Sen's (1999) critique of 'development as growth' rather than development as freedom. There is little doubt, by analogy, that globalization as growth, mediated through the self-serving expansion of some of the world's largest multinational companies, falls foul of the same strictures.

Globalization as freedom, by contrast, offers something very different, as spelled out in the Johannesburg Memo:

> *Broadly speaking, there are currently two concepts of globalization which have gained prominence in recent controversies. Corporate globalization, which aims at transforming the world into a single economic arena, allows corporations to compete freed from constraints in order to increase global wealth and welfare. This particular concept can be traced to the rise of the free trade idea in 18th-century Britain and has come, after many permutations, to dominate world politics in the late 20th century.*
>
> *Democratic globalization, on the other hand, envisages a world that is home to a flourishing plurality of cultures, and that recognizes the fundamental rights for every world citizen. The roots of this concept extend back to the late ancient Greek philosophy and the European enlightenment, with their perception of the world in a cosmopolitan spirit. We believe that the cause of justice and sustainability would be caught in quicksand unless it is elaborated upon in the framework of democratic globalization.* (Johannesburg Memo, 2002)

This is a debate that can only become sharper. I don't pretend to have given a comprehensively balanced view of what is, after all, a massively complicated and 'protean' phenomenon. Advocates of accelerated globalization – such as Johann Norberg (2001) in his persuasive *In Defence of Global Capitalism* or Martin Wolf (2004) with his hugely stimulating *Why Globalization Works* – point to a string of statistics about growing prosperity in many parts of the world. It must count for something, after all, that the number of poor people in East Asia as a whole has halved since 1975, and that since China started opening up to the global economy in the 1980s, more than 300 million of its people have been lifted out of poverty. Norberg and Wolf argue passionately that globalization is good for the poor, good for the environment and particularly good for technology transfer. And they are certainly right to point out that China and India are fashioning their own variants of global capitalism without having some standard model imposed upon them – including all sorts of features (such as 'selective protectionism' or strategic intervention by the state in certain sectors of the economy) which cut right across the standard Washington Consensus model. Which was precisely what countries like South Korea, Taiwan and Malaysia were able to do as they became serious players in the global economy.

But with the exception of China and India (very important exceptions, it has to be said), there is little evidence that globalization is producing any significant reduction *in relative income disparities*, as has always been claimed by conventional economists. Between 1970 and 2000 (the 'peak years' for the putative benefits of globalization to work their way through the system), things got a lot worse. In

1960, the income gap between the fifth of the world's people living in the richest countries and the fifth in the poorest countries was 30:1. In 1990, the gap had widened to 60:1. By 1998, it had grown to 78:1. By 2004, it was close to 108:1. Looking at current trends, it is difficult to imagine the point at which this trend will eventually bottom out.

It is, of course, difficult to disentangle cause and effect here. But in a world where the dice are so clearly loaded against the poor, global capitalism *as we know it today* would appear to be inherently incompatible with the pursuit of either ecological sustainability or social justice. Indeed, conceptualizing the journey from where we are today to an ecologically and socially sustainable model of globalization takes a lot of imagination. One of the organizations at the forefront of the 'reconceptualization challenge' is the New Economics Foundation, which over the years has helped to develop a formidable global network of sister organizations. Margaret Legum is the leading light in one of these (South African New Economics), and she has captured the 'before and after' effect of the various campaigns being waged by that network to ensure that the Washington Consensus is succeeded by a very different kind of consensus (see Figures 5.1 and 5.2). I will return to a number of these 'alternative scenarios' in Part III.

Whatever variations there may be in today's different movements against US-led corporate globalization, there is consensus on one point: the role played in the global economy by multinational companies lies at the very heart of the problem. It is not possible to answer the question about the compatibility of capitalism and sustainability without addressing the contribution made by today's multinationals to our current state – for good or ill – and then addressing the question of what to do about any dysfunctionalities that might be identified.

Confronting the multinationals

I am always amused by the fact that one of the very first campaigners against multinational corporations was Adam Smith in *The Wealth of Nations* back in 1776, where he warned that managers should not be trusted to steward other people's money, and that only 'negligence and confusion' would result. The corporation as we know it today is essentially a creature of Britain's imperial past, going right back to the establishment of the East India Company in 1600, just one of a series of corporate charters extended first by British monarchs and then by the English parliament to groups of investors. Each charter was slightly different, but essentially they limited the extent of any liabilities or losses suffered by the investors in return for certain obligations designed to serve the public purpose – including any share of profits accruing to the Crown. Gradually, these corporations were granted monopoly powers, either over whole territories (as with the East India Company or with the Hudson Bay Company) or over whole industries.

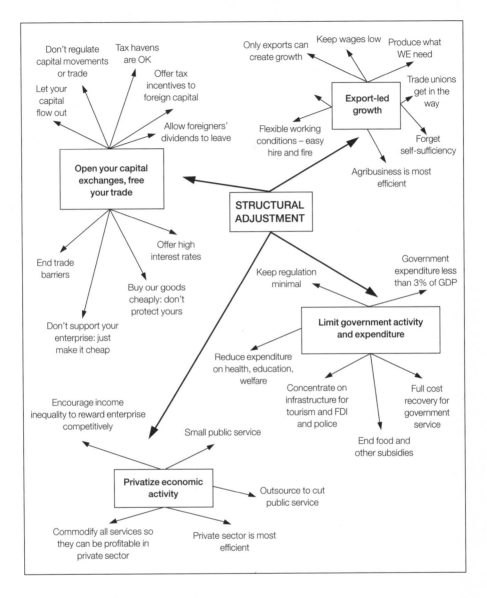

Don't regulate capital movements or trade

Tax havens are OK

Offer tax incentives to foreign capital

Let your capital flow out

Allow foreigners' dividends to leave

Open your capital exchanges, free your trade

Only exports can create growth

Keep wages low

Produce what WE need

Trade unions get in the way

Export-led growth

Flexible working conditions – easy hire and fire

Forget self-sufficiency

Agribusiness is most efficient

STRUCTURAL ADJUSTMENT

End trade barriers

Offer high interest rates

Buy our goods cheaply: don't protect yours

Don't support your enterprise: just make it cheap

Keep regulation minimal

Government expenditure less than 3% of GDP

Limit government activity and expenditure

Reduce expenditure on health, education, welfare

Concentrate on infrastructure for tourism and FDI and police

Full cost recovery for government service

End food and other subsidies

Encourage income inequality to reward enterprise competitively

Small public service

Privatize economic activity

Outsource to cut public service

Commodify all services so they can be profitable in private sector

Private sector is most efficient

Source: Legum (2002)

Figure 5.1 *The Washington Consensus: How it works*

During the 17th and 18th centuries, parliament then passed many new laws to extend these monopoly interests – and it was this slow accretion of power to the corporations that so irked Adam Smith. He saw the emerging nexus of influence between the state and corporations as wholly inimical to the competitive functions of the market. But during the 19th century, the power base of the multinationals

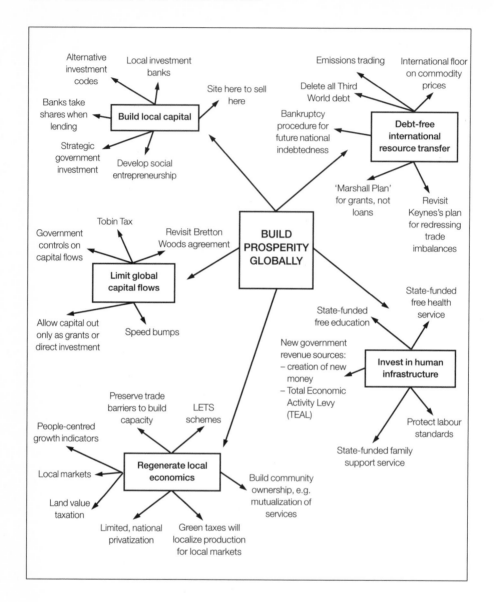

Source: Legum (2002)

Figure 5.2 *An alternative scenario to the Washington Consensus*

shifted to the US as it gradually overcame its hostility to the institution of the corporation, with individual corporations slowly gaining sufficient control over state legislatures basically to rewrite the laws governing their own regulation and the balance of their rights and responsibilities. By the middle of the 19th century, the detailed mechanics of 'limited liability' (limiting the losses an individual investor could incur, in the event of corporate failure, to the amount of money initially invested rather than to the total losses) was finally agreed upon – essentially as a way of attracting the middle classes into the business of buying and selling stocks. And in 1886, the US Supreme Court ruled that a private corporation could be treated as 'natural person' under the US constitution and was therefore entitled to all the protection afforded under the Bill of Rights. As David Korten points out:

> *Thus, corporations finally claimed the full rights enjoyed by individual citizens while being exempted from many of the responsibilities and liabilities of citizenship. The subsequent claim by corporations that they have the same right as any individual to influence the government in their own interest pits the individual citizen against the vast financial and communications resources of the corporation, and mocks the constitutional intent that all citizens have an equal voice in the political debates surrounding important issues.* (Korten, 1995)

This is one of the reasons why many campaigners remain so mistrustful of the concept of 'corporate citizenship'. History tells us that the likes of J. D. Rockerfeller, Cornelius Vanderbilt, Andrew Carnegie and James Mellon illegitimately arrogated to their enterprises the rights and entitlements of the individual citizen, while simultaneously diminishing the idea of any reciprocal 'public service' obligation on their part. Corporations are *not* citizens, and to abuse the concept of citizenship by attributing it to them is both misleading and unhelpful.

What has all this got to do with multinationals today, as the modern inheritors of all these legal privileges? There is a powerful school of thought which argues that multinationals (particularly over the last 30 years or so) have systematically increased their reach, scope and influence so that they are now *the* dominant social institution anywhere in the world. David Korten's 1995 classic *When Corporations Rule the World* lucidly analyses the build-up of corporate power, its progressive 'takeover' of political and legislative systems (particularly in the US, but now everywhere in the world), and the malign consequences of this for effective government, the more equitable distribution of wealth, and any attempt to set the global economy on a genuinely sustainable footing. Multinationals behave in this way because we continue to elect governments that continue, in effect, to license them to create wealth often at the expense of people and planet.

According to this kind of radical critique, any reform agenda is seen as a complete waste of time. Multinational corporations have slipped their constitutional leashes, feel that they now owe nothing to society apart from warm words about social responsibility, and are accountable solely to their shareholders, in whose interests profits must be maximized at all costs. For one reason or another, enough people are still sufficiently persuaded that this exercise of power predominantly in the interests of a tiny minority of human beings still serves the interests of the vast majority well enough – or, rather, better than anything else on offer. Corporate-dominated media (entrapped by their dependence on fat advertising budgets) shield people from the reality of what is actually happening, and an active propaganda machine seduces people into comatose consumerism as a substitute for real life and active engagement in the world around us. As Robert McChesney (himself inspired by the biting insights of Noam Chomsky) has written:

> As the mainstream media has become increasingly dependent on advert-
> ising revenues for support, it has become an anti-democratic force in
> society. The global commercial media system works to advance the cause
> of the global market, and promote commercial values, while denigrating
> journalism and culture not conducive to the immediate bottom line.
> (McChesney, 1999)

It is a powerful – and ultimately despairing – hypothesis. But does it really stack up? Of course the interests of shareholders come first: that is the way their legal and fiduciary obligations are currently framed. But it is misleading to argue that this *necessarily* and *automatically* demands corporate practices that degrade the environment, abuse employees and exploit local communities. Indeed, as we will see in Chapter 14, the underlying rationale of the so-called 'business case' for environmentally, socially and ethically responsible behaviour is a great deal stronger than most people allow for.

However, the intensity of the invective still levelled by most campaigners against the multinationals (as if there was still nothing to differentiate a BP from an ExxonMobil, a Unilever from a Nestlé) still comes as something of a surprise to those organizations (such as Forum for the Future) that work alongside such companies to accelerate the many different change processes which are already underway. Over the 14 years that the Prince of Wales's Business and the Environment Programme has been in existence, for instance, we have witnessed a profound shift in both attitudes and behaviours on the part of most of the big multinationals involved. As individuals, the 1500 or so senior business people who have been through the Programme's week-long seminar are often as concerned about the state of the world and its people as some of the campaigners lobbing brickbats at them. But they are constrained – by their bosses; by corporate inertia and bureaucracy; by the power of capital markets; by limited consumer and investor enthusiasm for using their purchasing power more sustainably; by muddled, procrastinating politicians.

For all of those reasons, there remains every reason to be extremely cautious about today's unbounded enthusiasm for the notion of corporate social responsibility (CSR). This has little to do with the *Economist*'s distaste for anything that seems to imply that contemporary capitalism isn't already doing a near-perfect job, and much more to do with the way in which CSR is interpreted by companies as a ragbag menu of nice-to-do add-ons that never really interrogate their core business model. This is easily demonstrated by the way in which some of the really difficult issues never get on to the menu in the first place.

Taxation and transfer pricing arrangements provide one such example for multinationals today, posing a challenge on both equity and transparency grounds. A narrow interpretation of a company's traditional fiduciary duties to its shareholders means that it should be doing everything in its power, within the law, to reduce the amount of tax it pays to any government and to maximize the financial benefits to be had from juggling prices, revenues and currency exchange across different markets. As a result, companies often end up paying tens of millions of dollars in legal fees to avoid as much of their tax burden as can legally be avoided, all the while talking enthusiastically about their benign influence on poor countries in terms of jobs generated, taxes paid and the 'multiplier effect' they purport to have on local economies. CSR sceptics have rightly pointed out that they could be much more of a 'force for good' if they simply paid over all the taxes owed in any particular country, rather than relying on quasi-philanthropic handouts ostentatiously offered up as a percentage of pre-tax profits. Understandably, Joel Bakan emphasizes the need for caution when assessing the potential significance of CSR:

> *Business leaders today say that their companies care about more than profit and loss, that they feel responsible to society as a whole, not just to their shareholders. Corporate social responsibility is their new creed, a self-conscious corrective to earlier greed-inspired versions of the corporation. Despite this shift, the corporation itself has not changed. It remains, as it was at the time of its origins as a modern business institution in the middle of the 19th century, a legally designated 'person' designed to valorize self-interest and invalidate moral concern. Most people would find its 'personality' abhorrent, even psychopathic, in a human being; yet curiously we accept it in society's most powerful institution.* (Bakan, 2004)

This kind of anti-corporate rhetoric causes huge offence to large numbers of business people. But critics such as Joel Bakan and David Korten are not talking about *individuals* in those companies, but about the *corporate persona* as such. By 'psychopathic', Bakan is referring to those traits that psychiatrists would expect to encounter in a psychopathic individual: a readiness to manipulate everything and everybody else; a lack of empathy; an obsession with being 'number one'; a refusal to accept responsibility for their own actions; an inability to feel any guilt or remorse.

Moreover, a growing number of business leaders have themselves commented on the fact that they are less in control of their companies' destiny than the outside world appears to recognize, bound as they are by the iron clad laws of short-term profit maximization. After listening to one Chief Executive bemoaning just how painfully his hands were tied by his shareholders, I offered him, in solidarity, the following ten Commandments:

> Thou shalt maximize economic growth.
> Thou shalt externalize all possible costs.
> Thou shalt minimize tax payments.
> Thou shalt discount the future.
> Thou shalt ignore natural limits.
> Thou shalt concentrate wealth in the smallest number of hands.
> Thou shalt elevate private gain over public benefit.
> Thou shalt set thy face against regulation.
> Thou shalt squeeze thy suppliers without mercy.
> Thou shalt smite thy competitors until they are vanquished.

If CSR can help, even on the margins, to mitigate those character traits, then we should do nothing to discourage that kind of engagement. But it is an illusion to think that responsibility for putting all this to rights lies predominantly with the companies themselves. If society wants companies to rebalance the respective interests of shareholders and other interested stakeholders (employees, local communities, environmental interests and so on), then it is society – through its governments – that must reframe their respective obligations. Governments, not companies, have the democratic mandate to intervene in order to shape market forces. If ministers are persuaded that there is sufficiently widespread public support for raising standards, or encouraging best practice, then they should intervene decisively to secure those public benefits without endlessly passing the buck back to business to do it on our behalf.

No one government can act on its own, however – hence the call from NGOs (represented most forcefully at the World Summit on Sustainable Development by Friends of the Earth International) for a Global Convention on Corporate Accountability. Although most NGOs acknowledge that multinational companies are already achieving a certain amount through voluntary mechanisms, they do not believe that this can possibly go far enough. A new Convention would include mechanisms to obtain redress for any stakeholders adversely affected by the impact of multinationals. Those individuals and organizations should be given legal standing to challenge corporations in their own home country. The Convention would identify clear social and environmental duties for corporations, which would include reporting on environmental and social performance in a verifiable fashion, seeking what is called 'prior informed consent' from affected communities, and defining rules for consistently high standards of behaviour wherever corporations are operating anywhere in the world. These rules would be based upon the principles enshrined in international environmental, social and human rights agreements.

The diversity of views on the 'reformability' of multinationals, as we have seen, covers a very wide span – all the way through from an uncompromising call for their total elimination, at one end of the spectrum, to a little bit of incremental tinkering (as favoured by most European governments) at the other, via various shades of moderate or radical reform in between. Many critics, however, believe that this debate still misses the point and that the real problems lie not so much in the corporate world as in the macro-economic and financial systems within which the corporations have to operate. David Korten again:

> *These forces have transformed once beneficial corporations and financial institutions into instruments of a market tyranny that is extending its reach across the planet like a cancer, colonizing ever more of the planet's living spaces, destroying livelihoods, displacing people, rendering democratic institutions impotent and feeding on life in an insatiable quest for money. As our economic system has detached itself from place and gained greater dominance over our democratic institutions, even the world's most powerful corporations have become captives of the forces of a globalized financial system that has de-linked the creation of money from creation of real wealth and rewards extractive, over-productive investment.* (Korten, 1995)

The idea of the relative powerlessness of multinational companies strikes many campaigners as counter-intuitive if not fantastical. But in a world where there are few restrictions on the movement of capital, and almost limitless opportunities for investors (both as listed institutions and as private operators) to move money at speed on the most marginal and most short-term of potential gains, multinationals really do not call the shots today as they may once have done in the past. This is something to which I will return in Chapter 11.

CONFRONTING POPULATION GROWTH

There remains one final global driver, about which all but a tiny number of campaigning organizations and individuals are in complete agreement. That driver is population, about which the overwhelming consensus is to say nothing and do even less.

This particular form of denial has fascinated me ever since I joined the Green Party in the mid-1970s. It's become a very personal issue since I made a TV documentary about population ('Sex, sin and survival') in 2000, and witnessed at first hand (in the Philippines, Egypt and Colombia) the terrible impact on poor people and on women in particular of the failure to provide for proper family planning.

Paradoxically, it's the one area of global politics where the facts are all but incontestable. When the UN brought out its latest projections, in March 2007, indicating that world population would grow from today's 6.5 billion to 9.1 billion by 2050 (which equates to roughly 80 million extra people every year), there was no storm of statistical controversy to match that which descended on the projections of the Intergovernmental Panel on Climate Change just a few weeks earlier. In fact, there was near silence.

That's partly because everyone now accepts that the UN projections in this area have proved to be extremely reliable, and partly because you can make a pretty good estimate of the numbers of people who will be around in 2050 simply by looking at the number of young people alive today. And that's where the insanity of what's happening today really hits you: nearly half of today's 6.5 billion people are under the age of 25, with an astonishing 1.2 billion between the ages of 10 and 19, the majority of them living in the new mega-city slums of the developing world.

This is a veritable 'youthquake', and the simple truth is that if we don't focus on enabling those young people to take control of their own fertility, that figure of 9.1 billion by 2050 could prove to be a frightening underestimate. Right now, around 350 million couples worldwide – that's about a *third* of all couples in their reproductive years – still lack access to a full range of family planning services. The evidence also tells us that as many as 50 per cent of the 500,000 women who die every year through unsafe induced abortion, pregnancy and childbirth would not have died if contraception had been available. Every minute of every day, 380 women become pregnant, and of those 190 did not plan to.

Please note that what I am talking about in this chapter has nothing to do with 'population control' – driven by some kind of choice-limiting, coercive agenda. The notoriety of China's 'one-child family' policy means that people believe this is the only effective way to reduce average fertility. Nothing could be further from the truth. All the best success stories (and there are many!) show countries like Mexico, Sri Lanka, South Korea, Morocco, Taiwan, Thailand, Vietnam, Costa Rica and Kerala in India reducing fertility to close to replacement level (2.1 children per family) as quickly as China did. Iran halved its average fertility from 5.2 children in 1988 to just 2.6 in 1996 – an 8-year transformation driven through by the country's political *and* religious leaders with great determination.

Mind you, it's sobering to work out what would have happened if China had not imposed its policy in 1979. The Chinese Government estimates that 138 million additional births have been prevented over the intervening 28 years. As we'll see in the next chapter, China's current emissions of carbon dioxide are 3.5 tonnes per person per annum. That's the equivalent of nearly 500 million tonnes of CO_2 averted every year and 330 billion tonnes since the policy was first introduced.

So you might imagine that all those environmental organizations campaigning so passionately to focus political attention on climate change would be equally focused on the critical importance of reducing average fertility – especially in those very poor countries crying out for help but getting nothing from the rich world. Wrong again. Leaders of our ever so politically-correct environment movement can barely bring themselves to utter the dreaded 'p' word. Yet this is spectacularly illogical. Just do the sums. The total annual amount of CO_2 that 6.5 billion of us put into the atmosphere today is around 30 billion tonnes. Very crudely, that works out at a personal CO_2 budget of 4.6 tonnes per person. If we achieve the current target of a 60 per cent cut by 2050 (bearing in mind that the target is almost certainly going to have to get a lot tougher over the next few years), that means we'll need to be emitting no more than 18 billion tonnes. But by 2050, there will be 9 billion of us, rather than 6.5 billion, which works out at a personal CO_2 budget of 2 tonnes per person. If global population was 7.5 billion, it would be 2.4 tonnes of CO_2; and at 6 billion, 3 tonnes. But reducing human numbers is *never* advanced as a solution to climate change.

If anything, leaders of today's development organizations are even more hostile than environmentalists to population being given any currency in international discussions. The Millennium Development Goals don't mention population. Tony Blair's Commission for Africa ignored it entirely, even though it's blindingly obvious that completely unsustainable population growth in most of Africa will keep it permanently, hopelessly stuck in deepest, darkest poverty. And I very much doubt that their minds will be changed by the February 2007 report from the All-Party Parliamentary Group on Population, Development and Reproductive Health (bringing together MPs and peers of all persuasions in the UK Parliament) which authoritatively demonstrates that every single one of the Millennium Development Goals will be harder to achieve because of continuing population growth. In its evidence to the Committee, the World Health Organization (WHO) spelled out the connection between fertility management and promoting gender equality – the third Millennium Development Goal: 'although women's ability to control their fertility is by itself not sufficient to gaining their full empowerment and gender equality, it is the first and most important step'. And the empirical correlation is pretty clear too: countries with a high contraceptive use have a higher proportion of girls in secondary schools.

The situation in Africa is particularly depressing. For instance, there are around 30 million people in Uganda today; by 2025, there will be around 55 million. If it keeps on down that track, Uganda will become the world's 12th largest country, with around 130 million people. President Museveni calls this 'a great resource' for his country; most sensible people see it as an unmitigated disaster. The persistent idea that it is somehow 'elitist' (in a 'rich world' kind of way), 'illiberal' or even 'oppressive' to urge massive extensions of good family planning in the world's poorest countries is ignorant, inhumane and destructive of women's rights. It cannot be long before the continuing neglect of this critical humanitarian challenge is exposed, once and for all, as a fundamental betrayal of some of the world's poorest and most exploited people.

As if the dogma and political correctness of the environment and development movements wasn't enough, we now have to deal with a resurgent 'pro-natalist' movement which is becoming increasingly influential within a number of governments. So concerned are they that their total fertility rate (TFR) has dropped below replacement rate (2.1 children per couple) that they're busily bribing women to have more children. In France, women get up to £670 a month during maternity leave to have a third child; in Australia, it's around £900 for *any* number of children. All this on the assumption that a declining population will create negative economic consequences and social dislocation of a very serious kind. This so-called 'demographic time bomb' has been massively exaggerated, however. With people living longer, working longer and staying healthier, the idea that one's productive (and earning) life comes to a juddering halt at 65 is simply archaic. I don't doubt that there will be issues around pensions (in terms of what it's fair to ask young people to contribute to the wellbeing of a much larger number of older people), but the idea that Western societies will somehow implode because of this shift strikes me as fantastical.

There's clearly also an important religious dimension to this. The day before the 27 members of the EU celebrated its 50th anniversary, the Pope declared that the entire continent could be set on the path to extinction because of the low birth rate in so many countries: 'From a demographic standpoint, Europe seems set on a path that could lead it to take leave of history,' he warned. Europe was 'losing faith in its own future'. Putting to one side the self-indulgent hyperbole, the Pope is certainly right (though I suspect for the wrong reasons) to direct our attention to the dramatic demographic transformation that is going on right now. By 2050, the population of 'the rich world' will be pretty much what it is today – around 1.2 billion people. And the total population of Europe could be down by as much as 50 million. At the same time, the population of 'the poor world' will have risen from around 5.3 billion today to around 7.8 billion.

This has massive implications for America, Europe, and Australia and New Zealand in particular. In 2005, the US Border Patrol arrested more than a million people who had gained illegal entry into the US across the Rio Grande in Mexico. The huge defensive wall along that border is now being extended over another few hundred miles, but few people believe it will have any serious effect on deterring those whose desperation will make them take any risk to escape a lifetime of crushing poverty.

In Europe, the situation is not so very different in terms of the borders between Southern Europe and North Africa. In the March 2003 issue of *Population and Development Review*, the French demographer Paul Demeny spells this out in the starkest terms: in 1950, Europe's neighbours had less than half Europe's population (163 to 350 million); by 2000, their population had almost quadrupled to surpass Europe's (587 to 451 million); and by 2050, according to the latest UN projections, their population will be more than three times larger than Europe's (1.3 billion to 401 million) (Demeny, 2003).

This, of course, is precisely the kind of outlook that is seized on by the likes of Jean-Marie Le Pen, leader of the Front National in France, and right-wing xenophobes across Europe. Images of being 'flooded out by an unstoppable tide of starving/black/Muslim/feckless/illegal immigrants from Africa' (insert your own combination of epithets) are used to justify draconian and racist policy proposals of every kind. Over the last few years, even the most liberal of European countries have been caught up in this wave of hostility to the poor and needy seeking to gain access to some of the relative wealth of their European neighbours. And it can only get worse, not just here in Europe, but also in the US, which is facing exactly the same pressures on its southern border, and in Australia, staring out across the Timor Sea at some of the poorest people in the world. Thomas Homer-Dixon again:

> *As population growth rates in poor countries remain far above those in rich countries, the proportion of poor people on the planet is rising fast. In 1950, there were about two poor people for every rich person on Earth; today, there are about four; and in 2025, when the world's population will be about 8 billion, there will be nearly six poor people for every rich person.* (Homer-Dixon, 2006)

This is one of the biggest issues of our time. Yet the majority of progressive voices in both Europe and the US have either ceded the ground to increasingly vocal right-wing and racist parties, or have adopted the same kind of harsh political tone and rhetoric while seeking to maintain some semblance of tolerant, inclusive and compassionate policies. And they are often urged on down that disastrous path by predominantly right-wing popular media, whose own language and imagery is subtly (and, in my country, not so subtly) honed to cultivating xenophobic, 'fortress' mentalities.

And that of course is one of the main reasons why all good environmentalists and progressives on the Left don't want to talk about population. They know that it's hard to address population in today's fracturing world without talking about flows of people between nations, and they're scared witless that they will end up sounding like an offshoot of the British National Party (BNP) here in the UK, or the Front National in France, or any number of right-wing, 'supremacist' groups in the US. This is a particularly pressing issue for the US and the UK, as ours are pretty much the only countries in the Organisation for Economic Co-operation and Development (OECD) where population is still rising, with increased immigration playing a major part in that growth.

According to the UK Government's 'Population trends', our population is projected to grow from just over 60 million today to around 67 million in 2031; 50 per cent of that increase is attributable to an assumed level of net inward migration, rather than because of a higher fertility rate (which is only slightly above the EU average of 1.8) or people living longer. For that reason (as a Patron of an organization called the Optimum Population Trust), I feel very comfortable with the idea of limiting immigration to the same number of people who leave the UK every year – around 350,000. Asylum seekers would obviously take priority under such a limitation, and then economic migrants and relatives of UK citizens. With declining fertility, that would mean a slow but steady decline in overall numbers over time. If we wanted a faster decline, then we would have to set a lower rate of net inward migration.

So what's the problem with that? Would it mean we'd be falling short of our international obligations? I don't think so, and make no apologies for arguing that one of the most overcrowded nations on Earth *must* factor that consideration into its immigration policy. Would it alienate existing immigrants and ethnic minorities? I very much doubt it. Perceptions of 'excessive' immigration are already having a seriously corrosive effect on social cohesion, and it will get a great deal worse as the BNP and the *Daily Mail* keep grinding away at peoples' fears and anxieties on this score. In short, I'm one of those who believe that strict, transparent and fair limitations on immigration are absolutely critical – indeed, a precondition of securing the kind of vibrant, cohesive multicultural society which the vast majority of people in this country are proud of and want to see flourish.

But for me, that's only the start. If we're going to be tough on illegal immigration in both Europe and the US, then we have to be equally tough on the *causes* of illegal immigration. And that means a radically different approach to building better relationships with Africa and South and Central America. Out would go those failed expressions of the kind of neo-liberal, ecologically-illiterate economic orthodoxy of the 1990s (in the shape of NAFTA and NEPAD – the North American Free Trade Agreement and the New Economic Partnership for African Development), and in would come new partnerships for achieving a genuinely sustainable future for some of the poorest countries on Earth. These partnerships would be based on the seven pillars of physical and human security: renewable energy; clean water and sanitation; adaptation to climate change; sustainable agriculture and land use; primary education for *every* child; dramatically improved healthcare services (including all the work being done on HIV/Aids); and access to a choice of contraception for *all* as part of a continent-wide drive to dramatically reduce average fertility. A reworking, if you like, of the Millennium Development Goals to make them rather more relevant in a millennium that is already beginning to look very difficult indeed. And to make this work, every OECD country would need to increase its commitment from 0.7 per cent of GDP to a minimum of 1 per cent – sold to their electorates not as old-fashioned philanthropic aid, but as a strategic investment in their own security and future wellbeing.

Unworldly? Insane even? Possibly. But having just finished reading the second part of the Fourth Assessment Report from the IPPC (2007), I just wonder what other kind of response politicians and their electorates now believe might be appropriate. If the level of devastation projected for Africa in particular begins to materialize over the next couple of decades, then the impact of this could be felt much sooner than even the most pessimistic have believed up until now. Combine all that with the continuing scourge of HIV/Aids, with some of the highest total fertility rates in the world, and with the harsh economic realities of oil either at or already past its 'peak moment', and it's difficult not to give way to a little bit of despair – as James Howard Kunstler did in a hard-hitting article in the *New Statesman* magazine in August 2005, describing exactly the kind of 'synchronous failure' referred to in Chapter 2:

> *Malthus (1766–1834), an English country clergyman, has been the whipping boy of idealists and techno-optimists for 200 years. His famous essay proposed that human population, if unconstrained, would grow exponentially while food supplies grew only arithmetically, and that therefore population growth faced strict and inevitable natural limits. I would argue that Malthus was correct, but that cheap oil has skewed the equation over the past hundred years while the human race has enjoyed an unprecedented orgy of non-renewable condensed solar energy accumulated over aeons of prehistory. The 'green revolution' in crop yields was minimally about scientific innovation in crop genetics, and mostly about dumping huge amounts of fertilizers and pesticides made out of fossil fuels onto crops, as well as employing irrigation at a fantastic scale, made possible by abundant oil and gas. The cheap-oil age created an artificial bubble of plenitude for a period not much longer than a human lifetime, a century. Within that comfortable bubble, the idea took hold that only grouches, spoilsports and godless maniacs considered population hypergrowth a problem, and that it was indecent even to raise the issue. I hazard to assert that as oil ceases to be cheap and world reserves move towards depletion, we will suddenly be left with an enormous surplus population that the ecology of Planet Earth will not support. No political programme of birth control will avail. The people are already here.* (Kunstler, 2005)

These days, it's not often you find anyone prepared to defend the much-maligned work of Thomas Malthus. Throughout my life as a sustainable development activist, I've been endlessly put down or even viciously attacked as a neo-Malthusian, and though I do not share Kunstler's apocalyptic conclusion in the quote above, I *do* share his bitter denunciation of all the cornucopian, politically-correct 'techno-optimists' who have basically betrayed an entire generation with their facile, intellectually corrupt escapism about population growth.

Taking stock

Despair in the face of such daunting problems is an understandable reaction, but not all that helpful. There are fewer and fewer people who seriously suppose that today's particular model of capitalism (dominated by a small number of hugely powerful interests, imposing upon the world a pattern of globalization that alienates millions, impoverishes hundreds of millions, further enriches an already inconceivably wealthy minority, and undermines our life-support systems in the process) can last for very much longer – on ecological grounds alone.

Indeed, there are those who argue, albeit against the run of the last 20 years or so, that the whole crazy edifice is a great deal more vulnerable than might ever be discerned from mainstream media coverage of the already visible cracks and faults in the system. Comparisons with the collapse of Soviet power in Eastern Europe are often made in this context. Even the remote possibility of such a collapse is stirring an ever larger number of enthusiastic capitalists to look far more purposefully to a reform agenda than ever before. But are they looking in the right direction?

Part II, 'A framework for sustainable capitalism', begins to explore what an alternative model of capitalism might look like. As I hope has emerged in the opening five chapters, the principal reason for taking on that challenge is the realization that today's particular model of capitalism simply won't get us to where we need to be: a world in which 9 billion people can live within the Earth's natural limits in a sufficiently equitable, just and healthy society.

The emergence of a sustainable variant of capitalism is certainly not going to happen overnight, with the world jumping instantly from one relatively stable state to another relatively stable state: it will be messy, incremental, controversial and very, very difficult. But that change process is already under way – in terms of our first faltering responses to climate change, the 'Make Poverty History' breakthroughs of 2005 on debt and aid, a growing awareness of our interdependence with all other nations and peoples, a better understanding of the scale of the technological challenges that now confront us, and so on.

What is at stake here is how fast that transition can be driven. I have tried to demonstrate in these first five chapters that we really don't have much alternative, given the state of the life-support systems upon which we depend, and have advanced the tentative hypothesis that there is no absolute 'deal-breaker' in terms of some inherent unsustainability within capitalism that would mean we could *never* arrive at a sustainable society via *any* capitalist economy. That hypothesis will, no doubt, be torn to shreds by more radical sustainable development activists who are still persuaded that there can be no accommodation whatsoever with capitalism, however 'tamed' and transformed a variant we might end up with.

To help generate that debate is part of the purpose in writing this book. To be leaders in this troubled world, we have to be able to offer as many messages of hope as of doom and gloom. We have simply got to get better at presenting the overwhelmingly positive benefits of a possible transition in terms of new opportunities for entrepreneurs, new sources of economic prosperity and jobs, a higher quality of life for people, safer, more secure communities, a better work–life balance, and so on. In other words, we have got to raise the *wellbeing* stakes (globally and individually) at the same time as we seek to put sustainability itself at the heart of progressive politics. It is only that powerful combination (necessity *and* desirability, sustainability *and* wellbeing) which is likely to drag the politics of sustainable development out of the margins and into the mainstream – a challenge which I seek to address in Part III.

Let me give one concrete example of what that combination might look like. On climate change, the UK has adopted a long-term target of achieving a cut in CO_2 emissions of 60 per cent by 2050. At the moment, that means almost nothing to most people – indeed, how could it, when most people have no real sense of where that CO_2 comes from in the first place? So let's get personal about this. When all the calculations are done in terms of concentrations of CO_2 in the atmosphere – stabilized emissions, threshold limits and so on – it all boils down to one simple number: assuming a population of around 9 billion by the middle of the century, each and every one of us will be able to emit the equivalent of approximately 1 tonne of carbon per annum. Welcome to the One Tonne World!

This is what is euphemistically known as a 'stretch target', given that we currently emit the equivalent of a great deal more than that – up to 7 tonnes per person per annum if you are a citizen of the US. At this point, environmentalists usually proffer the sackcloth and ashes, inviting people to contemplate a life of sober reflection, constant sacrifice and greatly reduced material wellbeing – and are a little taken aback when people rapidly decline the invitation. But what if that 'offer' was reworked – promising entry into the One Tonne World on the basis of better value for money, lower electricity and gas bills, better food, less hassle in terms of getting to and from work, improved health, more jobs in the cutting-edge industries of the future, cleaner air, more convivial communities, more time at home or reconnecting with the natural world? One Tonne – real fun!

There is a long way to go before we'll be able to reposition sustainability in that kind of way. And there's an equally long way to go before we get the politics of sustainable development properly sorted out. The case made here is that those interested in a sustainable future must get much more comfortable with some kind of engaged discourse about capitalism itself, and can no longer remain ideologically detached from the cut and thrust of that debate.

REFERENCES

All-Party Parliamentary Group on Population, Development and Reproductive Health (2007) *Return of the Population Growth Factor: Its Impact on the Millennium Development Goals*, report, available from www.appg-popdevrh.org.uk

Bakan, J. (2004) *The Corporation*, Constable, London

Demeny, P. (2003) 'Population policy dilemmas at the dawn of the twenty-first century', *Population and Development Review*, vol 29, no 1, March

Homer-Dixon, T. (2006) *The Upside of Down*, Island Press, Washington, DC

IPCC (Intergovernmental Panel on Climate Change) (2007) *Climate Change 2007*, the Fourth Assessment Report (AR4) of the IPCC, published online in four parts, available from www.ipcc.ch

Johannesburg Memo (2002) *Fairness in a Fragile World*, Heinrich Böll Foundation, Berlin

Klein, N. (2002) *Fences and Windows*, Flamingo, London

Korten, D. (1995) *When Corporations Rule the World*, Earthscan, London

Kunstler, J. H. (2005) 'As oil ceases to be cheap', *New Statesman*, 1 August

Legum, M. (2002) *It Doesn't Have to Be Like This*, Wild Goose Publications, Glasgow, UK

McChesney, R. (1999) *Rich Media, Poor Democracy*, University of Illinois Press, Urbana, IL

Norberg, J. (2001) *In Defence of Global Capitalism*, Timbro AB, Stockholm, Sweden

Northcott, M. (2004) *An Angel Directs the Storm: Apocalyptic Religion and American Empire*, I. B. Tauris, London

Scruton, R. (2002) *The West and the Rest: Globalization and the Terrorist Threat*, Continuum, London

Sen, A. (1999) *Development as Freedom*, Oxford University Press, Oxford

Smith, A. (1776) *An Inquiry into the Nature and Causes of the Wealth of Nations*, first published in London by W. Strahan and T. Cadell, printers, in two volumes. Numerous contemporary editions are available.

Stiglitz, J. (2002) *Globalization and Its Discontents*, Allen Lane, London

Wolf, M. (2004) *Why Globalization Works*, Yale University Press, New Haven, CT

PART II

A FRAMEWORK FOR SUSTAINABLE CAPITALISM

6

The Five Capitals Framework

INTRODUCTION

Behind the notion of *capitalism* lies the notion of *capital* – which economists use to describe a stock of anything (physical or virtual) from which anyone can extract a revenue or yield. Although it is true that many environmentalists and social justice campaigners remain wary of getting sucked too deep into the working practices and language of capitalism, the premise behind the idea of the Five Capitals Framework is that we can't reform capitalism without adopting some of its insights, tools and drivers. But most of today's 'reform agendas' (from the progressive left, for instance) simply refuse to face up to some of the issues covered in Part I of this book, unable to confront the challenge of learning to live within non-negotiable biophysical limits. So much for the theory. This chapter then looks briefly at the degree to which the Five Capitals Framework might be of relevance to a country such as China as it races towards becoming both the world's largest economy and the world's most terrifying ecological disaster.

GRAPPLING WITH THE CONCEPT OF CAPITAL

Although many critics of today's dominant capitalist paradigm would profoundly disagree with such a position, a viable *hypothesis* emerges from the analysis in Part I that there is no inherent, fixed or non-negotiable aspect of capitalism in general (rather than today's particular form of capitalism) that renders it for all time incompatible with the pursuit of a sustainable society. Moreover, it may well prove to be the case that the protean adaptability of capitalism (that has made it such a resilient and successful cultural phenomenon) will yet again prove to be its 'saving grace' in the face of the ever more pressing challenge of biophysical sustainability.

That makes it possible (intellectually and ethically) to subscribe to what was described earlier as a 'reform from within' strategy: identify those characteristics of today's dominant capitalist paradigm that most damagingly impede progress towards sustainability and set out to change them through the usual levers – government intervention, regulation of consumer preference, international diplomacy, education and so on. For those who have already been engaged in just such a reform agenda for the last few decades, that is hardly the most empowering conclusion to have arrived at. But how much worse would it be to be committed to a reform agenda if the system one sought to reform was inherently incapable of accommodating the necessary changes in the first place?

But exactly what kind of 'reform agenda' are we talking about here? There are literally hundreds of manifestos, declarations and high-level statements covering every shade of green or sustainability thinking. On individual causes, campaigns, themes and specific policy areas, the flow of reform proposals from countless organizations and individuals is unceasing. But most, perhaps inevitably, are symptom-oriented, dealing with the downstream externalities and impacts of an economic system that simply isn't 'tuned' to the world in which we now live. Few have attempted to address those downstream externalities from a more systematic approach to the economic system itself – capitalism.

As we have seen, capitalism has a number of important characteristics that distinguish it from other economic systems: private ownership of the means of production, reliance upon the market to allocate goods and services, the drive to accumulate capital, and so on. But the core concept of capitalism, from which it derives its very name, is the economic concept of *capital*. Capital is a stock of anything that has the capacity to generate a flow of benefits which are valued by humans. It is this flow – normally of goods and services of benefit to people – that makes the capital stock an asset, and the value of the asset is derived directly from the lifetime value of the flows to which it gives rise.

When people think of capital in this sense, they usually think of some of the more familiar 'stocks' of capital: land, machines and money. But in the description of the Five Capitals Framework that follows, this basic concept of capital (as in *any* stock capable of generating a flow) has been elaborated upon to arrive at a hypothetical model of sustainable capitalism. It entails five separate 'stocks': natural, human, social, manufactured and financial (see Box 6.1).

As we will see, people have different levels of familiarity with these five kinds of capital. We are all familiar with the concept of financial capital as we juggle with our own personal finances; manufactured capital is extremely familiar to business people, acquiring new assets and having to depreciate these through their annual accounts; human capital is in some ways a variation on the more familiar notion of human resources; the concept of social capital has caused a stir of academic interest over the last 20 years or more, but has had relatively little impact upon standard political discourse; and natural capital has been around for a long time as a handy abstraction to describe the uses which we humans make of the natural world. Such terminology is hardly controversial; but there are many who abhor the terminological reduction of the natural world to natural capital, or of people's unique talents and skills to human capital, or of the intricate pattern of networks, institutions and relationships that bind societies together to social capital. They may take some consolation from the fact that the concept of capital can only be used in relation to the fact that we derive a benefit of some kind (tangible or intangible) from a particular service. For example, sand on a beautiful beach is potentially natural capital because it could indirectly help to generate tourist revenues. The same sand in a desert would either not have the same value, or not have any value at all, in which case it cannot be described as capital. However, if technological changes meant that desert sand could be used in semi-conductors, then it would become capital, and its value would be related to the market value of the semi-conductors that it could be used to create.

This will not necessarily allay the concerns of many environmentalists. But if there is any genuinely sustainable variant of capitalism out there, then it will need to work within the conceptual and linguistic conventions that people are now so familiar with. The concept of capital serves not only to explain the productive power of capitalism; it also provides the clearest means of explaining the conditions for its sustainability.

Box 6.1 The five capitals

1 *Natural capital* (also referred to as environmental or ecological capital) is any stock or flow of energy and matter that yields valuable goods and services. It falls into several categories: resources, some of which are renewable (timber, grain, fish and water), while others are not (fossil fuels); sinks which absorb, neutralize or recycle waste; and services, such as climate regulation. Natural capital is the basis not only of production but of life itself.

2 *Human capital* consists of health, knowledge, skills and motivation (all of which are required for productive work), as well as an individual's emotional and spiritual capacities. Enhancing human capital (for instance, through investment in education and training) is central to a flourishing economy.

3 *Social capital* takes the form of structures, institutions, networks and relationships which enable individuals to maintain and develop their human capital in partnership with others, and to be more productive when working together than in isolation. It includes families, communities, businesses, trade unions, voluntary organizations, legal/political systems and educational and health bodies.

4 *Manufactured capital* comprises material goods – tools, machines, buildings and other forms of infrastructure – which contribute to the production process but do not become embodied in its output.

5 *Financial capital* plays an important role in our economy by reflecting the productive power of the other types of capital, and enabling them to be owned and traded. However, unlike the other types, it has no *intrinsic* value; whether in shares, bonds or banknotes, its value is purely representative of natural, human, social or manufactured capital.

Source: Forum for the Future (2000)

Historically, the first type of capital was undoubtedly natural capital – the capacity of the biosphere to use solar energy to build up and sustain ever more complex life-forms and ecosystems. All life-forms are totally dependent upon this continuing capacity, and humans are no exception. However, humans responded differently from other species in the use that they have made of the natural world's continuing provision of goods and services. Over the long march of evolution from *Homo Australopithecus* to modern times, humans have developed their own productive powers and, in the process, have become the repository of enormous amounts of human capital. This has many distinct elements, but is best defined as 'the physical, intellectual, emotional and spiritual capacities of any individual'.

With the agricultural revolution some 10,000 years ago, humans began to apply their human capital to the cultivation of natural capital, directing natural flows into crops and animals for human benefit. Well before that, however, humans had applied human capital to natural capital to create *manufactured* capital: artefacts fashioned out of resources which, combined with human skill, could increase human productivity still further.

Even before the creation and use of their earliest tools, humans had become aware, perhaps instinctively, of what was to become one of their greatest developmental strengths: humans are more productive organized in groups than as individuals. Many animals exhibit group behaviour, of course, and in some species it can become quite complex. But humans have taken organization to a quite different level of function and complexity, developing political, legal and financial systems, work patterns that permit ever more specialization and division of labour, and cultural institutions for sports, entertainment and the arts that increase enormously both the quantity and quality of what can be produced. This is *social* capital.

And one particular form of social capital that has acquired more immediate power in modern industrial capitalism than any other is *financial* capital. Money is, of course, a representation of value, rather than having value in itself, and depends for its power in production (or consumption) entirely upon the confidence that is placed in it. However, modern capitalism is now so complex that it could not function at all without a comparably complex financial system that commanded confidence.

These five forms of capital, judiciously combined by entrepreneurs, are the essential ingredients of modern industrial productivity. Natural capital, despite modern sophistications, is still required to maintain a functioning biosphere, supply resources to the economy and dispose of its wastes. Human capital provides the knowledge and skills which create manufactured capital and operate it effectively. Social capital creates the institutions that provide the stable context and conditions within and through which economic activity can take place, and which enable individuals to be vastly more productive. Financial capital provides the lubricant to keep the whole system operating.

All sorts of diagrammatic representations of the Five Capitals Framework present themselves; what matters most is to understand the interconnections and the interdependencies between the different kinds of capital (see Figure 6.1). Natural and human capital are undoubtedly the primary forms of capital, with social and manufactured capital both derived from natural and human capital. Financial capital is a means of exchange, reflecting all the other kinds of capital. The word 'economy' is used in Figure 6.1 in its original sense: the management of the home or household – in this context, planet Earth.

Any illustration must take proper account of what was referred to in Chapter 1 as the *preconditionality* of natural capital. But within that overarching system, there are no hard lines, especially when it comes to the reciprocal flows between human capital and social capital. All such categorizations are therefore more than a little arbitrary. In reality, there are only two sources of wealth in the world today: the wealth that flows from our use of the world's resources and ecosystems (our natural capital), all powered by incoming solar radiation, and the wealth that flows from the use of our hands, brains and spirits (our human capital). *All* else – money, machines, institutions and so on – is derivative of these two primary sources of wealth.

And to put everything in context, we ourselves are merely an ephemeral subset of that earthly natural capital, which itself is merely a subset of the incalculable material vastness of the whole cosmos!

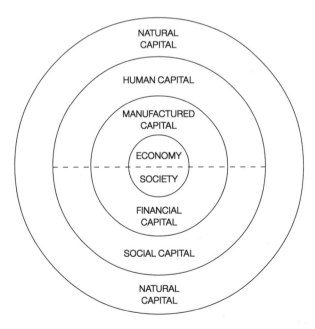

Source: Forum for the Future (2000)

Figure 6.1 *The Five Capitals Framework*

The rest of this section looks in more detail at each of the five capital stocks. But the connecting rationale is a powerful one:

> *Sustainability depends upon maintaining and, where possible, increasing stocks of certain kinds of capital so that we learn to live off the flows (the 'income') without depleting the stock of capital itself; if consumption is at the expense of investment, or results in net capital depletion so that the capital stock declines, then such consumption is not sustainable and will be reduced in the future.* (Forum for the Future, 2000)

THE CHALLENGE OF CHINA

It is a commonplace of sustainable development debates that they often end in the question: 'Well, that's all well and good, but what about China?' And it's the right question. The combined population of China and India is already 2.4 billion people and in 2050 will be around 3 billion people, approximately one third of total human numbers. Their economies are growing at rates that most mature OECD economies can barely credit (between 7 and 10 per cent per annum), and consumption levels are soaring. By the same token, the sustainability challenges that they face make our challenges in Europe pale into insignificance.

When quizzed by sceptics about the value of the UK going out on a limb on climate change (with the responsibility for just 2 per cent of global carbon dioxide emissions) when China is already responsible for 18 per cent and on track to take over pole position from the US (currently on 22 per cent) by 2009, Tony Blair's response sounds understandably resigned: 'Even if you were to eliminate all of the UK's emissions overnight, the growth in China's emissions would wipe out the difference in just two years.' True enough, though perhaps not the most appropriate way of getting UK citizens to see things in proportion: after all, we still emit around 7 tonnes of CO_2 per person, in comparison to China's 3.5 tonnes.

The linkage between population and climate change is an increasingly controversial one, as I sought to explain in Chapter 5. China calculates that its one child family policy has prevented the birth of around 138 million children over the last 30 years – meaning that there's a case to be made that this represents the biggest single contribution to averting dangerous climate change the world has ever seen. Especially as the numbers of middle-class, carbon-intensive consumers in China increases all the time: by 2020, the Chinese middle class is forecast to double from today's numbers (around 260 million) to around 530 million – roughly twice as many people as in the US today!

But to leap straight in on what China might be perceived to owe the rest of the world (in terms of its global responsibilities) is more than a little unfair. As I hope I've already made abundantly clear, sustainable development is *not* the same thing as environmentalism but with another name: it's absolutely about the balancing out of economic, social and environmental priorities. As one tries to get to grips with the challenges and opportunities for China in 'optimizing sustainable outcomes in managing *all* stocks of capital', one has to start with what it has done to address horrendous levels of poverty and deprivation. As the *Economist* puts it:

> *Since Deng Xiaoping launched his 'open door' policy in 1978, China has witnessed probably the most dramatic burst of wealth creation in human history. Its income per head has increased sevenfold in that time; more than 400 million people have been lifted out of severe poverty.* (*Economist*, 2004)

And it becomes all the more extraordinary when you work out what that entails in terms of sheer economic power. By 2002, China surpassed the US in annual consumption of grain, meat, coal, steel, fertilizer, cellular phones, TV sets, refrigerators, cement and aqua-cultured food – the US still leads on oil, personal computers and automobiles! In 2005, China used 26 per cent of the world's crude steel, 32 per cent of the rice, 37 per cent of the cotton, and 47 per cent of the cement. There have been massive social gains as well. To enjoy the fruits of living more sustainably, you first have to be able to stay alive! Average life expectancy in China in 1950 was just 35 years; by 2002, this had increased to 71 years. Again, no country in the world has ever been able to match that kind of net improvement in human wellbeing.

It's just a bit rich, therefore, when environmentalists leap in to make out that China is now the biggest single threat to a sustainable future for humankind when all it has done (as seen through the lens of 250 years of planet-trashing, ecologically-illiterate, no-holds-barred economic development) is to get to roughly the same place in 30 years that it took us 250 years to get to. Where, after all, were the alternative models of development for China to have adopted? Which of the richest nations in the world today achieved its material standard of living by 'nurturing its natural capital', cracking down on 'unacceptable' levels of pollution, distributing its wealth in impeccably fair and equitable ways? There seems to me to be something about beams and motes in the way people talk about China today.

However, it's precisely because China has concentrated what for us represents 250 years of growth, injustice and ecological mayhem into little more than 30 years that there is now no country in the world facing a more dramatic 'sustainability squeeze'. Such growth has come at a truly shocking price in terms of impacts upon stocks of natural capital. By China's own official assessments, 25 years of breakneck growth and resource depletion now threaten ecological meltdown, the early signs of which are already dramatically affecting people's livelihoods and health. Indeed, life expectancy has gone down over the last three years, predominantly because of air and water pollution, and the World Bank has calculated that pollution is costing China an annual 8 to 12 per cent of its $1.4 trillion GDP in terms of health bills, disaster relief, lost agricultural productivity and environmental clean-up. Both President Hu Jintao and the Prime Minister Wen Jiabao are warning that rates of economic growth will have to be severely curbed to prevent further loss of critical natural capital – 'balanced development', as measured by a brand new 'green GDP indicator', is the new aspiration, though no one is quite certain whether the official goal of quadrupling 2002 GDP by 2020 has been set aside as a result!

Pan Yue, China's outspoken and hugely impressive Deputy Environment Minister, sums it up as follows:

> [China's economic] miracle will end soon because the environment can no longer keep pace. Five of the ten most polluted cities worldwide are in China; acid rain is falling on one third of our territory; half of the water in China's seven largest rivers is completely useless; a quarter of our citizens lack access to clean drinking water; a third of the urban population is breathing polluted air; less than a fifth of the rubbish in cities is treated and processed in an environmentally sustainable manner. (Der Spiegel, 2005)

The impact on health has also been dramatic. An increasingly affluent lifestyle, with much more 'meat-intensive' diets, increased car use and far less exercise, has triggered a massive and rapid increase in obesity. China's National Nutrition and Health Survey back in 2002 found that 14.7 per cent of China's 1.3 billion people are overweight and 2.6 per cent are obese. That doesn't sound too bad compared, for instance, to the US, where around one third of people are obese, but it's the speed with which these figures are rising that has shocked public health officials: the prevalence of excess weight and obesity increased 28-fold between 1985 and 2000 in children aged 7 to 18. In one study of children in Shanghai, 8 per cent of 3 to 6-year-olds were identified as already obese.

It is because of the sheer scale of China, and the sheer speed of its economic development, that this 'growth and sustainability' showdown now looms so large in global terms. The knock-on effect of this for the rest of the world will be profound. China must feed 20 per cent of the world's population on just 7 per cent of the world's arable land. In 2004, China became a net importer of food for the first time in its history. Prime agricultural land was being lost so fast to urban and industrial development (at the rate of 0.6 million hectares a year) that China's leaders had to impose a moratorium on all 'green field developments', as we would call them, in 2004.

Not that this moratorium will do anything to prevent some of China's most fertile land in the north from further drying out after years of drought, rapidly declining water tables and chronic overgrazing. Desertification is a massive problem, with the Gobi Desert now within 240 kilometres of Beijing itself. As a direct consequence of that drought, exacerbated by climate change, huge dust storms regularly sweep through Chinese cities in the north and east and often have a serious impact upon Korea and Japan. In *High Tide*, Mark Lynas (2004) tells the extraordinary story of his visits to inner Mongolia and western China, witnessing at first hand the devastating impact of China's 'red clouds'.

If anything, China's water and energy constraints are even more severe than the constraints on its land. In some parts of northern China, including around Beijing, water tables have shrunk so fast that wells are now having to be drilled to a depth of up to a 1000 metres. The World Bank has predicted 'catastrophic consequences for future generations unless water use and supply can be restored to some kind of balance'. On the energy front, the International Energy Agency calculates that by 2020 China will be responsible for 40 per cent of all coal burned in the world, 10 per cent of all oil, 13 per cent of all electricity used – and 20 per cent of all energy-based CO_2 emissions. China is already planning to build around 550 coal-fired power stations between now and 2030 – that's roughly one every ten days! In 2002, 1 million new cars were manufactured and sold in China; sales in China up to 2012 will account for 20 per cent of *all* car sales anywhere in the world. More than 1100 new cars are driven on to the roads of Beijing every day.

At the 2007 G8+5 Summit in Germany, China's President made it very clear that economic growth took precedence over addressing the challenge of climate change. This is understandable at one level – China emits around 3 tonnes of CO_2 per person per annum, in comparison to the US figure of 20 tonnes – but with its huge population, that still leaves China with a massive responsibility. The International Energy Agency shocked the world in April 2007 when it announced that China would overtake the US as the world's largest emitter of CO_2 not by 2025 (the projection suggested in 2004), not by 2010 (its 2006 projection), but by the end of 2007 – emitting more than 6 billion tonnes in comparison to America's 5.9 billion tonnes. The fact that a substantial share of China's emissions can be attributed to the manufacture of exports for the rich world (40 per cent of them ending up in the US) is neither here nor there: Tony Blair was absolutely right when he pointed out at the Summit that the success or failure of international diplomacy around climate change depends utterly on how China and the US address their respective responsibilities.

With around \$470 billion of foreign reserves stashed away, China can obviously buy its way out some if its resource constraints, and that is exactly what it is doing on oil (importing more than 40 per cent of supplies), food, timber, steel, chemical feed stocks and so on – with a massive impact upon those global markets. But you can't buy fertile topsoil and you can't buy fresh, clean water.

The one thing China doesn't need to buy is coal, with reserves of around 190 billion tonnes at the last count. And it's now planning to use some of that coal to overcome perhaps its most critical energy constraint on future growth – namely, the availability of oil. In just a few years, China has become the world leader on what are known as 'Coal to Liquids' (CtL) technologies, converting coal directly into liquid fuels for transportation. As long as oil prices stay somewhere above the $50 a barrel mark, this makes sense in financial terms, which explains why 88 different CtL projects are included in the 11th Five Year Plan – with many more waiting in the wings.

Whether this makes sense from an environmental perspective is an altogether different question. Depending on which technology is used (direct liquefaction without gasifying the coal first produces a much dirtier fuel, higher in sulphur dioxide and other pollutants), and which particular fuel is actually produced at the end of the day (methanol is the current favourite), the environmental impacts can be dramatically different. Proponents of CtL technologies claim they allow the CO_2 which would otherwise be released to be captured more easily – but there's currently precious little sign of China being able to afford all the additional costs entailed in installing Carbon Capture and Storage (CCS) systems.

There's no doubt that China's energy constraints will drive an aggressive programme of innovation; companies like Shell and Sasol are not ramping up their investments in China out of the kindness of their hearts. China may even become a major exporter of these technologies in due course. But critics point out that it might make more sense to focus first on the chronic inefficiencies in the way China uses energy of every description. It takes at least seven times as much energy for China to produce the same amount of economic output as Japan – and three times as much as India, which itself is one of the most inefficient users of energy in the world. The Chinese Government is of course aware of this, and perhaps the single most important target in the new Five Year Plan is to reduce energy intensity by 20 per cent by 2010 – requiring annual efficiency improvements of 4 per cent. Last year (2006), it achieved just 1 per cent in increased efficiency. Like many governments the world over, including the UK, China is pretty good at setting stretch targets, but not so good on making them stick.

With China's population still growing (at somewhere between 8 and 10 million a year; it is predicted to peak in 2030 at 1.46 billion), with its cities still burgeoning (around 300 million people will move out of their rural areas into cities by 2020), and the purchasing power of the middle classes still soaring, this is a truly titanic struggle. As far as the simplistic worldview of the *Economist* is concerned, it's merely a question of whether China can get rich enough quick enough to curb pollution and deploy enough money to clean up the mess.

This kind of condescending banality obscures an infinitely more complex political challenge, as China's leaders weigh up conflicting imperatives on a colossal scale. Not only is the degradation of China's natural capital damaging the economy, it's also undermining social stability. Every year, there are literally tens of thousands of public protests all across China, and anger about pollution, 'land-grabs' and inappropriate development features more and more prominently in a dangerous cocktail of social dissent and grievance. In his 2007 Annual Report to Parliament, Prime Minister Wen Jiabao went out of his way to berate the failure of Provincial Governors and local officials to translate national policies and targets into practice on the ground. The Five Year Plan makes an unprecedented priority of these targets, and the Government is now seeking to strengthen governance arrangements in the provinces which will be required to turn fine words into serious deeds.

For the rest of the world, what's happening in China provides a window on the kind of resource constraints and natural capital dilemmas that we, too, will soon be facing. One can only hope that the Chinese leadership (many of whom are professional engineers) have the skills to balance all their different capital assets in a truly integrated and sustainable way.

It's not just in China that such vastly complicated 'balancing dilemmas' are now being faced up to. Development of the conventional kind (that traded off economic gains for 'acceptable' environmental and social costs) is no longer an available option either for governments or for the private sector. As we will see in the following chapters, adopting more integrated approaches can often be very demanding for decision-makers. But this idea of optimized outcomes (environmental, social and economic) instead of crude trade-off is the great prize available to both politicians and business leaders, the core methodological principle upon which the notion of *sustainable development as opportunity* rather than *sustainable development as constraint* ultimately rests. Before returning to that theme in Part III, we need first to review each of the five sets of capital assets in their own right.

REFERENCES

Der Spiegel (2005) interview with Pan Yue by Andreas Lorenz, published in *Der Spiegel*, 7 March (English translation by Patrick Kessler)

Economist (2004) 'China's growing pains', *Economist*, 21 August

Forum for the Future (2000) *Understanding Sustainability*, Forum for the Future, Cheltenham, UK

Lynas, M. (2004) *High Tide*, Flamingo, London

Natural Capital

INTRODUCTION

Approximately half of all humans now live in cities; by 2040, it will be 80 per cent. As people move away from the land, they become less and less mindful of the degree to which we are still totally dependent upon the natural world for energy, resources, food, fibre, water and so on. One way of describing that bounty from nature is 'natural capital' – and the way in which we now manage that natural capital is the biggest single determinant of whether a better life awaits us or a very much grimmer one. Unfortunately, most politicians have little understanding of our continuing dependence upon the natural world and have therefore ignored those pioneering economists who have been warning them for decades of the danger of not valuing nature properly. A huge amount of work is now being done to remove these political blinkers (for instance, in terms of assessing the hard-edged economic value of protecting species and habitats), reasserting in the process the critical significance of effective environmental regulation and planning systems that do, indeed, find effective ways of putting nature first.

DEFINING NATURAL CAPITAL

Natural capital (also referred to as environmental or ecological capital) is that part of the natural world which we humans make some use of or derive some benefit from – hence its definition (in economists' jargon) as any stock or flow of energy and matter that yields valuable goods and services. There are different kinds of natural capital: *resources*, some of which are renewable (timber, grain, fish and water), while others are not (fossil fuels); *sinks* that absorb, neutralize or recycle waste; and *services*, such as climate regulation. Natural capital is therefore not the same as nature, but it is the basis of all production in the human economy and the provider of services without which human society could not sustain itself.

At the heart of the current environmental crisis is the way in which current patterns of consumption and production are unsustainably depleting our natural capital so that its ability to support the projected levels of the human population (let alone at the standard of living of most people in the affluent industrialized countries) is seriously brought into question.

Although the debate about natural capital has become increasingly sophisticated over the last 50 years or so, there is an accessible simplicity about it that must not be lost. The relationship between ourselves and the natural world works at many different levels; but the essence of our evolutionary success as a species has been our ability to transform our natural capital into goods and services that satisfy our needs and improve our wellbeing. This natural capital provides a number of environmental functions which we make use of either directly or indirectly, particularly the flow of natural resources as inputs into our economy, the absorption of the by-products of that economy as wastes, and the provision of a number of critical 'environmental services' that underpin not just the human economy, but the whole of life on Earth. From that perspective, biophysical sustainability has been defined as the maintenance of these key environmental functions, which, in turn, depends upon their resilience and renewability.

Over time, that process of transforming natural capital has accelerated dramatically as human numbers and technological productivity have grown, fundamentally altering the relationship between the overall system (the biosphere) and the subsystem of the human economy. One of the reasons why there is still such abiding controversy about environmental issues is that there are very different views about the implications of that shift. The so-called 'contrarians' (such as Bjorn Lomborg and Wilfred Beckerman) argue that the key environmental functions referred to above are still largely unimpaired, and that all evidence to the contrary is either exaggerated or immaterial.

On the other hand, as we have seen, the vast majority of environmental scientists argue that the growth in the human subsystem now threatens the functional viability of the biosphere (the overarching system) itself – or, at least, certain aspects of it. This analysis leads on to a further proposition which the contrarians find even more abhorrent: that our species is moving from an era in which man-made capital (human, manufactured, financial) was the limiting factor, to one in which what is left of our natural capital will be the limiting factor.

NATURAL ADDED VALUE

In order to understand why we can no longer avoid this reality, we need to return again to the science that lies behind all this. As we saw in Chapter 3, the loss of natural capital should clearly be counted as a cost of economic growth, to be weighed against the benefits of that growth and reflected in our national accounts. That is a relatively easy exercise, although most countries are still failing to achieve even this modest goal. More complicatedly, we need to understand that we aren't actually consuming or using up that natural capital as such, merely its quality or its usefulness to us. Alfred Marshall was one of the first economists to understand what this means:

> *Man cannot create material things – his efforts and sacrifices result in changing the form or arrangements of matter to adapt it better for the satisfaction of his wants – as his production of material products is really nothing more than a rearrangement of matter which gives it new utilities, so his consumption of them is nothing more than a disarrangement of matter which destroys its utilities.* (Marshall, 1959)

To use the contemporary jargon, what's being consumed is the 'value added' – the structure that we humans (via our human, manufactured and financial capital) add to the natural capital. This means, of course, that new structure has to be added again before it can be consumed again. It is therefore more than a little surprising that in all their enthusiasm for the concept of 'value added', both economists and business people seem to show very little interest in exactly what it is that value is being added to. In fact, as Herman Daly has pointed out, we don't really appreciate that there are *two* elements to this added value: the bit that *we* put in, and the bit that *nature* puts in. Atoms of copper, for instance, spread uniformly in the crust of the Earth, are of little economic value to us; concentrated copper ore is much more useful for us to start adding our kind of value to the resource. By the same token: 'carbon atoms scattered in the atmosphere can receive value added from us only with the enormous expenditure of energy and other materials; carbon atoms structured in a tree can be rearranged much more easily' (Daly, 1996).

In effect, the more work nature does in advance, the less work we have to do to add the kind of economic value that makes our lives worth living. Unfortunately, we show nothing but contempt for this contribution from nature, valuing it at zero as some kind of free gift or subsidy, while blithely paying through the nose for the value added by *our* ingenuity, *our* technology and *our* financial resources. Having consumed the added value, we then dump what's left over back into the natural world, giving back (in thermodynamic terms) high entropy matter/energy in return for the low entropy matter/energy to which we added the value in the first place.

So why isn't our civilization overwhelmed by that loss of structure and quality? The answer is simple. While the Earth is a closed system as far as matter is concerned (almost all of the atoms that were here when the Earth was created 4.6 billion years ago are still here, as gravity does not allow matter to escape), it is an open system as far as energy is concerned – with around 10,000 times as much solar energy flowing into the system every year as the total amount of energy used by the whole of humankind.

Through photosynthesis, plants are able to use the solar energy that flows continuously into the Earth's system, gathering dispersed matter and assembling it into new structures. The uniqueness of plants lies in the fact that they obtain their energy from outside the system. Even nature's mechanisms could not function sustainably if the natural cycles were not fuelled by the sun's energy. Over time, nature has evolved to create the necessary conditions to support plants and animals, enabling the development of the living world as we know it today, in a wonderful array of complexity and diversity.

Ultimately, an improved understanding of the importance of natural capital has to cascade all the way through to decisions made by national regulators and local planning authorities. The Five Capitals Framework is one in which a balance can be achieved between potential economic, environmental and social benefits, between the wealthy and the poor (both here in the UK and between rich and poor nations), and between the interests of this generation and future generations. It is based upon what should be a clear and binding hierarchy for all regulators and planners: first, protect critical natural capital in all circumstances; then, wherever possible, seek to optimize mutually reinforcing economic, social and environmental benefits over time; where that is not possible, seek to minimize any potential damage to the environment, people and their communities; only then can one trade off potential economic benefits against unavoidable social and environment cost disbenefits.

As of now, very few countries have really sought to work out what it means 'to optimize mutually reinforcing economic, social and environmental benefits over time'. Cost–benefit methodologies remain crude and are so vulnerable to political abuse (where explicit or implicit 'political assumptions' distort the basis upon which any analysis is carried out) that their credibility has been severely undermined. Worse yet, at exactly the moment when we are beginning to relearn the critical importance to us of natural capital, we are simultaneously going through one of the most aggressively deregulatory periods of modern times. Many governments now eschew straightforward regulatory interventions in favour of voluntary approaches, negotiated covenants or quasi-legal agreements with business. And in the interests of protecting national or regional competitiveness, trade associations and business organizations have become increasingly strident in their denunciation of regulatory cost and burdens.

However, studies in both the US and Europe have exposed the way in which cost estimates prepared by business organizations massively and systematically exaggerate the putative scale of the additional burden of environmental regulations. The Confederation of British Industry (CBI) is one of the world's worst inflators of cost estimates; in 2003, for instance, it claimed that the EU Directive on Environmental Liability would cost UK business around £1.8 billion ('and will be the final nail in the coffin of British manufacturing'). In 2005, the UK Government announced that the costs amounted to no more than £50 million.

Most European governments appear to be terminally confused about developing a new strategic approach to environmental regulation. On the one hand, they endlessly parrot the huge value to Europe of the burgeoning world market in environmental goods and services (currently estimated at around $515 billion – comparable with the aerospace and pharmaceutical industries – and forecast to grow to $680 billion by 2010); on the other hand, they unthinkingly default to a much cruder competitiveness agenda to address the ever constant economic threat from China, India and other developing countries.

In some respects, this has become a battle for the heart of Europe itself. The crisis that engulfed Europe in 2005 after both France and The Netherlands rejected the new draft constitution was at least as much about what kind of economy Europe should be pursuing (the more inclusive, interventionist 'social market economy' favoured by the French and Germans, or the 'liberal market economy', with the emphasis on deregulation and competition favoured by the UK) as about the constitution itself. The UK's ideological fervour for the privatization, marketization and liberalization of anything that moves is well reflected in its EU Commissioner Peter Mandelson, whose personal crusade to downgrade the importance of environmental sustainability, social inclusion and better working conditions, and to put EU competitiveness before literally everything else has caused considerable controversy.

As a result, European electorates find themselves on the receiving end of great surges of excitable green rhetoric, only to discover that the self-same politicians are busy watering down the regulatory, fiscal and economic interventions that are so badly needed to create those innovative new markets. Here's one such surge from former Prime Minister Tony Blair himself:

> *We need to develop the new green industrial revolution that develops the new technologies that can confront and overcome the challenge of climate change. Just as British know-how brought the railways and mass production to the world, so British scientists, innovators and business people can lead the world in ways to grow and develop sustainably. I'm confident business will seize this opportunity. Cutting waste and saving energy could save billions of pounds each year. With about 90 per cent of production materials never becoming part of the final product, and 80 per cent of products discarded after single use, the opportunities are clear.* (Blair, 2004)

These words were uttered at almost exactly the same time as the UK Government was pressing for a more generous allocation of carbon credits through the EU's Emissions Trading Scheme (ETS) to keep the ever-moaning CBI off its back. The short-sightedness of this position (which was even more pronounced in other EU countries) became all too apparent in 2006, when the ETS all but collapsed. Governments had given away so many credits to industry through their respective National Allocation Plans that not a single company was forced to do anything more than it would have done anyway! With nobody needing to buy anybody else's credits, the price of a tonne of CO_2 plummeted, hitting a low of less than €0.30 in 2007. The Commission has learned an important lesson here (that markets only work when the product being sold is scarce enough to command a purchase price!), and there is no doubt that the next phase of the ETS (2008–2012) is being driven through a much tougher approach from the Commission on member countries' National Allocation Plans – and, happily, the UK has shown some real leadership here, this time resisting the special pleading from industry.

This ambivalence is a zero-sum game if ever there was one. From the ground-breaking work of Michael Porter in *The Competitive Advantage of Nations* (1990) – one of the very first works to advance the 'win–win hypothesis' that intelligent and carefully designed environmental regulations may be good for economic competitiveness – all the way through to Adair Turner's *Just Capital: The Liberal Economy* (2001) (as a former director-general of the CBI, Adair Turner's demolition of the 'myths and delusions' that lie behind much of today's defence of national competitiveness is particularly enlightening), the convergence of interest between promoting an innovative and productive economy, on the one hand, and securing a resilient and productive natural world, on the other, has been mapped out in great detail.

Politicians' resistance to this kind of analysis is symptomatic of a deeper problem. Although they have certainly woken up to the importance of some environmental issues, any deeper understanding of the nature of natural capital is still wholly absent in the thinking of Western governments today. Even as they address symptoms of a fundamental shift (over-fishing in the North Sea, the need to mitigate the potential impact of climate change, and so forth), the systemic reality that lies behind the symptoms (in terms of the preconditional importance of natural capital) remains all but invisible.

There are all sorts of reasons for this, some of which go right back to our evolutionary origins, to our Judaeo-Christian inheritance, and to a model of progress since the onset of the Industrial Revolution which set civilization *against* nature. Latterly, however, it has to be said that mainstream economists have done more to obscure physical reality in this area than any philosophical or historical factors. This is *not* because the concept of sustainability is alien to economists, as many environmental critics have claimed. In fact, the core meaning of sustainability is embedded within one of the 'seminal texts' of contemporary economics – namely *Value and Capital*, the work by J. R. Hicks in which was coined a definition of income that has been standard ever since: 'the maximum amount that a community can consume over some time period and still be as well off at the end of that period as at the beginning' (Hicks, 1946). In that respect, 'as well off' was defined by Hicks as having the same capacity to generate income in the next year – that is, maintaining capital intact.

Unfortunately, however, economists then proceeded to ignore natural capital (largely on the grounds that it was either not scarce or could not command a market value as it came to us 'for free'), and focused exclusively on the different aspects of man-made capital. Even when it began to dawn on them (at the persistent prompting of pioneers such as Herman Daly and David Pearce) that this was unwise, the key issue of *substitutability* still had to be confronted. Wealth creation is a process that judiciously combines different kinds of capital to produce the goods and services that people want (and therefore value). And there is obviously considerable scope for substitution between the different forms of capital, as evidenced by our own evolutionary success – converting natural capital into man-made capital. But there is a world of difference between maintaining constant the *sum* of all different kinds of capital, and maintaining each stock of capital constant in its own right. The former position (still dominant in contemporary economics) holds that it is fine to substitute one form of capital for another, and that in most cases there will be no problem, for example, in liquidating natural capital just so long as one invests to create equivalent value in manufactured capital or social capital.

Exponents of the latter position (maintaining each stock of capital in its own right) argue that natural capital and other forms of capital are *complementary but increasingly non-substitutable*, or at least only substitutable at the margins. Here in the UK, for instance, the Government's official advisers on biological diversity (English Nature) define environmental sustainability as 'maintaining the environment's natural qualities and characteristics and its capacity to fulfil its full range of functions'. These functions include the provision of resources, the disposal, recycling and sequestration of wastes, and the maintenance of a diverse, habitable and productive biosphere. English Nature stresses that achieving environmental sustainability often requires the *absolute* protection and conservation of particular components of natural capital, which it calls critical natural capital.

Kerry Turner was one of the first to characterize these different positions as weak sustainability and strong sustainability (Turner, 1992). He rapidly dismissed both very weak sustainability (which assumes complete substitutability across all capitals) and what he called 'absurdly strong sustainability' (which assumes no substitutability, with all natural capital maintained absolutely intact). There obviously has to be *some* substitution; but controversy still rages around how to define the acceptable limits to that constant trade-off process. This is why the kind of systemic approach adopted by organizations such as The Natural Step (TNS) is so important, defining strict biophysical limits for all human endeavour (see Chapter 2).

There is, of course, an important distinction between renewable and non-renewable resources. With regard to *renewable resources*, the science and economics of sustainable yield management are now much better understood, although inadequately practised wherever one looks. With agriculture, freshwater, forestry, fisheries and so on, maintaining 'cultivated' natural capital of this kind means constraining the annual yield to a level no greater than the annual regeneration capacity of the stock of natural capital concerned – a process that must take account of *all* the different environmental functions that stock of natural capital provides, including the maintenance of fundamental ecological services in that ecosystem from which we ourselves may derive no direct financial return.

Valuing nature capital

Again, putting a specific money value on the aggregated services we benefit from in terms of any ecosystem is a formidable challenge – and often provides a sufficient pretext for doing nothing. But this is already costing us very dear, especially as we stand by seemingly powerless as the world's forests continue to come crashing down. As Joseph Stiglitz points out, it's crazy to wait around any longer:

> *At current rates of deforestation, the combined contribution to greenhouse gas concentrations from deforestation in Brazil and Indonesia alone will offset some 80 per cent of the emissions reductions gained through the Kyoto Protocol. Moreover, some of the ancillary damage – the loss of old hardwood forest and biodiversity – may be irreversible if we do not act soon. It is urgent that we fix the problem now, and not accede to yet another impulse to delay.* (Stiglitz, 2006)

The problem, of course, is that most developing countries cannot afford *not* to cut down some of the remaining forests, let alone to protect them properly in order to prevent illegal logging or other development. A Greenpeace report in April 2007 ('Carving up the Congo') used the example of the Democratic Republic of the Congo, where the pressure for logging (both legal and illegal) is enormous. More than 40 million of the world's poorest people depend on those forests for their livelihoods, yet the Government knows that by granting logging concessions, it can raise the finance it needs for providing public services elsewhere. At the same time, this is also of direct interest to ourselves: 34 billion tonnes of CO_2 could be released if the Congolese forests are destroyed, equivalent to the UK's entire CO_2 output since 1946.

Without some kind of proper financial compensation, short-term economic needs will take precedence over long-term ecological stability. Unfortunately, the Kyoto Protocol is of very little use here; although it allows for 'carbon offsets' under its Clean Development Mechanism, including sequestering carbon by planting new forests, it says nothing at all about maintaining existing forests – in other words, maintaining intact the natural capital locked up in the forests of some of the world's poorest countries. However, this may change in the next round of Kyoto negotiations. A group of countries (including Costa Rica, Papua New Guinea and the state of Amazonas in Brazil) have come forward with a number of schemes for countries to sell carbon offsets for 'avoided deforestation' – with countries paid for every hectare of forest properly (and accountably!) protected rather than cut down for timber or to make way for soya or palm oil or subsistence farming. It has been calculated that the annual 'negative emissions' – in other words emissions of CO_2 avoided – of all the rainforest countries combined amounts to around $100 billion a year if CO_2 is priced at $30 dollars a tonne. That's a lot of money – but it's a lot of avoided warming too.

As to *non-renewable resources*, strictly speaking, there is no such thing as sustainable yield management. If there is only a given amount of some mineral or resource to be extracted from the Earth, it will – one day – run out, though as we will see in Chapter 10, there are ways of securing sufficiently high levels of reuse and recycling as to give us (in some cases) an all but sustainable yield. In the meantime, what we should be getting much better at is reinvesting a share of the receipts from liquidating our non-renewable natural capital in building up renewable stocks to generate sustainable yields in the future. In this regard, the failure of successive governments in the UK to direct even a small share of the billions of pounds from the exploitation of non-renewable hydrocarbons in the North Sea into renewable sources of energy for the UK (of which we have an astonishing abundance) contrasts starkly with the foresight of places such as Norway and Alaska, which every year set aside a proportion of their hydrocarbon revenues to create a permanent capital fund for the future.

Unfortunately, all of this knowledge about natural systems and the laws of thermodynamics still remains pretty alien for most economists. David Pearce et al's *Blueprint for a Green Economy* (1989) represented an important breakthrough in promoting different valuation techniques in terms of putting a money value on the use that we make of the natural world. Although it is true that some environmentalists still remain nervous about the whole idea of putting money values on things that are 'beyond price', this approach has, for the most part, greatly strengthened the hand of economists trying to bring 'the environment' closer to the heart of policy-making.

And it has moved on a long way since then. Even the somewhat vague notion of 'environmental services' (the third of the three categories of natural capital referred to at the start of this chapter) is being looked at from the point of view of their economic value to humankind. In 1997, Robert Costanza and colleagues at the Massachusetts Institute of Technology (MIT) set out 'to quantify the global value of ecosystem services consisting of flows of materials, energy and information from natural capital stocks which combine with manufactured and human capital to produce welfare' (Costanza et al, 1997). They identified 17 different services, including pollination, water supply and regulation, the assimilation of wastes, food production from the wild, genetic resources, climate regulation, and even 'cultural and spiritual values that are associated with ecosystems' – for example, eco-tourism, outdoor recreational activities and painting landscapes.

All sorts of valuation techniques were then applied to these 17 ecosystem services (including 'willingness to pay' calculations for some of the benefits derived from these services), and estimates were made of what it would cost to provide man-made substitutes for these services if we didn't get them for free from nature. The bottom line total (which came out at around $33 trillion per annum, with a margin of error of several trillion on either side!) is actually pretty academic: it's the demonstration of our massive dependence upon these ecosystem services that Costanza was trying to establish. This ground-breaking work was

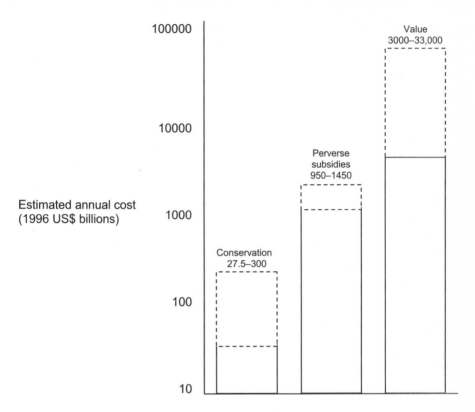

Source: Balmford (2002)

Figure 7.1 *The relative cost of conservation*

powerfully developed in the Millennium Ecosystem Assessment report (MA) described in Chapter 1.

Meta-calculations of this sort may not have any direct applicability to most decision-makers, but narrow the focus somewhat and the significance of this kind of approach to valuing natural capital becomes instantly apparent. Andy Balmford, of the Department of Zoology at Cambridge University, has been working away for many years to demonstrate just how good an economic bargain the protection of biodiversity really is. He reckons we already spend around $6 billion a year on conservation, but that we would need to increase that to around $27.5 billion to do the job properly (with up to 10 per cent of land area strictly protected, with half of that in special reserves) and provide proper compensation for those people 'losing out' in other ways through their land being used essentially for conservation. If we set out beyond that to protect biodiversity properly on farmed land outside the designated nature reserves, the costs rise steeply to a (loosely) estimated $300 billion.

Big numbers – but not that big. Balmford uses a handy little graphic (see Figure 7.1) to demonstrate why we shouldn't be overwhelmed by this, contrasting the potential costs of a properly funded global conservation strategy (between $27.5 billion and $300 billion) with two other related indicators. First, there is the cost to humankind of all the billions of taxpayer dollars we *already* dish out (on subsidies to farmers, energy producers, transportation, fisheries, water consumption and so on), which comes in at an astonishing total of between $950 billion and $1450 billion a year – according to the pioneering work done in this area by Norman Myers (Myers and Kent, 2001). What makes this figure all the more shocking is that the bulk of those subsidies contribute actively to the erosion and outright liquidation of natural capital all around the world. As Balmford and his colleagues say:

> *Implementing a global plan to conserve biodiversity should go hand in hand with the gradual removal of the subsidies. If subsidy reform was linked to investment in environmental protection, a small shift in government spending patterns would accomplish major conservation objectives. An effective global system of nature reserves would cost about 2 per cent of the annual expenditure on environmentally harmful subsidies. A truly comprehensive global conservation programme that incorporated biodiversity within all major natural resource sectors could be launched for only about 20 per cent of the cost of these subsidies.* (Alexander et al, 1999)

Second, the final indicator in the right-hand column takes us back to Bob Costanza's meta-calculation of the value to humankind derived from the 17 ecosystem services, set at around $33 trillion, with an absolute minimum in the most critical areas of $3 trillion. In effect, what this shows us is that we need an annual investment of around $300 billion to secure $33 trillion worth of natural services – not a bad return on investment, all things considered.

If this is still too abstract, we now have literally dozens of powerful examples, backed by hard-edged financial data, showing how investments in natural capital generate real value for money. In 2002, Gretchen Daily and Katherine Ellison published a summary of some of the most striking of these case studies under the arresting title *The New Economy of Nature*:

> *We still think of conservation basically as something to do for moral or aesthetic reasons – not for survival and certainly not for profit. Nevertheless, the record clearly shows that conservation can't succeed by charity alone. It has a fighting chance, however, with well-designed appeals to self-interest. The challenge now is to change the rules of the game so as to produce new incentives for environmental protection,*

geared to both society's long-term wellbeing and individuals' self-interest.
(Daily and Ellison, 2002)

Perhaps the best known example that they use was the decision by New York City in 1997 to invest around $1.5 billion in rehabilitating the city's principal source of freshwater – the Catskill/Delaware watershed – rather than spending even more billions of dollars (around $5 billion) in constructing a new generation of costly, energy-intensive filtration plants to bring the water quality up to the standards set by the US Environmental Protection Agency. The Catskill/Delaware watershed is an area of around 2000 square miles of farmed valleys and forested mountains, with around 50,000 inhabitants. The system had worked fine throughout most of the 20th century, but since the 1980s, growth in tourism and housing started to take off in a big way, while farming systems became ever more intensive and sewage treatment plants struggled to cope. Water quality started to decline.

Given that New York City owns only a small fraction of the total land area, it has proved to be a huge effort bringing everyone on board, persuading them (and paying them) to manage their land and their use of water in ways that keep New York's water pure and fit for use all year round. It is early days still, in terms of evaluating the success of the programme; but it is already inspiring many other towns and cities in the US to think about similar projects. Some experts have calculated that up to 12 per cent of the entire land area in the US could be managed in this way to secure pure, high-quality water for its citizens. But the majority of politicians and economists still can't see the logic in this kind of approach; for them, the best and safest thing to do is to keep on pouring the concrete, relying on costly, high-tech, energy-intensive engineering schemes.

But does all this only work because it is taking place in one of the wealthiest enclaves anywhere in the world, richly endowed with generations of New York dollars and countless individual millionaires? Environmentalists are regularly assaulted with the accusation that 'you have to be rich to be green', and that all 'this environment stuff' means nothing to the billions of poor people struggling to improve their material standard of living all around the world, with no time to worry about 'the luxury of a clean environment'. Given that the vast majority of these people still depend directly upon natural resources – clean water, fertile soils and healthy forests – for their livelihoods, this is too absurd a charge to spend much time on. What is much more interesting is the way in which many rural communities in the developing world are starting to think very differently about making better use of their natural heritage. And they are doing that precisely to improve their material standard of living.

One such community is Torra in the remote north-west of Namibia. It is a huge area, with just a few hundred very poor farmers struggling to eke out some kind of livelihood from their herds of cattle and goats. In 1998, with the support of the World Wide Fund for Nature (WWF), they established a special conservancy based on a very simple deal: the community protects the local wildlife (including a thriving population of black rhino) in return for a share of the revenues earned through tourism and strictly controlled hunting rights. It's not a huge amount of money that they earn; but it is distributed across the whole population, and it's more than enough to underpin new business activity.

This is just one of 70 wildlife conservancies that have been established in Namibia since its independence from South Africa in 1990, based on the robust principles of community-based natural resource management, including formal bylaws to ensure that the conservancies are run democratically at the lowest possible level in the community. More than 250,000 people are now involved, covering around 7 million hectares of land. The journalist Mike McCarthy (of the *Independent* newspaper in the UK) visited Namibia in 2004 to assess what sort of impact this innovative approach was having in one of the world's poorest countries – where there's little to stop desperately poor people mushrooming in numbers and struggling to exist, eating and poaching their wildlife out of existence:

> *Only a truly radical gesture can answer the problem: turn the wildlife over to the people and let them use it. Local people handle their own wildlife; they handle their own money; and, thus, they handle their own future. The farmers of Torra are longing for more tourism, and if you go there you will see the great wild animals of Africa in a setting that you will never forget: a pristine, semi-desert wilderness of harsh but astonishing beauty. But maybe you will see something else too: the hope that Africa's people and its wildlife may live together into the future to the lasting benefit of each other.* (McCarthy, 2004)

There are, of course, 'none so blind as those who will not see'. A basic lack of understanding of how natural systems work lies at the heart of most politicians' and economists' ecological illiteracy, compounded by the fact that catastrophe (as in widespread ecological meltdown) would until now appear to have been averted. But ecosystems often remain productive even as their resilience continues to decline, masking the inevitability of future collapse unless those systems are allowed to regenerate properly. Although some changes are reversible, many are not. And given our relative ignorance as to the workings of nature, especially when exposed to the impact of exponential economic growth, a much more precautionary approach is clearly advisable. This is of course problematic to those intent on maximizing the short-term value to be derived from converting natural capital into man-made resources.

From a philosophical perspective, this is all horribly instrumentalist, as if there was nothing more to the natural world than its direct economic value to just one species. As Janine Benyus's hugely inspiring *Biomimicry* (1997) keeps on reminding us, such arrogance is unwise:

After 3.8 billion years of research and development, failures are fossils, and what surrounds us is the secret to survival. The more our world looks and functions like this natural world, the more likely we are to be accepted in this home that is ours, but not ours alone. (Benyus, 1997)

Benyus defines biomimicry as 'a new science that studies nature's model, and then imitates or takes inspiration from these designs and processes to solve human problems'. Her book is stuffed full of stories of scientists working away at that particular cutting edge – on photosynthesis, self-sustaining ecosystems, natural medicines, self-assembly processes and so on. She is keen to emphasize the difference between this kind of approach and the way in which so many scientists and industrialists still set about their task of dominating or even 'improving' nature. 'This respectful imitation is a radically new approach, a revolution, really. Unlike the Industrial Revolution, the biomimicry revolution introduces an era based not on what we can extract from nature, but on what we can learn from her' (Benyus, 1997).

Biomimicry provides one of the most visionary approaches to meeting the overarching challenge of aligning humankind's model of progress and growth with nature's systems and processes (about which, as we have said, we have no choice). Although much of this chapter is about different ways of *valuing* nature, the thrust of this particular philosophical orientation is that we will only benefit from tools like cost–benefit analysis if we simultaneously rethink our relationship with the natural world – if we learn, in E. O. Wilson's words, 'to affiliate with life' in a much more profound way. Our artificially constructed technosphere, however ingenious and powerful it may be, cannot operate independently of the biosphere. It is still embedded deep within that biosphere and is still subject to the laws of nature.

REFERENCES

Alexander, J., Gaston, K. and Balmford, A. (1999) 'Balancing the Earth's accounts', *Nature*, vol 401, 23 September

Balmford, A. (2002) Presentation to Business and the Environment Programme, Cambridge, UK, March

Benyus, J. (1997) *Biomimicry: Innovation Inspired by Nature*, Quill, William Morrow, New York

Blair, T. (2004) Speech to Prince of Wales's Business and the Environment Programme, London, 14 September

Costanza, R., Cumberland, J., Daly, H., Goodland, R. and Norgaard, R. (1997) *An Introduction to Ecological Economics*, CRC Press, Boca Raton, FL

Daily, G. and Ellison, K. (2002) *The New Economy of Nature: The Quest to Make Conservation Profitable*, Island Press, Washington, DC

Daly, H. (1996) *Beyond Growth*, Beacon Press, Boston, MA

Hicks, J. R. (1946) *Value and Capital*, Oxford University Press, Oxford

Marshall, A. (1959) *Principles of Economics*, Macmillan, London

McCarthy, M. (2004) 'Where animals can build a community', *Independent*, 13 December

Myers, N. and Kent, J. (2001) *Perverse Subsidies: How Tax Dollars Can Undercut the Environment and the Economy*, Island Press, Washington, DC

Pearce, D., Markandya, A. and Barbier, E. B. (1989) *Blueprint for a Green Economy*, Earthscan, London

Porter, M. (1990) *The Competitive Advantage of Nations*, Free Press, New York

Stiglitz, J. (2006) *Making Globalization Work*, Allen Lane, London

Turner, A. (2001) *Just Capital: The Liberal Economy*, Macmillan, London

Turner, R. K. (1992) 'Speculations on weak and strong sustainability', CSERGE Working Paper, University of East Anglia, Norwich, UK

Human Capital

INTRODUCTION

There was a time during the late 1990s when the world suddenly woke up to the allure of the 'knowledge economy'. Politicians boldly declared that the future prosperity of their countries would depend far more upon companies' intellectual and human capital than upon their manufacturing and financial capital. It has all died down a bit since then; but the traditional and often undervalued business of managing human resources in any organization gained new stature. As explained in this chapter, the Five Capitals Framework defines human capital in terms of any one individual's physical, intellectual, emotional and spiritual capacities – in other words, what each one of us brings to any working, playing, nurturing or loving relationship. All organizations (for-profit or non-profit) are now keen to find ways of enhancing their human capital, although there's a lively debate as to how best to measure this – or indeed whether it is worth measuring in the first place.

DEFINING HUMAN CAPITAL

The Five Capitals Framework unhesitatingly asserts the primacy (or 'preconditionality') of natural capital: after nearly 4 billion years of life on Earth, of which we've been around for just a few tens of thousands of years, that has to be the right way of looking at things.

But the fact that we are the first species (so far as we know) capable of reflecting upon our place in the natural order is just one of the characteristics that makes humankind more than a little special. When it comes down to it, our capacity to create wealth, solve problems, reach for the stars or constantly seek to improve the lot of our fellow human beings depends upon a combination of the natural capital out of which our complex industrial civilization is fashioned and the human capital which generates the designs, systems and assembly processes that make it all happen.

The definition of human capital that we use in the Five Capitals Framework is a simple one: 'the physical, intellectual, emotional and spiritual capacities of any individual'. But human capital has come to mean many different things to different people. Ask an economist, an educationalist and a human resources professional what the term means to them, and each will have their own slightly different definition and explanation. And as with the concept of natural capital, there are some people for whom the words 'human' and 'capital' just shouldn't be used together – the connotation of even putting a quasi-financial value on each person's head makes them feel uneasy (an issue of *New Internationalist* in 2001 gently mocked the World Bank's use of the term: 'Do the World Bank economists go home at night and tuck up their own units of human capital before reading them a bed-time story?').

Physical capacities

At the societal level, we can say that stocks of human capital will be greater if we manage to increase healthy lifestyles and healthy life expectancy figures. At the organizational level, investing in the physical wellbeing of employees through offering health education or encouraging sports and physical activity has been shown to improve both productivity and emotional wellbeing. And at an individual level, each of us is able to lead a more fulfilling life if we invest a little time and effort into making our own lifestyle healthier.

This is clearly not the place for a lengthy analysis of the degree to which different societies effectively promote health strategies that nurture this critical aspect of human capital. There is growing awareness of the huge contribution that public health makes to the pursuit of sustainable development and vice versa. And as with so many areas of public policy, this means radically changing the paradigm of what healthcare really means. Both public health campaigners and sustainable development activists have long argued that these are just two sides of the same coin. It is clearly possible to achieve improved health outcomes by pursuing less destructive patterns of economic development, and it is clearly possible to achieve a more sustainable (and equitable) society by reducing health inequalities, using resources more efficiently and more strategically, and focusing on preventing illness as far upstream as possible. During the 20 years between the mid-1970s and the mid-1990s, the gap in life expectancy between the most well-off and the least well-off in the UK increased by 5½ years to an astonishing 9½ years – just one aspect of the legacy of Mrs Thatcher that people rarely refer to. Anna Coote, Health Commissioner on the UK Sustainable Development Commission, sums it up as follows:

> *The evidence tells us that social isolation, poor education, fear of crime, disrupted family life and unhappiness are bad for health – happy people live, on average, seven years longer than unhappy people. Likewise, poverty, joblessness, powerlessness and economic insecurity are bad for human health. And these, of course, are the social and economic*

dimensions of sustainable development. Equally, environmental damage is bad for health – air pollution, contaminated water, poor food supplies, heavy road traffic, dislocated neighbourhoods, poorly designed buildings. What's more, these health risks tend to pile up in the lives of the poor and dispossessed in ways that are vividly reflected in health statistics. Poor people get ill more often and die much younger than people who are well off. (Coote, 2005)

The connection between good health and access to the natural world constantly bubbles along under the surface in all sorts of different ways. The pioneering work by Professor Ulrich in the US demonstrated that patients in hospitals who were able to see green spaces from their windows made a more rapid recovery from gall-bladder surgery than those whose windows faced on to a brick courtyard. Here in the UK, the British Trust for Conservation Volunteers has successfully demonstrated that involving people recovering from either physical or mental illness in practical conservation schemes has a marked (and measurable) impact upon recovery rates. Doctors in a growing number of general practices have started to formally prescribe conservation work and outdoor activity as part of their treatment toolkit – building on extensive research carried out by English Nature on the whole question of 'natural and psychological wellbeing'.

What we're addressing here, throughout the rich, urbanized world, is the pervasive and increasingly costly phenomenon of 'nature-deficit disorder'. This would come as no surprise to Theodore Roszak, whose 1993 book *The Voice of the Earth* outraged the psychotherapy establishment in the US by accusing them of exacerbating the problems of their clients in ignoring the contribution that their alienation from the natural world was making to those problems. The obvious solution is to reconnect people to the natural world as part and parcel of any long-term healing or therapy process:

What would it mean to 'prescribe nature' as part of therapy? Therapists, tied to the city by their careers and their bank accounts, cannot be expected to treat their clients anywhere but in the city. The troubled soul locked in a tortured ego will never be coaxed to look out and around at something greater, more lordly, more ennobling: a state of nature that invites the mind to contemplate eternal things. Yet, common experience tells us that a solitary walk by the river or ocean, a few calm hours in the woods, restores the spirit and may produce more insight into our motives and goals than the best labours of the professional analyst. The quiet contemplation of the night sky before one turns to sleep and dreams might do more to touch the mind with a healing grandeur than weeks, months, years of obsessive autobiographical excavation. (Roszak, 1993)

Lest this sounds like tree-hugging escapism for the pampered middle classes, it is worth bearing in mind that environmental campaigners have struggled long and hard to demonstrate the link between health inequalities in deprived areas and environmental inequalities. There is now a mountain of evidence that people who suffer from environmental injustice (in poor-quality, toxic, polluted, run-down environments) are much more vulnerable to a host of health problems. The upside of this is the increasingly widespread experience that engaging local communities in improving their own local environment can succeed where many other strategies fail.

Those problems, however, pale into insignificance beside those of many developing countries. The scale of the challenge here and the sheer numbers of people suffering from disease or chronic ill health (intoned with a sense of almost fatalistic dread at one global gathering after another) have led some people to conclude that this is just how it is and how it will always be. But as Gro Brundtland (former executive director of the World Health Organization) reminded people in a speech at the 2002 World Summit on Sustainable Development: 'Very small investments (by Western standards) in primary healthcare can make a very big difference, not just to the individuals that benefit directly but to the whole nation.'

Intellectual capacities

In 1912, the German psychologist William Stern noticed that even though the gap between mental age and chronological age widens as a child matures, the ratio of mental age to chronological age remains constant. He dubbed this ratio the 'intelligence quotient'; since then, testing of IQ remains one of the most widely used (and controversial) forms of measurement of our intellectual abilities. But our mental powers are more than just a number. Our intellectual abilities include, among other things, our knowledge, our creativity and our linguistic ability. IQ tests, however, measure only a particular kind of intellectual ability – rational, linear intelligence, of the kind best suited to solve particular types of logical problems.

It is to this aspect of human capital that the lion's share of research investment has been dedicated over the last few decades. From a sociological perspective, human capital has come to be associated almost exclusively with the capacity of governments and other organizations to intervene in the lives of individuals to enhance opportunities for learning and education – formal or informal. It is therefore wholly appropriate that efforts to enhance individuals' intellectual capacities through formal education feature prominently in almost all indicator sets designed to demonstrate progress on sustainable development.

From a business perspective, the corollary of this is the capacity for companies to intervene in the lives of their employees to facilitate access to training and other educational opportunities. In particular, there has been much interest of late in the idea of *intellectual capital*. This term was first coined back in 1969 by J.

K. Galbraith, but only gained widespread currency during the mid-1990s, when pioneering companies such as Skandia (the Swedish financial services group) and Dow Chemicals started to measure, manage and report on their flows of intellectual capital. Since then, there has been a flood of books and articles on the subject, and many of the large management consultancies still offer specialist services in this area.

With the growth of the knowledge economy has come an important change in the relationship between employers and employees. Human capital is not owned but rented. In Marxist terms, the means of production are now inside the heads of the workers. As a result, investment in the intellectual capacities of employees is a serious priority for successful companies, not least because of powerful evidence that it generates significant returns. One study by the US Government found that a 10 per cent average increase in the educational level of employees led to an 8.6 per cent gain in total productivity. By contrast, a 10 per cent increase in investment in equipment increased productivity by only 3.4 per cent – suggesting that the marginal value of investing in intellectual capital is three times that of investing in equipment.

Emotional capacities

Our emotional abilities include our skills in empathy, conflict management, relationship-building and organizational awareness. Without them, we are less able to participate in the society around us, and less able to function effectively among those with whom we work and live. Emotional abilities are also involved to a great extent in creativity. Musicians, artists and performers show high levels of emotional awareness.

Daniel Goleman is the most high-profile advocate of the theory of emotional intelligence, which came to prominence during the 1990s. He was the first to hypothesize that human emotions are an important factor in human intelligence; if our emotions are healthy and mature, we use whatever IQ we have more effectively. He states that businesses that learn to invest in the emotional abilities of their employees will see greater success since it is our emotional skills which enable us to work effectively in teams and deal with customers in such a way as to secure their loyalty.

Emotional abilities are particularly key to leadership; the most successful leaders use their emotional intelligence to create a working climate that nurtures employees and encourages them to give their best. In the UK, a study of 42 schools found more positive teacher attitudes and higher pupil exam grades in the schools with head teachers with greater emotional abilities, and underperformance at the schools where the head teachers relied upon lesser emotional abilities. In a study of US insurance companies, companies whose CEOs exhibited more emotional competencies showed better financial results as measured by both profit and growth.

It sounds so obvious, from a company perspective, that one wonders how (under the current shareholder model of capitalism) the critical importance of nurturing both intellectual and emotional capacities among employees can be so consistently and damagingly devalued by such a large number of companies. Interestingly, it is often those companies that have made the clearest commitment to sustainable development that have withstood shareholder pressures to abuse their employees' human capital. At Dow Chemicals, for instance, the very first commitment within the Sustainable Development Operating Plan is 'the implementation of a comprehensive people strategy'. And this is far more than a standard human resources plan – it is a comprehensive strategy that articulates priorities around developing the workforce, defining the obligations of both Dow and its employees. As Michael Parker, former CEO of Dow Chemicals, put it:

> *Let us, once and for all, deflate the myth that shareholder and employee interests are somehow mutually exclusive. Using a business model rooted in sustainable development – with its triple bottom line of economic prosperity, environmental stewardship and corporate social responsibility – we now have a framework that validates the intuitive notion that employees' 'intellectual capital' is as essential to an enterprise's success as shareholders' invested capital.* (Parker, 2002)

Spiritual capacities

Although there are many for whom the very idea of spiritual capacity will trigger intellectual disdain or outright hostility, others have suggested that the Five Capitals Framework should really be a *six* capitals framework – with spiritual capital or moral capital designated as a separate capital stock of its own. That is very much the line taken in works such as Stephen Young's *Moral Capitalism* (2003) or Peter Heslem's *Globalization and the Good* (2004), where moral capital is defined as the norms, values, and ethics ('often formed by religion') that underpin any community or society.

The decision of Forum for the Future to treat this whole area of human experience as a subset of human capital rather than as a separate stock of capital in its own right may well reflect higher than usual levels of scepticism about such an approach here in the predominantly secular society of the UK. That does not alter the fact that the vast majority of humankind still subscribes to one form of religious belief system or another; empirically, such beliefs constitute a critical part of what it is that makes us human. In talking about spiritual capital, however, it is important to stress that the word 'spirituality' has no formal connection with institutionalized religion. In that context, I have much sympathy with Danah Zohar's understanding of spirituality as an enhancement of our daily lives, based on the Latin *spiritus*, that which breathes life or vitality into a system:

Spiritual capital adds the dimension of our shared meanings and values and ultimate purposes. It addresses those concerns we have about what it means to be human and the ultimate meaning and purpose of human life. It is the cultivation and sharing of our truly ultimate concerns that acts as the real glue in society. It is only when our notion of capitalism includes spiritual capital's wealth of meaning, values, purpose and higher motivation that we can have sustainable capitalism and a sustainable society. (Zohar, 2004)

Take just two of today's most pressing sustainability challenges: how to counter the all-but-universal seduction of consumerism (a theme which I return to in Chapter 15) and the need for people to go beyond rational respect for the natural systems upon which we depend by developing a much more humble, reverential ethos. There are few sources of authority (let alone wisdom) in addressing these two challenges that are not derived from religious or spiritual sources. Yet that critical inheritance is deemed illegitimate by many of those who continue to exhort people to 'respect nature' and 'consume responsibly' from the stony ground of self-indulgent, secular materialism. In *Natural Alien: Humankind and the Environment*, Neil Evernden wrote:

Although they seldom recognize it, environmentalists are protesting not at the stripping of natural resources, but at the stripping of earthly meaning. I have suggested elsewhere that environmentalism, like romanticism in a previous century, actually constitutes a defence of values. I am now asserting an even more fundamental role for environmentalism – namely, the defence of meaning. We call people 'environmentalists' because they are moved to defend what we call the environment; but at the bottom, their action is actually a defence of the cosmos, not of scenery. (Evernden, 1993)

What we are talking about here are some of the 'ultimate ends' that give meaning and purpose to the lives of billions of people. For more and more people, the business of nurturing our spiritual capacity is now a serious priority. At the heart of this endeavour is the idea of finding 'a new story', enabling us to reconnect with our evolutionary origins, going back over 4 billion years of unfolding life, to understand better our place in creation, and to experience that sense of interconnectedness and interdependence with the rest of life on Earth – the loss of which now imperils our very future.

VALUING HUMAN CAPITAL

Human capital is a morally neutral concept. The uses people make of their individual capacities may or may not be benign in societal and environmental terms. Intelligence can be used for purely selfish reasons to harm others, or to accelerate environmental degradation; spiritual capacities can be deployed to worsen religious intolerance and social divides; even good health, in terms of superior physical strength, can be used to abuse women, bully children or dominate 'weaker' colleagues.

But it is, of course, the benign 'flows' from our net stock of human capital that the focus should be on in any model of sustainable capitalism: good health that liberates people to fulfil their own and other people's aspirations; parenting skills; providing caring, nurturing, emotional support; creativity – works of art, novels and poetry; productive work of every kind; spiritual practice, compassion, humanitarian devotion; new ideas – design, innovations; the capacity for empathy. When thinking about the flow of benefits and 'free gifts' from people's human capital in such broad terms, it is clear that it cannot possibly be measured in financial terms. Indeed, in most instances, it's not even possible to quantify it in any serious way.

During the 1990s, however, companies such as Skandia devoted considerable resources to developing appropriate intellectual capital metrics. For several years, it produced comprehensive annual reports to demonstrate the value to shareholders of its intellectual capital, defined as 'the sum of a company's intangible assets or, more simply, the difference between a company's net worth and its market value' (Skandia, 1997). In *Intellectual Capital: The New Wealth of Nations*, Thomas Stewart (1997) defined intellectual capital as 'the sum of everything everybody in a company knows that gives it a competitive edge'.

This was, of course, the period when people who really should have known better were getting almost hysterically overexcited about the dotcom boom – or dotcom bubble, as we now know it to have been. Politicians and business people waxed equally lyrical about the knowledge economy and the importance of being able to quantify 'the rental value of any individual's intellectual capacities'. Most companies simply use a combination of qualitative indicators (motivation or empowerment indexes, staff satisfaction surveys) and standard quantitative indicators (turnover, average years of service, training costs per employee and so on).

And there is, of course, a completely different way of looking at human capital inside a company, drawing far more upon the moral and emotional capabilities of employees, seeing business as a 'vocation' to serve humankind as well as a means of creating wealth and generating profits for shareholders. Although many individual business people will feel distinctly ill at ease about such a 'touchy-feely' way of looking at the role of business in the world today, it is important to bear in mind that the current, somewhat brutal and reductionist view of what makes for business success may not reign supreme for ever. Danah Zohar likes to challenge her business clients by inviting them to think of themselves as 'servant leaders' in signing up to the following 'credo':

> *I believe that global business has the money and the power to make a significant difference in today's troubled world, and that by making that difference it can help itself as well as others. I envision business raising its sights above the bottom line. I envisage business becoming a vocation, like the higher professions. To make this possible, I believe that business must add a moral dimension, becoming more service- and value-oriented, and largely eliminating the assumed natural distinction between private enterprise and public institution. I envisage business taking responsibility for the world in which it operates and from which it creates its wealth. And I envisage myself becoming one of those business leaders who are 'servant leaders' – leaders who serve not just stockholders, colleagues, employees, products and customers, but leaders who also serve the community, the planet, humanity, the future and life itself.* (Zohar, 2004)

For many non-profit organizations, by the same token, there is something inherently suspicious in deploying too heavy-handed a set of metrics. In Forum for the Future, a small educational charity employing around 70 people, we went to some lengths to get to grips with understanding the dynamics of our own human/intellectual capital as part and parcel of our integrated sustainability management system (see Figure 8.1). But ours is definitely a qualitative rather than a quantitative approach!

Outside of the controlled work environment, it is even harder to track, let alone measure, what is happening to people's stocks of human capital. Unfortunately, it's a great deal easier to see when things are going wrong with them: when stress-related illnesses proliferate, when more people become addicted to drugs or alcohol, when the incidence of child abuse or crimes of violence increases, or when neglected, unloved children go on to become neglectful, unloving parents. As we will see in the next chapter, all of these things have a damaging impact upon stocks of social capital; but they originate in the failure to create the conditions in which each individual can fulfil his or her own potentiality to the full.

The quite proper focus for government and international bodies is therefore to create those conditions, starting with measures to ensure minimum standards of healthcare, nutrition, education and material wellbeing. Governments can't make people happy, healthy or rich – but they can invest in those institutions, systems and services that best enable individuals to make the most of their life chances. They can systematically build up social capital that nurtures and underpins each individual's human capital.

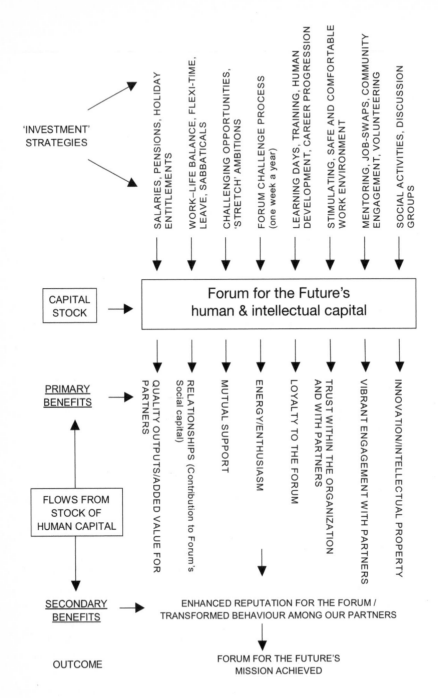

Source: Forum for the Future

Figure 8.1 *Forum for the Future's human and intellectual capital*

REFERENCES

Coote, A. (2005) 'Public health and sustainable development', unpublished speech, Sustainable Development Commission, London

Evernden, N. (1993) *Natural Alien: Humankind and the Environment*, Oxford University Press, Oxford

Heslem, P. (2004) *Globalization and the Good*, SPCK, London

New Internationalist (2001) 'Enduring terrors', *New Internationalist*, November

Parker, M. (2002) 'The shareholder–employee balance: Beyond the rhetoric', *New Academy Review*, vol 1, no 2

Roszak, T. (1993) *The Voice of the Earth*, Bantam Press, London

Skandia (1997) *Skandia Annual Report*. Available at www.skandia.com/en/ir/orderprint fininfo.jsp

Stewart, T. A. (1997) *Intellectual Capital: The New Wealth of Nations*, Nicholas Brealey, London

Young, S. (2003) *Moral Capitalism: Reconciling Private Interest with the Public Good*, Berrett-Koehler, San Francisco, CA

Zohar, D. (2004) *Spiritual Capital: Wealth We Can Live By*, Bloomsbury, London

Social Capital

INTRODUCTION

QUESTION: *When does one person's stock of human capital become a community's stock of social capital?*

ANSWER: *It doesn't really matter, as long as they are mutually reinforcing and help to secure a better quality of life for the greatest number of people in any particular area.*

Although the concept of social capital is beginning to receive real traction in both policy-making and business circles, it is still struggling somewhat to cast off its aura of academic theorizing about what it is that binds communities and societies together. This is unfortunate; in many ways, social capital lends itself far more to the development of concrete, measurable interventions by business than the aggravatingly elusive determinants of corporate social responsibility (CSR). In essence, it all comes down to things that we are all very familiar with in both our personal and working lives: good networks, trust, shared initiatives and solidarity – the 'social glue' that keeps things bound together, often in the teeth of increasingly 'atomized' lifestyles, with each individual going his or her own way regardless of the impacts upon society, community or family.

DEFINING SOCIAL CAPITAL

The links between human capital and social capital are clearly very strong. Leading politicians talk passionately about the importance of community. Sociologists stress the role of 'friendship networks' for getting jobs. More and more funding for regenerating run-down neighbourhoods supports community groups, as well as investments in new infrastructure. International institutions such as the World Bank are increasingly promoting community groups, NGOs and the 'building blocks' of civic society as crucial to economic and social development. Why such interest in community and civic organizations? Advocates argue that they make two important contributions to a sustainable economy and society. First, friends, family and mutual groups can provide people with practical support, from looking after children and old people to lending money or providing informal counselling. During an era in which state resources continue to be tight and trust in state institutions is often low, many commentators see such informal support as increasingly important.

Second, broad social networks and civic organizations are perceived to foster cooperation between people. They increase trust, which, in turn, helps people to enjoy a higher quality of life and entrepreneurs to do business. They provide structures for discussing and agreeing ways to overcome shared challenges, such as how to run a school, reduce crime or protect the environment. In contrast, a socially fragmented society finds it difficult to engage in the kind of debate that is essential for democratic government.

Advocates argue that such mutual support, trust and the ability to work together to solve common problems contribute as much to a country's success as do its material resources (natural and manufactured capital) or the skills of its population (human capital). Consequently, they have dubbed these attributes *social capital*.

Although the first usage of 'social capital' has been traced back to 1916, it was the American sociologist Robert Putnam who was responsible for popularizing the concept and bringing it into mainstream political debate. Putnam's book *Bowling Alone* (2000) takes bowling clubs as a defining example of activities that previously helped to sustain the social fabric of life in the US, but which are now in decline. He draws on a vast body of data and research to show that the past 40 years have seen a dramatic decline in participation in social structures, from the church and political parties to parent–teacher associations and bowling leagues.

Putnam defines social capital as the 'features of social life – networks, norms and trust – that enable participants to act together more effectively to pursue shared objectives'. Other 'features' often referred to in the literature are institutions, relationships, values, levels of participation, reciprocity and community cohesion – though it is important to point out that there is far more to the concept of social capital than is captured in the notion of community. To develop a more nuanced understanding of the different dynamics within social capital, Putnam distinguishes between two types:

1 *Bridging* (or inclusive) social capital: this is outward looking and encompasses people from different social groups. Examples include the civil rights movement and ecumenical religious organizations.
2 *Bonding* (or exclusive) social capital: this is inward looking and tends to reinforce exclusive identities. Examples include urban gangs, church-based women's reading groups and fashionable country clubs.

Bonding social capital creates in-group loyalty and solidarity, and offers strong support for less fortunate community members. Bridging networks tend to be more useful for accessing external assets and contacts. Putnam summarizes the differences as follows: 'Bonding social capital constitutes a kind of sociological superglue, whereas bridging social capital provides a sociological WD-40' (Putnam, 2000).

All commentators on social capital are quick to point out that this too, just like human capital, is a 'value-neutral term'. All forms of social capital can produce negative effects as well as positive effects, and the academic literature identifies a wide range of possible downsides to social capital. As one critic pointed out: 'Wouldn't it be better if Timothy McVeigh *had* gone bowling alone?' – since McVeigh, whose bomb in Oklahoma killed 168 people, gained valuable advice from the network of friends he used to go bowling with. Putnam acknowledges that the positive consequences of social capital – mutual support, cooperation and trust – can often be matched by negative consequences, such as sectarianism (dividing rather than uniting communities or societies), ethnocentrism, corruption, and creating barriers to social inclusion and social mobility. Indeed, there is a substantial body of academic work in the US which supports one of Robert Putnam's more controversial hypotheses that geographical areas with high levels of ethnic and social diversity will display *lower* levels of social capital over a wide range of indicators – including trust and civic engagement.

Despite a growing body of academic work, social capital still remains a fairly nebulous term, difficult to pin down and even harder to implement. By way of a summary, the prevailing view suggests that a society can be said to have high stocks of social capital if it has:

- high levels of trust between people;
- high membership of civic organizations;
- high levels of volunteering and charitable giving;
- high levels of participation in politics, including membership of political parties;
- high levels of participation in religious groups; and
- high levels of informal socializing.

These should all help people to give each other mutual support, cooperate to solve common problems, establish a system of good government and do business together. Societies with high membership of civic organizations also tend to have higher trust, more informal socializing and political participation.

The evidence to back up the importance of social networks and civic organizations is fairly strong. States in America whose residents have high levels of informal socializing, volunteering, community groups and trust of others tend to have lower crime and relatively good schools, health facilities and government. Individuals with good social connections tend to prosper. There is also some evidence that countries and regions with low social trust have relatively poor economies.

Robert Putnam (2000) has further attempted to pick out the factors that have accounted for the decline in social capital over the last four decades in the US. He tentatively estimates that changing patterns of work account for 10 per cent of the decline; suburbanization accounts for another 10 per cent decline because people live further away from each other and their work, and spend more time commuting. Television accounts for a quarter of the decline because it provides a more isolated form of entertainment. The majority of the rest of the decline he attributes to a rather vague change in the cultures of different generations. For example, those who lived through World War II appear to have established patterns of political and social engagement which their children never learned.

Other researchers agree with Putnam that Americans are becoming more socially isolated and less civically engaged; but they suggest different root causes. Amitai Etzioni, an influential sociologist, argues that communities have been undermined in Western countries because governments have given people too many individual rights. Individualism has become rampant, he claims, because everyone has been given rights to free healthcare, education, a minimum income, privacy, divorce, compensation for almost any wrong and so on, without any corresponding duties and responsibilities.

William Julius Wilson, one of the leading writers on ghetto culture, claims that poor urban areas in the US have suffered a breakdown in community. Trust has declined, civic organizations have withered. Those social groups which thrive – such as gangs – are very exclusive and contribute little to cooperation between all residents. But he attributes the root cause of this not to the time pressures of work, nor a culture of individual rights, but to the economic dislocation caused by the flight of stable employment from such neighbourhoods.

Building social capital

As interest has increased in social capital, numerous questions have been asked about how it can be fostered. How can trust be developed, community groups supported and networks expanded? This institutional focus has also been the basis of most attempts to stimulate social capital over the last decade. Governments are increasingly funding programmes that aim to strengthen the *capacity* of civic organizations – for example, by giving their members training. Internationally, much of the support given to emerging democracies in Eastern Europe has been to help them develop civic institutions, from funding small community centres upwards. Even those, such as Robert Putnam, who attribute the decline in social capital to economic, cultural and technological factors believe that the way to foster social capital is to create new community and civic institutions.

In April 2002, the UK Prime Minister's Strategy Unit carried out an intriguing review (Cabinet Office Strategy Unit, 2002) of the many different ways in which the concept of social capital is permeating political discourse in the UK and elsewhere. In seeking to answer the question 'Why is social capital important?', it advanced six potential areas of economic and social benefit – in the terminology of the Five Capitals Framework, these represent hypothetical flows from the stock of social capital from which the whole of society (as well as many individuals) benefits.

1 Social capital is important because it may facilitate higher levels of GDP

The efficient functioning of markets requires clear definition of property rights, the ability easily or cheaply to enforce contracts or other negotiated agreements, low transaction costs and good information. (Fukuyama, 1995)

This was the principal thesis advanced by Francis Fukuyama in his article 'Social capital and the global economy' (1995). Robert Putnam (2000) argues that there is now detailed empirical evidence from Tanzania to Sri Lanka to Italy to Russia which demonstrates that economic development can be, and often has been, boosted by enhanced stocks of social capital. In one small but intriguing manifestation of this, the 1997 World Values Survey shows that countries where trust of strangers is high also tend to be countries with high GDP. All of these correlations have proved to be particularly important in explaining variations in economic development in developing nations.

2 Social capital is important because it may facilitate the more efficient functioning of job markets

The level and duration of unemployment is partly a function of search costs. The networks and contacts that make up social capital can provide highly cost-effective mechanisms for facilitating job search. (Cabinet Office Strategy Unit, 2002)

The evidence here is strong. Those who live in particularly disadvantaged neighbourhoods are even less likely to get jobs and break out of any poverty cycle than individuals with similar qualifications and characteristics living in better neighbourhoods – a conclusion reinforced by studies that show more unemployed people find jobs through friends and personal contacts than through any other route.

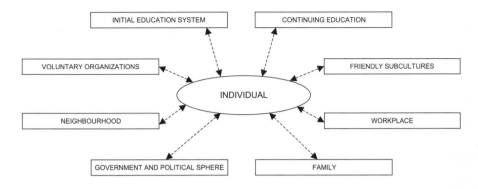

Source: adapted from Baron et al (2000)

Figure 9.1 *Sources of social capital that influence the attainment of education*

3 Social capital is important because it may facilitate educational attainment

> *At the individual level, there is a strong positive association between levels of social capital, measured by the size and diversity of social networks, community engagement and social trust, and levels of educational attainment.* (Cabinet Office Strategy Unit, 2002)

Figure 9.1 demonstrates the different sources of social capital influencing educational attainment in individuals, with a balance of both formal and informal learning sources.

4 Social capital is important because it may contribute to lower levels of crime

> *Within criminology, this is sometimes known as 'social control theory' – social networks and bonds to mainstream society are what prevent people from offending – and has been impressively demonstrated by longitudinal studies at both the individual and neighbourhood level.* (Cabinet Office Strategy Unit, 2002)

For many people living in the cities of both rich and poor countries, crime (or fear of crime) is one of the most significant factors in a reduced quality of life. Higher levels of social capital acting both as a deterrent (before any crime is committed) and a support network (after a crime is committed) can make an enormous difference to people's levels of wellbeing.

Indeed, financial support by either local or central government for initiatives along the lines of Neighbourhood Watch may well prove to be an extremely cost-effective way of making a real difference in people's lives. There are therefore few more disturbing manifestations of low levels of trust and social capital in urban areas than the emergence of 'gated communities', with more and more wealthy individuals choosing to withdraw behind various kinds of physical barrier to put themselves as far beyond the reach of criminal or anti-social elements as possible.

5 Social capital is important because it may lead to better health

> *Wider social relationships may have an impact on health through their impact on individuals' perceptions of their social status; stress; the strength of social affiliations; 'daily hassles'; and more general feelings of safety and fear. Social capital provides tangible assistance and care, and also creates a sense of wellbeing and belonging, whereas its absence leads to isolation and depression.* (Cabinet Office Strategy Unit, 2002)

Sociologists have demonstrated time after time the importance of bonding relationships on health – particularly in childhood and in old age. Even when they are well cared for in orphanages (with a good diet, comfortable facilities and so on), children's development can be badly affected by the lack of love and trust provided in normal family relationships.

The Worldwatch Institute's 2004 *State of the World* comments on just how significant this can be when assessing ways of securing a better quality of life for people:

> *People who are socially connected tend to be healthier – often significantly so. More than a dozen long-term studies in Japan, Scandinavia and the US show that the chances of dying in a given year, no matter the cause, is two to five times greater for people who are isolated than for socially connected people. For example, one study found that in 1234 heart attack patients, the rate of a recurring attack within six months was nearly double for those living alone. And a Harvard study of health and mistrust in the US concluded that moving to a state with a high level of social connections from a state where the level is low would improve a person's health almost as much as quitting smoking.* (Worldwatch Institute, 2004)

6 Social capital is important because it may improve the effectiveness of institutions of government

Governments and politicians nowadays are widely distrusted and ignored. In many European countries, politicians at all levels of government command the outright trust of less than one tenth of the population. Well over half of young people do not bother to vote in any elections. Democratic legitimacy is diminishing rapidly all over the Western world. Revitalizing systems of governance is a critical part of the challenge of sustainable development, and it is clear that investments in social capital can do much to help achieve this purpose.

The Strategy Unit's review concludes that there is an array of *possible* policy interventions for 'positively stimulating the creation of social capital', some of which are already in place, with many more under consideration.

From a sustainability perspective, the concept of social capital offers an exciting new way of thinking about and measuring the social dimensions of sustainability. But despite the wealth of research on natural capital and environmental sustainability, there have been surprisingly few attempts to explore the links between social capital and social sustainability.

Yet there are some hints of convergence. Ismail Serageldin and Christiaan Grootaert of the World Bank have argued that social capital 'is best studied in the context of the contribution it makes to sustainable development' (Serageldin and Grootaert, 2000). They set social capital alongside natural, human and manufactured capital, and explore ways of measuring the stocks and flows of all these capital types. Using a 'back of the envelope' calculation, they estimate that in 192 countries, human and social capital equals or exceeds natural capital and manufactured assets combined (the only exceptions to this rule being a few large exporters of raw materials). Manufactured capital represents only 16 to 20 per cent of the wealth of most countries; but, as they rightly point out, it is this small slice of the cake that nearly all economic policy is focused upon.

Environmentalists may take issue with the rather low valuations that Seregaldin and Grootaert place on natural capital; but most would agree with their conclusion – that an overhaul of economic policy and the introduction of more sophisticated metrics for valuing different capital types will be critical if we are to achieve sustainable development. There are the beginnings here of a powerful synthesis, and academics and practitioners in both areas should endeavour to strengthen the intellectual and political links between their work.

The thrust of this chapter has been to look at ways in which governments can both conceptualize social capital and bring forward specific initiatives to help build social capital at different levels in society. Beyond that, there are equally important opportunities for the *private sector* to re-conceptualize what is now a rather soft and even flabby CSR agenda in terms of social capital, taking a much more rigorous approach to understanding the stocks of social capital for which it is responsible (and from which it derives considerable benefits) and the most effective ways of securing constant value from them. Companies are often unaware that they may be involved in building or depleting social capital as the terminology is rarely used in business or management literature, or by CSR practitioners. For many business people, the definition used in this chapter would need to be reworked to give it a much more grounded relevance – something along the lines of social capital being seen as 'the sum of social channels, networks and norms which expedite action on the part of any company pursuing its legitimate business interests'.

I will be returning to this specific theme in Chapter 14 as part of a broader analysis of what leading companies are doing to implement as much of the Five Capitals Framework as is now available to them under current company law and other legislation. However, it is worth commenting at this stage that there are already a substantial number of case studies exploring both the business and societal value of corporate engagement on social capital issues – particularly with reference to the role of big multinationals in developing countries, where some of the socio-economic challenges are a great deal more pressing than conventional environmental issues. The Worldwatch Institute's 2004 *State of the World* describes why this has become so important to them:

> *Stephen Knack of the World Bank warns that low levels of societal trust may lock countries in a 'poverty trap,' in which the vicious circle of mistrust, low investment and poverty is difficult to break. Knack and his colleagues tested the relationship between trust and economic performance in 29 countries included in the World Values Survey. They found that each 12-point rise in the survey's measure of trust was associated with a 1 per cent increase in annual income growth, and that each 7-point rise in trust corresponded to a 1 per cent increase in investment's share of GDP.* (Worldwatch Institute, 2004)

The simple truth of it is that, without high and stable levels of social capital, no society can achieve its collective aspirations, companies and entrepreneurs find it much harder to transact their day-to-day business, and fewer individuals have the opportunity to develop to their full potential.

REFERENCES

Baron, S., Field, J. and Schuller, T. (eds) (2000) *Social Capital: Critical Perspectives*, Oxford University Press, Oxford

Cabinet Office Strategy Unit (2002) *Social Capital: A Discussion Paper*, Cabinet Office Strategy Unit, London

Fukuyama, F. (1995) 'Social capital and the global economy', *Foreign Affairs*, vol 74, no 5, September/October, pp89–103

Putnam, R. (2000) *Bowling Alone: The Collapse and Revival of American Community*, Simon and Schuster, New York

Serageldin, I. and Grootaert, C. (2000) 'Defining social capital: An integrating view', in P. Dasgupta and I. Serageldin (eds) *Social Capital: A Multifaceted Perspective*, World Bank, Washington, DC, pp40–58

Worldwatch Institute (2004) *State of the World 2004: Progress Towards a Sustainable Society*, Earthscan, London

Manufactured Capital

INTRODUCTION

Ever since the publication of *Limits to Growth* (Meadows et al, 1972), sustainable development pragmatists have convincingly argued that the best hope of averting ecological meltdown is pervasive technological innovation: keep on driving down the environmental and social impacts of each unit of production, in whatever sector, through incremental improvements in resource efficiency. This, after all, is going to be a lot easier than trying to get on top of the population challenge (in the shape of around 80 million new citizens arriving on planet Earth every year), or trying to persuade consumers to reduce their levels of personal consumption. Eco-efficiency and eco-innovation have been the response. However, not only are governments *not* driving the resource productivity challenge with sufficient clarity or purposefulness, but even if they did, efficiency gains would barely keep up with burgeoning increases in consumption all around the world. A much more radical approach can be found in concepts such as 'biomimicry' or 'cradle-to-cradle wealth creation' – all of which depend upon a profound transformation in the way in which we see ourselves as embedded absolutely at the heart of the natural world, rather than somewhat detached observers of it from afar. Technology alone can't get us out of a hole: we have to re-engineer our mindsets at the same time.

DEFINING MANUFACTURED CAPITAL

The two remaining stocks of capital (manufactured and financial) are probably the most familiar to people. However, manufactured capital is not quite as simple a concept as it sounds. It is made up of material goods that contribute to the production process, but do not become embodied in the output of that process. The main components of manufactured capital include buildings (the built environment of villages, towns and cities); infrastructure (the physical fabric supporting social and economic life, including transport networks, schools, hospitals, media and communications, energy, and sewerage and water systems); and technologies (the means by which goods and services are produced, from simple tools and machines to information technology, biotechnology and engineering).

But the underlying 'story' is much easier to grasp. Children the world over are brought up on the same evolutionary account: that it was humankind's capacity to use tools that first helped us to establish our ecological niche, and that this slowly evolved into an increasingly powerful ability to assemble raw materials extracted from nature into objects, machines, buildings and so on. For most of our short history, this conversion process (from natural capital into manufactured capital) was relatively modest, localized and mostly low impact as far as the environment was concerned. But from the mid-18th century onwards, the Industrial Revolution transformed the balance of that relationship between the biosphere and the technosphere. The availability of cheap fossil fuels from the middle of the 20th century onwards has further increased the dependence of human beings upon countless different sources of manufactured capital.

It's within the broad concept of manufactured capital that the whole debate about the role of technology and sustainability has been subsumed. This is certainly not the place to attempt a résumé of one of the most important areas of intellectual divergence within green thinking over the last 40 years, but before launching into any analysis of the *potential* contribution that manufactured capital may make to achieving a just and sustainable society, it's important to remember that for some environmentalists, it is *technology* itself that is the problem. As far back as 1971, the eminent American activist Barry Commoner pointed the finger of blame at 'the sweeping transformation of production technologies since World War II', and argued that this transformation would have to be 'redone in order to bring the nation's productive technology much more closely into harmony with the inescapable demands of the ecosystem' (Commoner, 1971).

Perhaps the most consistent articulation of this perspective over four decades has been Teddy Goldsmith's eloquent laments in the *Ecologist* magazine at the usurpation of the biosphere by the technosphere, leaving humanity stripped of any proper connectedness with the natural world, and leaving society rushing headlong into an increasingly destructive frenzy of exploitation and consumption. The insult of choice for such campaigners is 'neo-Luddite', and they still find themselves on the receiving end of an incredibly rich vein of invective from today's cornucopians, who quite literally see technology as the answer to *all* our problems. In some quarters, particularly in the US, it's all but impossible to raise a cautionary voice against some new development without being dismissed as a green fundamentalist, or 'rejectionist', notwithstanding the fact that many carefully researched books (such as Edward Tenner's 1996 *Why Things Bite Back*) have, over the years, demonstrated convincingly just how beneficial a little more precaution would have been along the way.

To listen to these technophiliacs, you might think the entire green movement was made up of such rejectionists. In fact, such voices have always been in a minority – an influential minority (especially in terms of the image that people may now have of environmentalists' overall attitude to technology as a result), but a minority for all that. Over the last decade, it is much closer to the truth to say that the dominant intellectual force in this debate has been fundamentally pro-technology and increasingly focused on the benign potential for technological transformation. Indeed, some of the most eloquent and influential advocates of sustainable development today (Lester Brown, Paul Hawken, Amory and Hunter Lovins, Bill McDonough, Ernst von Weizsacker, Paul Ekins and many more) start from the premise that the only way of achieving sustainability is through a 'second Industrial Revolution', entailing the wholesale transformation of the way in which we think about manufactured capital.

Put at its simplest, this all goes back to the equation first promulgated by Paul Ehrlich in the 1960s to encapsulate the sustainability dilemma: $I = P \times C \times T$, where I represents total environmental impact, P is population, C is per capita consumption, and T is the technological efficiency with which that consumption is generated (impact per unit of consumption).

For a host of different reasons covered earlier in this book, most contemporary politicians have proved themselves incapable of addressing population issues (however blindingly obvious it may be that the more people there are on Earth, the harder it is going to be to fashion a genuinely sustainable future for each and every one of us), and remain extremely reluctant to engage in any debate about limits to consumption – other than to subscribe (implicitly or explicitly) to the horribly flawed notion that the more people consume, the happier they must be. The consequences of these two variables – lower population and reduced consumption – effectively being ruled 'off-limits', as far as contemporary political debate is concerned, has had a huge impact upon the way in which people have addressed today's sustainability challenges, with a quite disproportionate emphasis on the third variable – technology.

With global population rising to around 9 billion in the second half of this century, and per capita consumption likely to go on rising (especially in today's poorer developing countries), the challenge of getting more (in terms of economic value) out of less (in terms of the throughput of energy and raw materials) becomes all important – which explains the current wave of enthusiasm for concepts such as eco-innovation, resource efficiency, dematerialization, zero waste or zero emissions, carbon neutrality and so on.

How much more we can squeeze out remains a moot point. Calculations by Paul Ekins (2000) in his *Economic Growth and Environmental Sustainability* demonstrate that environmental impact per unit of consumption would need to fall by at least 90 per cent to achieve genuine environmental sustainability – the much talked-about 'Factor 10' improvement in resource productivity. Others argue that this is the absolute minimum required. As Lester Brown points out:

> *If China were to have a car in every garage, American style, it would need 80 million barrels of oil a day – more than the world currently produces. If paper consumption per person in China were to reach the US level, China would need more paper than the world produces.*

> *There go the world's forests. If the fossil fuel-based, automobile-centred,*
> *throwaway economic model will not work for China, it will not work*
> *for the other 3 billion people in the developing world – and it will not*
> *work for the rest of the world.* (Brown, 2003)

However, advocates of a new 'green industrial revolution' believe that this kind of efficiency transformation *is* perfectly viable – as you will have seen in Amory Lovins's feisty Foreword to this edition of the book, where he takes me to task for not being sufficiently enthusiastic about the efficiency revolution that could be ours for the taking! In sector after sector, scenarios are now bandied about showing how our existing stocks of manufactured capital must be replaced as soon as possible with buildings, infrastructure, investments and new technologies that will enable an efficiency revolution of this kind. Two important questions remain regarding the likelihood of this kind of transformation in our stocks of manufactured capital: How viable is it economically? and How likely is it politically? Opinions differ enormously on economic viability.

The optimists look to a sequence of win–win technological transitions that both help to reduce environmental damage and generate economic growth in the process. By contrast, pessimists view such a scenario as improbable. Ultimately, one way or the other, given that there is no real choice, we will have to pay whatever price it takes to get humankind onto a genuinely sustainable path. The shift from hydrocarbons to solar/renewable technologies is one of the most interesting areas to test out these respective positions.

RENEWABLE ENERGY

When you've nothing better to do on a wet Friday afternoon, just try and imagine what the world would be like without any fossil fuels: no coal, no oil, no gas, nothing. No stored solar energy of any description. It's quite daunting, simply because of the omnipresence of these particular energy sources in our lives, and because of the immense concentration of power in them, and in oil in particular. I recently learned from Thomas Homer-Dixon that three large spoonfuls of crude oil contain about the same amount of energy as eight hours of human manual labour, and when we fill our cars with gas (or petrol over here in the UK), we're pouring into the tank the energy equivalent of about two years of human labour! As Colin Campbell constantly reminds us, 'it's as if each of us had a team of slaves working for us for next to nothing'.

Without those metaphorical slaves, life would obviously be very different. For one thing, there would be far fewer of us: the vast increases in human numbers over the last 100 years or so can be correlated almost exactly with the availability of cheap oil and gas. Apart from hydropower (and assuming we still hadn't cracked the technological challenge of being able to extract large amounts of hydrogen from water without any fossil fuel energy to hand) and geothermal power, we would be entirely dependent on energy from the sun and on the ability of plants and trees to convert that solar radiation into usable forms of energy.

But there would still be all sorts of human civilizations thriving on the planet, just as there were before the discovery of fossil fuels. Our ingenuity (which is not of itself the product of fossil fuels!) would by now have found ways of maximizing the usefulness of that endless supply of energy from the sun. There would no doubt have been a few more Easter Island disasters along the way (as we overexploited nature's conversion capacity and collapsed into thermodynamic disequilibrium), but *theoretically*, the sum of intellectual capital that our species has built up and deployed over centuries would have been available to us to create immensely sophisticated solar civilizations. And given that enough solar energy reaches the surface of the Earth in just *one hour* to meet all of our current energy needs for an *entire year*, life probably wouldn't be that bad.

That's basically what we're going to have to do now. We'll always be able to use a certain amount of fossil fuels every year (especially if we can learn to store away the carbon dioxide which would otherwise be released into the atmosphere), but we've already overloaded the system so badly that we need to bring down that 'permissible quotient of fossil fuel usage' as rapidly as we possibly can. We need to let nature get on with its own sequestering (in soils, biomass and the oceans) without making it any harder than it's already going to be. And we're going to have to execute this transition in such a way as to deliver those solutions to 9 billion of us by 2050 – rather than (say) the 2 or 3 billion that might have been here on Earth without the use of fossil fuels over the last hundred years.

As it happens, this is the one sustainability challenge about which I feel uncomplicatedly and hugely optimistic. Indeed, I get heartily sick of the misery-guts whose brains have been so corrupted by years of psychological dependency on fossil fuels that all they can do is to point out the problems and the costs involved in any alternatives. Threaten to take away their security blanket, and they collapse in a heap of bed-wetting, 'can't be done' fatalism. The absurdity of it is that we absolutely know it *has to be done*, that nuclear power will only ever make a small contribution to our total energy needs (assuming it survives this troubled age of mega-terrorism, which, in my opinion, is extremely improbable), and that we've got no more than 10–15 years to get it sorted before we pass that point of irreversibility explained on page 28.

Unlike theirs, therefore, my spirit soars every time I read about prospective breakthroughs and real blue-sky solutions, about massive improvements in the efficiencies of photovoltaic cells at hugely reduced costs; about the work being done to harness the power of photosynthesis itself at Massachusetts Institute of Technology (MIT) and Arizona State University; about prototype technologies to convert CO_2 itself into an energy source via bio-reactors packed with algae; about magnetic-levitation trains; about ultra-efficient hydrogen-powered fuel cells; about the cars of the future running on plain old water (with hydrogen produced on board by reacting water with boron or some other element); about distributed energy systems both liberating people already connected to the grid (with every roof tile and every pane of glass in our houses operating as PV panels), as well as providing an equivalent level of energy services to the 1.6 billion people in the poor world not yet connected to the grid – and never needing to be either.

Just so many 'pies in the sky', I hear those oil-fixated sceptics claiming. But go back to Sir Nicholas Stern's principal description of climate change as 'the greatest market failure the world has ever seen'. He wasn't just talking about the insane subsidies that OECD governments still hand out to their fossil fuel industries (to the tune of around \$75 billion dollars every year!), but about the systematic market failure caused by us not paying a realistic price for every tonne of CO_2 we emit into the atmosphere. It is this global, wholly illegitimate subsidy for *all* fossil fuels that totally distorts today's energy markets. Hence the increasingly urgent drive to put a price on a tonne of CO_2, through trading schemes (like the EU's Emissions Trading Scheme – ETS), or taxes or other economic instruments.

As explored in Chapter 1, the world is making very slow progress on this – yet if there was just one thing those G8+5 world leaders could do in 2008 now that they have agreed to come forward with a new global agreement to succeed the Kyoto Protocol by the end of 2008, it would be to set the price of CO_2 in 2020, arbitrarily (because there's no perfect, science-based calculus as yet available here) setting a *minimum* figure, in other words the price that would be paid for every tonne emitted *come what may* at a given point in the future. The UK Treasury currently works on the basis of £70 a tonne for some of its long-term calculations, and that was well before the Fourth Assessment Report of the Intergovernmental Panel on Climate Change (IPPC) in 2007, so let's settle for the time being on a price of \$100 dollars a tonne.

My own belief is that the price of CO_2 will be much, much higher than that in 2020, as the impacts of accelerating climate change kick in over the next few years. But agreeing a minimum price *now* would start to correct the market failure Stern refers to, and create sufficient certainty for investors massively to ramp up their investments. Investment in 'cleantech' in the US in 2006 topped \$70 billion (43 per cent up on 2005), and it will nearly double again in 2007. But that is still only a fraction of what will be needed to transition the global energy economy from hydrocarbons to renewables. There are obviously huge risks associated with this (some people are already talking of the inevitability of a 'wattcom boom', to match the earlier 'dotcom boom'), as crazy money pursues flaky technologies that haven't a hope in hell of breaking through. But these risks are nothing compared to the risks of today's 'can't-be-done' fatalism.

At \$100 a tonne, Carbon Capture and Storage (CCS) also becomes much more viable, although this is development to which many radical environmentalists are strongly opposed on the grounds that it merely prolongs our dependency on fossil fuels. I think this is misguided: we may not like CCS, but we certainly need it. Much more importantly, with CO_2 at \$100 a tonne, a wide range of different renewable sources of energy will become available to us with CO_2 priced at that level. Just take PVs: the 'too expensive' argument completely ignores the fact that as manufacturers scale up production, prices will start to fall dramatically. And the spur of innovation will drive brilliant new ideas. As Jeremy Leggett, Chief Executive of Solar Century has said:

> *PV is a classic example of a disruptive technology, capable of invading the trillion-dollar global energy market with the same speed the personal computers invaded the mainframe market. Companies tend not to spot such invasions of their core market. Horse traders laughed at the first automobiles, shortly before going out of business. IBM failed to realize that the mainframe was under threat until late in the day. In fact, never in the history of commerce has a company with core interests in threatened areas commercialized the disruptive invader.* (Leggett, 2003)

And PV is not the only disruptive technology which will transform our world. At long last, people are beginning to talk about Concentrated Solar Power (CSP), a technology which has been operating successfully in the Mojave Desert in California for nearly 20 years. Large parabolic mirrors concentrate the solar radiation on an 'absorber' – a large tower or vessel which contains either water, gas or oil, and acts as a heat exchange generating steam to power a conventional steam turbine. The potential is enormous: every square kilometre of desert sands receives the solar equivalent of 1.5 *million* barrels of oil every year. Costs are already 'manageable' – the cost of producing the solar thermal equivalent of 1 barrel of oil is today about $50 (less than the current price of oil), and will fall dramatically as economies of scale kick in in terms of the manufacture of all the different component parts. If CO_2 were to hit $100 a tonne, this would become something of a no-brainer.

New CSP schemes *are* now being developed in Israel, Australia, the US (where a 64 megawatt in the Nevada desert came on stream in June 2007), the United Arab Emirates, Algeria and Spain (with a new 11 megawatt 'power tower' just commissioned in the south of the country and with several much bigger projects to follow). Investors *are* starting to wake up, but there's still no real sense of the massive potential of CSP if it can be linked to new, high-voltage, direct-current (HVDC) power lines – which is where the real investment will be needed. A recent study commissioned by the German Federal Ministry for the Environment shows how Europe (including even the most northerly countries) could theoretically meet all its needs for electricity and cut emissions of CO_2 by 70 per cent by 2050 through CSP projects in both North Africa and the Middle East. Better yet, some of the energy generated in this way could either be used to produce hydrogen, or to power desalination plants all around the Mediterranean and the Middle East, where water shortages already loom as a massive problem for the future.

The Government of Yemen's recent decision that it was going to have to relocate its capital away from Sanaa to a new city on the coast, simply because Sanaa is running out of water, is just a small indication of the devastation that lies ahead.

No breakthrough technology of this kind is ever quite as good as its proponents make out. There would be massive problems, not least in terms of establishing a completely new DC grid alongside today's AC transmission systems. And there would be environmental impacts: 'empty deserts' is a phrase that makes desert ecologists' blood run cold, as they're never quite as empty as they seem! And they're often extremely difficult environments to work in. Even so, in the light of what we now know about climate change, it remains incomprehensible to me that CSP is being treated as 'an eccentric gleam in the eye', warranting miniscule amounts of government R&D budgets, let alone political leadership.

By contrast, in November 2006, 30 of the world's richest countries committed an initial sum of £7 billion on an experimental fusion reactor which, even according to its exponents, will not produce any commercial electricity for at least another 30 years. Too late! What's more, fusion power has *always* been another '30/40 years away', and in contrast to the most powerful fusion reactor we already have (namely, the sun itself!), will *never* make a serious contribution to our energy needs. As many critics have pointed out, fusion power is basically a job creation scheme for plasma physicists. Wouldn't it make a lot more sense (bearing in mind the points raised earlier about population growth, chronic poverty and very high levels of employment, particularly among young men in much of Africa and the Middle East, with huge security implications for the whole of Europe) to be putting that kind of investment into technology that will bring massive and almost immediate benefits to some of the poorest countries in the world, rather than into yesterday's sad and discredited nuclear pipe dreams? Why aren't Gordon Brown and Angela Merkel out there right now building political momentum around CSP if they believe a fraction of their own rhetoric about climate change, about threats to Europe's security, and about the importance of achieving greater equity in a divided world?

As I think the broad thrust of this book bears out, I have always resisted giving way to crude conspiracy theories about why we continue to resist 'the blindingly obvious' which is already available to us. But on CSP (and renewable energy in general), I'm no longer so sure. Organizations like the International Energy Association seem to swallow the hydrocarbon propaganda of the big energy companies as if that was their pre-ordained duty. Future energy projections showing fossil fuel consumption continuing to grow strongly for the next 30 years, even though we know for sure that is guaranteed to tip us over the edge into 'dangerous climate change', still dominate the energy debate. Claims that we simply can't grow renewable energy businesses any faster than we're already doing are simply lies – and it really doesn't take long to work out who the principal beneficiaries of that institutionalized dishonesty are likely to be.

So here we are in 2007 with untold billions of dollars still going into new fossil fuel investments (as we saw in Chapter 3), with a new generation of nuclear reactors about to be foisted upon us (at God knows what cost and at what risk to people today, let alone future generations having to cope with the nuclear waste), with a trillion-dollar biofuel bonanza unfolding in our midst which in the first instance will do little to address the problems of climate change (while pushing up the cost of food for hundreds of millions of the world's poorest people), and with the equivalent of *next to nothing* being done on renewables. (I have focused here on solar technologies, but I could have made a similar case for wind power, wave power, tidal power, small-scale hydropower, geothermal, genuinely sustainable biomass and so on.)

ALIGNING NATURAL AND MANUFACTURED CAPITAL

As to political feasibility, optimism does not come easily here either. Levels of ecological illiteracy remain so deep as to beggar belief after 40 years of accumulating evidence that all is not well with our dominant model of progress. Symptoms, not systems, remain the political order of the day. There is little, if any, applied understanding among politicians of how natural systems work; the laws of thermodynamics obtain only in engineering textbooks; and frontier mentalities (based on an atavistic assumption that there are no real limits to what the human species can aspire to do) have proved astonishingly resilient.

This is precisely the kind of challenge that some of the world's most progressive companies are facing as they seek to reduce the overall impact of their products – to really work the 'T' variable in the $I = P \times C \times T$ equation in order to get us closer to something resembling sustainable production systems. One of the most popular tools used by companies to achieve these efficiency gains is lifecycle analysis, assessing the impact of a product from manufacture through to final disposal, reuse or recycling. It sounds simple, but it's still proving very difficult to move society towards a better understanding of what is now required. Linear models of resource use – *make, use and dispose* – are still dominant. Unlike the cyclical resource flows of natural systems, which result in no net accumulation of waste, human-induced resource flows *inevitably* lead to an accumulation of waste and to a build-up of entropy. Statistics that bear out the scale of this systems dilemma provide even more telling illustrations: if Americans had recycled the 32 billion cans of fizzy drinks they threw away in 2002, for example, they would have saved 435,000 tonnes of aluminium – enough to rebuild the world's entire commercial air fleet more than 1.5 times. Americans use and throw away 2.5 million plastic bottles every hour. The scale of the problem is extraordinary. More than 90 per cent of all the materials extracted to manufacture ordinary consumer products ends up as waste; only 10 per cent – and sometimes a lot less – ends up in the product itself. And given the success that some manufacturers have had in ensuring that their products don't last very long (through built-in obsolescence), the lifetime of many of those products is very short before they are rejected and replaced, meaning that only around 1 per cent of *all* materials flowing through the US economy ends up in products still being used six months after manufacture. One leading DIY business in the UK, for instance, reckons that the average domestic power tool is used for just ten minutes! As Ed Douglas puts it:

> *Most will serve 'conscience-time', gathering dust on a shelf in the garage, but the end is inevitable: thousands of years mouldering underground. A power tool consumes many times its own weight of resources in its design, manufacture, packaging, transportation and disposal, all for a shorter active life span than that of the adult mayfly.* (Douglas, 2007)

For reasons such as these, there are many who remain sceptical that even the most systematic re-engineering of our manufactured capital over a 20- to 30-year period will deliver a genuinely sustainable economy for humankind. But given that this is the most practical, deliverable and economically manageable way of getting us at least some way down that track, not to engage urgently in that process as our number one sustainability priority represents a shameful lack of political leadership and vision. That's a view strongly shared by a new generation of designers who are trying to think through the whole problem from a much more thoughtful perspective, digging deep into the psyche of those whose behaviour – without them really understanding it – is accelerating the onset of an environmental disaster. Jonathan Chapman of the University of Brighton in the UK likes to contrast this kind of 'adulterous consumption', where there is simply no 'relationship' at all between the product and the purchaser, with what he calls 'emotionally durable design', breaking through that desperately wasteful cycle of desire and disappointment by enabling consumers to feel as much connectedness with the products that they buy as they might with a favourite pair of jeans – or even with their childhood 'teddy bear', if they still have one!

It's clear that there remains a big problem in the way in which we frame this whole question of waste and resource management. The lion's share of the work that goes into the crafting of new policy or new economic instruments has, as its principal objective, 'the reduction of waste'. Because this in itself is hard enough (in an age where simply chucking things away regardless has become standard human behaviour in far too many countries), no attempt is made to think that challenge through in terms of total resource flows, compatibility with natural systems and so on. So we tend to get very worked up about levels of recycling as the sole benchmark of success in this area without necessarily asking the more difficult questions about whether or not recycling makes much sense in either economic or thermodynamic terms. Sometimes it does, but sometimes it doesn't.

This, of course, gets very problematic for both politicians and the citizens whom they are seeking to influence on waste and recycling issues – or, indeed, on any other sustainable development issue for that matter. Try telling people that recycling can sometimes be 'bad for the environment' and there's a serious risk that people will just want to give up on the whole thing.

One of the most stimulating voices in this debate is that of Bill McDonough, an American architect and visionary who is less and less tolerant of conventional environmental thinking. In *Cradle to Cradle* (2002), co-authored with Michael Braungart, there is a subtext of 'why being less bad is actually no good', given the scale of the challenge we now face, and why our current 'cradle-to-grave' thinking is leading us down a very dangerous blind alley. McDonough and Braungart also take a serious swipe at the World Business Council for Sustainable Development's (WBCSD's) most treasured concept – namely, eco-efficiency:

> *Eco-efficiency is an outwardly admirable, even noble, concept; but it is not a strategy for success over the long term because it does not reach deep enough. It presents little more than an illusion of change. We do not mean to lambaste those who are working with good intentions to create and enforce laws meant to protect the public good. In a world where designs are unintelligent and destructive, regulations can reduce immediate deleterious effects. But, ultimately, regulation is a signal of design failure. In fact, it is what we call 'a licence to harm': a permit issued by a government to an industry so that it may dispense sickness, destruction and death at an 'acceptable' rate. But as we shall see, good design can require no regulation at all.* (McDonough and Braungart, 2002)

The challenge, then, has to be articulated in terms not of being 'less unsustainable' but of being 'genuinely sustainable', in every particular. In advancing the alternative concept of 'eco-effectiveness', McDonough and Braungart remind us that we have to become as effective as nature in imitating the cradle-to-cradle systems of nutrient and resource flows upon which the entire system depends. 'To eliminate the concept of waste means to design things – products, packaging and systems – from the very beginning in the understanding that waste does not exist', or must cease to exist if the metabolism of the human species is eventually to align with the metabolism of the natural world.

The only way in which the biosphere and the technosphere can co-exist is for the technosphere to become biologically compatible with the rest of life on Earth. Our economies are ecosystems in themselves and, like any ecosystem, take in energy and materials and transform them into products. The problem is that we do it by way of linear transformation, whereas nature's transformation is cyclical.

Our economy/ecosystem is also at a very immature stage of development – what is referred to by ecologists as the 'colonizing' or 'pioneer' phase in any organism's evolution. Acting on the twin assumptions that there were no limits to our use of the natural world, and that we could lay claim to as much of its productivity and resource flow as we saw fit, the human species has opportunistically set out to colonize all but the most inhospitable habitats on Earth. In that process, we have behaved as if we were just passing through, grabbing anything we could get our hands on in the short term without any particular concern for what happens next.

We have now reached the outer limits of that ecosystem, having pretty much filled up the world in the process, and are now having to think very differently given that we've got nowhere else to move on to – which means 'living on the Earth as if we intended to stay here'. Or, as ecologists would put it, we have to evolve out of being a pioneer species into a mature species by learning to be 'self-renewing right where we are'. Again, Janine Benyus has found a compelling way of capturing what it would mean for the human species to mimic nature in that very broad systems approach:

> *Over billions of years, natural selections come up with winning strategies adopted by all complex mature ecosystems. The strategies in the following list are tried-and-true approaches to the mystery of surviving in place. Think of them as the ten commandments of the Redwood clan. Organisms in a mature ecosystem:*
>
> 1 *use waste as a resource;*
> 2 *diversify and cooperate to fully use the habitat;*
> 3 *gather and use energy efficiently;*
> 4 *optimize rather than maximize;*
> 5 *use materials sparingly;*
> 6 *don't foul their nests;*
> 7 *don't draw down resources;*
> 8 *remain in balance with the biosphere;*
> 9 *run on information;*
> 10 *shop locally.* (Benyus, 1997)

As we will see in Chapter 14, there are now a large number of companies intent on internalizing at least some of these ten commandments in the way that they deploy their manufactured capital. But this doesn't come without a substantial investment of human and intellectual capital, backed by an equally substantial financial involvement. It is to that final stock of capital that we must now turn.

References

Benyus, J. (1997) *Biomimicry: Innovation Inspired by Nature*, Quill, William Morrow, New York

Brown, L. (2003) *Plan B*, W. W. Norton, New York

Commoner, B. (1971) *The Closing Circle: Nature, Man, and Technology*, Random House, London

Douglas, E. (2007) 'Better by design', *New Scientist*, 6 January

Ekins, P. (2000) *Economic Growth and Environmental Sustainability*, Routledge, London

Leggett, J. (2003) 'Here comes the sun', *New Scientist*, 6 September

McDonough, W. and Braungart, M. (2002) *Cradle to Cradle*, North Point Press, New York

Meadows, D., Meadows, D., Randers, J. and Behrens III, W. W. (1972) *Limits to Growth*, Universe Books, New York

Stern, N. (2007) *The Economics of Climate Change: The Stern Review*, Cambridge University Press, Cambridge

Tenner, E. (1996) *Why Things Bite Back*, Fourth Estate, London

Financial Capital

INTRODUCTION

Economists will tell you that financial capital shouldn't really be included in any model of this kind since it's not a capital stock in its own right, but just a means of exchange between other kinds of capital. That may be so, but the uses to which financial capital are put have a huge impact upon the prospects of us ever achieving a genuinely sustainable society – from the role money plays in our own lives, all the way through to the way today's capital markets operate, with their increasingly destructive emphasis on short-term profit maximization in the service of disloyal and footloose investors. That makes it all the harder for companies to balance the interests of other stakeholders, even if (as we will explore in much greater detail in Chapter 14) there now exists a robust and persuasive 'business case' for companies getting themselves sorted on their key social, environmental and ethical responsibilities. And there are still those, of course, who believe that money is indeed the root of all evil – the principal source of psychological alienation and unsustainable lifestyles in today's consumer capitalism.

DEFINING FINANCIAL CAPITAL

The role of financial capital is perhaps the least understood of all the categories of capital now seen as essential to a sustainable economic system. Indeed, it is usually excluded from such models on the grounds that financial capital has no intrinsic value, is not *essential* for the production of goods and services, and simply provides a means of exchange for the fruits of other categories of capital. Paper assets that make up the stocks of money, bonds and equities have no value in themselves, but are simply derivatives of the underlying manufactured, natural, social or human capital stocks. In that fundamental sense, financial capital is *not* a separate category to the other capital stocks, but, as will be explained in this chapter, an aspect of social capital.

But that's not the whole story. In a world where all businesses and consumers had perfect information and foresight, exchange in the marketplace would be a simple matter. Businesses seeking to invest in new manufactured capital would know who had surplus funds, and the saver or lender would know that the borrower would be able to repay the loan in the future. There would be no transaction costs associated with combining the right amounts of manufactured, human and natural capital to produce the goods and services desired. There would be no need for banks to attract and agglomerate surplus funds, or to select and monitor the projects or businesses to which they might lend. In fact, there would be no need even for the paper assets of money, bond or equity since investors would know who has surplus human or natural capital to construct the new bit of machinery required. The reason that this is not the way the world works is information or, rather, its imperfections. Imperfect information gives economic and social value to the paper assets, markets, institutions and, most importantly, social conventions that make up the stock of financial capital.

Imperfect information means that there will always be an important role for financial capital to play in the production of goods and services. That comes from the role financial markets and institutions play in allocating funds between different businesses and individual borrowers. It also derives from the social conventions that enable the paper assets, financial markets and institutions to function. Recall Putnam's (2000) definition of social capital as being 'networks', 'norms' and 'trust'. Financial markets and institutions are networks with built-in norms; and 'trust' forms a key element of financial capital. Financial markets are therefore 'network capital' in the same sense as those networks described in Chapter 9 on social capital.

Institutions such as retail and commercial banks, investment banks, asset managers and insurers provide the stocks of specialist information and expertise. They have accumulated organizational and individual knowledge on how to attract the resources from savers to provide to borrowers, on how to select and monitor projects or businesses to lend to, and on how to transfer, share, pool or diversify the risks inherent in making a loan that may not be repaid (see Figure 11.1).

Social conventions are the final facet of financial capital. As with trust and norms in relation to social capital, these are also an important (if not the most important) aspect of financial capital. Dogs' teeth in the Admiralty Islands, seashells in parts of Africa, gold during the 19th century, token (notes and coins) and IOU (bank deposits) money today, internet money, time dollars in the US – all are examples of money. What matters is not the physical commodity, but the social convention or norm that it will be accepted without question as a means of payment.

Financial capital, like all other forms of capital, depreciates as it is used and can be degraded if abused. It needs investment and good stewardship to continue to provide the flow of services required at the same rate and quality. The role of governments in shaping financial markets should therefore never be underestimated, whatever the prevailing deregulatory rhetoric may seem to imply. Above all, incentives need to be designed in such a way that private self-interest

Source: Forum for the Future

Figure 11.1 *Stocks of financial capital*

is not incompatible with securing socially beneficial outcomes. As Stephen Young says:

> For incentives to be properly aligned, governments must do their part. Title to property and a marketable interest, such as ownership of inventions, must be secure; contracts must be enforced; currencies must be stable; corruption must be prevented; bankruptcy laws must permit smooth realignment of interests after misjudgements have brought on business failure; information necessary for accurate valuation of assets and correct pricing must be provided openly; and financial institutions must be prevented from funding speculative bubbles. (Young, 2003)

GOVERNANCE FAILURES

So much for the basics, in terms of understanding the role of financial capital in today's global economy. But this is not the value-free, depoliticized terrain that many would have us believe: issues regarding both the ownership and the use of financial capital go right to the heart of what sustainability means, and to the prospects of fashioning a genuinely sustainable future for humankind.

As suggested in Part I, there are many aspects of contemporary capitalism that are in direct conflict with the pursuit of sustainability. There is still considerable debate as to whether these incompatibilities are structural and permanent (in other words, inherent, unavoidable elements in all models of capitalism) or temporary, aberrant phenomena that can be transformed into a different set of system characteristics that *would* be compatible with the pursuit of sustainability. The working hypothesis in this book is that compatibility is *theoretically* available to us, even though the political and economic challenges in engineering that convergence are daunting.

In the *Divine Right of Capital*, for instance, Marjorie Kelly (2001) challenged the dominant model of contemporary shareholder capitalism in an attempt to develop a new consensus. For her, many of the fundamental attributes of capitalism (supply and demand, competition, profit, self-interest, private property and free trade) are, indeed, fine – 'sturdy, healthy and well worth keeping'. But the whole complex edifice of capitalism is for her threatened by the contemporary obsession with maximizing returns to shareholders:

> *To judge by the current arrangement in corporate America, one might suppose capital creates wealth – which is strange, because a pile of private capital sitting there creates nothing. Yet capital providers – stockholders – lay claim to most of the wealth the public corporations generate. Corporations are believed to exist to maximize returns to shareholders. This is the law of the land, much as the divine right of kings was once the law of the land. In the dominant paradigm of business, it is not in the least controversial. Though it should be.* (Kelly, 2001)

Part of Kelly's analysis as to why this approach to investment has become so dysfunctional depends upon scotching the myth that it is shareholders who create wealth through the investment they make in companies. According to figures from the Federal Reserve in the US, about $1 in $100 trading on Wall Street actually reaches companies. The other $99 are all speculatively invested. In 1999, the value of new stock sold was $106 billion; the value of all shares traded was $20.4 trillion. By the time stock buy-backs are taken into account, as well as dividends paid by companies to shareholders, an extraordinary picture emerges:

> *New equity sales were a negative source of funding in 15 out of the 20 years from 1981 to 2000. In other words, when you look back over two decades, you can't find any net stockholder money going in – it's all going out. The net outflow since 1981 for new equity issues was $540 billion. Rather than capitalizing companies, the stock market has been de-capitalizing them. Stockholders for decades have been an immense cash drain on corporations. They are the deadest of dead wood. It's inaccurate even to speak of stockholders as 'investors', for more truthfully*

they are 'extractors'. When we buy stock, we are not contributing capital:
we are buying the right to extract wealth. (Kelly, 2001)

This analysis has been powerfully reinforced by Henry Mintzberg in a 'Memo to CEOs', written for *Fast Company* in June 2002. Reminding CEOs of the origins of corporations and the initial rationale behind granting them their charters – to serve society – he suggests that shareholders have essentially 'muscled out' all other stakeholders whom a company must deal with, and that CEOs have been complicit in this (inadvertently or not) given that their own remuneration over the last decade has become more and more closely tied to share price and shareholder return through stock options and other performance incentives.

There might be some justification for this approach if the majority of shareholders had any long-term commitment to the companies in which they invest – of which they are the 'theoretical' owners. But in reality, investment markets today are dominated by huge funds that buy and sell millions of shares on a daily basis following a variety of tracker indexes, or by day-traders out for tiny shifts in share price. Boards of directors are in thrall to institutions and individuals who have no concern for their companies, their products and services, let alone their employees or the communities in which they are based.

As many commentators have pointed out since the collapse of Enron and other huge US companies, this servitude to detached and indifferent shareholders (mediated through hugely influential market analysts) has led to a pattern of self-serving, irresponsible and illegal behaviour that would beggar belief if it was not such a logical consequence of everything that's been going on over the last 20 years. In terms of the balance between different kinds of capital (particularly financial capital and human capital), this makes it a great deal harder to deploy capital to secure equitable and genuinely sustainable outcomes. As Henry Mintzberg says:

Shareholder value thus drives a wedge between those who create the economic performance and those who harvest its benefits. It is a wedge of disengagement, both between the two groups and within each. Those who create the benefits are disengaged from the ownership of their efforts and treated as dispensable, while those who own the enterprise treat that ownership as dispensable and so disengage themselves from its activities. Can we have healthy corporations, and a healthy society, without commitment? (Mintzberg, 2002)

These concerns have been exacerbated by the extraordinary growth in two categories of financial products over the last few years: hedge funds and private equity. Although the scale of both may still be relatively small (it is believed, for instance, that only about 3 per cent of the world's total investment assets are controlled by hedge fund managers (that's somewhere between £600 billion and

£750 billion), it is the combination of increased risk and reduced transparency that is now commanding unprecedented attention. With investment banks and even pension funds ever more anxious to provide even quite questionable hedge funds with all the borrowing they are looking for, any downturn in the fortunes of these funds could have incredibly damaging impacts all across the system. (When the firm Long Term Capital Management collapsed in 1998, for example, it was believed to have borrowed more than 50 times the assets it had under management.) And few are persuaded that financial regulators either in the US or in Europe are sufficiently well prepared to cope with the complexity and secrecy of an industry that prefers wherever possible to keep itself out of the limelight.

As indeed did the world of private equity until it renounced its relative obscurity to move into the full glare of publicity with a growing number of huge takeover bids for major companies in both the US and Europe. This has plunged it into unprecedented controversy, with a growing coalition of trade unions, politicians, academics, media commentators and NGOs campaigning against 'unaccountable capital' of every kind, becoming increasingly outspoken in their condemnation of 'asset-stripping locusts' – as such funds are often described in Germany.

This may be a little unfair, but evidence is indeed mounting that stocks of natural, social and human capital (evidenced, for instance, by severe cuts in research, training and personal development), are being even more severely depleted than would be the case if the enterprises involved had remained as publicly-traded companies (since as such, they would have been subject to the kind of scrutiny and third-party stakeholder pressure which mandates far higher standards of transparency and accountability). There is also growing concern, especially in the UK, that private equity owners have so successfully manipulated tax laws that they are depriving the Treasury of billions of pounds. There was a frisson of shock in May 2007 when one of the grandees of the private equity world broke ranks with his peers in acknowledging that the executives running private equity firms 'are paying less tax than a cleaning lady'.

A much more benign role for private equity emerged in February 2007 when two huge private interests in the US (KKR and Texas Pacific) based their proposed buyout of the Texas-based energy firm TXU on an uncompromisingly 'green' proposition. It agreed to scrap seven out of the 11 new coal-fired plants that TXU had been planning (which would have emitted 78 million tonnes of carbon dioxide every year!), to support an emissions trading programme and to invest massively in energy efficiency schemes. This was hailed by environmental organizations as a signal that capital markets (and private equity interests in particular) were at last waking up to the realities of a carbon-constrained world.

That's all well and good, but it's difficult to see, on a more global basis, how today's huge extensions of what has understandably been dubbed as 'casino capitalism' are likely to make the global economy more resilient, let alone more sustainable. In effect, it's becoming clearer and clearer that we've wasted the best part of 20 years pursuing to the point of utter exhaustion a model of capitalism that can only succeed by liquidating the life-support systems that sustain us and systematically widening the 'inequity gaps' upon which any kind of social cohesion depends in the long run. It seems impossible to imagine that people will be prepared to condone such a system for very much longer; but it is a sobering thought that it's now at least 20 years since a generation of eminent economists (such as J. K. Galbraith, Robert Heilbroner and Fred Hirsch) flagged the inevitability of this particular model's failure.

These chronic dysfunctionalities now cast such a pall over the workings of the world's capital markets as to prejudice the efforts of all those working to secure a more sustainable utilization of capital within the existing system. It is an extraordinary irony that at exactly the same time as a large number of deeply immoral corporate executives were doing everything they could to line their own pockets, often at the expense of their companies and the entire system of wealth creation that supported them, a quite different group of people (made up of other business leaders, academics and progressive NGOs) has been seeking a radically different business model for more sustainable wealth creation.

The business case

The evolution of the so-called 'business case for sustainable development' represents an interesting shift towards 'a more successful capitalism', and has generated a growing amount of coverage over the last few years. At the heart of this business case is a simple but powerful proposition: if it can be demonstrated that the interests of shareholders, over time, are best served by companies that seek radically to improve their social, environment and ethical performance, then capital could be allocated against a different set of criteria, and short-term profit maximization would cease to be the driving force (creating an inherently destructive model of capitalism). This, it has to be said, makes the business case for sustainable development a rather more interesting concept than those who see it primarily in terms of saving small amounts of money by installing a few energy-efficient light bulbs.

It's possible to be cautiously optimistic about such an hypothesis. In a piece of research commissioned by the Co-operative Insurance Society in 2002, conducted by Brian Pearce, Forum for the Future's Centre for Sustainable Investment found that the majority of academic studies carried out from the 1970s to the 1990s were able to demonstrate evidence of a positive correlation between environmentally and socially responsible business practices and financial performance (Pearce, 2002). This is not as definitive and substantive a correlation as many people are looking for. But for those who can remember the days in which any environmental investment or any decision to practise more socially responsible business behaviours was dismissed as anti-business and a constraint upon competitiveness, such findings (confirmed by a large number of studies over the last ten years) are certainly significant.

There is, of course, a conundrum here. If a reconciliation between the pursuit of profitability and the achievement of genuine sustainability seems at least potentially feasible, looking at this collective experience, why are politicians so slow to drive those policy measures that would accelerate such a convergence? And if there would appear to be no threat to the paramount interests of shareholders (with investments in those pioneering companies generating at least average returns and possibly even some small additional premium), why are the world's capital markets still so slow to ensure that capital is being allocated in such a way as to reflect the desirability of securing the Earth's life-support systems even as we secure a good return on our investments?

Paul Gilding and his colleagues at the Ecos Corporation suggest that the answer to this problem lies in the flawed advocacy of those promoting the business case, with an overdependence on moral imperatives and an inappropriate appeal to values and ethics. For him, the exclusive focus should be on the financial *value* to be had in designing and implementing corporate sustainability strategies (Gilding, 2002).

As we will see in Chapter 14, there are, indeed, many companies intent on pursuing that hard-nosed approach to defining a competitive business case for their shareholders. For other companies, that just doesn't work culturally, in terms of the values through which they run the business. Matsushita, for instance, still follows the precept of its founder Konosuke Matsushita, embodying the notion that a company is a 'public entity of society'. Its basic management objective – 'Recognizing our responsibilities as industrialists, we will devote ourselves to the progress and development of society and the wellbeing of people through our business activities, thereby enhancing the quality of life throughout the world' – doesn't even mention shareholders. In refreshing contrast to most companies' stodgy corporate responsibility/sustainable development reports, Matsushita is quite happy to wear its heart on its sleeve in terms of its ambitions to relieve world poverty and achieve 'material and spiritual prosperity'.

One way or another, most companies are now seeking out a balance between the interests/demands of their shareholders and their responsibilities to other stakeholders. Few, though, have thought as systematically about those responsibilities as the Danish healthcare and pharmaceuticals company Novo Nordisk. In annual sustainability reports, they provide admirable summaries as to why this kind of strategic approach now works so well for them (see Figure 11.2). Interestingly, Novo Nordisk is one of the few global companies to have tried to tease out the difference between its financial performance and its broader economic performance. As mentioned in Chapter 2, far too many companies have interpreted the financial element of their triple bottom line accounting in very narrow terms: profits, net present value, productivity, return on investment and

Examples of our stakeholder engagement

Meetings with neighbours to reduce environmental impacts at production sites

Evaluating suppliers' social and environmental performance

Personal meetings between employees and patients

Partnerships with NGOs on animal welfare

Memberships of business organisations to promote sustainable development

Raising public debate on stem cell research and the need for revised legislation

Putting diabetes on the agenda in the European Parliament

Stakeholders

Business organisations
Local communities
Media
Investors
Universities
Authorities
Healthcare professionals
Citizens
Government
Patients
Novo Nordisk
Suppliers
NGOs

Novo Nordisk's approach

In today's complex society, Novo Nordisk's world view is but one among many different perspectives. Our stakeholder engagement is founded in a reflective understanding of others' positions and motives. Relations with stakeholders are not static, but depend on the nature of the relationship.

The multi-stakeholder approach helps Novo Nordisk align with different views and focus on the issues that are central to earn our societal licence to operate and innovate.

Figure 11.2 *Novo Nordisk's engagement with its stakeholders*

Source: Novo Nordisk (2002)

so on. But economic performance is *not* the same thing as financial performance, as is now much more clearly laid out in the latest version of the Global Reporting Initiative's *Sustainability Reporting Guidelines*. Companies are now expected to provide information on where they generate their income, on taxes paid, on how different stakeholders benefit from their activities and on other 'economic multipliers'.

This recognition of the importance of addressing *all* externalities (social, economic and environmental – both positive and negative) will clearly allow companies to give a much better account of the way in which they are managing their financial capital.

In 2003, under growing pressure from NGOs, some of the world's largest financial institutions (including ABN AMRO, Bank of America, Barclays, Citigroup, HSBC, Standard Chartered and the Royal Bank of Scotland) developed a new framework for managing environmental and social impacts in financing new projects that have a total capital cost of $50 million or more. The so-called 'Equator Principles' have already had a marked impact upon the way in which foreign direct investment is being managed to secure 'optimized benefits for the long term' rather than short-term economic gains – although it has to be said that many NGOs remain extremely sceptical about the degree to which behaviour has really changed at the end of the day.

But how best to determine which actions will most powerfully reinforce such a business case? From the perspective of natural capital, I have already suggested that The Natural Step (TNS) framework offers one of the few authoritative ways of assessing whether or not any proposed new investment will be working to maintain or enhance stocks of natural capital. From a financial perspective, there are familiar techniques that are just as relevant here as with any other investment decision, including return on capital employed, economic value added, weighted average cost of capital and discounted cash flow.

There has been much discussion about the business case for sustainable development over the last few years, but surprisingly few hard-edged attempts at measuring it in any serious way. The Co-op Bank and BT (see Chapter 14) have made notable efforts at measuring the value to their shareholders of their ethical and corporate social responsibility (CSR) policies. However, the numbers revealed are usually small, and the response of analysts whom they are trying to impress has usually been 'So what? This tells me nothing of what is *really* driving the success of your company.' A huge opportunity is being missed by the concentration on eco-efficiency, cost savings and 'green premiums' by most valuation efforts to date. The real *business* value of sustainability must come from the added value it generates for the particular company, from the ways in which it protects and develops that company's strategic assets, and from the competitive advantage that flows from the responsible use of all five stocks of capital.

BRINGING FINANCIAL CAPITAL DOWN TO EARTH

All of this is genuinely encouraging in terms of promoting more environmentally and socially responsible behaviour within the existing economic and financial structures. But if those structures are themselves dysfunctional and incapable of delivering genuine sustainability, then what we're really talking about here is damage limitation rather than transformation. In that case, we cannot any longer put off the need for far more radical proposals regarding the way in which financial capital is created, distributed, owned and used. David Korten doesn't beat around the bush in identifying the root cause of our current problems:

> *The problem is this: a predatory global financial system, driven by the single imperative of making ever more money for those who already have lots of it, is rapidly depleting the real capital – the human, social, natural and even manufactured capital – upon which our wellbeing depends. Pathology enters the economic system when money, once convenient as a means of facilitating commerce, comes to define the life purpose of individuals and society. The truly troubling part is that so many of us have become willing accomplices to what is best described as a war of money against life. It starts, in part, from our failure to recognize that money is not wealth. In our confusion, we concentrate on the money to the neglect of those things that actually sustain a good life.* (Korten, 1997)

But what can we do about it? Some, as we saw in Chapter 8, prescribe a decade-long process of 'metaphysical reconstruction' (as Fritz Schumacher described it) to restore a proper sense of value and balance in people's lives; others, as we've seen, dream of a great global movement gathering enough momentum to compel politicians to dethrone both the elites and the redundant economic orthodoxies that still dominate out lives; most campaigners chip away at the edges, looking for the occasional opening that allows the breadth of more radical reform to enter into what they see as a seriously corrupted system. But it is extremely difficult for most people to get a sense of the ferment of ideas that is going on out there given that our mainstream media rarely, if ever, reach out beyond the completely safe confines of financial orthodoxy.

Why is it, for instance, that we are never invited to think more creatively about the question of monetary reform and the impact that today's monetary system has upon the pursuit of sustainability? Social justice campaigners are understandably focused on questions of debt, aid and trade in their tireless efforts to find a more equitable set of global financial arrangements – but rarely question the monetary system itself. Environmental campaigners focus on taxation issues, perverse subsidies, improved accounting systems and so on, but are about as interested in monetary reform as they are in the issue of population.

James Robertson has been proposing radical ideas ever since his ground-breaking book *The Sane Alternative* in 1978. His most recent publication is *Monetary Reform: Making it Happen*, co-authored with John M. Bunzl (2003), focusing on the utterly perverse way in which money supply is managed in almost all countries. For instance, about 97 per cent of the UK's money supply is created by commercial banks more or less out of thin air as interest-bearing (profit-making) loans; the remaining 3 per cent is created debt-free by the Bank of England and the Royal Mint as bank notes and coins. The banks in the UK make about £20 billion a year in interest from this arrangement.

Few people really understand the links between indebtedness, economic growth and sustainability. But at every level in the economy (from national debt to corporate debt to farm debt to personal debt), the growth imperative is that much more powerful because increases in economic growth are in part needed in order to pay off the interest on those debts. In the UK, the most indebted country in Europe, personal debt now exceeds £1.3 trillion, with more than 1 million people in real and present danger of being tipped over into insolvency in the event of the economy going into any kind of downturn. UK banks are already increasing their provision for bad debts, and more and more politicians are beginning to question the wisdom of building an economy on such shifting sands – 'an economy built on borrowed money is built on borrowed time'.

It is pretty much the same story all around the world, and one wonders quite how we've allowed ourselves to get into this situation – as J. K. Galbraith himself put it: 'The process by which banks create money is so simple the mind is repelled [...] where something so important is involved, a deeper mystery seems only decent' (Galbraith, 1975). The money supply created in this way is not linked to real resource use or to the amount of goods and services in the national economy – it is based entirely upon the banks' commercial judgement about the ability of an individual or an enterprise to repay their loans. The more money there is, the more debt there is; as the money supply increases, so does a nation's indebtedness.

Robertson's proposal (backed by a growing number of experts in this area) is a simple but comprehensive one: take away this power from the commercial banks and transfer it to the Bank of England, which can then give the money debt free to the government to spend into circulation. In one fell swoop, taxation can either be substantially reduced or public spending substantially increased; a debt-free money supply will help reduce levels of public and private debt; the economy will become more stable; the Bank of England will be better able to control inflation; and, lastly, environmental stress will be reduced. When, as now, almost all of the money we use is debt, people have to produce and sell more things in order to service and repay debt than they would if money were put into circulation debt free.

Many now believe that without that kind of monetary reform, we are un-likely to sort out the huge problems that confront benefits and welfare systems throughout the rich world. Over the last few decades, there have been all sorts of proposals to replace intensely complicated, costly and fundamentally unfair benefits systems with some kind of 'citizens' income' – also known as the basic income, social dividend or negative income tax. One stalwart in these debates is Clive Lord, whose short primer (*A Citizens' Income: A Foundation for a Sustainable World*, 2003) on this neglected yet critical area of radical reform raises a profound challenge for mainstream political parties in the UK:

> *The citizens' income is based on the principle that every man, woman and child should receive a weekly sum sufficient to cover the basic needs of food, fuel, clothing and accommodation. It will be tax-free, paid to individuals and unconditional. So everyone will keep it whether they are working or not, or even whether they need it or not. The citizens' income will replace all existing social security benefits and income tax allowances for the able bodied. In short, the citizens' income is the unconditional provision of basic necessities for all from a common fund, provided by members of the community as a whole according to their ability to pay.* (Lord, 2003)

Again, this is not something that most environmentalists (or even, it has to be said, most campaigners for a more equitable economy) have paid much attention to. It just doesn't seem to command the same level of political engagement, even though, over the years, a surprising number of eminent economists have ended up acknowledging just how significant a reform this could be – including those polar opposites of Milton Friedman, on the one hand, and J. K. Galbraith, on the other. As Margaret Legum (2002) points out in *It Doesn't Have to Be Like This* (which includes one of the best expositions of the benefits of a citizens' income or basic income), there are now groups actively involved in researching or promulgating similar approaches in Holland, Ireland, Spain, Sweden, France, Germany, New Zealand, Australia, Brazil, Canada and the US – as well as the UK. By her reckoning:

> *Brazil is out in front. Some municipalities are already paying something like a basic income grant as a monthly payment to households, not individuals. Research already shows that where the household grant is in place, employment rises and crime drops.* (Legum, 2002)

On the whole question of ownership, we would appear yet again to be stuck in some very predictable tramlines. If private property is one of those fundamental characteristics of capitalism (as briefly explored in Chapter 4), then a constant examination of the ease with which people can get access to the ownership of land and other assets, or the use of credit, is obviously critical. I have already mentioned the work of the Peruvian economist Hernando de Soto, whose hugely stimulating book *The Other Path* (1989) documents in great detail how lack of secure title for poor people in developing countries seriously inhibits economic development. By his calculation, there are around $9 trillion worth of undeclared assets across the world's poorest people – 'undeclared' because they belong to squatters without legal title – which cannot be leveraged to encourage self-reliant entrepreneurial activity. As one concrete example of what a difference this can make, he cites a study showing that investment in home improvements increased nine-fold when squatters in townships around Lima gained title to their homes. Throughout South America, land on which there is no secure title is often overexploited by peasant farmers who have no expectation of settled residence; 'land stewardship' becomes a meaningless nonsense without that kind of security.

Closer to home, the American lawyer and activist Jeff Gates has campaigned strenuously to show how extending access to various ownership opportunities can work directly for a more sustainable economy. *The Ownership Solution* (Gates, 1998) is an extraordinary book that starts from the premise that the real problem with capitalism today is that there are so few practising capitalists! Ownership of assets is restricted to such a tiny number of people that the momentum towards increased inequity and injustice is all but unstoppable. Starting with the already familiar (employee share-ownership schemes, for instance, or co-operatives), he then reviews a battery of different ways in which 'a pragmatic ownership strategy could weave a broader web of personal, economic and civic participation'.

Some of the alternatives are already quietly getting on with things out of the public eye. Perhaps the best known of these in the UK is the John Lewis Partnership, or, in the US, United Airlines, which is 55 per cent employee owned. One of my favourites is the Scott Bader Commonwealth, a successful chemical company founded in 1921 and reconstituted as a charitable trust in 1951. Its founder, Ernest Bader, believed passionately that 'a world where capital employs labour is not sustainable, and that labour should employ capital, acknowledging the quality of everyone as individuals'. Membership of the Commonwealth, and with it co-ownership of the various operating companies, is open to all employees once they have worked for the company for a specific period of time. It remains a successful enterprise – and a hugely inspiring example that it really is possible to do things differently.

But there is so much more that could be done in this area, especially by those who are concerned for the future of capitalism itself. As Jeff Gates says:

> *Today's capitalism embodies a curious and dangerous inconsistency. It extols the necessity of private ownership. Yet, while the capital is there and so is the capitalism, what's missing are people who can rightly be called capitalists. The reason for this is poorly understood: contemporary capitalism is not designed to create capitalists, but to finance capital. Without political will those dramatically different goals will never be combined. A more participatory capitalism could gradually displace today's exclusive, detached and socially corrosive ownership patterns.*
> (Gates, 1998)

Many people have commented on the arrogance of the capitalist establishments in the Western world, particularly in New York and London, with their constant barrage of propaganda about the ineffable superiority of their particular model of capitalism. In fact, we might have just as much to learn from other countries as they do from us, and the inspiring example of the Grameen Bank in Bangladesh provides an excellent example of that kind of reverse flow of intellectual capital. One of the pioneers of today's micro-credit movement, the Grameen Bank makes small loans available to groups of women who don't meet conventional loan criteria simply because they don't have enough collateral. The bonds between the women in each group provide the critical social capital, based upon informal networks and trust as well as the final sanction that the members of the group accept joint responsibility for repayment.

The success of the micro-credit movement provides perhaps the best example of how capital can be used in radically different, empowering and redistributive ways. But it's little more than a pinprick set against the power of today's global capital markets. Unfortunately the majority of people controlling or managing those markets are among the most greedy, self-obsessed and ecologically-illiterate people on the face of the Earth. Their denial of the true state of the Earth and its people is one of the greatest barriers we are up against today.

REFERENCES

de Soto, H. (1989) *The Other Path,* Harper & Row, New York
Galbraith, J. K. (1975) *Money: Whence It Came, Where It Went*, Houghton Mifflin, Boston, MA
Gates, J. (1998) *The Ownership Solution*, Penguin, London
Gilding, P. (2002) *Sustaining Economic Value*, Ecos Corporation, Sydney, Australia
Kelly, M. (2001) *The Divine Right of Capital*, Berrett-Koehler, San Francisco, CA
Korten, D. (1997) 'Money versus wealth', *Yes! A Journal of Positive Futures*, spring, www.hackvan.com/pub/stig/articles/yes-magazine-money-issue/Korten.html
Legum, M. (2002) *It Doesn't Have to Be Like This*, Wild Goose Publications, Glasgow, UK
Lord, C. (2003) *A Citizens' Income: A Foundation for a Sustainable World*, Jon Carpenter Publishing, Charlbury, UK
Mintzberg, H. (2002) 'Memo to CEOs', *Fast Company*, June
Novo Nordisk (2002) 'Sustainability report 2002', available at http://susrep2002.novonordisk.com/sustainability/default.asp
Pearce, B. (2002) *Sustainability Pays*, Centre for Sustainable Investment, Forum for the Future, Cheltenham, UK
Putnam, R. (2000) *Bowling Alone: The Collapse and Revival of American Community*, Simon and Schuster, New York
Robertson, J. (1978) *The Sane Alternative*, James Robertson, Cholsey, UK
Robertson, J. and Bunzl, J. M. (2003) *Monetary Reform: Making it Happen*, International Simultaneous Policy Organization, London
Young, S. (2003) *Moral Capitalism: Reconciling Private Interest with the Public Good*, Berrett-Koehler, San Francisco, CA

PART III

BETTER LIVES IN A BETTER WORLD

12

Confronting Denial

INTRODUCTION

Sticking with the hypothesis that it's theoretically possible to transform the workings of contemporary capitalism in order to achieve a sustainable economy, you have then got to ask why it is proving so difficult to address that transformative challenge – bringing us back to the uncomfortable but pervasive phenomenon of *denial*. As we saw in Part I, it's all but impossible to ignore the accelerating decline in our life-support systems; yet politicians seem paralysed by the immensity of the changes required. They've started to get climate change, but they still absolutely don't get any deeper analysis of our total dependence on the natural world. What this means is that we have to completely rethink our understanding of *security*. The billions of dollars we currently spend on arms and military security (not least on the increasingly costly 'war against terror') are systematically undermining the ecological and social conditions upon which our long-term security actually depends. The continuing dependence of the US upon wholly unsustainable supplies of oil, particularly in the Middle East, inflicts massive direct and indirect costs on both its own citizens and the rest of the world, hampering efforts to address issues of chronic poverty in developing countries and equally pressing issues of collapsing natural systems.

THE CAPACITY FOR DENIAL

The Five Capitals Framework presented in Part II draws upon ideas from many different disciplines: economics, ecology, sociology, psychology and so on. This does not as yet constitute a fully worked-up reform agenda for capitalism; but what it does seek to do is provide the context within which that all-important question about the compatibility between capitalism and sustainability can be pursued. I fear that still won't make it appealing to mainstream politicians, though. Their capacity for denial remains extraordinary, not so much in terms of denial of the empirical environmental and social data (which is now largely undeniable), but rather denial of the *implications* of that data. For most, the basic model of progress (achieved through unfettered growth in an increasingly global economy) still remains sound, requiring only a little bit of market-based corrective action for the environment and more concerted efforts to address poverty in the world's poorest countries. A few, however, are beginning to question and even lose faith in the model itself; and one particular aspect of our latter-day Faustian bargain (that it is acceptable to go on trashing the planet for a better life today) looks increasingly suspect. But why do these voices still command relatively little traction in politics and the media today?

The field of cognitive psychology tells us that even at the best of times most humans have real difficulty coping with uncertainty and complexity; when overwhelmed, we tend to fall back on familiar 'rules of thumb', reassuring habits and defensive routines. It's only human to want to maintain a worldview or a way of life that suits us, and to block out that which puts it at risk. Emotionally, it's even harder to cope with grave threats to our wellbeing or to those we love, especially if we feel there's little we can do about it – and often default to 'sanity-maintaining' mechanisms of repression, denial, detachment, hopelessness or anger. 'Denial' does not need a conspiracy to make it work; it just needs normal people who like the way their world is organized. In the face of today's portfolio of environmental 'horror stories', Thomas Homer-Dixon points to the three layers of defensive barriers that people erect:

> First we might try **existential denial**: in this case, we'll say the environmental problem in question – for instance, climate change – simply doesn't exist. But if the weight of evidence becomes impossible to ignore, we can turn to **consequential denial**. Here, we'll admit the problem exists, but say it really doesn't matter. Finally, if we can't credibly deny both the problem's existence and its consequences, we might say we can't do anything about it. **This is fatalistic denial.** For the die-hard environmental sceptic, fatalistic denial is a last and all-but-impenetrable line of psychological defence. (Homer-Dixon, 2006)

Each of these mechanisms can be powerfully reinforced in the face of *apparent* uncertainty ('perhaps all this stuff will just go away after all'), and continuing controversy ('if so-and-so believes that, and I trust so-and-so, then we'll probably be OK'), even when it's patently obvious that much of that controversy can be traced back to people and organizations with deeply vested interests in keeping people in denial. This poses a serious problem for educators and advocates for change: straightforward scientific evidence – however authoritative and objectively convincing – will not necessarily be sufficient to stimulate changed attitudes and behaviours, unless that evidence can be 'framed' in such a way that it also makes sense at a deeper 'values-based' level. As Ian Christie says:

> What we see here are a series of 'culture wars'. The climate debate is a culture war, for sure. And the broader struggles over sustainable

development are also of this kind. At stake are basic beliefs about the relationship between people and planet, the values that should underpin human society and striving, and the place of the money economy in our lives. Seeing sustainability as the focus for a culture war helps us understand why the accumulating evidence of unsustainable development makes so little difference to politics and business as usual. Deep-rooted cultural factors make it all too easy to live in denial of unsustainability. (Christie, 2004)

But we can't make sense of this particular 'moment in time' without that scientific evidence either. So let's just take stock – before moving on to much more positive perspectives in the final chapters – of the full weight of the evidence that so many people continue to deny the significance of.

NATURE DENIED

It remains the case that the debate about the scale and speed of today's ecological crisis is not an easy one to track, and because it has been rumbling on for more than three decades – albeit episodically and inadequately – there is an understandable assumption across society that so much worrying away at something *must* have got it all sorted out by now. As we saw in Chapter 1, some things do, indeed, get sorted – such as the gradual recovery of the protective ozone layer after prompt action was taken nearly 20 years ago to eliminate the use of most ozone-depleting chemicals. However, the fact that it will take at least another 40 years to restore the ozone layer to its proper state is a cautionary aspect of this success story that all too often gets overlooked. Indeed, recent evidence from the United Nations Environment Programme (UNEP) on the scale of smuggling in ozone-depleting chemicals demonstrates that even this isn't quite the 'done deal' that it is customarily portrayed as.

Beyond that, in the developed world at least, the consequence of at least 30 years' worth of environmental regulation has ensured significant improvements in the quality of our drinking water and bathing waters, a reduction in the use of toxic chemicals, some improvements in local air quality (in most, if not all, places) and so on.

There are, therefore, enough success stories to encourage the so-called 'cornu-copians' (those who trust in the 'limitless bounty' of the Earth and in its capacity for self-healing) to continue to dismiss environmentalists as an irritating swarm of whining Cassandras and Jeremiahs with nothing better to do than promise imminent doom. One of the most outspoken of these cornucopian contrarians is Bjorn Lomborg, whose book *The Skeptical Environmentalist* (2001) created an absolute furore about the degree to which the natural world was or wasn't falling to pieces.

Lomborg was a gift for most countries' predominantly right-wing media, allowing them to vent their accumulated spleen at a global environment movement that has consistently chipped away at their own complacency and subservience to big business. Unfortunately for them, their star contrarian flew a bit too close to the sun and plummeted Icarus-like to Earth when the Danish Committee on Scientific Dishonesty came to the conclusion that his book was 'clearly contrary to the standards of good scientific practice. Objectively speaking, the publication of the work under consideration is deemed to fall within the concept of scientific dishonesty.' This won't necessarily deter future media-savvy contrarians. They know only too well how easy it is to play to the media's love of engineering a good debate: now that there is almost universal consensus about the seriousness of today's ecological crisis, the dissenters inevitably become much more interesting even as they become more extreme and more detached from the data, as we saw in Chapter 1 in relation to climate change.

However, it may just be that the seriousness of climate change has at last fixed itself in the minds of enough decision-makers to warrant more of a sense of urgency about the need for change. The extraordinary climatic events that we see more and more of every year can just about be dismissed as 'extreme but still entirely natural phenomena, the like of which have been seen many times before'; but as we saw in Chapter 1, it's getting harder and harder to get away with this kind of denial.

But many other issues are not on the agenda. It is clear, for instance, from reports coming in from all over the world and particularly from Indonesia and other countries in Southeast Asia, that the world's tropical forests are being destroyed at as fast a rate today as when Friends of the Earth first forced this issue onto the global agenda during the mid-1980s. Twenty years on, and the forests are still coming down.

Unfortunately, that's true of all too many global issues, as the Earthwatch Institute's authoritative *State of the World* reports make clear year after year. We may have slowed the rate of decline, but almost *all* of the principal indicators of planetary wellbeing are still heading in the wrong direction. It's clear, for example, that there is far less awareness of the direct damage to our collective self-interest caused by the loss of biodiversity than there is for climate change. There's no active sense of the direct and indirect benefits we derive from the proper functioning of natural systems, as explained in Chapter 7, and no real awareness that the loss of these services could *directly* imperil our prospects. The only way I've ever been able to communicate this powerfully enough is by talking about bees – and all the other pollinators working away out there on our behalf.

Without pollinators, plants cannot produce the seeds that ensure their survival – and ours. More than 90 per cent of the world's 250,000 flowering plant species are pollinated by animals – birds, bats and lizards, but mostly insects. Eighty per cent of the world's cultivated crops are pollinated by wild and semi-wild pollinators; it's been calculated that honeybee pollination services are 60–100 times more valuable than the actual honey they produce, and the total value to agriculture runs into hundreds of billions of dollars – the price we would have to pay if the bees and other insects didn't do it for us. And yet, many farmers have little interest in this hidden source of economic value. The use of insecticides and herbicides (which destroy plants that pollinators need for their own food) can be devastating. Destruction of habitat further reduces pollinator numbers (contrary to people's instincts, only 15 per cent of our major crops are pollinated by domesticated bees), and in many parts of the world these man-made threats to bees (combined with the growing incidence of diseases of one kind or another) are already very serious. As Albert Einstein said, 'When the bees go extinct, it won't be long before the humans follow.'

Again, we're back to that core intellectual failing that lies at the heart of so many of today's environmental problems: a failure to recognize *systems*, and the importance of multiple complex relationships between organisms in those systems. In essence, because we only see each individual species in its own right, we have no idea what impact the damage we do to that species will have on *other* species: the system may look resilient right up to the point where one final assault from us precipitates total collapse. Paul Ehrlich used to compare this to popping rivets out of an aeroplane's wing: you can pop just so many and everything still seems fine, with the plane flying along absolutely as normal, but at some point there'll be one popped rivet too many, at which point the wing will fall off. And Thomas Homer-Dixon reminds us just how we've fallen into this massive misunderstanding of how systems really work:

> *At the heart of this view is the assumption that the economy is separate from nature, and operates much like a machine. The machine's behaviour is linear, predictable and reversible, so it can be managed by a planet-wide class of technocrats – including central bankers and government officials – trained in the arcane science of economics. An alternative theory would recognize that the economy is intimately connected with nature and its flows of energy. This larger economic–ecological system often doesn't act like a machine at all. Instead, its behaviour is marked by threshold effects, and often neither predictable nor controllable. An alternative view would also recognize that there are no good substitutes for some of the most precious things nature gives us, like biodiversity and a benign climate.* (Homer-Dixon, 2006)

In *Collapse*, Jared Diamond (2005) explores the phenomenon of denial in relation to earlier societies and civilizations (such as the Mayan civilization) which disappeared off the face of the Earth because of a failure to manage natural resources properly. His most lovingly developed case study is Easter Island ('the clearest example of a society that destroyed itself by overexploiting its own resources'), which he invites the reader to see as a 'metaphor, a worst-case scenario for what may lie ahead of us in our own future'. How could this particular collapse have happened? Or, as one of Diamond's students put it to him, 'What do you suppose the islander who cut down the last tree on Easter Island said to himself as he was doing it?' Given that in this instance there was no extreme shift in the island's climate at that time and no hostile invaders, why would any group of people commit 'ecocide' in such a dramatic fashion?

Diamond advances a number of potential explanations to that question in relation to *all* of the different collapses and near collapses that he explores. And a number of these explanations have direct relevance to our own ecological crisis: a failure to anticipate future consequences; an inability to read trends or see behind the phenomenon of 'creeping normalcy', with each year things getting just a little bit worse than the year before, but never bad enough for anyone to get too agitated; and the disproportionate power of detached elites, particularly when they condone or even positively promote what Diamond describes as 'rational bad behaviour' on the part of those who manage or use natural resources.

In Chapter 14, I will be focusing on the more benign influence of multinationals in promoting a more sustainable world. But their role as 'rational bad actors' over the last 40 years or more cannot go un-remarked, not least because of the horrifying legacy (environmental, social and economic) that their activities have left behind (on a continuing basis) in literally dozens of developing countries which they purported to be assisting. We should never forget this unedifying chapter in corporate history, much of which goes back to the phenomenon of 'licensed cost externalization', where governments set standards so low (and consumers settled for correspondingly low expectations) that companies could quite legally pollute, degrade, exploit, and cause irreversible ecological damage and lasting social misery.

There are now many accounts of this kind of 'rational' bad behaviour. I've already commented on Robert F. Kennedy's extraordinary book *Crimes Against Nature* (2004), which lays bare a litany of corporate greed and malpractice. But John Perkins's *Confessions of an Economic Hit Man* (2004) digs even deeper into the warped psychology of the individuals involved in this asset-stripping 'corporatocracy', revealing in extraordinary detail the conjunction of interests between an imperialistic US and large American companies securing massive development and infrastructure contracts all around the world – with America's 'national interest' top of the list of priorities:

> *The 'corporatocracy' is not a conspiracy, but its members do endorse common values and goals. One of the corporatocracy's most important functions is to perpetuate and continually expand and strengthen the system. The lives of those who 'make it' and their accoutrements – their mansions, yachts and private jets – are presented as models to inspire us all to consume, consume, consume. Every opportunity is taken to convince us that purchasing things is our civic duty, that pillaging the*

Earth is good for the economy and therefore serves our higher interest.
(Perkins, 2004)

At an individual level, most would consider such behaviour to be a deeply immoral example of personal denial, however rational it might be. But as we have seen, denial of this kind depends, in part, on maintaining the myth of the *amoral* corporation and on the 'separation of functions' which allows the same person to behave one way in his/her business life and quite differently as a mother or father or 'pillar of the local community'. The deeper irrationality usually lies elsewhere – in those who license such behaviour for perverted ideological reasons (such as the neo-conservative empire-builders in Washington today), notwithstanding the growing body of evidence that this particular model of economic warfare is entirely unsustainable in both ecological and social terms, and in those who continue to elect such governments even as they turn a blind eye to the symptoms of chronic failure all around them.

Having reviewed a wide range of collapses and near collapses, Jared Diamond spends an equal amount of time dissecting those 'irrational' manifestations of denial. The often irreconcilable clash between the pursuit of short-term gratification and the defence of future generations' long-term interests features prominently in many of his collapse case studies – the concept of 'intergenerational justice' was clearly no more compelling to some of these long-gone societies than it is for us today. What's more, the greater the level of change required to a society's core values, the easier it becomes to lapse into systematic and falsely reassuring denial. Anticipating a wide range of rebuttals to his central hypothesis (that the kind of collapse experienced by many cultures and civilizations during the past could easily happen to modern-day societies), he reminds people that we are *already* witnessing the conditions for collapse in a number of different countries:

> *Just as in the past, countries that are environmentally stressed, over-populated or both become at risk of getting politically stressed, and of their governments collapsing. When people are desperate, undernourished and without hope, they blame their governments, which they see as responsible for or unable to solve their problems. They try to emigrate at any cost. They fight each other over land. They kill each other. They start civil wars. They figure that they have nothing to lose, so they become terrorists, or they support or tolerate terrorism.* (Diamond, 2005)

Many of us can more or less recognize this from afar as an emerging set of responses in our own world, a highly probable set of generic consequences that may have already been set in train by policies and events stretching back over many decades. The sight of more than a million people marching through the streets of London (and millions more around the world) in opposition to the war in Iraq in 2003 provided powerful testimony that very large numbers of people remain entirely unpersuaded by the geopolitical game plan being played out by Washington and its more compliant allies. But there is still enough residual comfort in 'better the devil you know than the devil you don't' mindsets to ensure that the lessons of history often go ignored.

This same combination of constant but low-level ill ease, compounded by a somewhat fatalistic sense of there not being very much that anyone can do about it, can be seen to be operating at the personal level as well as the geopolitical level. Surveys across the world (in rich and poor countries) demonstrate that people do, indeed, care about the state of the environment, particularly in terms of their own local environment. Where once environmental damage was accepted as the inevitable price to be paid for economic progress, there is now far less willingness to accept this as an unavoidable trade-off: why can't we have both economic progress and a secure, healthy environment?

However, there is also a school of thought (predominantly but not exclusively associated with the more extreme fringes of today's neo-conservative ideology) that this kind of meta-trade-off – humankind prospering, planet degrading – is rational, legitimate and not immoral. For such people, the concept of intergenerational justice (what one generation owes future generations) is philosophically flawed and a dangerous irrelevance; if people today are that concerned about the future, then they should reflect this in their own behaviour as an individual consumer and not expect governments to 'distort' markets today in the forlorn hope of protecting the interests of people tomorrow. In these terms, politics is about nothing more than the maximization of short-term individual gratification – a somewhat dispiriting reflection on that Enlightenment ideal of the perfectibility of humankind.

JUSTICE DENIED

When it comes to the reckoning, when we finally have to pay the bills for this systematic abuse of our natural wealth over the last few decades, it is one of the cruellest ironies that the poor will end up paying a far higher price than the rich. As we've seen, one of the most shocking aspects of the Fourth Assessment Report of the Intergovernmental Panel on Climate Change (IPCC) is its judgement that the impacts of rising temperatures and sea levels will hit poor countries faster and more furiously than those countries which have the resources to invest in some kind of adaptation.

Even without that massive additional burden, it's not hard to feel overwhelmed at the existing scale and persistence of poverty in so many parts of the world. But one of the great things about the Make Poverty History campaign in 2005, and all the new energy brought to bear on debt relief and trade issues over the last couple of years, was the constant refrain that there really is something we can still do about this. Over the last few years, far too many people have settled into a somewhat fatalistic state of mind about this state of affairs. Here's the dominant rationale: such poverty is certainly unfortunate and disturbing, but probably inevitable; after all, the poor have always been with us; a lot of it is 'their own fault' anyway – because of endemic corruption, political incompetence and a continuing failure to get on top of the problem of rising populations – so does it really make much difference what we do when we can do so little? And is there really any chance of delivering against all those 'motherhood and apple pie' declarations in the Millennium Development Goals? (See Box 12.1.)

Box 12.1 Goals and targets agreed at the United Nations Millennium Summit

- Halve the number of people living on less than $1 per day, currently 1.2 billion, by 2015.
- Achieve universal primary education, including the 113 million children with no access to primary schools.
- Eliminate all gender disparities by 2015 – for example, by narrowing the gap between genders in literacy, refugees and employment.
- Reduce by two-thirds the number of children dying before their fifth birthday, currently 11 million a year, by 2015.
- Reduce by two-thirds the ratio of women dying in childbirth (today the risk is 1 in 48 in developing nations).
- Halt and begin to reverse the spread of HIV; combat malaria and other diseases.
- Reverse the loss of environmental resources by 2015, including halving the population without access to safe drinking water.
- Develop a global partnership for development, including an open trading and financial system that includes a commitment to good governance, development and poverty reduction, tackling debt problems, provision of work for youth and access to affordable essential drugs in developing countries, and make available the benefits of new technologies – especially information and communications technologies.

Source: UN (2000)

Development organizations and developing world charities have to struggle against this downbeat and often deliberately distorted worldview. It's fair to say, however, that the balance sheet of the international development movement is not a brilliant one 60 years on from that extraordinary moment in human history when world leaders came together in the aftermath of World War II to fashion a new international order that (it was hoped) would eliminate poverty and keep all conflicts in check:

> *Half a century is enough for the system to have proved itself, and while there are a few well-publicized success stories, there has been no*

general gain in prosperity or security. We still live in a world scarred by absolutely poverty, with 1.3 billion people living on less than $1 a day), rising inequality both within and between counties, and continuing ethnic conflict. Foreign aid is declining almost everywhere, assailed by critics from across the ideological spectrum. The end of the Cold War has not revitalized international cooperation, as many had hoped, and support for military intervention in conflict zones has fallen away since the debacles in Somalia and the Balkans. The United Nations and other international bureaucracies are under constant threat: and even support for NGOs – the darlings of the development world – seems to have peaked. The international business of helping is in serious trouble.
(Edwards, 1999)

That summary is taken from *Future Positive: International Co-operation in the 21st Century*, a lively and insightful account of development issues by Michael Edwards. Since its publication in 1999, foreign aid as a percentage of GDP appeared to be on the rise again, until the 2006 Annual Review of Aid from the Organisation for Economic Co-operation and Development revealed that aid *fell* by 5 per cent in 2006 to $104 billion – the first fall in real (inflation-adjusted) terms since 1997. This includes aid for Africa, which also fell by 5 per cent, excluding debt relief, which development organizations insist should not be included in aid budgets. This was all the more devastating a blow given the firm commitment made by G8 leaders at the Gleneagles Summit in 2005 to provide an extra $50 billion a year in financial assistance by 2010. Worse yet, it looks as if the figures for 2007 will be even lower, unless Germany (which holds the 2007 G8 Presidency) is able to wring more action out of world leaders than former Prime Minister Tony Blair has been able to do despite his constant exhortation and pressure. The musician and campaigner Bob Geldof described this simply as 'a grotesque abrogation of responsibility'.

Development organizations are only too familiar with these ups and downs. If 2006 was a bad year, 2005 was a good one, shaped as it was, paradoxically, by the worst natural disaster in living memory. In December 2004, the world looked on aghast as the horrifying impacts of the Indian Ocean earthquake and resulting tsunami filled our television screens night after night. More than 300,000 dead, 5 million people homeless. Economic damage ran into untold billions of US dollars. The response of people across the developed world was extraordinary. In the UK, hundreds of millions of pounds were raised in just a few weeks in response to a constant stream of images of suffering and loss. Disaster-hardened professionals were almost as astonished at the scale and intensity of this response as they were at the scale of the disaster itself, reflecting somewhat wearily upon the intensity of the response to the tsunami compared to the 'slow burn' of shifting public opinion on the critical urgency of dealing with chronic poverty across the world.

In the aftermath, the Make Poverty History campaign in the UK re-energized a development movement that appeared to have got somewhat stuck in a very deep rut. Jacques Chirac led an increasingly influential campaign to raise substantial sums of new money for development investments by imposing a levy on international financial transactions (the so-called Tobin Tax) or, as an alternative, on international air travel – much to the irritation of the US and the UK! Gordon Brown's debt forgiveness campaign for the world's poorest countries, combined with a new International Finance Facility, secured the support of the majority of G8 nations, raising the prospect of a real and lasting improvement in the lives of millions of people.

On all these issues, no one can accuse the UK of double-talk. Our aid budget went up by 13 per cent in 2006, putting the UK firmly on track to reach the UN target of 0.7 per cent of GDP by its agreed target date of 2010. Yet again, the worst laggard is the US, which gives just 0.17 per cent of GDP – a massive blow to international efforts to reduce poverty given its standing as the world's richest nation. Of course, aid is only one part of a much bigger picture when looking at differences in GDP and per capita income across the world today. Much better progress has been made by the G8 on debt relief (19 of the world's poorest countries have now secured 100 per cent debt relief, and a further 44 are eligible for relief in the future). Trade reform also has a huge part to play (though there has been mighty little progress on that front over the last two years), as does foreign direct investment in developing countries. And these days, remittances sent home by emigrants make an increasing contribution: the Inter-America Development Bank published figures in March 2007 demonstrating that the 25 million Latin Americans living outside the region sent back nearly $50 billion in 2006 – a sum which dwarfs foreign direct investment in those countries. For some of the poorest of them, in the Caribbean and Central America, remittances are contributing more than 10 per cent of total GDP.

But for all that, the soaring promises made by the champions of globalization over the last 50 years are sounding more and more hollow. Huge benefits were supposed to accrue to the world's poorest countries through ever closer integration of those countries into the global economy, through the increased flow of goods, services and capital, raising living standards throughout the world. The evidence is now overwhelming that globalization has completely failed to live up to those promises, and though many believe this has far more to do with the political agenda of those shaping today's globalization imperative, the model itself is now under unprecedented scrutiny.

In 2004, the World Commission on the Social Dimension of Globalization (WCSDG) came out with a devastating summary of just how deep this sense of failure now runs:

> *The current process of globalization is generating unbalanced outcomes, both between and within countries. Wealth is being created, but too*

many countries and people are not sharing in its benefits. They also have little or no voice in shaping the process. Seen through the eyes of the vast majority of women and men, globalization has not met their simple and legitimate aspirations for decent jobs and a better future for their children. Many of them live in the limbo of the informal economy without formal rights, and in a swathe of poor countries that subsist precariously on the margins of the global economy. Meanwhile, the revolution in global communications heightens awareness of these disparities. These global imbalances are morally unacceptable and politically unsustainable. (WCSDG, 2004)

The Commission found that 59 per cent of the world's people are living in countries with growing inequality, and just 5 per cent in countries with declining inequality. Even in most developed countries, the rich are continuing to get richer, while the poor are barely holding their own. Confirmation of this, in the US, was published by the US Census Bureau in 2002, revealing the share of aggregate income received by each fifth of the population – and by the top 5 per cent of US families (see Figure 12.1).

Joseph Stiglitz, former Chief Economist of the World Bank, was a member of the WCSDG, and has since brought out a stirring and powerful appeal for a root and branch rethink about globalization. *Making Globalization Work* (Stiglitz, 2006) pulls few punches in its analysis of the grisly inadequacies of

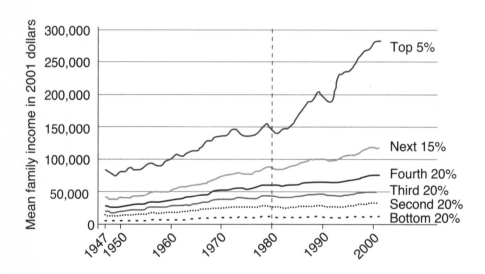

Source: US Census Bureau (2002)

Figure 12.1 *Share of mean family income 1947–2000*

international agencies (including the International Monetary Fund, the World Trade Organization and the World Bank itself) in clumsily imposing on scores of nations what has come to be known as the Washington Consensus. It's those countries that have managed to stay out of the clutches of the IMF in particular that have most prospered in the global economy – Malaysia, Indonesia, South Korea, China, Singapore, India – opening up their economies at their own pace, protecting key industries where that seems appropriate, taking what they want from the global systems being set in place rather than having the entire package imposed upon them.

Most of the rest of the poor world has not been so fortunate. Here's Stiglitz's summary:

> *The world is in a race between economic growth and population growth, and so far population growth is winning. Even as the percentages of people living in poverty are falling, the absolute number is rising. Outside of China, poverty in the developing world has increased over the past two decades. Some 40 per cent of the world's 6.5 billion people live in poverty (a number that is up from 36 per cent in 1981), a sixth (877 million) live in extreme poverty. The worst failure is Africa, where the percentage of the population living in extreme poverty has increased from 41.6 per cent in 1981 to 46.9 per cent in 2001. Given its increasing population, this means that the number of people living in extreme poverty has almost doubled, from 164 million to 316 million.*
> (Stiglitz, 2006)

Having rubbed his readers' noses in this chronic and continuing failure, the rest of *Making Globalization Work* is devoted to creative and forthright ideas for getting globalization back on track – in effect, rescuing it from the neo-conservative ideologues in the US who have used the power of globalization to enhance their own political and increasingly imperialistic interests. Tellingly, however, Stiglitz is modest in his recommendations for reforming the institutions themselves, even though a growing number of NGOs in both Europe and the US are persuaded that they are basically 'beyond reform', and should in fact be decommissioned to make way for new international financial institutions. The World Development Movement's 2006 report *Out of Time* makes a compelling case for 'starting over' (WDM, 2006).

That would still leave the WTO, and its massively problematic influence in the global economy today. The stand-off between those who sincerely believe that the WTO model of world trade (which, in effect, is the model of OECD member governments) will help address serious poverty in developing countries (in both the short and the long term), and those who see the WTO as the most pernicious institutional embodiment of a global economy that is destroying the world, is absolute:

> *Expansion of the free trade mandate, and the power and jurisdiction of the WTO, is a mortal threat to development, social justice and the environment. It's the goal we must thwart at all costs, for we might as well kiss goodbye to sustainable development if the big trading powers and their corporate elites have their way.* (Bello, 1999)

That outburst from Walden Bello (one of the most influential campaigners against the current model of globalization) pretty accurately captures the 'anti' position.

Because of the continuing impasse over the Doha Round, any 'reform' agenda for the WTO has been pushed to the margins. But the WTO is *so* far off the pace, *so* detached from current realities about climate change, inexorable eco-system degradation, worsening levels of inequity, perverse subsidies and the all but unconstrained actions of today's 'corporatocracy', as to make one wonder how any reform process could ever haul this institutional monstrosity back into the real world – not least as the disconnect is not between the WTO and its elite member governments, but between the WTO and the rest of the world.

This debate means very little to most people, for whom the rows about managing trade-offs between trade and economic development on the one hand, and sustainability and social justice on the other, are just so many irrelevant abstractions. This titanic struggle about starkly differentiated models of promoting improved wellbeing for the world's poorest people has to be grounded in real-life stories, of which I offer just one to exemplify the complexities involved. UK consumers are enthusiastic purchasers of roses grown in Kenya – particularly for 'special occasions' such as Valentine's Day, 14 February. But so great are people's current concerns about 'rose miles' (a variation of food miles, looking at the amount of carbon dioxide emitted by the aircraft bringing the roses from Kenya to the UK), that no less an authority than the Secretary of State for International Development in the UK had to reassure all right-on romantics that they shouldn't worry – that air-freighted flowers and fresh produce from the whole of sub-Saharan Africa contributed no more than 0.1 per cent of the UK's total CO_2 emissions, and that emissions from growing flowers in Kenyan sunshine were less than one fifth of emissions from flowers grown in greenhouses in The Netherlands.

So far, so good – and it would indeed be ridiculous to cut off all trade with Africa (and all the economic benefits it generates) on such a limited case. But then you have to dig a little deeper down into that particular trade, and look at its impact on a place like Lake Naivasha in Kenya, once a 'must-visit' tourist destination, now an ecological and social disaster zone in the making. To provide the labour for the rose industry, the population has grown ten-fold in just 25 years, the lake has lost 25 per cent of its water and is now seriously polluted, and the surrounding hills have been completely denuded for firewood and charcoal. Stocks of fish have been massively overexploited. Workers are paid utterly miserable wages to keep costs down for Western consumers, local taxes go unpaid by unscrupulous companies, and the surrounding villages have become dirty, violent places.

Just one more special place sucked into the great grinder of global trade, with the life slowly being squeezed out of it. Local environmentalists (one of whom was recently murdered) reckon there's another ten years of squeezing to be done, before the lake completely collapses, at which point the flower industry will have to move on to do exactly the same thing somewhere else. It's more than 35 years since Dr Seuss wrote *The Lorax*, his devastating parable of mindless, short-term environmental destruction. It should be required reading, even now, for everyone who works for the WTO and every department of so-called 'international development'.

CLOSER TO HOME

As the world falls to pieces, and most of the poor stay poor, a lot of people are getting very rich. In a report published in December 2006, the World Institute for Development Economics Research (a UN body) revealed that the richest 1 per cent of people in the world own 40 per cent of the world's wealth; the richest 10 per cent own 85 per cent. At the other end of the scale, half the world's adult population owned less than 1 per cent of global wealth. These findings confirm those of the annual 'World Wealth Report' published by the investment bank Merrill Lynch: the 2006 report showed that at the end of 2005 there were 8.7 million 'High Net Worth Individuals' (people with liquid assets of more than $1 million) around the world, up 6.5 per cent on 2004. Total wealth between them: $33 trillion. And that includes roughly 800 billionaires with a combined wealth of $2.6 trillion. There were big increases not just in the US (obviously), but in Russia, India, South Korea and Brazil. As ever, apocalypse pays well, for some.

The UK is holding its own in this Super League, relative to population. Six per cent of the super-rich live here in the UK (compared to 37 per cent in the US and 27 per cent in Japan), with the number of High Net Worth Individuals up 7 per cent between 2000 and 2005, at around 450,000 people. Many of these High Net Worth Individuals will be the beneficiaries either of a massive boom in house prices, which have tripled in England over the last few years, adding £2.5 trillion to the wealth of those owning residential property, or of the grotesque bonuses paid to high-earners in the City, which reached a record £19 billion in 2005 (16 per cent up on 2004), and are likely to go even higher in 2007. One per cent of people in the UK own 25 per cent of total wealth. On average, across the population as a whole, UK citizens have £64,000 in assets.

Things are far from rosy at the other end of the scale – the bottom 50 per cent of UK citizens own just 6 per cent. For the first time in a decade, poverty in the UK worsened in 2006. Those living on less than 60 per cent of average income (the threshold for defining relative poverty and equating to around £217 a week for a single person) increased from 12.1 million to 12.7 million. The number of children living in poor families rose by 200,000 to 3.8 million – making a massive dent in Gordon Brown's commitment to lift another 1 million out of child poverty by 2010. There was a marginal fall in pensioner poverty, but even here (another of Labour's priority commitments), the outlook for pensioners is not good.

There's no doubting the Chancellor's sincere efforts in addressing these issues, and most Labour MPs (when kicked hard enough) recall that redistributing wealth is one of the foundations on which their party used to stand. But their failure to make that much progress on undoing the horribly regressive effects of 18 years of the Tory Party implementing economic policies at the expense of the poor is a serious indictment of the Labour government's record since 1997. Progressive voices (many of which have joined together under the left-of-centre pressure group called 'Compass') are less and less prepared to take this worsening inequality as an inevitable price to be paid for success in the global economy – with globalization used to justify both runaway salaries and bonuses at the top end of the scale (in order to retain 'mobile talent' in an increasingly competitive world) and the miserable wages at the bottom end of the scale (battling against low-cost producers elsewhere in the world and harsh, government-imposed pay constraints).

The truth of it is, however, that this has been a fiercely anti-tax age. As the Fabian Society's ongoing campaign to reassert 'the social value of fair and pro-portionate taxation' has shown, the legacy of more than 25 years of vitriolic condemnation of the business of raising and spending taxes has taken a serious intellectual toll. Even now, the Government's lack of enthusiasm for overtly redistributive policies is compounded by unremitting anti-tax propaganda from the UK's predominantly right-wing media; there are mighty few politicians or economists prepared to make the case for higher levels of taxation in the face of such public hostility. Yet it's a mystery to many political commentators how anybody imagines that this country can go on improving its health and education services, restore its transport infrastructure, or improve the state of both the natural and the built environment, let alone do more to help developing countries, protect the global environment and create the necessary conditions for lasting security in countries currently ravaged by war and conflict, *without higher taxes*. But any debate on this score remains strictly off-limits. In the 2007 Budget, Gordon Brown declared that the standard rate of income tax would be reduced by 2p, with the shortfall made up from other sources, including increased 'green taxes', which brought a wry smile to the face of most environmentalists. Unless something much more radical is done, the equality gap will go on widening – not least because those with properties are able to wipe out much of their increased tax liability simply through the increase in property values, a hidden benefit simply not available to the poorest 20 per cent of people who rent accommodation rather than own property.

This has led some to call for a tax on land value – an idea first proposed by Adam Smith more than 200 years ago, and taken up (in different ways) by countries like Denmark, Sweden and Australia. It could be introduced so as not to increase the total tax burden (by reducing council tax, for example, or even income tax), and would be very hard for even the richest – with their cohorts of tax advisers – to avoid. Alternatively, there are many people (including myself) who would like to see a Labour government increase the top rate of taxation or bring in a new band for those with incomes of over £100,000 a year. Perhaps the swing of capitalism's pendulum to which I have referred elsewhere will make it easier to argue the case for maintaining and enhancing social, human and natural capital through fair and proportionate taxation. And if the moral case for a more equitable society (or family of nations) doesn't do it for electorates, then the appeal to 'enlightened self-interest' would appear to be getting more powerful by the day.

SECURITY DENIED

On the international stage, this kind of appeal to enlightened self-interest has also started to resonate somewhat more persuasively, albeit against the less than propitious backdrop of the 'war against terror'. In November 2001, with memories of 11 September and its 3000 victims still very fresh in people's minds, the *New Internationalist* (2001) provocatively set out to remind its readers of how hard it is to get any proper perspective on such events by making a series of somewhat poignant comparisons (see Box 12.2).

BOX 12.2 THE WAR AGAINST TERROR IN CONTEXT

ENDURING TERRORS

- Number of people who died in attacks on the Twin Towers, 11 September 2001: 3000.
- Number of people who died of hunger on 11 September 2001:*24,000.
- Number of children killed by diarrhoea on 11 September 2001:*6020.
- Number of children killed by measles on 11 September 2001:*2700.
- Number of malnourished children in developing countries: 149 million.
- Number of people without access to safe drinking water: 1100 million.
- Number of people without access to adequate sanitation: 2400 million.
- Number of people living on less than $1 a day: 1200 million.
- Number of African children under 15 living with HIV: 1.1 million.
- Number of children without access to basic education: 100 million.
- Number of illiterate adults: 875 million.
- Number of women who die each year in pregnancy and childbirth: 515,000.
- Annual average number of people killed by drought and famine, 1972–1996: 73,606.
- Annual average number of children killed in conflict, 1990–2000: 200,000.
- Annual average number of children made homeless by conflict, 1990–2000: 1.2 million.

Note: *Assuming annual deaths were evenly spread across the year.
Source: New Internationalist (2001)

As we saw in Chapter 5, the rich world's standard response to these enduring and truly terrible problems is to work towards an accelerated process of market liberalization and the promotion of Western values. This has clearly brought some benefits to some people in some countries; but as a universal model for addressing these 'enduring terrors', it is, at best, hopelessly inadequate and, at worst, a form of economic medicine that often makes things worse. As Roger Scruton so powerfully argues in *The West and the Rest: Globalization and the Terrorist Threat* (2002), it is precisely the imposition of that model of corporate globalization that fuels the fires of Islamic extremism and pretty much guarantees an eventual 'clash of civilizations' *unless* the current model of globalization is radically reformed.

It is in this context that the synergistic convergence of some of the 'radical discontinuities' referred to in earlier chapters becomes so threatening. Our addiction to oil, for instance, is not only environmentally unsustainable, but – as with any addictive habit – inevitably leads to rash and potentially violent actions in an effort to satisfy our cravings. It may be unfair to ascribe the whole of Western strategy on Iraq to no more than a thirst for oil; but you would have to have your head buried deep in the sands of Saudi Arabia not to spot a certain confluence of interests. And whatever people think of Vice President Dick Cheney, the man certainly deserves points for honesty for having argued *openly* as long ago as 1998 (together with the likes of Paul Wolfowitz) for the overthrow of Saddam as a means of boosting American oil supplies.

Both Europe and America are set to become increasingly dependent upon imported oil and gas supplies – much of them from politically volatile regions with little reason to love the West. Indeed, despite enthusiastically pursuing the development of what's left of its own reserves in Alaska and elsewhere, the US is expected to rely upon the Middle East for no less than 70 per cent of its oil by 2025. That reliance, of course, is the prime reason for US military presence in Saudi Arabia and Iraq – a presence which provides Osama bin Laden with the strongest possible pretext for continuing to wage war (in his terms) on US imperialists. Our need for oil makes us all insecure. A minor diplomatic contretemps between Iran and the UK in March 2007 (with 15 British troops illegally taken into custody and then released a week later) was enough to add $10 to the price of a barrel of oil.

It's not beyond hope, therefore, that sooner rather than later we might all wake up to the realization that true independence means a decisive shift away from fossil fuels in favour of a combination of renewables and improved efficiency – both of which offer huge scope for progress. Energy guru Amory Lovins calls efficiency gains 'the rapid deployment energy resource': it takes years to discover and develop a new oil field, but just months to make sufficient efficiency savings to make it redundant before it even starts pumping.

In *Winning the Oil Endgame*, Lovins (2005) gives us a comprehensive account of the way in which US dependence on oil not only imperils its own national security, but inflicts on US taxpayers a huge bill in terms of both direct and indirect costs. If ever there was a time for the US Administration to free itself of that dependency, it has to be now: the imported proportion of US oil will rise from around 50 per cent today to around 70 per cent by 2025 (compared to 66 per cent in the EU), and policy-makers are well aware that even today's figure is *twice* the level of imports in 1973 at the time of the first Organization of the Petroleum Exporting Countries (OPEC) oil shock. In 2000, these imports cost $109 billion, accounting for a full 25 per cent of the US trade deficit, which has become such a major headache that it is eroding the value of the dollar – which, in turn, boosts the price of oil.

But Lovins (2005) emphasizes that the *indirect* costs are, if anything, more of a problem than the direct costs. A quarter of US imports come from OPEC countries and one seventh from Arab OPEC countries. Reliance upon such unstable sources means huge costs in terms of having to protect access and maintain a substantial US presence throughout the Middle East. By analysing US Department of Defense figures, Lovins comes to the conclusion that the annual cost to US taxpayers through the 1990s was anywhere between $54 billion and $86 billion dollars, which means 'the US pays two to three times as much to maintain military forces poised to intervene in the Gulf as it pays to buy oil from the Gulf'.

Mind you, even those huge sums have to be set against *global* military spending, which has been rising rapidly since the onset of the war on terror: $956 billion in 2003, and well in excess of $1.2 trillion in 2005. Military expert Chris Langley reminds us of the devastating implications of that kind of chronic misallocation of capital:

> *The economic, social and environmental cost to the world of this military procurement and development is immense. Much of it is borne by poorer countries in Africa, the Middle East and Latin America, where most of the world's wars are taking place and many of the weapons are concentrated. These three regions spend $22 billion a year on arms, many of which are supplied by the G8 countries, such as the US and the UK. The result, inevitably, is instability – a consequence the arms-supplying nations seem to have ignored. Noticeably lacking from most of the military–research partnerships are conflict-resolution or peace-building strategies. In 2004, only 6 per cent of the UK Ministry of Defence's budget went towards conflict resolution.* (Langley, 2005)

Perhaps we might all feel better about this level of expenditure if there was any sense that it was actually increasing global security. But there are just so many opportunities for addressing some of the root causes of growing instability in the world that every extra billion dollars on arms has to be seen as another setback. The Worldwatch Institute's 2005 *State of the World* was devoted entirely to the linkage between security issues (as conventionally understood) and today's converging environmental, resource and social issues. It summarizes the full extent of those costs:

> *Surprisingly modest investments in health, education and environmental protection could tap the vast human potential now shackled by poverty and break the vicious circles that are destabilizing large areas of our planet. Estimates suggest that programmes to provide clean water and sewage systems would cost roughly $37 billion annually; to cut world hunger in half, $24 billion; to prevent soil erosion, another $24 billion; to provide reproductive healthcare for all women, $12 billion; to eradicate illiteracy, $5 billion; and to provide immunization for every child in the developing world, $3 billion. Spending just $10 billion a year on the global HIV/AIDS programme, and $3 billion or so to control malaria in sub-Saharan Africa, would save millions of lives. All this adds up to a little more than half the $211 billion likely to be appropriated for the Iraq War by the end of 2004.* (Worldwatch Institute, 2005)

Critics of this kind of 'opportunity costs analysis' claim it is extremely naïve: just because mosquito nets could be bought to protect hundreds of thousands of children against the scourge of malaria for five years for the price of just one day's worth of military expenditure in the US, doesn't make it wrong, necessarily, to carry on with the military expenditure. It just means the money for the mosquito nets has to be found elsewhere. This is facile. Not only are all public expenditure budgets in OECD countries under constant pressure; it's also the case that the bloated defence budgets are almost the only source available for strategic, security-related redirection.

That's what makes the Labour government's decision in 2007 to update the UK's nuclear weapons capability (to the tune of tens of billions of pounds over the next 20 years or so) so utterly reprehensible – morally and geopolitically. Here's a government that prides itself (rightly) on its leadership on climate change (acknowledging we have no more than 10–15 years to put in place a global programme for mitigating the impacts of future climate change and for adapting to the impacts of existing climate change), and on a better deal for the Third World in terms of debt relief, increased aid budgets, financial support for Africa and so on. And yet it still finds it wholly acceptable to sink up to £60 billion into a weapons system that is anachronistic (the threats we face today, post-Cold War, are of a very different kind), massively prejudicial to the Nuclear Non-Proliferation Treaty (a big welcome for Iran to the world's nuclear club!), and completely redundant in that there's *no* conceivable situation in which the UK will be likely to use its nuclear weapons where the US didn't already have its finger on the button.

This is power politics ('keeping our seat at the table') of the worst kind, a defining moment of betrayal, effectively consigning the UK to the role of a bit-part player in the massive challenge to create a sustainable world over the next few decades. A very different 'table', to be sure, but the only one worth being seated around for a country with any serious global aspirations.

And there's no doubt that the US and the UK bear a very special responsibility in this area. Far from making the world a more secure place, let alone delivering that elusive 'hammer blow' to international terrorism, the war in Iraq has set back both those crucial strategic objectives by a very long way. Even US security experts have been compelled to admit that the occupation of Iraq and the continuing failure to address the tragic plight of Palestine have dramatically accelerated the radicalization of many Islamic countries, while re-energizing the Al-Qa'eda network in many parts of the world. Here in the UK, Tony Blair's protestations that our foreign policy (especially the role of British troops in Iraq and Afghanistan) has not contributed significantly to the alienation of Muslims all over the world, and particularly in the UK, take denial on to a completely new and surreal plain. In a quite shocking poll carried out by Channel 4 in the summer of 2006, nearly one third of young British Muslims agreed with the suggestion that 'the 7 July London bombings were justified because of British support for the war on terror'. That is, of course, utterly reprehensible. But the tragic reality is that the Bush/Blair global war on terror has come to be seen by many Muslims as a global war on Islam. It's easy to dismiss this as a 'ludicrous misrepresentation' (as both governments have sought to do), but many see this as a direct consequence of decisions taken by the US and the UK to lump together *all* manifestations of violent opposition to Western interests as part and parcel of the same global conspiracy. If we go on portraying all Muslim opponents of our misbegotten role in the world today as one homogenous enemy, then that is exactly what they will become.

The stupidity of this is quite startling. It's hard to imagine a course of action more finely honed to play right into the hands of Muslim fundamentalists. Their 'single narrative' is one that depends on persuading moderate Muslims to interpret the whole of human history as an ongoing Christian and Jewish plot against Islam. It's precisely for that reason that they choose to separate themselves from the main body of Islam, on the grounds that the moderates have betrayed Islam in making too many concessions to the West and to the onward march of modernity. The very strong emphasis placed by Islam on the importance of justice and solidarity means that many Muslims feel both oppressed and humiliated by what is happening in Iraq, Palestine and Afghanistan – which we, astonishingly, continue to treat as 'different fronts in a common struggle'.

Meanwhile, the Middle East continues down its spiral of decline. Environmental degradation and social injustice are increasingly feeding off each other, exacerbated by very high levels of average fertility and chronic unemployment among young men. You don't need a degree in environmental management to spot that the refugee camps of the Gaza Strip, for example, are an object lesson in unbearable unsustainability, or to conclude that people who are forced out of their rural homelands and into squalid urban squatter camps due to water shortages, soil erosion, climate change and civil conflict – the sort of runaway environmental and social breakdown that is happening right across Africa and Asia – will make a ready audience for fundamentalist firebrands. In Maoist terms, it's those pressures which fill up the 'sea of sympathy' in which the fish of Al-Qa'eda and the like can swim.

And you can't dry out that sea by force of arms. Military might can kill individual terrorists; it rarely saps their support. For proof, look at Palestine, where decades of Israeli *force majeure* have only fed increasingly violent uprisings. If we are to drain that sea of sympathy, we have to address the root causes of injustice and degradation with a resolve which we have sadly lacked to date. And therein lies another searing irony: while the fruits of the global economy are far from equitably distributed, the hype about its supposed benefits increasingly is. The world's refugee camps and squatter homes are increasingly alive with the flickering seduction of television images portraying Western consumerism in all its elusive, bloated glory; the streets of developing world cities are lined with hoardings holding out the promise of the same. For several years through the 1990s, the most watched TV programme across the world was *Baywatch*. And for the vast majority, the gulf between their daily reality and the astonishing wealth on display is unimaginably huge, a distant, shimmering dream jealously guarded by the military and financial muscle of America and its allies. So should we really be surprised if the world's 2 billion people surviving on less than $2 a day end up responding with a mix of anger, envy and intense bitterness? Or that some adopt ideologies which wholly reject Western values, and, *in extremis*, end up as conscripts in the extremists' *jihad*? As James Wolfensohn, former president of the World Bank, puts it: 'The idea that a rich world and a poor world can co-exist without dramatic implications collapsed along with the Twin Towers on 11 September.'

In short, we cannot divorce our own physical security from that of the world's poor. If we want a long-term future that is safe, we shouldn't be worrying just about the threat from rogue states, but about the yawning gulf between the over-indulged world and the dispossessed. If we want to feel more secure ourselves, we should start by improving the security of the poorest. And doing that simultaneously means doing right by the environment: tackling climate change which, unchecked, is helping to cause the droughts and storms which destroy poor peoples' chances of making a living on the margins; investing in clean water supplies and decent sanitation, and in non-polluting, small-scale renewable energy, all of which can make it possible for vulnerable communities to stay on their land and earn a living from it, rather than join the drift to the city slums. Almost without exception, technologies which are more sustainable are less prone to being hijacked, in any sense of the word, by those intent on inflicting harm. No terrorist is going to make governments tremble by threatening to bomb a wind turbine or release clouds of compost over our cities. Compare that to the destructive potential of nuclear power and toxic chemicals. A more sustainable world is, indeed, a safer world.

Such sustainability-related concerns about global security are matched in equal measure by concerns about some of the technologies that have been developed over recent decades. It's not just environmentalists who are sounding the alarm bells these days, but many of those who have been working at the very heart of these cutting-edge innovations. Perhaps the most pessimistic of these is Bill Joy, co-founder of Sun Microsytems, whose article in *Wired* in 2000 ('Why the future doesn't need us') fast-forwarded several decades to look at some of the implications of that troika of technologies that will shake the very foundations of the 21st century: genetics, robotics and nanotechnology. Just as some climatologists have flagged the possibility of 'runaway climate change' (where natural feedback mechanisms combine to accelerate processes in ways that simply can't be foreseen), Bill Joy focuses on the 'runaway potential' of computers and robots surpassing human control to the point where they actually take us over. Michael Crichton's fictional account of self-replicating 'nanobots' threatening to reduce all life on Earth to a 'grey goo' (in Eric Drexler's words) has provided for many a 'working model' of Bill Joy's theoretical concerns, however dreadful a novel it may be.

For me, however, the pessimism of Sir Martin Rees, Astronomer Royal and most eminent of contemporary cosmologists, hits home a lot harder. His book *Our Final Century* (Rees, 2003) speculates about every conceivable kind of meltdown or Doomsday scenario for humankind, from the illicit use of plutonium or enriched uranium from the former Soviet Union through to asteroid impacts and comets, from climate change through to catastrophic disasters caused by experiments in today's particle accelerators. But by far the most worrying sections of the book focus on the likelihood of what he calls 'bio-error or bio-terror' – the accidental or deliberate release of micro-organisms, pathogens, 'designer viruses' or other biological agents that could have a devastating effect on humankind. In June 2002, the US National Academy of Sciences reminded politicians just how high the stakes are at this stage in human history:

> *Just a few individuals with specialized skills and access to a laboratory could inexpensively and easily produce a panoply of lethal biological weapons that might seriously threaten the US population. Moreover, they could manufacture such biological agents with commercially available equipment – that is, equipment that could also be used to make chemicals, pharmaceuticals, food or beer – and therefore remain inconspicuous. The deciphering of the human genome sequence and the complete elucidation of numerous pathogen genomes allow science to be misused to create new agents of mass destruction.* (US National Academy of Sciences, 2002)

And that's the nub of it. The self-same techniques that are so enthusiastically promoted by both big business and government as promising huge benefits (in terms of agriculture, health, waste management and so on) inevitably become available to those for whom the advancement of humankind is a pathetic irrelevance. Within just a few years, the genetic blueprints of large numbers of species (including bacteria and viruses) will be as easily available via the internet to latter-day Dr Strangeloves as to the likes of John Sulston and others who worked so tirelessly to unlock the secrets of the human genome for the betterment of the human species. Dozens of biotech firms now offer to synthesize complete genes from the chemical components of DNA; only rarely do they carry out any checks on what they are being asked to make, or by whom. As an avid reader of *New Scientist*, I've been following with growing concern the stories about 'dual-use biology' – essentially, research intended to combat disease, but which could easily be misused by bio-terrorists or enemy states. The problem is that it is difficult, if not impossible, to pursue such work without potentially helping others design bio-weapons. A *New Scientist* survey in October 2006 illustrated the difficulties faced by the US National Science Advisory Board for Biosecurity when asked to approve projects, for instance, to tweak the anthrax toxin to render experimental drugs ineffective, to turn a harmless rodent virus into a deadly pathogen, to enhance the potency of botulinum toxins, or to transfer genes that help viruses evade the human immune system from one pathogen to another.

And if bio-error or bio-terror don't get us, then the measures taken to try and ward off such horrors very well may. We have already seen the first signs of what this might mean. The response to the events of 11 September 2001 has already seriously eroded civil liberties in the US, the UK and many other countries; constitutional and legal 'niceties' have been unceremoniously set to one side in the interests of national security. But to what end? As Martin Rees points out:

> *An organized network of Al-Qa'eda-type terrorists would not be required: just a fanatical social misfit with the mindset of those who now design computer viruses. There are people with such propensities in every country – very few, to be sure, but bio- and cyber-technologies will become so powerful that even one could well be too many.* (Rees, 2003)

So is there anything that can be done about this seemingly inexorable slide into terror met with oppression met with terror and so on? Martin Rees reviews the various possibilities in terms of slowing the speed of technological advance in these areas – through more regulation, voluntary moratoria and increasingly intrusive surveillance. But none seems feasible. This may well account for the fact that he once staked $1000 on a bet 'that by the year 2020 an incidence of bio-error or bio-terror will have killed 1 million people'.

In these circumstances, it makes little sense dumping total responsibility for this nightmarish vision on today's rudderless world leaders, weakened as they so clearly are by the unmanageability and complexity of both society and technology. But whenever I hear world leaders telling us that 'we have no choice', in the interests of economic growth and international competitiveness, but to push on ever faster and ever more furiously with genetic research, biotech, nanotech or whatever the next 'tech' may be, I wince at the sheer scale of tribute that the great god of economic growth now demands of us. I am not suggesting that 'genies' such as these can be put back into their bottles; indeed, why would we want to, given that humankind will undoubtedly benefit greatly from some of the uses to which these technologies will be put? But I do believe that today's obsessive pursuit of economic growth at all costs makes those genies much less controllable than they might otherwise be.

All of this draws us back yet again to the critical notion of *interdependence*. This means acknowledging the degree to which security for any one country or community can only be achieved by making others more secure in their countries and communities, not just by reinforcing commercial and cultural interconnectedness, but by stressing mutual dependency. In advocating a rapid shift to 'the politics of resilience', Martin Wright, Editor of the magazine *Green Futures*, makes the point in a suitably provocative way:

> *The emphasis in the future should be on a more integrated agenda of positive security and shared resilience. This recognizes the links between areas such as resource conflicts, energy policy and climate change, on the one hand, and our approaches to issues like failed states, terrorism, global governance and poverty relief, on the other. And, crucially, it identifies ways in which these can be tackled simultaneously. It shows how a community wind farm on a Welsh hillside is, in its way, as much a part of a counter-terrorist strategy as an ID card; how a shift to sourcing hospital food in the UK from local farms can help bring about a more secure future for African villages; how a scheme to tackle obesity among school children can cut our dependence on oil from the Gulf.* (Wright, 2005)

SCIENCE DENIED

As we saw in Chapter 2, one of the reasons why there's been such slow progress on the international climate change agenda has been the refusal of the Bush Administration to accept the prevailing scientific consensus. President Bush himself has done everything he could, personally, to confuse the American people as to the reality of climate change all the way through his Presidency. Part of this is just good old-fashioned oil politics as practised in the US over many decades;

Vice-President Dick Cheney (Chief Executive of Halliburton between 1995 and 2000) has been the undisputed ringmaster of a network of relationships shot through and through with secrecy, vested interests, cronyism, no-bid contracts, manipulation of science (both in terms of policy and official US institutions like the Environmental Protection Agency), grotesque subsidies to the oil industry and the nuclear industry, and so on.

It's difficult to imagine that history's judgement on Dick Cheney's role will be anything other than utterly damning – not least because his erstwhile company, Halliburton, outraged the US public by declaring in March 2007 that it was moving its corporate headquarters from Houston to Dubai in the United Arab Emirates. The timing of this may have been coincidental, but with the company at the centre of numerous enquiries into alleged accounting malpractices, sanctions-busting, over-charging, corruption, improper payments and massive incompetence in carrying out up to $25 billion worth of what are euphemistically described as 'reconstruction contracts' in Iraq, many Americans have come to their own conclusions.

When it comes to climate change, however, Halliburton has nothing on ExxonMobil, the world's largest oil company with annual profits of around $350 billion – that's more or less $100 million every day – and an unrivalled hold over the White House and the Department of Energy. In 2007, the Union of Concerned Scientists in the US brought out a report (under the title of 'Smoke, mirrors and hot air' by the investigative journalist Seth Shulman) that exposes nearly 20 years' worth of planned, systematic and utterly unscrupulous efforts by ExxonMobil to derail the emerging scientific consensus around climate change. It makes riveting but deeply depressing reading, as it lays bare how the company spends between $2 and $3 million a year to fund a network of 'front' organizations and phoney think-tanks to peddle any variety of junk science just so long as it serves to undermine the consensus on climate change. From the moment where ExxonMobil claimed the credit for persuading George Bush to pull out of the Kyoto Protocol in 2001, to its enthusiastic support for the comprehensively discredited work of Henrik Svensmark (claiming that it is increased solar radiation that is entirely responsible for climate change), ExxonMobil's is a truly shameful record.

So much so that in September 2006, the President of the Royal Society (the UK's most prestigious scientific institution) wrote publicly to ExxonMobil to make a formal complaint about its continuing support for dozens of organizations 'which have misrepresented the science of climate change by outright denial of the evidence', and for its own 'inaccurate and misleading statements on climate change'. This was the first time the Royal Society has ever had to take a company to task for such systematic scientific dishonesty, and its intervention should certainly strengthen the hand of all those campaigners seeking to find a way of holding ExxonMobil to account in law in due course. Meanwhile, ExxonMobil remains unmoved. Its latest report shows that in 2006 it handed over $1,767,500 to 26 organizations on the Royal Society's hit list.

Oil politics as usual, in other words! Equally disturbing, but harder to pin down, has been the influence on the White House of the same evangelical churches that have had such a powerful influence on key social issues like abortion, gay rights and so on. As we saw in Chapter 2, it has taken a concerted and highly effective campaign by progressive evangelicals to bring the majority of evangelical churches into a formal recognition of the seriousness of climate change, and of the duty of individual Christians to exercise their responsibility as 'stewards of God's creation' and to address their own personal responsibility for walking more lightly on the Earth.

However, this is just one small aspect of a much more profound attack on science among fundamentalist Christians. According to the National Center for Science Education, 13 states are now embroiled in legal and political battles over the way in which evolution is taught in schools and colleges. For the last 20 years or more, Christian fundamentalists have been seeking to have evolution described as 'a theory' so that their version of creationism (the belief that God created the Earth and all its species – and, indeed, all its fossils! – in just six days around 6000 years ago) can be taught as a rival theory alongside it. The teaching of creationism in American schools was explicitly outlawed in 1987 when the US Supreme Court confirmed that it was unconstitutional to bring any such religious perspectives to bear on the school curriculum. Since then, however, the religious right has regrouped and, under the new banner of 'intelligent design', is now intent on challenging what it sees as the atheistic domination of science in American education. Intelligent design maintains that there is no definitive proof for the theory of evolution, and that the complexity and diversity of life on Earth can only be explained in terms of some purposeful act of creation by 'an intelligent designer'.

As of now, the National Centre for Science Education and dozens of local groups have managed to hold the line in a host of different fire fights. But they are under no illusions that this is the new battleground for the religious right. And there's no firm agreement as to how best to counter it: should they embrace the idea of 'teaching the controversy', by bringing intelligent design into the classroom in the hope that the strength and rigour of the scientific method, properly understood, would see off this transparently unscientific interloper? Or should they stand firm, resisting any accommodation on the grounds that once this Trojan horse is inside the system, there would be no undoing its malign influence? And why give any credence to intelligent design by suggesting that there might be something wrong with Darwin's theory of evolution by natural selection? As the *New Scientist* put it in one of its editorials on this subject:

> *There is no scientific controversy between intelligent design and evolu-tion. The case for teaching them as valid alternatives is no stronger than the case for teaching students about some supposed controversy between astrology and astronomy. Let's be honest. This is creationism by another name. Tell a class of teenagers that the tail of a bacterium did*

> *not evolve, but was 'designed', and who will they think the 'designer' is?*
> *Intelligent design may qualify as a religious belief, but it is not science.*
> *Teach it in philosophy or sociology by all means. Its proper resting place,*
> *however, will be in history. (New Scientist, 2006)*

But not, one suspects, for quite a while. Evangelical Christians have opened 'a second front' to reinforce their attempts to gain legal access to the formal educational system. It's reckoned that there could be up to 2.5 million children in the US who are now being home-schooled, and that the parents of around three quarters of those children have made this decision because of their desire to provide what they see as proper religious and moral education. Having started out as a bit of a hippie, counter-cultural movement in the late 1960s, home-schooling has now been well and truly colonized by the religious right and by organizations like the Home School Legal Defence Association. Home-schooled children often go on to universities run along the same moral and religious precepts, some with quite specific objectives to prepare 'the leaders of the future'. An organization called the 'Exodus Mandate' is actively proselytizing to persuade Christian parents to pull their children out of public schools, meaning that the number of home-schooled children could double or even triple over the next few years. This can only exacerbate an already deeply troubling contempt for science (polls show that as many as 50 per cent of Americans already reject the theory of evolution) and few people doubt that the new $27 million 'Creation Museum' in Petersburg, Kentucky, will prove to be a rip-roaring success despite being more about supernatural history than natural history.

Creationism and intelligent design have had much less of an impact elsewhere in the world, though that may be only a matter of time. Emmanuel College in the north-east of England (financed by the Christian fundamentalist Peter Vardy) was the first school to teach both evolution and creationism in science classes, and Vardy has since funded two further 'academies' following the same approach. An astonishing survey of UK students in August 2006 (by Opinionpanel Research) showed 56 per cent favouring Darwinian evolution, 19 per cent intelligent design and 12 per cent out and out creationism. A third of those who said they were Muslims and a quarter of those who said they were Christians favoured creationism.

Scientists like Richard Dawkins and Steve Jones see this as tantamount to a return to the Dark Ages, blaming not just the influence of Christian fundamentalism in the US, but the political cowardice of UK teachers who feel they have to 'give space' to divergent beliefs, particularly to Muslims. And it's certainly the case that support from Muslim fundamentalists is the mirror image of support for creationism from Christian fundamentalists. In Pakistan, evolution is no longer taught in universities, and in Turkey, creationism is now a standard element in all school textbooks. Karen Armstrong highlights this as one of the key similarities between Christian and Islamic fundamentalism: 'they reveal a deep disappointment and disenchantment with the modern experiment [...] they also express real fear, and are convinced that the secular establishment is determined to wipe religion out' (Armstrong, 2006).

Fortunately, that is not the view of the vast majority of moderate Christians and Muslims all around the world. For them, there is no fundamental incompatibility between their faith and the theory of evolution, seeing the hand of the creator/designer to have been at work at the moment the universe came into being (according to Big Bang theory), unleashing in the process the power of natural selection over billions of years of life evolving here on Earth. Even the Vatican (in its position paper of 1996) acknowledged that humankind did not spring ready-formed from God during the course of the last 6000 years, but emerged from a gradual evolutionary process.

Much of the commentary today, in a religious context, is about a potential 'clash of civilizations' between Christianity, on the one hand, and Islam, on the other. But in many respects, it's 'the clash of Christianities' that is at least as important, with liberal, progressive Christians needing to fight on a number of critical sustainability-related issues: for instance, with regard to the absolutist 'moral' intolerance of the Catholic Church against women and responsible family planning (is it really possible that a new 21st-century Pope will perpetuate the incomprehensibly cruel dogma of his predecessor in decreeing that the use of condoms cannot even be condoned within a conjugal relationship where one partner has contracted HIV/AIDS and the other has not?), or against the millenarian madness of huge numbers of Christian fundamentalists in the US.

The fact that former Prime Minister Tony Blair, himself a profound and genuine Christian, should have found himself so closely aligned politically with an American Administration so powerfully influenced by millenarian fundamentalism is a source of continuing bemusement to those who see him as a strong, moral and decent man. Did his security advisers ever brief him properly on the Project for the New American Century, on the implications of the influence of pre-millenarian fundamentalism on US foreign policy, and on the views of Dick Cheney, Paul Wolfowitz and President Bush himself? Michael Northcott brings forward a powerful indictment on that score:

> *Political economists who describe modern government in terms of rational constitutions, social contracts and the 'laws' of supply and demand disable a proper understanding of the apocalyptic spirit that drives the politics of American empire, the civil religion that sacralizes it and the idolatrous rituals of consumerism which it sustains. Like so many of the emperors and monarchs of what came to be known as Christendom, Bush and his speech writers use a distortion of Christian apocalyptic, combined with American civil religion, to legitimate and sacralize imperial violence.*

> *That Christian ethics can be put to such use is perhaps the greatest indictment of Christianity for many secular humanists in the first decade of the third millennium. Were more Christians in America, Britain and beyond to recover the radical Christianity of the founder, then the abuse of religion by political leaders and by terrorists to sacralize their wars, and their apocalyptic divisions of humanity into the wicked and the righteous, would be undermined.* (Northcott, 2004)

ARE ENVIRONMENTALISTS IN DENIAL TOO?

All in all, this chapter does not offer us a happy global prospect. 'Don't rock the boat' may sound wise advice against such a backdrop. But there's rocking and there's rocking. Cast your mind back over the communiqués of the last half dozen G8 meetings, or EU summits, or world trade conferences, or even the Johannesburg Plan of Implementation from the 2002 World Summit on Sustainable Development, and the level of denial involved beggars belief.

So what's going on? The worst possibility, of course, is that a significant proportion of Western leaders are now so thoroughly co-opted by a tiny but hugely powerful business and political elite that they couldn't start to question the paradigm that serves that elite so well even if they wanted to. Berlusconi's Italy provided the living embodiment of that malign convergence. In the US, the Bush Administration makes no secret of its unyielding allegiance to such an elite, as evidenced both by its devotion to the deepest of pork-barrel politics and by its continuing tax cuts that serve only to enrich the already very rich.

But once the conspiracy theories are put to one side, the principal reasons offered for the phenomenon of this continuing, utterly perverse denial on the part of politicians are these: ignorance (however improbable that may seem for any politician, business person, community leader or media commentator able to see the world as it really is); dogmatic adherence to the 'revealed truth' of post-World War II materialism (certainly a powerful contributory factor, as covered in Chapter 3); and the hypothesis that the challenge of governance itself in a demanding, complex, interconnected and increasingly individualistic society has become all but impossible.

Such analysis commands a growing following in contemporary political circles. But what if a substantial slice of this apparently unmanageable complexity is, in essence, a *consequence* of the failure of politicians to realize that the dominant paradigm of progress through exponential economic growth, at almost any cost, is now generating as many disbenefits as genuine benefits? Were that to be the case (as many advocates of sustainable development now believe it to be), then no amount of 'modernization' in the way policy is implemented is likely to make all that much difference if the 'meta-narrative' of contemporary politics remains unchanged. At that level, politicians of all mainstream parties continue to subscribe, with varying degrees of enthusiasm or reluctance, to the suffocating embrace of 'There Is No Alternative'.

Even to contextualize an alternative approach within a pro-market, democracy enhancing, reforming framework looks, at best, subversive and highly risky (as in former Chancellor Kohl's charge that all green ideas are like tomatoes: 'they may start out green, but they all end up the deepest red') and, at worst, revolutionary. We are back, it seems, to the apparent impossibility of looking at economic growth and development in a very different way. But are such fears justified? Is the level of political pain and electoral risk really so high if one focuses in the near term on some of the most important *transitional strategies* that present themselves pretty much as no-brainers for anyone still intent on reconciling the non-negotiable long-term imperative of biophysical sustainability with the highly desirable short-term dynamism and creativity of capitalism? Politicians certainly think it is, and environmentalists have had relatively little success over the last 25 years in persuading them to change their minds.

The fate of Europe's green parties reflects this *realpolitik* all too clearly. In 2000, green parties were involved in coalition governments in 5 out of the 15 EU states; in 2006, that had shrunk back to two (the Czech Republic and Finland), with Greens holding a total of just 240 parliamentary seats in 18 countries. Environmentalists like to reassure themselves by seeing things in terms of gently rising curves of environmental awareness and action, incrementally moving nation states towards a greener, safer way of living. That's simply not the case. In many places things are moving rapidly backwards – in the US, for instance, in the EU, as a whole, and particularly in Germany.

And it's here we must confront denial of a different kind, not on the part of politicians, big business, the world's major religions or the general public, but on the part of the environmental movement itself. Our denial lies in the simple fact that we have done very little over the last few years to change our conventional ways of campaigning and lobbying, despite 'the evidence of relative failure' being all around us. The most recent example of this was the 2005 general election in the UK, where environmental issues (including climate change) received as close to zero attention as it's possible to get. Although public support for environmental issues is very broad, it is also very shallow. Politicians have learned that they can get away with doing as little as is necessary, while deferring, downgrading and diluting the range of interventions open to them, in the sure knowledge that consistent underperformance in this area will not bring people out on to the streets or even affect their electoral chances. Only small minorities vote in elections because of their environmental concerns, as evidenced by the difficulties of the European green parties to extend their supporter base much beyond a hard core of 5 to 10 per cent of voters. Only rarely do European environmentalists ask themselves how much of this failure can be attributed to our own underperformance rather than to the failure of everyone else. There is always just enough going on (in terms, for example, of new EU processes, occasional 'victories' and incremental policy shifts) to justify the kind of 'stick to the knitting, do what we do best' tactics that have served environmental organizations reasonably well over so many years. This makes for a very muted and ineffective kind of debate.

Not so in the US, where a lively debate about the future of environmentalism has been going on for some time. Michael Schellenberger and Ted Nordhaus, the authors of 'The death of environmentalism' (2005), made themselves deeply unpopular by coming up with a fundamentally different analysis of why the neo-conservatives in the US had been so successful in portraying environmentalism as an anti-American niche for extremists and drop-outs.

Their analysis of the principal obstacles to making progress on big issues such as climate change is very different from that of conventional environmental thinking – though much closer to the broad approach adopted in this book:

- *our failure to articulate an inspiring and positive vision;*
- *our inability to craft legislative proposals that shape the debate around core American values;*
- *the radical right's control of all three branches of the US Government;*
- *trade policies that undermine environmental protection;*
- *the influence of money in American politics;*
- *poverty;*
- *overpopulation; and*
- *old assumptions about what the problem is and what it isn't.*
(Schellenberger and Nordhaus, 2005)

By 'old assumptions', Schellenberger and Nordhaus are referring to the fact that the standard approach of US environmentalists has not changed much in the 40 plus years since the publication of Rachel Carson's *Silent Spring* (1962): first, define a problem as specifically 'environmental'; then work up a whole set of technical policy solutions to that specific environmental problem; and then persuade legislators to adopt those policies. Their contention is that although this worked really well for 25 years or so, it's brought very little success since the neo-conservatives started out on their crusade to be seen as the defenders of core US values and virtues. By allowing the environment to be seen as just another special interest, to be ranked alongside every other special interest vying for public attention, environmentalists have boxed themselves into a very narrow corner from which it is proving extremely difficult to escape:

> *The marriage between vision, values and policy has proved elusive for environmentalists. Most environmental leaders, even the most vision oriented, are struggling to articulate proposals that have coherence. This is a crisis because environmentalism will never be able to muster the strength it needs to deal with the global warming problem as long as it*

is seen as a 'special interest'. And it will continue to be seen as a special interest as long as it narrowly defines the problem as 'environmental' and the solutions as technical. (Schellenberger and Nordhaus, 2005)

I will return to this question of the balance between vision, values and policy in Chapter 16. Although it simply isn't true (in Europe, anyway) that environmentalists have always put 'the technical policy cart before the vision-and-values horse', the naivety of some environmentalists regarding the scale of the culture war and the ideological battles that they are engaged in has been a problem for a very long time. In a strange sort of way, over-reliance on the assumed power of evidence and on the rational consideration of long-term, collective self-interest to shift political systems has proved to be something of a mistake.

The alternative that is now being pushed much more actively in the US entails the building of a much broader coalition of interests, including trade unionists, industrialists and economists, to crack climate change by creating new jobs in renewables and energy efficiency (rather than appearing to threaten old jobs), and reducing energy costs in the long run by securing much greater energy security. As referred to before, this has been Amory Lovins's crusade for more than two decades, and the subtitle of his latest book makes no bones about his game plan: 'innovation for profits, jobs and security'. He provides a stirring vision:

> *Our energy future is choice, not fate. Oil dependence is a problem we need no longer have – and it's cheaper not to. US oil dependence can be eliminated by proven and attractive technologies that create wealth, enhance choice and strengthen common security. This could be achieved only about as far in the future as the 1973 Arab oil embargo is in the past. When the US last paid attention to oil, in 1977–1985, it cut its oil use 17 per cent while GDP grew 27 per cent. Oil imports fell 50 per cent and imports from the Persian Gulf by 87 per cent in just eight years. That exercise of dominant market power – from the demand side – broke OPEC's ability to set world oil prices for a decade. Today we can rerun that play, only better. The obstacles are less important than the opportunities if we replace ignorance with insight, inattention with foresight, and inaction with mobilization. American business can lead the nation and the world into the post-petroleum era, a vibrant economy and lasting security – if we just realize that we are the people we have been waiting for.* (Lovins, 2005)

Amory Lovins puts enormous emphasis on the role of the business community. And it's certainly true that engineering the transition to a more sustainable world will require the best efforts of business people, professionals, religious and spiritual leaders, NGOs, educationists, the media and so on. But it is clearly politicians who have to make the most decisive interventions to enable others to play a fuller part in that transition. It's governments that win democratic mandates from electorates; it's governments that frame the legal and constitutional boundaries within which individual citizens and corporate entities must operate; it's governments that set the macro-economic framework through the use of fiscal and economic instruments; and it's governments (by and large) that set the tone for public debate and that can take the lead on controversial and potentially divisive issues.

Yet that kind of government-first hierarchy is distinctly out of fashion – for all sorts of reasons. All nation states, for instance, have already ceded a certain amount of national sovereignty to supranational bodies – to the EU, to the UN and to bodies like the WTO. Many governments are now predisposed against decisive interventions in the marketplace, look on regulation as the 'policy instrument of last resort', and greatly prefer the use of voluntary instruments or old-fashioned exhortation to try to change individual or corporate behaviour. What's more, governments have become adept at shedding both risk and responsibility – on to businesses, quangos, arm's length executive agencies, community bodies, citizens and, of course, 'the market' itself.

This is particularly true in the realm of promoting environmentally and socially responsible behaviour in the corporate world. The increasingly authoritative 'business case' for companies voluntarily to reduce their negative environmental and social externalities has come as manna from heaven to today's business-friendly, deregulation-inclined governments. If it can be shown that companies really do end up doing better (for example, by way of market share, performance and shareholder return) by championing corporate responsibility, why shouldn't governments just sit on the sidelines cheering them all on, doing a bit of 'naming and shaming' to encourage the others?

Unfortunately, the *current* approach to corporate responsibility simply isn't up to the task in hand. Indeed, in certain crucial respects, it reinforces patterns of denial among those who really should know better by providing some superficial reassurance that today's massive environmental and social problems really are being taken seriously by the business community. But they aren't.

Although responsibility for bringing about the necessary changes is, indeed, shared between different parties, the *primary* responsibility for making it all happen still lies with government – and that's where our attention must now turn to investigate the scope for bringing forward some short-term but still effective measures to get the transition to a more sustainable economy properly under way.

REFERENCES

Armstrong, K. (2006) 'Violent Islamic radicals know they are heretical', *Guardian*, 8 July

Bello, W. (1999) 'Architectural blueprints, development models and political strategies', paper presented at Economic Sovereignty in a Globalized World conference, March

Carson, R. (1962) *Silent Spring*, Houghton Mifflin, Boston, MA

Christie, I. (2004) 'Culture war', *Elements*, June, Environmental Council, London

Diamond, J. (2005) *Collapse: How Societies Choose to Fail or Succeed*, Allen Lane, London

Edwards, M. (1999) *Future Positive: International Co-operation in the 21st Century*, Earthscan, London

Homer-Dixon, T. (2006) *The Upside of Down*, Island Press, Washington, DC

Joy, B. (2000) 'Why the future doesn't need us', *Wired*, April

Kennedy, R. F. (2004) *Crimes Against Nature*, Penguin, London

Langley, C. (2005) 'The best defence', *New Scientist*, 22 January

Lomborg, B. (2001) *The Skeptical Environmentalist: Measuring the Real State of the World*, Cambridge University Press, Cambridge, UK

Lovins, A. (2005) *Winning the Oil Endgame: Innovation for Profits, Jobs and Security*, Rocky Mountain Institute, Snowmass, CO

New Internationalist (2001) 'Enduring terrors', *New Internationalist*, November

New Scientist (2006) 'Preach your children well', *New Scientist*, 11 November

Northcott, M. (2004) *An Angel Directs the Storm: Apocalyptic Religion and American Empire*, I. B. Tauris, London

Perkins, J. (2004) *Confessions of an Economic Hit Man*, Berrett-Koehler, San Francisco, CA

Rees, M. (2003) *Our Final Century*, William Heinemann, London

Schellenberger, M. and Nordhaus, T. (2005) 'The death of environmentalism: Global warming politics in a post-environmental world', *Grist Magazine*, www.grist.org

Scruton, R. (2002) *The West and the Rest: Globalization and the Terrorist Threat*, Continuum, London

Stiglitz, J. (2006) *Making Globalization Work*, Allen Lane, London

UN (2000) The Millennium Assembly of the United Nations, 6–8 September. Further details available at www.un.org/millennium/summit.htm

US National Academy of Sciences (2002) *Biological Weapons*, National Academy of Sciences, June, Washington, DC

WCSDG (2004) *A Fair Globalization: Creating Opportunities for All*, World Commission on the Social Dimension of Globalization, London

WDM (2006) *Out of Time: The Case for Replacing the World Bank and IMF*, World Development Movement, London

Worldwatch Institute (2005) *State of the World 2005: Global Security*, Earthscan, London

Wright, M. (2005) *Positive Security: A New Politics of Resilience*, Forum for the Future, London

13

Changing the Metrics

INTRODUCTION

One of the best ways of overcoming denial is to show people more clearly exactly what's going on in terms of the constant trade-off between economic progress and environmental damage. Gross Domestic Product just doesn't do that – indeed, it wasn't designed to do that. Simon Kuznets, one of the pioneers of GDP as we know it today, warned the US congress way back in 1934 that the US Administration should be very careful in the way it used measures of national income: 'the welfare of a nation can scarcely be inferred from a measurement of national income.' By 1962, he was getting even more anxious: 'distinctions must be kept in mind between quantity and quality of growth. Goals of "more growth" should always specify more growth *of what* and for *what purpose*.' Though he went on to win a Nobel Prize in 1961, Kuznets's advice was ignored then and still is today.

So we need to develop parallel measures of economic success and quality of life, and to move well beyond our total reliance upon economic metrics by taking proper account of individual wellbeing. In due course, when we start to get really serious about climate change, we will need to become as conscious about carbon as we are about cost, measuring and even trading in the amounts of carbon dioxide that each and every one of us causes to be emitted as we go about our daily lives. But it's *price* that remains the most powerful source of information in a market economy, and politicians will need to think far more systematically about 'ecological tax reform' and other interventions to start penalizing the things we want less of (waste, CO_2 emissions and so on), while reducing the tax burden on things we want more of – jobs, livelihoods, new business start-ups and so on. There has been a lot of talk about this over the years; but politicians never quite seem to find the courage to make it stick in practice.

GROSS DOMESTIC PRODUCT

In Chapter 3, I reviewed some of the critical concerns that economists and activists alike have about the use of GDP as our principal indicator of economic success. There have been many, many attempts made over the years both to provide alternatives to and to adjust GDP so that its influence might be less pernicious. The key factors that these initiatives have sought to take account of include crime (GDP counts as progress the money people spend deterring crime and repairing the damage it causes), other 'defensive expenditures' (cleaning up after pollution incidents, for example), the household and volunteering economy (which remains entirely ignored in calculations of GDP), resource depletion and the degradation of 'natural capital' (as explored in Chapter 7), the distribution of income (a rising tide of GDP emphatically does *not* 'lift all boats'), and a number of lifestyle issues such as work–life balance. None of these initiatives has been entirely successful, but few economists deny that they have raised important concerns which between them constitute a compelling critique of our dependence on GDP today.

So why is it, after ten years of a supposedly radical and fresh-thinking government, that the amount of political will available to address this lamentable state of affairs is all but non-existent? The Labour government boldly produced some 'satellite accounts' in 1998, essentially designed to see what would happen if they deducted the depletion of non-renewable natural capital from GDP. It did that for two years, but then gave up, claiming it was a lot more complicated than it had at first thought. And that's the last that's been heard of this initiative since then.

To be fair, it's *not* all that easy. Campaigners' favoured alternative to GDP is the Index of Sustainable Economic Welfare (ISEW); many others, however, are not entirely persuaded that any single aggregated index can do the job. At this stage, we probably need a much more pluralistic approach, developing a number of different metrics to get people used to the fact that there's more to national success than GDP.

Given all the concerns about the wrong kind of economic growth, it might be imagined that the best prospects for an environmentally sustainable economy would be provided by a no-growth economy. That was the underlying thrust of the debate during the 1970s, and is a view still espoused by a small minority of radical greens today. However, the vast majority of alternative economists have acknowledged that capitalist economies need growth of some description if they are not to be thrown into massive social hardship. All the evidence suggests that a capitalist economy that is not growing at all may not be economically viable. Nor is it necessarily even environmentally benign. This suggests that 'no growth' under capitalism would not further the cause of environmental sustainability as such, but would, in fact, be more likely to put it further beyond reach.

In the broad sweep of human history, it seems most improbable that capitalism will prove to be the last word in humanity's organization of its economic affairs. But it is all that is credibly on offer at present, and if capitalism needs economic growth, then the only chance for social and environmental sustainability in the coming decades is to make that growth consistent with sustainability, rather than conjuring fanciful visions of how to do without it. This is the principal challenge that stands at the core of the concept of sustainable development and the principal problem behind the idea of just 'getting rid of GDP'. As any child psychologist would point out, it is very unwise for parents forcibly to separate their child from his or her security blanket: better by far to divert that child's attention with other compellingly interesting toys or activities.

The inadequacy of GDP stems, in part, from the failure of accounting systems to fully account for 'natural capital'. As we saw in Chapter 7, natural capital can be thought of as the exploitable resources of the Earth's ecosystems – its oceans, forests, mountains and plains – that provide the raw material inputs, resources and flows of energy into our production processes. It also consists of a range of 'ecosystem services', including the maintenance of a stable climate, a protective ozone layer, and the absorptive capacities to disperse, neutralize and recycle the material outputs and pollution generated in ever increasing quantities from our global economy. While some account is taken of the depletion of resources in the calculation of GDP, no account is taken of the degradation of what has been described as 'critical natural capital', the essential ecosystem services without which our lives would look very different.

Evidence of this incomplete accounting is abundant. For example, while governments may account for the timber which is extracted from its forests, they do *not* account for the ecosystem services provided by that forest. These include water storage, soil stability, habitat maintenance, and the regulation of the atmosphere and climate. Unfortunately, the costs of losing these essential ecosystem services only become apparent when they start to break down. In China's Yangtze Basin in 1998, for example, deforestation triggered flooding that killed 3700 people, inundated 24 million hectares of farmland and disrupted the lives of 225 million people. This $30 billion disaster forced a logging moratorium and a $12 billion emergency reforestation programme.

The logic for adjusting our national income calculations to take account of such factors is unanswerable. National income is defined as the amount that may be consumed during the accounting period while leaving the consumer (a nation, in the case of national income) no worse off at the end than at the beginning of the period. Income, therefore, represents a quantity which is, by definition, sustainable precisely because its consumption has not affected the capital stock from which it is derived. However, national income will only faithfully reflect this inherent sustainability of income if the deductions from GDP for capital consumption are an adequate approximation of the *total* consumption of capital that has taken place. At the moment, national income is computed by subtracting capital depreciation from gross income, or GDP. Given that natural capital, in exactly the same way as manufactured capital, makes a significant contribution to the production of GDP, the negative effects on it from that production should, in principle, be subtracted from GDP in exactly the same way as depreciation is subtracted.

It won't be perfect. Calculations would inevitably be very rudimentary to start with. But as any finance director or accountant will tell you, calculations of depreciation on manufactured capital are not exactly state-of-the-art either.

INDEX OF SUSTAINABLE ECONOMIC WELFARE

In 1989, Herman Daly and John Cobb came up with what has since become the favoured alternative among many critics of the status quo: the ISEW. With regard to the US, their conclusion was stark:

> *Despite the year-to-year variations in ISEW, it indicates a long-term trend from the late 1970s to the present that is, indeed, bleak. Economic welfare has been deteriorating for at least a decade, largely as a result of growing income inequality, the exhaustion of resources and the failure to invest adequately to sustain the economy in the future.* (Daly and Cobb, 1989)

In 1994, this work was replicated here in the UK by Professor Tim Jackson, who came to much the same conclusion as Daly and Cobb. The research was then taken up in a big way by the New Economics Foundation, which has done much to popularize the value of the index as a full-blown alternative to GDP. As well as adjusting for the loss of natural capital, the ISEW also seeks to provide a better measure of *welfare* than GDP by adding to it some measures of un-traded benefits (such as unpaid domestic work), by subtracting the value of activities which are traded but do not contribute to human welfare (such as the treatment of pollution-related illnesses), and by correcting for income inequality. ISEW calculations for several other developed countries all show the same overall pattern of levelling off and decline. This overall shape is robust over a wide range of weightings of the contributory factors – a partial answer to valid criticisms that the ISEW is something of a methodological mongrel, made by arbitrarily aggregating those proverbial 'apples and pears'!

In international terms, perhaps the best known and simplest of alternative indicators is the United Nations Development Programme's Human Development Index (HDI), which has some similarities with the ISEW. The HDI is calculated annually for the UNDP's *Human Development Report* to allow simple comparisons to be made between different countries. It is based on three essential dimensions: longevity (as measured by life expectancy at birth); knowledge (as measured by adult literacy and enrolment ratios at primary, secondary and tertiary levels); and prosperity – as measured by GDP per capita.

From the point of view of biophysical sustainability, the key measure is how much economic value we can derive from ever lower levels of material throughput. And from an international perspective, that should indeed be the principal comparator of relative economic success and competitiveness, rather than GDP, if we are going to start getting serious about resource efficiency.

Given global population growth and current aspirations for increased material prosperity, Paul Ekins (2000) and others have calculated that to achieve environmental sustainability in an affluent industrial country would require a reduction in the environmental intensity of consumption (the environmental impact per unit of consumption) by a factor of about ten (that is, a 90 per cent reduction) by about 2050. Thereafter, if economic growth continues, the environmental intensity of consumption will have to continue to decrease, at least at the rate of economic growth for those impacts that are at the threshold of sustainability.

It has to be said that the current picture on *overall* resource consumption in industrialized countries is reasonably encouraging. Research by the Wuppertal Institute in Germany showed that the UK's 'total material requirement' grew by just 12 per cent between 1970 and 1999, while GDP increased by 88 per cent during the same time, a 'decoupling' of economic growth and resource use that has surprised many commentators given the enormous difficulties that the UK has had in implementing effective waste policies. Much of the decoupling effect, however, can be attributed to the shift from manufacturing to services (which tend to have a far lower environmental impact per unit of GDP), and the export or 'off-shoring' of much of our most polluting economic activity. A 'win' for us, perhaps, but certainly not for the global environment. Governments around the world are going to have to get much more serious about 'decoupling' GDP from resource consumption, over and above more conventional measures of economic success such as growth per se, jobs, productivity and so on.

AND WHAT ABOUT WELLBEING?

Lastly, any consideration of metrics must address the vexed issue of how people are feeling about all this – their perception of 'life satisfaction', level of contentment, happiness, call it what you will. For a long time, alternative economists have pointed out just how important it is to look at whether or not people are actually getting any happier as a consequence of all this astonishing economic growth and increased prosperity, and the disturbing reality (described in Chapter 3) would appear to be that we are not. Policy-makers in rich countries are, in effect, confronted with a double dilemma: increased economic growth is generating more and more negative externalities that threaten to overwhelm the life-support systems upon which we depend; yet, at the same time, increased economic growth isn't necessarily making people any happier. You'd think that devastating combination might stimulate some rather more creative thinking (particularly in Her Majesty's Treasury) but, so far, no such luck.

Elsewhere, all sorts of efforts have been made to construct a specific 'wellbeing index' to take a nation's pulse, as it were, in terms of levels of contentment and people's general satisfaction with their work, personal life, achievements and so on. Apart from Bhutan's measure of 'Gross Domestic Happiness' as a direct alternative to GDP, most of these are similar to the ISEW, focusing on national, social and economic indicators.

What is still missing, of course, is the much more subjective, impressionistic feelings that individuals experience year on year, though it's questionable whether there is any real value in trying to quantify subjective perceptions of that kind in any way other than by 'big picture generalization' – along the lines of 'more or less happy/content' at any particular moment. Quantification often obscures the subtlety of all the different factors involved in making us feel up or down about our lives. Professor Tim O'Riordan and I, for instance, have been exploring a 'wellbeing map' for use by UK local authorities as they develop their sustainable community strategies, showing the principal influences on a cluster of key determinants (see Figure 13.1). But imagine what it would take, first, to measure each of those influencing factors in its own right, and then to aggregate them into a single indicator!

The UK-based think-tank New Economics Foundation has just pioneered a new set of metrics looking both at key environmental and social indicators, and at perceptions of happiness. The Happy Planet Index measures for the first time both human life and happiness, and the impact of an economy on the sustainability of planet Earth. Hence 'happy' and 'planet' in the title – however naff that may sound. Objectively measurable indicators include, on the social side, income distribution, longevity, infant mortality and levels of education; and on the environmental side, the use of both renewable and non-renewable resources, as well as the objective quality of the natural environment including air, water and soil. 'Happiness' is measured by a set of subjective questions about how people experience the quality of their lives, including how participative people think their democracy is.

The richest countries in GDP terms come pretty low on the Happy Planet Index – and not only because their developed economies create such large ecological footprints. Their people experience a relatively low level of life satisfaction as well. For that reason, Britain comes 108th, and the US 150th. The Pacific Island of Vanuatu comes top, with its citizens enjoying long lives and a laid-back lifestyle, embedded in flourishing local economies with a low environmental impact, and New Zealand comes second.

But the big question lurking behind any consideration of wellbeing is not so much whether it can be measured (for if it can't be measured, it's difficult to plan for strategic policy interventions to improve it), but whether politicians should be getting stuck in here at all. At one level, it's perfectly obvious they should, as reflected in these two comments from Tony Blair – 'Money isn't everything. Delivering the best possible quality of life means more than concentrating solely on economic growth' – and David Cameron – 'We should all be thinking not just about what is good for putting money in people's pockets, but what is good for putting joy in people's hearts'. On the other hand, the default, laissez-faire position – that the job of governments is simply to maintain the rule of law and to engineer an efficient, competitive and reasonably fair economy – still commands a lot of support in a nation that has an almost paranoid aversion to anything resembling a

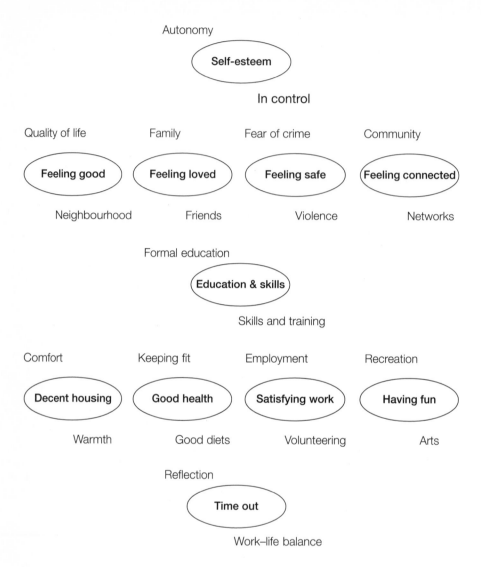

Source: Sustainable Development Commission

Figure 13.1 *The components of wellbeing*

'nanny state'. Since wellbeing and happiness are such slippery, subjective concepts, impossible to pin down let alone to measure, shouldn't governments just keep their noses out of it?

There's an appealing simplicity to this approach, but it conveniently overlooks the empirical evidence that relying exclusively on increases in economic growth and per capita income is having a direct *negative* influence on people's wellbeing – in other words, governments are not acting as neutral ring-holders, but are *actively* stacking the odds against people enjoying more balanced and contented lives. The complete disregard on the part of government ministers for soaring levels of personal debt here in the UK, despite clear evidence of the impact debt has on levels of stress and poor health, for instance, is surely taking laissez-faire just a little too far?

Perhaps all this already represents 'index overload' anyway? But we badly need a short, sharp statistical shock to the system if we are to challenge the continuing, but wholly illegitimate, supremacy of GDP. 'Surfacing the data' is the first step in this transitional process; interpreting it and using it to transform government policies and practices is obviously even more important. This is sometimes called 'mainstreaming sustainability', and although it's hardly the stuff of headline grabbing news coverage, it would probably have a bigger impact upon changing the culture and institutions of government than dozens of one-off, ad hoc, 'just do it' initiatives.

PRICE SIGNALS AND TAX REFORM

To move towards environmental sustainability, capitalist economies will need to ensure that they use the forces of structural change to shift away from environmentally intensive sectors and develop new, comparative advantages and capabilities in technologies and sectors with low environmental impact – or, even better, in technologies and sectors concerned with environmental restoration and improvement. Such an economy will earn income and sustain livelihoods even as it improves environmental performance, one of the great win–win opportunities offered by the new imperative of achieving biophysical sustainability.

Prices are the key to this transformation. Prices are fundamental both with regard to the present allocation of resources and in influencing the direction of economic development in the future. But as we have seen, prices today rarely reflect full environmental costs. For markets to operate efficiently, we need environmental taxes to help internalize those costs. As Paul Ekins (1997) points out, environmental taxes also have a fundamental role in moving an economy towards environmental sustainability and keeping it there:

- *By charging for the use or depletion of resources, they signal the end of 'environmental free goods', whether the goods in question are water, air (as a dump for pollutants) or soil. Perceptions of scarcity are among the strongest motivations in markets for the development of substitutes and of more efficient technologies.*
- *An escalating price signal not only weakens or removes the rebound effect, it strengthens incentives for further efficiency gains. In a growing economy, an escalating price is also necessary to maintain the cost of using the environment relative to incomes.*

- *Charging for use of the environment stimulates structural change away from environmentally intensive sectors towards those that are less damaging.*
- *Environmental taxes raise revenues which, even when they are successful in dampening demand for the object of the taxation, can remain substantial. This allows other taxes, in particular taxes on labour, to be reduced. This stimulates employment.*

Such price signals would simultaneously stimulate continuous technological change, reinforce consumers' environmental awareness, counteract any rebound effect, strengthen incentives for increased environmental efficiency, offset the income effect of economic growth, and change the structure of the economy in favour of environmentally neutral or beneficial sectors. It may confidently be predicted that a fiscal shift of this sort will be an essential element of any transition by capitalism to biophysical sustainability, and it is now one of the highest priorities of all those organizations around the world seeking to promote a new economic paradigm – often in the teeth of ecologically-illiterate governments.

In political terms, however, it's not quite that simple! Seeking increased environmental efficiency simply by raising the price of key resources will, where these resources provide for basic needs, be likely to be regressive – that is, the poor will pay a higher proportion of their income in meeting that tax than the rich. That is politically unacceptable. However, regressive effects can *always* be removed by complementary measures if there is the political will. And there is more than one social justice issue at work here. When the present generation's unwillingness to face up to these issues causes it to fail to pay the full environmental costs of its own activities, these costs are simply shifted onto future generations, which is, in effect, as inequitable as failing to remove regressive effects in the present.

Environmental policy, especially when implemented through environmental taxes, does not need to be regressive, however. When raising revenue from the relatively rich as well as from the poor, there is always enough money from the tax to give rebates to the latter so that regressivity is removed. Alternatively, regressivity may be removed by exempting from the tax an initial *tranche* of use of the resource – a minimum entitlement, as it were, to ensure that basic needs are properly met in all households. This is done with water in some parts of Portugal and with domestic energy in The Netherlands.

Policies to remove any regressivity in environmental policy are not an optional extra, but a prerequisite for successful policy-making. Environmental policy that bears harder on the poor than the well-off in order to generate benefits for, or fulfil obligations to, future generations makes no sense in terms of social justice, and is obviously completely 'unsellable' in today's political climate. If policies to achieve and maintain environmental sustainability are to be implemented, they must both be socially just *and* be seen to be socially just.

Given the overarching significance of pursuing this process of 'ecological tax reform', it is disappointing that progress is currently so slow in so many countries. If there was one thing that the UK Government could do to kick-start the transition to a more sustainable economy, it would be to get serious about eco-taxation. *Guarantee* fiscal neutrality (so that eco-taxes are not seen as cynical revenue-raisers for governments that care little about the state of the environment), map the scale of the changes required, give business plenty of time to gear their investment decisions to the new fiscal environment, disregard the whingeing of narrow, backward-looking business interests (as we saw in Chapter 7, research going back over the last 30 years shows that the *real* costs to business of environmental improvements and higher standards is a fraction of the *projected* costs that business organizations invent to keep such improvements at bay), and get on with it.

In some areas, decisive action *is* being taken in the UK: landfill tax, for instance, will increase by £9 per tonne per annum (from 2008 onwards) – still much less than in many other European countries, but a clear enough signal of the need for dramatic changes in our waste management strategy. In other areas (such as pesticide reduction or ending the anomaly that no taxes are paid on aviation fuel), it is all talk still, with no real intent to get to grips with the different problems. The doubling of Air Passenger Duty in 2006 was an example of exactly how *not* to use fiscal interventions, with the extra £1 billion it raises going straight into general tax receipts, providing little if any incentive for change, and leaving consumers either deeply aggrieved or completely cynical.

The astonishing increases in air travel over the last few years have stimulated intense debate not just about national (or European) measures to compel at least partial internalization of the environmental costs of flying, but about a global scheme to levy a charge on *all* international flights to generate additional income for international aid – at the kind of scale that is now required. The French Government has been particularly active in promoting a Europe-wide Airline Ticket Levy, a proposal eventually trumped in 2006 by the decision to bring aviation into the EU Emissions Trading Scheme (ETS) in 2011. There remains considerable controversy over whether or not this will have *any* impact on holding down demand for aviation, and many more see the advocacy of this route (both by governments and by some airlines) simply as a means of delaying things as long as possible or warding off much tougher sanctions such as a global kerosene tax.

By contrast, the other well-known idea for a new global tax (the so-called Tobin Tax) on the value of all foreign exchange transactions continues to command substantial support, with the Canadian Government formally committed to such a measure and many European countries actively investigating the feasibility of it. Professor Tobin (a Nobel laureate for economics) first came up with the idea during the late 1970s, with the dual intention of reining in market volatility and raising revenue for international development. Since then, the problems associated with foreign exchange transactions have intensified. In 1983, the *daily* volume of foreign exchange trading was around $550 billion; now it is over $2 trillion and growing by around 20 per cent a year – whereas real physical trade grows by little more than 5 per cent per annum. Of that $2 trillion, as much as 95 per cent is purely speculative, moving from one trader to another in a virtual economy all of its own.

Despite the enormous scale and potential of this proposal (estimates made by the Stamp Out Poverty campaign suggest that a 0.005 per cent charge on transactions of the world's most heavily traded currencies could generate between $35 billion and $40 billion a year without making any serious dent in banking sector profits), there is still a very long way to go before this proposal makes further progress, with countries such as the UK and the US predictably hostile. The situation is rather more encouraging on other reform issues – there are, for instance, at least eight European countries that have introduced a carbon tax of one kind or another.

However, on the equally pressing issue of eliminating the wide range of 'perverse subsidies' that still dog so many economies, progress remains very slow. As Norman Myers has argued, these perverse subsidies are particularly damaging (in terms of the environment) in six main sectors: fossil fuels (exacerbating acid rain, urban smog and global warming); road transportation (causing local and national air pollution, and contributing to congestion and road accidents); agriculture (promoting unnecessary production and causing every conceivable kind of environmental impact, from soil erosion to loss of biodiversity); forestry (supporting over-logging in every corner of the world); water use (encouraging inefficiency in agriculture and industry, and reducing already scarce supplies); and fisheries (with numerous fish species now on the verge of commercial if not biological extinction and a cost to taxpayers for this area alone of around $20 billion a year) (Myers, 2002). As Myers points out, this borders on the insane:

> If perverse subsidies were to be reduced, there would be a double divid-end. First, there would be an end to the formidable obstacles imposed by such subsidies on sustainable development. Second, there would be a huge stock of funds available to give an entirely new push to sustainable development – funds on a scale unlikely to become available through any other source. In the case of the US, for instance, they would amount to $550 billion. An American pays taxes of at least $2000 a year to fund perverse subsidies, and then pays another $1000 through increased costs for marketplace goods and through environmental degradation.
> (Myers, 2002)

The principal reason for this kind of backsliding, as we saw in earlier chapters, is that taking cost internalization and resource productivity seriously (that is, systematically driving down resource and energy consumption across the entire economy) is not as pain-free as it first appears. There are losers as well as winners, and unavoidable political consequences. However disconcerting it may be for relatively affluent, well-educated environmentalists, most people not only enjoy the benefits of a cheap-energy, consumer-driven economy, but would appear to be relatively unconcerned about the impact of this upon future generations. They are undoubtedly *not* out dancing in the streets at the news that such an economy's days are numbered in the interests of intergenerational equity!

However, it is equally misguided to underestimate the huge economic benefits that will accompany many of the necessary shifts. The single most important requirement for structural change required for biophysical sustainability is a shift from fossil fuels to renewable energy sources. The EU has estimated that the renewables business in the EU will be valued at 37 billion euros by 2010, with a further 17 billion euros from exports in the expanding world markets. The World Energy Council has projected that cumulative global investments in renewables from 2000 to 2010 will be in the range of $200 billion to $500 billion. This makes renewables likely to be the biggest single market opportunity to emerge in this field (or, indeed, in any other) through to the middle of this century. It suggests that while the shift to renewables may, indeed, be an absolute prerequisite for capitalism to become more environmentally sustainable, it also provides an unparalleled opportunity for the kind of entrepreneur-driven technological change in the generation of which capitalism excels.

There will be many other opportunities. Today's technology optimists draw attention to a dazzling array of possibilities across the whole range of environmental impacts, which could serve to reduce these impacts by the amounts required for environmental sustainability. Some of the possibilities are already available and only require that businesses become aware of them and governments stimulate their introduction for them to become fully competitive in the marketplace. Others still need development. However, over time and given a favourable framework of public policy, there seems to be no reason why these should not quite naturally become part of the next generation of infrastructure and industrial production. Closed-loop production processes with zero emissions, producer responsibility for material flows through to the end of the life of all products, and full re-use or recyclability of these products could cause today's problems of waste disposal and toxic pollution to be viewed, from the vantage point of 2020, in the same light as urban pollution from horse manure in the 1880s or the London smogs of the 1950s.

THE METRICS OF CLIMATE CHANGE

A growing number of commentators have recently been advocating even more radical approaches, especially in the face of growing concern about the impacts of climate change. One of the most interesting of these is the idea of 'personal carbon allowances', with each individual above a certain age being allocated an annual carbon quota to cover all personal consumption. Everyone would receive exactly the same quota, regardless of income, and as the quota was gradually brought down (in response to the need to reduce global emissions), individuals could either sell whatever fraction of their quota they didn't need, or buy the extra allocation they required to make possible a more carbon-intensive lifestyle.

For a radical new idea to work in today's highly controversial climate change debates, it has got to work on many different levels. This one does. Internationally, the arguments have already started regarding what is going to come after 2012 – the final year covered by the current Kyoto Protocol agreement. Some countries favour a relatively straightforward reworking of Kyoto, with much tougher targets for OECD countries, including the US, and first-time targets for developing countries (that currently are not included). Others have already written off this kind of process on the grounds that the US will never have anything to do with it, now or in the future, and are exploring an 'equal rights for all' approach. Each person on Earth would have an equal right to emit a given amount of CO_2 equivalent (in effect, an equal share of the capacity of the atmosphere to absorb those greenhouse gases), with each country's national allocation calculated according to its population.

The assiduous campaigning over the last decade by the Global Commons Institute (based on its idea of 'contract and converge', under which the rich nations undertake to reduce emissions even as developing nations are permitted to grow their emissions until such time as per capita emissions converge at the same level) has given this kind of approach some real credibility. So, too, has the growing readiness of developing countries such as Brazil, Indonesia and Argentina to accept emissions targets for their own counties – not least because they too are already beginning to feel the impacts of climate change.

The real strength of this approach is that it is based upon a trading system, with rich nations needing to purchase additional carbon credits from poorer nations. This appeals a lot to those campaigning for global economic justice: a global trading system in carbon would begin to shift substantial resources from rich countries to poor countries as nations with wasteful, carbon-intensive lifestyles have to purchase additional carbon credits from nations with low-carbon economies.

One of the indirect benefits of personalizing it in this way (through individual allowances) is that it makes transparent what is currently completely hidden from most people – that we are all, in one way or another, complicit in the growing emissions that are contributing to climate change. The reality is that carbon is going to have to become almost as important a measure of value as money, with people instinctively taking account not just of the cost of something, but of its carbon intensity – the amount of carbon embedded in any product or service. Such parallel 'carbon metrics' will be quite a stretch for people brought up in an age where the environment counted for literally nothing in the pursuit of an ever higher material standard of living, but will rapidly become second nature for young people more and more alert to the implications of climate change in terms of their own future prospects. Indeed, I wager that it won't be long before the latest mobile phone comes fully equipped with its very own 'carbon calculator' to give young people an instant take on the amount of carbon 'embedded' in a particular pair of jeans or CD! And with three of the largest retailers in the UK now firmly committed to 'carbon labelling' on all their products, this is rapidly becoming a commercial reality rather than a distant pipe dream.

However, it's already abundantly clear that any trading system (on a global, regional, national or even personal basis) is inevitably going to be very complex, with all sorts of 'weak links' in the systems which may lead to serious under-performance, false or double accounting, and 'carbon scams' of every variety. The EU's own ETS has performed very poorly in its first (voluntary) phase between 2003 and 2007, primarily because governments played fast and loose with setting their own national limits in order to protect their own industries. Fortunately, the EU Commission has now got its act together in terms of regulating for the legally-binding period between 2008 and 2012, and there is growing optimism in the carbon markets themselves that the ETS could now begin to deliver the goods. In geopolitical terms, that's crucially important; with the US Congress now actively contemplating what a cap-and-trade scheme might look like for the US (with the strong encouragement of many US companies), it's clear that the US will not re-enter international negotiations for what happens after 2012 unless proposals are based on some kind of trading system.

As we've already seen in Chapter 1, that may not be the most effective way of determining a price for carbon. Many economists believe it would be simpler, more transparent and less vulnerable to abuse to levy a charge or tax on the carbon content of *all* sources of energy at the point where they enter the economy. Those additional costs would then be passed on to all users of those different kinds of energy until they eventually (as ever!) reach the consumer. There's more to this than just another spat between economists. Trading systems (including personal carbon allowances) will undoubtedly encourage higher levels of 'carbon literacy', involving all organizations and individuals in the decisions taken at different levels in society to reduce CO_2 emissions. Tax-based systems, imposed as far upstream in the economy as possible and involving very few corporate players, may well be more effective, but would almost certainly obscure personal responsibility for reducing CO_2 emissions. Some liken this to the difference between an 'open source' carbon economy based on trading, and a 'Microsoft Windows', one-size-fits-all carbon economy based on taxation.

Personalized carbon allowances, in this 'dual currency' world, will clearly have a huge impact upon the business community, directing companies into ever more ingenious ways of getting the carbon out of whatever it is that they are selling. As with any initiative to create a genuinely transparent and fair market by eliminating historical distortions caused by the refusal of previous governments to come down hard on systematic cost externalization, there will be the usual fall-out in terms of winners and losers. In *How We Can Save the Planet* Mayer Hillman (2005) presents a balance sheet under a low-carbon economy (see Table 13.1). Hillman himself prefers to talk about 'carbon rationing' as a less mealy-mouthed way of getting people to understand what's really going on:

> In comparison with food rationing, carbon rationing would, in some respects, be less prescriptive and intrusive in everyday life. People could select from a range of ways in which to adjust their lifestyles and energy use in order to reduce their personal carbon dioxide emissions. However, the need for carbon limitation is likely to be less clearly felt than the need for food rationing. This was necessary to ensure that populations remained well fed at a time of national crisis and restricted food supplies. Education has a key role to play so that the public understands why rationing is being introduced and for that reason supports it as the only fair and realistic way of responding to climate change. (Hillman, 2005)

However much one may doubt the wisdom of wartime mindsets and the language of sacrifice, Hillman is right to bring it all back to education and to the complex psychology of transforming people's attitudes and lifestyles. As the

Table 13.1 *Balance sheet of a low-carbon economy*

Winners	Losers
Manufacturers of efficient appliances, lights, cars, etc	Manufacturers of inefficient appliances, lights, cars, etc
Construction industry, other than the transport sector	Construction industry for the transport sector
Renewable energy manufacturers – for example, of wind turbines and solar water heating	Manufacturers and suppliers of fossil fuel energy stations
Biofuel companies	Fossil fuel companies
Bus and bicycle manufacturers	Car manufacturers
Organic and other UK farmers	Energy-intensive agriculture
Domestic tourism	Overseas tourism
Bicycle repair shops	Garages and petrol stations
Local shops and businesses	Regional shopping centres
Service and knowledge economy	Short-life goods economy
International communication systems	Airlines
Businesses offering low energy/carbon solutions – for example, zero-energy homes	Businesses selling high-energy systems – for example, domestic air conditioning
New technologies such as micro-combined heat and power (CHP), electric heat pumps, hybrid cars and airships	Old technologies such as direct heating

Source: Hillman (2005)

American economist Lester Thurow has written: 'The proper role of government in capitalist societies is to represent the interests of the future to the present.' Yet, in many ways that gets harder and harder in a world seemingly obsessed with instant gratification and short-term profit maximization – which puts the pressure not just on governments to act today 'in the interests of the future', but on those who create the wealth that enriches the lives of so many hundreds of millions of people.

REFERENCES

Daly, H. and Cobb, J. (1989) *For the Common Good*, Beacon Press, Boston, MA

Ekins, P. (1997) 'Sustainability: The challenge for capitalism in the new century', unpublished paper for Forum for the Future

Ekins, P. (2000) *Economic Growth and Environmental Sustainability*, Routledge, London

Hillman, M. (2005) *How We Can Save the Planet*, Penguin, London

Myers, N. (2002) 'Sustainable development: Tackling problems – Or sources of problems?', in H. van Ginkel and B. Barrett (eds) *Human Development and the Environment*, United Nations University Press, Tokyo

14

Business Excellence

INTRODUCTION

Companies started to come under pressure from governments to reduce their impacts upon the environment and society more than 30 years ago, giving rise to a continuing swathe of regulation to oblige them to internalize more and more of the costs they once imposed upon society. But all of today's progressive companies have now moved way beyond the regulated minimum, and are voluntarily seeking out a more durable convergence between their shareholders' interests and broader societal interests. Some of this is serious; some is still in the green-wash mode – or 'bluewash' in the case of the United Nations Global Compact. Recent initiatives, all underpinned by a strong business case, have stimulated more creative partnerships to help fashion sustainable livelihoods for some of the world's poorest people. The real test, however, is to gauge just how successful companies have been in 'mainstreaming' these sustainability behaviours through more integrated management practices and better metrics and accounting. This is hardly the high point in today's sustainable development debates – but crucial in understanding what's really happening in practice.

REVIEWING THE BUSINESS CASE

I would argue that the kind of opportunity-driven agenda outlined in Chapters 10 and 13 gives the lie to right-wing commentators, conservative think-tanks and defensive trade associations that sustainable development must, by definition, be anti-business and anti-prosperity. What one suspects that they don't like is the idea that the self-same market forces which they venerate may well turn out to be the most powerful driver of change in our inevitable transition to a sustainable economy.

So, is the role of business just to sit back and wait for government and international bodies to change the rules of the game, restructure markets and rebalance the short-term interests of profit-maximizing shareholders with the longer-term concerns of other stakeholders? In the strictest sense, the answer to that question has to be 'yes': only governments have the democratic mandate

Table 14.1 *The business benefits of sustainable development*

Eco-efficiency	1	Reduced costs
	2	Costs avoided (design for environment, eco-innovation)
	3	Optimal investment strategies
Quality management	4	Better risk management
	5	Greater responsiveness in volatile markets
	6	Staff motivations/commitment
	7	Enhanced intellectual capital
Licence to operate	8	Reduced costs of compliance/planning permits/licences
	9	Enhanced reputation with all key stakeholders
	10	Influence with regulator/government, etc
Market advantage	11	Stronger brands
	12	Customer preference/loyalty
	13	Lower costs of capital
	14	New products/processes/services
	15	Attracting the right talent
Sustainable profits	16	Option creation
	17	New business/increased market share
	18	Enhanced shareholder value

Source: Prince of Wales's Business and the Environment Programme (2005)

to re-engineer the macro-economic framework in that sort of way. However, the onus is increasingly on companies to be proactive rather than reactive, to anticipate inevitable change, to fill the space available to them for much more environmentally and socially responsible actions, and to lobby government in favour of faster change, rather than oppose it at every turn.

The idea of there being a specific business case for sustainable development (one that is framed and articulated in terms of business priorities and using business-friendly language) goes back to the creation of the World Business Council for Sustainable Development (WBCSD) in the run-up to the 1992 Earth Summit in Rio de Janeiro. Looking back on that early documentation, one can see just how crude a concept it was at that time, with almost all of the emphasis on 'savings to the bottom line through eco-efficiency', or on the importance of 'earning the licence to operate in society'. As Table 14.1 shows (this is now the standard potential benefits list we use in both Forum for the Future and the Prince of Wales's Business and the Environment Programme), things have moved on a long way since then.

All sorts of companies have found their own way of assessing their own particular business case, drawing on a combination of different benefits to demonstrate the clear convergence between shareholder interests and increased environmental and social responsibility. And an ever wider range of academics and business consultancies has sought to provide some coherent intellectual underpinning to what has been, in effect, a pretty pragmatic process of promoting changed behaviour. One of the most persuasive of these is the 'shareholder value model' developed by Stuart Hart (see Figure 14.1).

With the warning that 'firms must perform well in all four quadrants of the model if they are to continuously generate shareholder value over time' (and those two little words 'over time' are very important in the context of the debate about short-term profit maximization and building long-term shareholder value), Hart proceeds to fill out the different boxes in the model (see Figure 14.2).

For those suspicious of business school models of this kind, the good news is that huge progress has been made in terms of 'operationalizing' ideas of this kind over the last few years. Perhaps the best overview of this can be found in Dan Esty and Andrew Winston's *Green to Gold*, which came out at the end of 2006 and provides a massive wealth of detail about companies (predominantly US-based) making the business case work for them. It offers a very applied 'how to/how not to' primer for companies intent on moving this agenda forward, and demonstrates quite clearly that the only way to maximize the benefits of the business case is to move the whole agenda into the corporate mainstream, rather than leaving it marooned in the hands of a small group of corporate social responsibility (CSR)/ sustainable development professionals – however dedicated and skilled they may be.

Fifteen years on from the Earth Summit in Rio de Janeiro (where the World Business Council for Sustainable Development first articulated the business case for sustainable development), it is now possible to start drawing some conclusions about the nature of business leadership that is driving these shifts in corporate behaviour. Some very big players have emerged along the way, and some have inevitably fallen by the wayside. None bigger than Bill Ford of the Ford Motor Company, whose massive losses and shutdowns in 2006 have caused a number of analysts to question whether the company has any kind of long-term future at all. What makes this fall from grace so riveting is the very direct part that sustainability (or, rather, the lack of it) has played in this process, with Ford entirely misreading the market all the way through the 1990s as it continued to rely on gas-guzzling SUVs and light trucks for the lion's share of its profitability. Even before Hurricane Katrina in 2005, gas prices had begun to rise and ever larger numbers of US motorists went in search of much more fuel-efficient vehicles, causing SUV sales to plummet. That explains, in part, the astonishing rise of Toyota, whose hybrids and eco-friendly reputation have led to record profits and a serious challenge both to Ford and to General Motors (GM) for ascendancy in the US market. Dan Esty is scathing about Ford's leadership failure:

> Ford's blue and white logo once embodied America's industrial might.
> It now stands as a symbol of short-sighted management. It isn't the only
> company to have been blindsided by the 'Green Wave' washing over the
> business world, but it is ironic that just-departed CEO Bill Ford, who
> is known for his environmental interests, never succeeded in getting

Source: Hart (2005)

Figure 14.1 *The shareholder value model*

Source: Hart (2005)

Figure 14.2 *The second shareholder value model*

> *his leadership team to understand the need to make the environment*
> *a core element of the company's business strategy. Ford had several*
> *eco-initiatives on the go, but they failed to address the company's real*
> *vulnerabilities. The market shift towards more eco-friendly and efficient*
> *cars caught Ford flat-footed with a product line heavy on fuel-chugging*
> *and pollution-spewing behemoths like the Expedition and Navigator.*
> (Esty, 2006)

It's an unforgiving world for leaders in corporate sustainability. Even John Browne, the redoubtable former Chief Executive of BP whose bold initiatives to reposition BP as the most progressive and environmentally conscious of all the oil companies have seized people's imagination throughout the last decade, saw his star wane by the end of 2006. BP's 'Beyond Petroleum' gambit came under severe pressure at that time when the disaster at the BP Texas City Refinery and serious operational failures on its Alaska pipelines and elsewhere took the shine off BP's green credentials. Critics began to contrast the limited impact of its commitment to invest around $400 million a year in its renewable energy portfolio with the much bolder strategic commitment of General Electric (GE) in creating its Ecomagination business in 2004. GE's revenues from renewables, energy-efficient and environmentally advanced products soared from $6.2 billion in 2004 to more than $17 billion in 2006, and GE is going flat out to command an ever higher share in the 'cleantech markets' opening up all around the world – particularly in China and India.

But the company which has really seized the attention of 'corporate watchers' in the green movement is Wal-Mart. In October 2005, its Chief Executive Lee Scott announced perhaps the most ambitious 'greening' programme ever seen from a leading US company. With images of Hurricane Katrina still resonating in his mind (he has described today's environmental disaster as 'Hurricane Katrina in slow motion'), Lee Scott committed the company to a wide range of 'stretch targets' affecting both its own direct operations and all its supply chains:

- *Trucks/Shipping*
  - *+25 per cent efficiency gains in 3 yrs, +50 per cent in 10*
    (=$310m saving by 2015)
  - *1 mpg improvement in its fleet*
    (=$52m saving per annum)
- *Stores*
  - *Reduce CO_2 emissions from existing stores by 20 per cent*
    in 7 years
  - *30 per cent lower emissions from new stores*
- *Waste*
  - *Recycle as much plastic as possible – to save $28m per annum*
  - *Reduce solid waste by 25 per cent in 3 years*

- *Products*
  - *Organic cotton at no on-cost to consumers*
  - *MSC certified seafood in all US stores as soon as possible*
- *Operations*
  - *Wal-Mart senior executives now have their rewards directly linked to the delivery of sustainability goals.*
  - *Suppliers who collaborate with Wal-Mart on this agenda will be 'rewarded'.*

If this is for real (and *all* Wal-Mart's main suppliers, who are now on the receiving end of the familiar Wal-Mart 'squeeze', focused this time on 'price plus sustainability' rather than just price, have all commented just how 'real' it feels from their perspective!), then it represents a huge step forward. NGOs understandably find this very hard to stomach, not least because the equally serious *social* impacts of Wal-Mart's global operations remain entirely unaddressed. Charles Fishman's *The Wal-Mart Effect* and Robert Greenwald's excoriating documentary about Wal-Mart (*Wal-Mart: The High Cost of Low Price*) have both stripped the Wal-Mart success story right back down to its basics: low wages, constant ill-treatment of its employees, a disregard for local communities, a fanatical hatred of trade unions, and an utterly ruthless approach to squeezing suppliers (Fishman, 2005; Greenwald, 2005).

Wal-Mart may not even be out of the woods on the green front, with a fierce battle now underway in the US between those NGOs like Environmental Defense and the Natural Resources Defense Council (NRDC) who are working with Wal-Mart to ensure it delivers on all its commitments, and more radical NGOs and campaigners who are convinced that no amount of 'greening around the edges' could offset the massive damage caused by Wal-Mart in the kind of business model it has. Here's Stacy Mitchell on that score:

> *In January 2007 alone, Wal-Mart opened 70 stores in the US. At current growth rates, by 2015, Wal-Mart will have enlarged its domestic footprint by 20,000 acres, turning CO_2-absorbing fields and forests into stores and parking lots. Big-box stores make incredibly inefficient use of land. These new stores will use more electricity than its energy-efficiency measures will save. By making its existing outlets 20 per cent more efficient, Wal-Mart says it will cut CO_2 emissions by 2.5 million metric tonnes by 2013. But new stores built this year alone will consume enough electricity to add about 1 million metric tonnes of CO_2 to the atmosphere.* (Mitchell, 2007)

Whichever way you look at this (breakthrough or outrageous greenwash), there's no doubt the Wal-Mart initiative has had a big impact on retailers around the world. Here in the UK, Tesco has moved from a position based on doing as little as it needed to in order to keep its customers happy, to a much more proactive stance where it's seeking to work with customers to help them reduce their own environmental footprint – for instance, halving the price of all energy-efficient light bulbs. But there's still something 'added on' about the Tesco model, in clear contrast to the Marks and Spencer 'Plan A', a £200 million five-year plan to transform the way it does business across all its activities. This 100-point action plan is without doubt the most radical mainstream strategy that Forum for the Future has been involved in, with some of the targets (carbon neutral by 2012, zero waste needing to go to landfill, sustainable supply chains throughout the business, increasingly targeted interventions on healthy eating and living and so on) necessitating some massive shifts in business behaviour.

Looking at case studies such as these, one gets the distinct feeling that we are on the very edge of a sea-change in corporate behaviour. What counts as CSR today will soon be seen as the palest imitation of genuinely sustainable behaviour. And those in the CSR industry who currently prosper by peddling superficial add-on palliatives to inherently unsustainable business models need to check out their own business model if they have their own sustainability in mind.

THE SEDUCTIVE ILLUSION OF CSR

When it comes to 'filling the space available' to companies (the territory between the regulated minimum and the point where shareholder interests are jeopardized by behaving uncompetitively or too riskily), the difference between today's prevailing band-aid CSR and an integrated, strategic commitment to becoming genuinely sustainable, over time, couldn't be greater. The very fact that the majority of companies still opt for CSR (or, increasingly, just 'CR' without the 'S') as the self-contained box into which to pack all their 'good stuff', while they continue to pursue their core business (quite legally and, indeed, quite logically, given the failure of politicians to change the rules) without the remotest likelihood that they or their products/services will ever become genuinely sustainable, reveals all one really needs to know about the empty, seductive illusion that is CSR.

That may be a bit harsh. Like its predecessor, the triple bottom line, CSR may well help to raise awareness, to enable people to reach the first base camp along the road to sustainability. And there is certainly no denying the fact that countless good deeds are done in the name of CSR, by an ever growing army of companies, and that the world is a marginally better place for it – but *only* if it paves the way for a much more serious analysis on the part of business leaders of the challenge the for-profit sector now faces in today's increasingly unsustainable world.

As an extreme example, it's instructive to look at the CSR efforts of companies like BAE. In 2006, the Campaign Against Arms Trade became understandably incensed when BAE announced that it would be launching a new range of 'environment-friendly' weapons, including 'lead free' bullets, rockets with reduced toxins and grenades that produce less smoke. There have even been experiments to see if explosives can be converted into manure! BAE executives were of course persuaded that they were 'doing the right thing' in marginally reducing their environmental footprint, while staying true to their particular business model: making as much money as possible flogging weapons of deadly destruction to whomsoever is prepared to buy them – entirely legally, of course.

It is hard to imagine a better way of explaining the difference between CSR and corporate sustainability. BAE will no doubt be looking for plaudits in the world of CSR indexes and reports, and may well get them, on the grounds that it's obviously preferable for combatants to die or be wounded in a clean environment rather than a polluted hell-hole. But by any serious measure of sustainability, it's just plain ridiculous. In 2005, as we saw in Chapter 12, global expenditure on arms topped $1 trillion, completely undermining whatever paltry efforts we are currently making to re-direct the global economy onto a more sustainable path. Not only does that $1 trillion entail the consumption of enormously high levels of fossil fuels, raw materials and precious metals; it represents an opportunity cost of staggering proportions when one looks at what $1 trillion could buy in terms of enhancing *real* security around the world today – by way of combating desertification or deforestation, providing access to drinking water and sanitation, or addressing the kind of preventable diseases that are still killing around 35,000 children under the age of 5 every day – rather than undermining it.

It is of course a bit tough to stick a burden such as this on one miserable company. But dealers in death (such as tobacco companies, for example) are best advised to dispense with any CSR fig leaves, however expensively fashioned they may be. If your definition of 'unsustainable' does not include wilfully facilitating the premature demise of millions of people, then it's literally worthless.

Many campaigners today are now intent on holding other unsustainable sectors to account, however 'responsible' they may claim their business operations to be. For instance, there's a growing debate about ways in which the big oil companies could be held to account for the increasingly severe impacts of climate change. In 2004, Greenpeace calculated the *net* contribution on the part of ExxonMobil to climate change over its lifetime ('from 1882 to 2002, ExxonMobil's emissions of CO_2 totalled an estimated 20.3 billion tonnes of carbon – or between 4.7 per cent and 5.3 per cent of global CO_2 emissions'), looking ahead to the possibility of future legal action against ExxonMobil on the part of those whose lives are destroyed by rising sea levels or climate-related disasters – on the same sort of basis as tobacco companies have been sued by people whose health has been destroyed by smoking. And any number of tokenistic, add-on charitable initiatives – such as the new ExxonMobil Energy Challenge working with reputable NGOs like Community Service Volunteers to help address fuel poverty issues in the UK – won't make a blind bit of difference on that score. If anything, they just make people even more cynical.

This threat of legal action is far from theoretical, as Jonathan Lash and Fred Wallington pointed out in the March 2007 issue of the *Harvard Business Review*:

> *In an unprecedented case spearheaded by the former New York Attorney General Eliot Spitzer and currently being considered by the US Second Circuit Court of Appeals, eight states and New York City have sued five of America's largest power companies, demanding that they cut carbon emissions. In a Federal District Court in Mississippi, plaintiffs are suing oil and coal companies for greenhouse gas emissions, arguing that they contributed to the severity of Hurricane Katrina. Claims in that case include unjust enrichment, civil conspiracy (against the American Petroleum Institute), public and private nuisance, trespass, negligence, and fraudulent misrepresentation.* (Lash and Wallington, 2007)

Oil companies absolutely hate any analogy between themselves and tobacco companies as dealers in death and destruction. Indeed, they're astonished at the hypocrisy of people who greatly enjoy the benefits of their products (in terms of driving, flying and so on), but reckon it's the oil companies that should be held responsible for all the costs. People know what they're doing when they fill up their tank, and petrol and diesel are hardly addictive in the way that cigarettes are.

I sympathize with that; it's far too easy for us to dump *our* own responsibilities onto those wicked multinationals. However, there is a massive mismatch between a 'socially responsible fossil fuels company', on the one hand, and a 'genuinely sustainable energy company' on the other. BP and Shell (usually considered to be the most socially responsible oil companies today) continue to talk blandly of oil and gas remaining dominant sources of energy through to 2050. By contrast, the emerging scientific consensus on climate change is that we have a *far* shorter period of time to wean ourselves off our dependency on fossil fuels if we are to avoid runaway climate change – perhaps no more than ten or fifteen years. In that respect, the percentage of new investment going into renewable energy rather than into more and more oil and gas developments is becoming the single most important measure of a company's commitment to a genuinely sustainable energy future. Now that we know that emissions from the combustion of fossil fuels constitute the biggest single threat to the future of humankind, managing existing oil and gas assets (or developing new assets) as responsibly as possible just won't cut it.

And on renewables, the record of the major oil companies is seriously poor, both on a historical basis and in terms of share of new investment. BP's $8 billion investment over the next ten years into its new Energy Alternatives business represents the biggest commitment to date, but this is still a fraction of the total effort required and half of it isn't about renewables at all, but about generating electricity from gas. It may of course be unrealistic to look to the big oil and gas companies to grow the next generation of renewable energy technologies that will inevitably, at some point in the future, displace our use of fossil fuels. And they may already be losing any kind of controlling role anyway; spending on renewables in China in 2005 was in excess of $5 billion, and investment in venture capital funds covering renewables is soaring all around the world.

Sweeping market transformations of this kind go absolutely to the heart of how sustainability is going to impact on the business community. Climate scientists talk more and more of the likelihood of 'non-linear climate change' – the point at which the gradual build-up of greenhouse gases in the atmosphere triggers dramatic rather than gradual changes in the climate. That's what the climate record, deduced from ice-core samples going back over hundreds of thousands of years, has revealed with startling clarity. The threat of non-linear climate change demands a non-linear leap in leadership quality, and comfortable, complacent, incremental CSR is completely incapable of driving such a shift.

Before now, people have tended to use CSR and corporate sustainability interchangeably, as if they were one and the same thing. They aren't. And in a world that now knows itself to be imminently threatened by climate meltdown, a different kind of leadership is clearly called for. Unfortunately, the dominant business model for most companies today remains 'business as usual' with CSR strategies retrospectively welded on. Just as politicians are now having to address the utter inadequacy of their 'progress as usual' political models, based essentially on cranking up levels of economic growth at almost any cost to society and the environment, so any serious business leader is going to have to renounce that 'business as usual' model, and start working out what *real* corporate sustainability looks like in a changing world.

There are now serious questions about the efficacy of many of today's voluntary efforts to promote CSR. Perhaps the grandest of these is the United Nations Global Compact, personally brokered by former Secretary-General Kofi Annan back in 1999 to help create 'a more sustainable and inclusive global economy by fostering a more beneficial relationship between business and societies'. Drawing on some of the 'landmark' international agreements, such as the Universal Declaration of Human Rights, the Compact asks its signatory companies 'to embrace, support and enact a set of core values' in the following areas:

- Support and respect the protection of internationally proclaimed human rights.
- Avoid complicity in human rights abuses.
- Uphold freedom of association and the effective recognition of the right to collective bargaining.
- Eliminate all forms of forced and compulsory labour.
- Effectively abolish child labour.
- Eliminate discrimination with respect to employment and occupation.
- Support a precautionary approach to environmental challenges.

- Promote greater environmental responsibility.
- Promote development and diffusion of environmentally friendly technologies.
- Businesses should work against all forms of corruption, including extortion and bribery.

There are currently hundreds of signatories to the Global Compact from all around the world. But as NGOs have pointed out, there are no mechanisms for assessing the degree to which any one of them is complying with those principles *in practice*, leading to the inevitable (and not excessively cynical) conclusion that many of those signatories are just in it for the UN badge – the phenomenon known as 'bluewash' as contrasted with the more conventional 'greenwash'.

There are many who believe that the bar should now be raised on all such voluntary initiatives. Here in the UK, the Co-op Bank is actively campaigning for all participants in the well-established Corporate Responsibility Index of Business in the Community (BITC) to publish the self-assessments upon which the rankings in the index are based – and has led the way on that score itself. Few have followed the lead. The concerns of the Co-op Bank were amplified early in 2005, when one of BITC's most progressive members (the small brewer Adnams, which won BITC's Small Company of the Year Award in 2003) resigned on the grounds that not enough was being done to challenge *in public* poor performing members of BITC, and to strip away the 'public relations fig leaf' that so many companies have come to wear so elegantly.

That's a tough call for BITC, which would pretty soon find itself in an uncomfortable financial position if it started taking some of its 700 members to task in public. But Adnams is right about one thing: companies very rarely break ranks to criticize poor performance in their sector or industry. 'There but for the grace of God go we' seems to be the dominant, risk-averse mindset, ensuring that the general public rarely gets a chance to understand that there are substantial divergences (ideological as well as tactical) among business leaders today, including very different ways of articulating what it is that business owes to society for its continuing licence to operate in our midst.

This takes us promptly back to the Five Capitals Framework. Forum for the Future finds itself in a privileged, trust-based position with a number of leading companies in the UK with whom it has collaborated to develop the Framework. Companies such as BAA and Wessex Water have engaged seriously in matching the Five Capitals Framework against their own long-term visions – not always with total consensus emerging as the end result, but always with improved understanding. The Framework can be used both conceptually (to help envision what a genuinely sustainable company in a particular sector would look like) and practically (to help prioritize 'indicative strategies' in terms of changed policy and practice).

However, addressing the *business* case for sustainable development in isolation can be both limiting and illusory. It is true that NGOs working with the business community have no option currently but to 'sell in' sustainability on the back of such a business-friendly approach. But it's important to realize that this is, in essence, no more than a tactical ploy; the non-negotiable *imperative* of sustainability sometimes makes such approaches appear pretty limited. It must therefore be possible to demonstrate the closest possible correlation between the increasingly familiar business case for sustainable development and what might be described as the 'societal case for sustainable development'. In an ideal world, *all* actions taken by a company to enhance its own commercial success should simultaneously generate benefits for society *over and above* those that come directly through the use of that company's products and services.

EXTENDING THE LICENCE TO OPERATE

We are, of course, a very long way away from that kind of reciprocity, given the degree to which the interests of shareholders have been systematically prioritized by governments over the interests of all other stakeholders. Crude trade-off remains the name of the game in far too many instances. However, as Tables 14.2 and 14.3 demonstrate, the Five Capitals Framework at least makes it possible to envisage a business environment (in which governments could regulate or motivate investment strategies for a company) which does, indeed, generate both direct and indirect benefits for society.

And this really wouldn't be as risky and uncompetitive – to use the language of the current debate in the EU – as most Organisation for Economic Co-operation and Development governments would have their electorates believe. No less an authority than the redoubtable US economist Joseph Schumpeter constantly reminded politicians that the real driving force of capitalism is *disequilibrium*, based on new combinations of technology, opportunity, information and shifting demand. He described this phenomenon as 'creative destruction' and urged governments not to intervene in markets to protect sectors or individual companies that were being overwhelmed by the transformative power of capitalism seeking out the next best way of generating better returns. As we know, this process of creative destruction can be very painful, especially as older industrialized economies (which are often very labour intensive) give way to different (more capital-intensive) models of creating value.

As Stuart Hart (2005) has pointed out in *Capitalism at the Crossroads*, this debate about creative destruction has a direct bearing on the way in which different companies are responding to the respective threats and opportunities posed by today's sustainability challenge. On the one hand, there's a cautious, modest process of continuous improvement under way (formalized in management systems such as ISO 14001), providing plenty of reassurance and comfort for those companies whose core business models evolved in an era of cheap energy, abundant raw materials and no sense of physical limits. On the other hand, one

Table 14.2 The Five Capitals Framework: benefits for business

Five Capitals	Business Strategies	Direct Business Benefits →	← Indirect Business Benefits	Aggregate Benefits
Natural Capital	Eco-efficiency Climate Change Strategy Design for Sustainable Development Biodiversity Action Plans Product Stewardship	• Lower costs • Future costs avoided • Stimulate increased innovation	• Reputation enhanced • Regulatory impact avoided • Better risk management • Take advantage of government incentives	Enhanced Reputation
Social Capital	Corporate Community Investment Communications for Sustainability Proactive Stakeholder Engagement Human Rights Policy	• Reduced cost of compliance • Local business links • Community goodwill • Reduced costs of getting planning permission	• Long term 'licence to operate'/'licence to grow' • Enhanced reputation with Government/Regulators • Lower transaction costs • Favourable communications	Stronger Brand Customer Preference
Human/ Intellectual Capital	Employee Rights and Entitlements Process Innovation Quality Management Values-led Leadership Personal & Professional Development	• Loyalty/staff motivation • Easier to recruit top talent • Staff productivity • Retention of key staff • Improved Health & Safety record	• New products and services • Enhanced knowledge networks • Improved customer services	Market Advantage
Manufactured/ Technological Capital	Eco-innovation Reduced Energy Intensity Dematerialization Closed Loop Process Virtualization (move from Product to Service)	• Constant refinement of product range • Minimize impact of new taxes/charges, etc • Innovation flourishes • Creativity brings its own reward	• New products and services • Business opportunities identified early	Risk Reduction
Financial Capital	Performance Measurement Transparency & Accountability Best Practice Corporate Governance Green Accounting/Cost Internalization Investment Criteria (Pension Funds, etc)	• Reduced cost of capital • Improved cost controls • Reduced insurance costs	• Better risk management • High standing with Socially Responsible Investment analysts • 'Future proofing' • Lower transaction costs	Option Creation (responsiveness to changing world)

Source: Forum for the Future

Table 14.3 *The Five Capitals Framework: societal benefits*

Five Capitals	Business Strategies	Direct Societal Benefits →	← Indirect Societal Benefits	Aggregate Benefits
Natural Capital	Eco-efficiency Climate Change Strategy Design for Sustainable Development Biodiversity Action Plans Product Stewardship	• Cleaner, safer environments • Reductions in mortality/morbidity • Improved air & water quality	Life-support systems protected • Aesthetic recreational benefits • Obligations to the future met •	Social/Environmental Security
Social Capital	Corporate Community Investment Communications for Sustainability Proactive Stakeholder Engagement Human Rights Policy	• Participation/engagement • Human/civil rights reinforced • Inequalities diminished • Local economic multipliers	Companies have to earn their "licence to operate" • Companies acting as 'Good Neighbours' • Enhanced community spirit • Cultural diversity honoured •	Community Cohesion
Human/ Intellectual Capital	Employee Rights and Entitlements Process Innovation Quality Management Values-led Leadership Personal & Professional Development	• Employees' rights/entitlements protected • Access to training/learning opportunities • Improved working environment • Opportunities for more challenging/rewarding work	Better work–life balance • Life-long learning • Better educated workforce/society •	Improved Quality of Life
Manufactured/ Technological Capital	Eco-innovation Reduced Energy Intensity Dematerialization Closed Loop Process Virtualization (move from Product to Service)	• Better value for money from goods & services • Reduction in unforeseen risk • Easier to reuse & recycle • 'Smarter' products & services	Extended range of options • Easier to act as responsible consumers • Reduced environmental/social footprint •	Greater Access to Economic Opportunities
Financial Capital	Performance Measurement Transparency & Accountability Best Practice Corporate Governance Green Accounting/Cost Internalization Investment Criteria (Pension Funds, etc)	• Prices internalize their full social/environmental costs • Better informed consumers/investors	Economic/employment opportunities spread more widely • Increased opportunities for Socially Responsible Investment • Greater trust between companies and their stakeholders •	Personal Needs/Aspirations Met

Source: Forum for the Future

can now identify a growing number of new entrepreneurs more interested in bringing on 'disruptive' technologies or processes with a view to making those old business models entirely redundant – however much incremental 'greening' they may go in for. Hart draws an interesting analogy here:

> *Just as nature enables some species to out-compete others through a process of natural selection and succession, so the sustainability revolution will enable those firms with more sustainable strategies to outperform – and, ultimately, replace – those with outmoded strategies and damaging technologies. No amount of greening will save firms from the gales of creative destruction that are likely to ensue in the coming decades. Greening perpetuates the current industry structure; it fosters continuous improvement rather than reinvention or fundamental innovation. Given the velocity of technological change and the growing significance of sustainability, this no longer appears to be a viable strategy: creative destruction appears to hold the key not only to the growth industries of the future, but to corporate survival.* (Hart, 2005)

A classic example of this dilemma can be seen with today's chemicals industry. In 2003, I found myself as the sole representative of 'civil society' on the UK Chemistry Leadership Council – a body set up by the UK Department for Trade and Industry (DTI) to lift the sights of the chemicals industry by pressing the case for much smarter innovation, better training and a serious commitment to the notion of sustainable chemicals. The game plan was to reach out beyond the industry's own trade associations to engage with big users of chemicals and chemistry (pharmaceutical companies, car manufacturers, retailers and so on), as well as the industry's wider stakeholders. It proved to be an extraordinary challenge, working against a backdrop of depressed industry expectations, rising NGO and consumer demands, big problems in recruiting high-quality staff, and intense competitive pressures as more and more of the production of bulk commodity chemicals shifts to China or the Middle East.

All of this has resulted in the dominance of highly defensive, reactive mindsets throughout large parts of the industry. Spokespeople for the industry feel that it has already 'cleaned up its act'; indeed, as a consequence of those external pressures, the industry has, step by tortuous step, improved its social and environmental performance, built better relationships with the communities in which its plants are based, and become far more transparent in both data management and reporting. In other words, classic incremental greening, best represented in the global industry by the Responsible Care programme, a 15-year-old voluntary initiative that has had a big impact upon all large chemical companies. Within a limited framework, Responsible Care has worked: it has helped to reduce the industry's collective environmental and social externalities, and helped to present a 'better case' to its respective stakeholders. But it has *not* helped the industry to focus on *genuine sustainability* in that it has not asked what changes are now required to ensure that the use of chemicals in society, at every level, can be secured within nature's limits.

The Chemistry Leadership Council took on that challenge, and produced a vision for the industry (or, rather, for the much wider chemistry-using supply chain) based upon the Five Capitals Framework and looking at a very different pattern of creating wealth through chemistry:

> *These trends are pushing the industry towards adding value in very different ways, with many companies becoming smaller, faster, more consumer-oriented and more flexible as they focus on the 'knowledge content' of products and processes. This is being accelerated by the convergence between different scientific disciplines as biologists, bio-chemists, chemists, chemical engineers, geneticists, systems engineers, and IT and computer specialists combine forces in a sometimes bewildering array of new research and product development configurations. Achieving sustainability will mean that those who have responsibility for specifying materials or designing products will need to have a much fuller understanding of the need for radical 'dematerialization' and the far more efficient use of materials and energy.* (Chemistry Leadership Council, 2005)

For governments and business to start thinking in this way will strengthen the general case that sustainable development is fundamentally not about trade-offs: it is first and foremost about win–win outcomes, in a real sense, and only then about unavoidable trade-offs. Moreover, the alignment that is proposed here is not so much the conventional triple bottom line alignment, but the aligning of business ('private') interest with societal ('common') interests in a far more challenging interdependence. In that respect, such an approach to the business case would, in essence, re-present the case first made by Adam Smith, and more recently by Herman Daly and John Cobb (1989) in *For the Common Good*, that wealth creation should be so organized as to simultaneously optimize both profit *and* social wellbeing. It does not, however, go as far as Paul Hawken (1993), who has argued that the *primary* purpose of business is to increase social wellbeing, with profit playing a secondary role. That seems an ideological bridge too far at this point in the evolution of our capitalist systems.

It is interesting how reluctant business leaders are to publicly engage in this kind of broad debate. They effortlessly fall back on the old 'division of labour argument': that this isn't really legitimate territory for them since it is up to governments using their democratic mandate to regulate the social, environmental and economic framework within which business then creates the wealth that society needs. Yet it is not disputed that all large multinational companies are lobbying away furiously to persuade governments that you couldn't put a cigarette paper between their interests and the interests of society as a whole – even though this is transparently not proven in the majority of cases. The very concept of 'corporate citizenship' (which seems to imply the same kind of balance between rights and obligations for a company as for an individual citizen) turns to ashes when one contemplates close up some of the flagrant abuses of 'citizenship' carried out by some of today's least responsible multinational companies.

As we have seen, many business leaders (particularly in the US) do, indeed, see sustainable development as a serious threat to today's neo-liberal, corporate-led economy, not least because any serious rebalancing of the interests of shareholders and other stakeholders would have a marked impact upon their own financial prospects. But few of them any longer speak out about this in public. Lecturing at Boston College's Chief Executives Club in March 2005, Peter Brabeck-Letmathe, Chief Executive of Nestlé, gave rare voice to what one suspects many chief executives may still feel in private: 'What the hell have we taken away from society by being a successful company that employs a lot of people?' He went on to pour scorn on the notion of any company having any additional obligations to a community over and above creating jobs and profits, and to argue that any 'charitable work' a company engages in should be geared exclusively to helping make more money for investors. Such an unyielding approach may explain why, for many environmental and social justice campaigners, Nestlé remains one of the most criticized and heavily targeted multinationals in the world today.

It may also explain why Stephen Viederman, president of the Jessie Smith Noyes Foundation, argues that 'corporations and sustainable development are simply incompatible since these corporations have no commitment to community or place, to future generations, to democracy, to equity or to alleviating poverty'. I don't accept that irreconcilable incompatibility, as I have already made clear in Chapter 5; but Viederman's certainly right in pointing out that multinational companies have a very partial perspective on corporate responsibility, especially on issues such as corporate governance, taxation and even macro-economic concerns such as overall levels of employment.

In this respect, there remains an extraordinary mismatch between the power of multinationals and their contribution to global employment. The top 300 corporations own an estimated 25 per cent of the world's productive assets; the top 500 account for 75 per cent of all commodities traded. Despite that, the world's top 200 corporations (accounting for 28 per cent of global economic activity) employ less than 0.25 per cent of the global workforce. Estimates vary, but the top 500 employ less than 1 per cent of the global workforce – a figure which has not increased for more than two decades. Yet, for most people in the developed world (and increasingly in the developing countries), access to a job is still the principal mechanism for improving one's material standard of living. For many people, the fact that multinational companies play such a minute role in creating direct job opportunities while controlling such a huge share of total productive assets raises a serious question mark over their so-called 'licence to operate'. As we have seen elsewhere, there are many who believe that they are simply not paying enough for that licence.

ENGAGING WITH THE BASE OF THE PYRAMID

World-class companies are increasingly aware of the way in which societal expectations are rising on issues of this kind. Ever since C. K. Prahalad and Stuart Hart published their influential article 'The fortune at the bottom of the pyramid' in 2002, growing attention has been paid to the challenge of addressing the needs of the poorest 4 billion people in the world today. This strategic thrust has been championed by the WBCSD, which brought out an excellent booklet in 2004 (*Doing Business with the Poor: A Field Guide*) demonstrating the different ways in which multinational companies are already trying to 'blend financial and social value'. It is clear that a number of global trends are now encouraging companies to start thinking far more proactively about engaging with 'the base of the pyramid' to help promote sustainable livelihoods:

- Many companies now see a need to break out of mature markets with their near-glutted profile and seek new opportunities in emerging, more dynamic markets.
- Enabling conditions in many developing countries are improving in terms of legal structures, investment conditions, less corruption and so on.
- Global communications are improving all the time, making the world a smaller and easier place for businesses to operate in.
- It's getting easier to find the right kind of partners to experiment with more innovative, cross-sectoral approaches.
- Many more countries now see foreign direct investment as an important way of helping to address poverty, reinforcing aid flows rather than undermining them.
- There is a much clearer realization that business can make a genuine difference, and that it badly needs to; as the WBCSD puts it: 'Business cannot succeed in a society that fails.'

I have to admit that I remain somewhat sceptical about this 'base-of-the-pyramid' stuff. It seems to me that a lot of it is pretty flimsy, and much more about coming up with smart new ways of flogging more things to more people than about addressing real poverty or sustainability issues. Stuart Hart's latest book, *Capitalism at the Crossroads* (2005), however, has at least caused me to rethink that scepticism in that he's come up with a far more compelling and inspirational rationale for base-of-the-pyramid strategies than anything I've seen before:

> *Over the past few years, it has become apparent that there is a large prospective market to be served in the base of the pyramid. It has also become clear that the prospect transcends mere market potential: The opportunity is to use commerce as a driving force for human betterment and environmental restoration – to literally raise the base of the pyramid. Attempts to adapt the top of the pyramid model for use at the base, however, appear destined to fail. Only through a concerted focus on the base of the pyramid will it be possible for large corporations to combine a humanitarian, even activist, orientation with the conventional motivations of growth and profitability.* (Hart, 2005)

The case studies that Stuart Hart uses to demonstrate that this kind of shift is already manifesting itself in all sorts of different ways are also very motivational. Although the critics of multinationals quoted elsewhere in this book would still be inclined to dismiss all such case studies as a 'green veneer' on an otherwise unreconstructed and fundamentally unsustainable business model, a more positive approach (especially for governments trying to work out their own role in promoting more socially and environmentally responsible business engagement) would be to distil critical success criteria from these case studies and to work hard to promote them elsewhere – as is already happening through today's Base of the Pyramid Learning Laboratory. The story of Cemex, a Mexican cement company, for example, demonstrates important aspects of this new approach, even as critics around the world would point out that Cemex is by no means a paragon of virtue on many sustainability issues (see Box 14.1).

One of the most interesting aspects of Stuart Hart's argument is that the base of the pyramid is likely to prove a far more welcoming test bed for some of the bolder, disruptive technologies upon which our sustainable future depends. Mature OECD economies are often so fixed in their ways, so deeply trapped in fixed infrastructures and decades' worth of sunk capital investments, that the prospective losers in any 'disruptive transition' towards a more sustainable economy fight like fury to protect their own (and their shareholders') vested interests. In many base-of-the-pyramid contexts, such vested interests do not command such blocking rights, opening up opportunities for far more radical market creation strategies. One particularly important example of this relates to the emergence of a host of new technologies designed to generate electricity at the point of use – the home, the office, the hospital, school or factory. These so-called 'distributed generation' or micro-generation technologies (including mini-wind turbines, mini-CHP (combined heat and power) plants, photovoltaic fuel cells, ground source heat pumps, biomass boilers and biogas digesters) are not dependent upon grid connection, and could make a huge difference in terms of securing reliable and low-carbon supplies of energy.

Indeed, in Schumpeterian terms, it's hard to imagine a more necessary process of 'creative destruction' than this one. Not surprisingly, however, the principal

BOX 14.1 CEMEX: A MEXICAN CEMENT COMPANY

Cemex, Mexico's largest cement company, provides a glimpse into how to go about constraint identification as a vehicle for reaching the BOP (base of the pyramid). The 1994 financial crisis in Mexico was a major blow to the company's domestic business, which constituted nearly half of Cemex's cement sales at the time. However, Cemex executives noted that whereas revenues from upper- and middle-class customers dropped by half, cement sales to the poorest tier of the population were hardly affected. Given that cement sales to the poor constituted 40 per cent of Cemex's Mexican business and that the company knew little about this customer segment, corporate leadership decided that it was worthy of further investigation.

In 1998, a team of Cemex employees began to explore this issue in greater depth. They began by issuing a Declaration of Ignorance, an open admission that the company knew virtually nothing about 40 per cent of its Mexican market. They then resolved to learn all they could about the needs and problems of the people in the urban slums and shantytowns where demand for the company's cement was the strongest. To accomplish this, the team lived in the shantytown for six months. Their mission was to better understand the context in the BOP, not to sell more cement.

At first glance, the shantytowns appeared to be chaotic assemblages of half-built squatter homes stretching as far as the eye can see. But after spending several months living in this context, the team came to realize that the people were doing the best possible job that could be done, given the constraints and the circumstances. Poor, do-it-yourself homebuilders in the shantytowns, they learned, often take 4 years to complete just one room and 13 years to finish a small four-room house. The reason is that banks and other businesses will not engage with poor residents of informal settlements where the legal status of their property ownership is murky. Haphazard design, combined with material theft and spoilage, conspire to make home construction a costly and risky proposition. Vendors prey upon the poor, selling them off-quality goods in quantities that are inappropriate because they have little bargaining power or ability to complain. The Cemex team came to realize that if these constraints could be removed, it might be possible for the poor to build much better-quality homes in less time, while also saving money on material in the process. And, yes, they might also grow the cement business as well.

To accomplish this end, the team created a new business model. Through its programme called *Patrimonio Hoy*, which, roughly translated, means Equity Today, Cemex formed savings clubs that allowed aspiring homebuilders to make weekly savings payments. In exchange, Cemex provided material storage and architectural support so that homes could be well designed and built in sensible stages. Given its clout as a major buyer, Cemex could negotiate with material suppliers for the best possible prices and quality, something that the shantytown dwellers themselves were unable to do. Participants in the programme built their houses three times faster, with higher-quality materials and designs, and at two-thirds the cost. *Patrimonio Hoy* has been growing at a rate of 250 per cent per year and has enrolled more than 20,000 poor families since its inception. The goal is to reach 1 million families in Mexico in five years.

Source: adapted from Hart (2005)

power-brokers in today's energy industries have been less than enthusiastic about investing in the research and development required to bring these alternatives to market. Obstacles confront pioneers of distributed energy systems at every turn. So why not look elsewhere, suggests Stuart Hart:

> Distributed generation faces few of these obstacles among the rural poor in the developing world. It may be decades before the electrical grid system is extended to provide service to those who currently lack access to dependable electric power. As a consequence, the rural poor spend a significant portion of their income – as much as $10 per month – on candles, kerosene and batteries to have access to lighting at night and periodic electrical service. Furthermore, generating electricity using kerosene and batteries is expensive, costing $5 to $10 or more per kilowatt hour. If offered a viable substitute, these people might abandon these dangerous, polluting and expensive technologies in favour of clean, efficient and renewable electric power. Yet few producers of distributed generation have targeted the rural poor at the base of the pyramid as their early market for these technologies, despite the fact that the market is potentially huge and is populated by people who would be delighted with technologies that cannot compete along the metrics used in developed markets. (Hart, 2005)

Case studies of this kind have begun to influence multilateral bodies like the World Bank and United Nations Development Programme (UNDP). In April 2007, the World Resources Institute (in partnership with the International Finance Corporation) launched the first serious analysis of the potential base-of-the-pyramid markets: *The Next 4 Billion* (WRI, 2007) looked at eight strategic business sectors (health, electricity, water, housing, energy, food, financial services and transportation) to identify both how much is already going on (often not very much, it has to be said) and how much is in the pipeline – quite a lot. With an aggregated household income of around $5 trillion across all base-of-the-pyramid countries, it's not surprising that a lot of companies are gaining confidence in designing appropriate interventions in different parts of the world – in ways that can be quite disturbing to development NGOs and public officials. The authors of *The Next 4 Billion* explain some of the differences that exist between traditional approaches and base-of-the-pyramid strategies:

> There are distinct differences between a market-based approach to poverty reduction and more traditional approaches. Traditional approaches focus on the very poor, proceeding from the assumption that they are unable to help themselves, and thus need charity or public assistance. A market-led approach starts from the recognition that

being poor does not eliminate commerce and market processes: virtually all poor households trade cash or labour to meet much of their basic needs. A market-based approach thus focuses on people as consumers and producers, and on solutions that can make markets more efficient, competitive and inclusive – so that the base of the pyramid can benefit from them.

Traditional approaches tend to address unmet needs for health care, clean water or other basic necessities by setting targets for meeting those needs through direct public investments, subsidies or other handouts. The goals may be worthy, but the results have not been strikingly successful. A market-based approach recognizes that it is not just the very poor who have unmet needs – and asks about willingness to pay across market segments. It looks at solutions in the form of new products and new business models that can provide goods for services at affordable prices. (WRI, 2007)

Four overarching success criteria emerge for base-of-the-pyramid interventions: first, the companies need to develop *unique* products, services and technologies for the base of the pyramid, completely re-imagining their new business model, rather than taking an existing product and tweaking it for a base-of-the-pyramid segment; second, it's crucial to rethink supply chains at the local level, and where necessary to invest in capacity-building and training within the communities that have the most to gain; third, the success depends as much on creating new financial models as on the products or services themselves; lastly, unconventional partnership agreements (breaking out of the usual sectoral silos) are often a precondition for bringing the right mix of skills to the table.

It goes without saying that any such vision would depend upon developing a completely different kind of stakeholder strategy; it is not just disruptive technologies that this business model requires, but disruptive processes – particularly when it comes to new patterns of partnership. Some of the most creative partnerships these days are cross-sectoral, particularly when it's a question of negotiating management of community assets or biological diversity. And this can be very difficult territory. The business of providing clean water and sanitation services in developing countries, for instance, has caused intense controversy over the last decade or more as Western countries and multilateral institutions have sought to advance privatization as the solution to all such problems. The scale of the problems, as recognized in the Millennium Development Goals, is not in dispute: at least 1 billion people lack access to safe water, and 2.6 billion suffer from inadequate sewerage. According to the 2006 Human Development Report, 2 million children die every year for want of clean water and sanitation – that is nearly four children every minute of every day. But the solution to these problems certainly *is* in dispute, not least because most multinational water companies have become very wary about making huge new investments in developing countries. Many of them have had their fingers very badly burned, with poor returns, inadequate regulatory enforcement and high political risk.

It was partly because of that gloomy prospect that Thames Water decided to try something very different, convening an international consortium made up of itself, Halcrow, Unilever, Care International, the World Wide Fund for Nature (WWF) and WaterAid to establish the Water and Sanitation for the Urban Poor (WSUP) project. The basic idea is to use international aid funding and contributions in kind from the members of the consortium to identify and develop projects in conjunction with local community organizations and local authorities.

Although it's early days, it is hoped that the areas where assistance will really be brought to bear will include project management of infrastructure works, as well as assistance in the development of sustainable, locally managed arrangements for operating and maintaining the system. Emphasis will be on building the capacity of the local service authority staff and on the sustainability of that service. Local people will fill key positions, and external assistance will only be provided when and where necessary. None of the organizations involved in the different project consortia will seek long-term commercial involvement in the project locations, thereby opening up opportunities for the local private sector. And once the consortium has achieved its purpose, which it is assumed will generally take three to five years, it will hand over the project to the local service provider or community.

The first WSUP project is under way in Bangalore to provide 70,000 residents of urban slums with safe water and effective sanitation. That, of course, is just a drop in the proverbial ocean of need in developing countries; but at least the WSUP is trying to break out of the deadlock over water privatization that has bedevilled innovative thinking in this area for more than a decade. And the principal victims of the deadlock have been poor people themselves. As C. K. Prahalad and Al Hammond (2002) have so convincingly demonstrated, the urban poor often end up paying anywhere between twice and 20 times as much for water (and, indeed, other basic services) as consumers 'at the top of the pyramid'. Essentially, the poorer you are, the more you are likely to pay. Exploitative local vendors, corrupt local government officials and utterly ruthless local moneylenders often combine forces to deprive some of the world's poorest and most vulnerable people of basic services. Any major initiative that begins to combat that nexus of exploitation has to be an important step forward.

A key characteristic that many such case studies have in common is a much less risk-averse approach to finding the right partners for any project. The concept of 'coalitions of the willing' emerged from the World Summit on Sustainable Development in Johannesburg in 2002 as a way of overcoming some of the usual barriers to progress; many companies are, indeed, much more willing to pool both learning and risk by taking forward new ideas in conjunction with others, especially in areas of particular controversy. This is very much the thinking behind the UNDP's initiative 'Growing Sustainable Business for Poverty Reduction'. This emerged out of Kofi Annan's Global Compact in 2002 in order to prove that 'business-led enterprise solutions to poverty' can provide practical resources for the advancement of the Millennium Development Goals.

TOWARDS A MORE BALANCED SCORECARD

Nevertheless, it is easy to get seduced by the allure of the individual project, ignoring the fact that such projects are often unrepresentative (in that they do not necessarily reflect core business behaviour or affect the dominant business model) and ephemeral – failure rates are high. Though it's much less 'sexy' in media terms, and therefore far less visible to the outside world, the real test of a company's intentions in this area can only be gauged by scrutinizing in detail the management systems and practices by which it seeks to mainstream sustainable development/corporate responsibility into the *whole* of the company. To what extent are companies developing a more sophisticated, balanced scorecard to take proper account of these complex societal and ethical issues?

A lot of this comes back to the old adage that 'what can't be measured can't be managed'. Because so many business impacts upon the environment and society have remained obstinately outside any 'measure it to manage it' framework, most companies still don't know the degree to which their notional end-of-year profits are, in part, inflated by their ability to go on externalizing costs and drawing large subsidies from the natural world or the 'social capital' upon which they depend.

Hence the critical importance of environmental accounting – and the more innovative and integrated approach embodied in the broader concept of sustainability accounting (see Box 14.2).

There is no reason why sustainability accounting shouldn't become a standard procedure for any well-managed company. It provides a mechanism to unlock 'hidden value', and to reduce impacts and enhance profits through more complete and transparent accounting for aspects of an organization's environmental performance. These eco-efficiency savings can be significant. Baxter Healthcare, for example, has reported that environmental investments instituted as early as 1992 have yielded approximately $86 million per annum in savings and cost avoidance. In December 2003, Sir John Browne, Chief Executive of BP, updated shareholders on BP's own emissions reduction programme: 'Within the first three years, we added $650 million of value, for an investment of around $20 million.' Examples of this kind (and there are many) clearly provide a very powerful signal to boards of directors to initiate further sustainability investments and to replicate identified good practice across their organizations.

Eco-efficiency savings and risk management are just two aspects of the overall business case for sustainable development. For some companies, more value is

---

BOX 14.2 WHAT IS SUSTAINABILITY ACCOUNTING?

Using an accounting approach anchors sustainability considerations in data that goes far beyond simple indicators. By converting environmental – and, eventually, social – benefits and costs into monetized values, a company can account for its contribution to sustainability in a way that is consistent with other business activities. Financial environmental accounting can help to make the link between financial and environmental performance and therefore give management the information they need to come up with win–win decisions.

Environmental accounting has three different faces:

1   *Tracking the benefits and costs to the company of its initiatives.* The costs of environmental activities are all too prominent, but the benefits are often hidden. Many projects have environmental and financial benefits: avoiding fines, creating cost efficiencies or leading to new sources of revenue while increasing resource productivity and reducing waste. More intangible benefits come from motivating employees and enhancing a company's reputation. Unless these benefits are brought to management's attention, environmental activities only look like a cost centre. Bringing the costs and benefits of environmental activities together allows companies to build the business case.
2   *Measuring the externalities created.* An externality is the cost borne by other people, now and in the future, from an activity which was not included in the transaction price. It is now possible to calculate the externality a company is creating; but because externalities are by definition outside of the market's price-setting process, any valuation is judgemental.
3   *Calculating the cost and benefit to the company of avoiding its environmental impacts.* A company needs to know the financial exposure of having to internalize its externalities. Companies can be quickly asked to reduce their environmental impacts – either through regulation and taxes (such as the Climate Change Levy or Landfill Tax) or from changes in stakeholder expectations (disposal of oil rigs such as the Brent Spar). With an account of how much it would cost the company to avoid or restore its main environmental impacts, a company can move to limit its exposure, improve its decision-making and report progress to stakeholders.

Forum for the Future has worked with a number of partners to develop a technique to account for the cost of avoiding or restoring environmental impacts. The results of our work were published with the Chartered Institute of Management Accounting (CIMA) in *Environmental Cost Accounting: An Introduction and Practical Guide* (2002).

Source: Forum for the Future

---

likely to be derived from the *intangible* benefits associated with greater social and environmental responsibility. These include the impact upon brand value and reputation, the ability to attract and retain the best people, higher productivity from a motivated and inspired workforce and access to new markets (and maintenance of existing markets) (see Table 14.1 for the intangible benefits associated with the business case for sustainable development). Innovative work by the Co-op Bank,

Table 14.4 *The Co-operative Bank's ethical and sustainability positioning (percentage pre-tax profit)*

	Profitability contribution made by customers who state that ethics is the most important factor	Profitability contribution made by customers who state that ethics is an important factor
2001[i]	14%	25%
2002[ii]	13%	24%
2003[iii]	17%	29%
2004[iv]	20%	34%

Notes: i Profit before tax as reported in the Co-operative Bank's interim results to 28 July 2001: £60.2 million.
ii Profit before tax as reported in the Co-operative Bank's full year results: £122.5 million.
iii Profit before tax as reported in the Co-operative Bank's full year results: £130.1 million.
iv Profit before tax as reported in the Co-operative Bank's full year results: £132.0 million.
Source: CFS (2005)

for example, investigates the link between their ethical policies and the bank's overall profitability. Table 14.4 shows how they reported the results in their *2005 Partnership Report.*

Suffice it to say, in conclusion, that there is a lot going on in the business world which is genuine (*not* driven by public relations), substantive and long term. As evidence of this, one only has to take account of the proliferation of new books published over the last four or five years analysing the impact of sustainable development/corporate responsibility thinking on the business community, highlighting the progress that is being made, and exemplifying that progress through literally dozens of case studies on every conceivable area of concern. One of the most authoritative and accessible of these hands-on tracts is the WBCSD's *Walking the Talk: The Business Case for Sustainable Development* (WBCSD, 2002), which is still highly relevant for those trying to track down what is actually happening in practice. And Dan Esty and Andrew Winston's *Green to Gold* (2007) references dozens of corporate success stories achieved through reduced environmental impacts – although it has little if anything to say about the social dimensions of sustainable development.

And there is further encouragement from a new generation of business leaders who are prepared to speak out much more trenchantly on the need for more effective government–business relations to advance better policy-making. In a speech that former Prime Minister Tony Blair gave in September 2004 to mark the tenth anniversary of the Prince of Wales's Business and the Environment Programme, he challenged the business community to start thinking more proactively about its role in getting serious on climate change. I suspect he may well have been somewhat taken aback when a consortium of 13 chief executives of major international companies (convened as the Business and the Environment Programme's Corporate Leaders Group) came right back at him with a response in June 2005, in effect offering a new kind of partnership between business and the UK Government:

> *At present, we believe that the private sector and governments are caught in a 'Catch 22' situation with regard to tackling climate change. Governments tend to feel limited in their ability to introduce new policies for reducing emissions because they fear business resistance, while companies are unable to take their investments in low-carbon solutions to scale because of lack of long-term policies.*
>
> *In order to break this impasse, we are proposing to work in partnership with the government in order to:*
>
> - *support the development of a world-leading climate change policy framework capable of enabling a step change in private-sector investment in low-carbon technology in the UK;*
> - *significantly increase support for action on climate change from UK businesses, the public and other governments and businesses internationally; and*
> - *dramatically scale up investment in low-carbon technologies and processes by our companies and others in response to a new policy.*
> (Prince of Wales's Business and the Environment Programme, 2005)

Since then, the Corporate Leaders' Group has engaged with President Barroso of the EU (to help persuade him to 'act tough' with member states on the next phase of the Emissions Trading Scheme) and will now seek to mobilize European companies to start taking an equally proactive stance.

There is nothing too dramatic in all of this, it's true; but compare this kind of positioning with that of the Confederation of British Industry (CBI), and a different kind of business leadership begins to emerge. I've already mentioned the emergence on the US scene of the US Climate Action Partnership – a potentially powerful coalition of big, carbon-intensive companies and a few business-friendly NGOs. It wants to see a cap-and-trade scheme introduced in the US with mandatory caps imposed by government, something which President Bush has steadfastly fought against on the grounds that it would damage US businesses! In May 2007, GM became the first big car company to join the Partnership, with indications that Ford would follow suit in the near future – especially after its decision to sell both Jaguar and Land Rover, its gas-guzzling (and very carbon dioxide intensive) brands based in the UK. If the US Environmental Protection Agency gets its act together and decides to regulate emissions of CO_2 as a polluting gas (which the Supreme Court has confirmed it is entirely within its rights to do), then both GM and Ford would be obliged to go a great deal further than signing up to a voluntary, relatively pain-free Partnership.

However, the combined effect of all these examples of business engagement has yet to win over many critics of the role of multinationals in today's global economy. As we saw in Chapter 5, only a much more fundamental downsizing and reconfiguring of the limited liability corporation is likely to placate that much deeper hostility. It is only governments that can reframe those boundary conditions, and governments are currently unlikely to commit to anything other than piecemeal, incremental reform, nudging the pendulum of capitalism away from an almost exclusive shareholder focus back towards the interests of society and a wider group of stakeholders. The pace and depth of that reform depends, in turn, upon just how much pressure governments come under from their electorates – and from consumers – to demand more of their wealth creators in terms of higher standards and more sustainable business practices. Here, too, we will find a somewhat ambivalent picture.

REFERENCES

CFS (2005) *2005 Partnership Report*, Co-operative Financial Services, Manchester

Chemistry Leadership Council (2005) *The Sustainable Production and Use of Chemicals*, Forum for the Future, London

CIMA (2002) *Environmental Cost Accounting: An Introduction and Practical Guide*, Chartered Institute of Management Accountants, London

Daly, H. and Cobb, J. (1989) *For the Common Good*, Beacon Press, Boston, MA

Esty, D. (2006) 'Greener pastures', *Wall Street Journal*, 29 December

Esty, D. and Winston, A. (2006) *Green to Gold*, Yale University Press, New Haven, CT

Fishman, C. (2005) *The Wal-Mart Effect: How an Out-of-Town Superstore Became a Superpower*, Allen Lane, London

Greenwald, R. (2005) *Wal-Mart: The High Cost of Low Price*, Brave New Films, official website at www.walmartmovie.com

Hart, S. (2005) *Capitalism at the Crossroads*, Wharton School Publishing, University of Pennsylvania, Philadelphia, PA

Hawken, P. (1993) *The Ecology of Commerce*, Weidenfield and Nicholson, London

Lash, J. and Wallington, F. (2007) 'Competitive advantage on a warming planet', *Harvard Business Review*, March

Mitchell, S. (2007) 'Keep your eyes on the size: The impossibility of a green Wal-Mart', Soapbox, *Grist* website, 28 March, www.grist.org/comments/soapbox/2007/03/28/mitchell

Prahalad, C. K. and Hammond, A. (2002) 'Serving the world's poor, profitably', *Harvard Business Review*, September

Prahalad, C. K. and Hart, S. (2002) 'The fortune at the bottom of the pyramid', *Strategy and Business*, no 26

Prince of Wales's Business and the Environment Programme (2005) *Corporate Leaders' Group on Climate Change*, University of Cambridge Programme for Industry, Cambridge, UK

WBCSD (2002) *Walking the Talk: The Business Case for Sustainable Development*, World Business Council for Sustainable Development, Geneva

WBCSD (2004) *Doing Business with the Poor: A Field Guide*, World Business Council for Sustainable Development, Geneva

WRI (2007) *The Next 4 Billion: Market Size and Business Strategy at the Base of the Pyramid*, World Resources Institute, Washington, DC

15

Civil Society

INTRODUCTION

Free market zealots (who object to *any* increase in the powers of the state) would have us believe that the only way to secure a genuinely sustainable economy is for enough consumers to be using their purchasing power (or withholding it by saving rather than consuming) in order to ensure that markets deliver sustainable development as a by-product of consumer sovereignty. It's a wonderful notion *if* one believes that we live in a world of perfect information. But given how disempowered, manipulated and deceived (not least by prices that don't reflect true costs) today's consumers really are, the concept of 'consumer sovereignty' needs to be exposed to rather more stringent analysis. This uncertainty often leaves governments uncertain of their own role – not just in terms of regulation and other direct interventions in markets, but through sustainable procurement in the public sector and other ways of 'walking the sustainable talk' rather more proactively. It doesn't help that governments (with the active connivance of today's progressive left) now choose to define all citizens as consumers – of the party brand, of policy packages, of political choices. This 'consumerization' of politics has widened the governance gaps that are already causing such concern in terms of voter disengagement and disaffection.

CONSUMERS AND CITIZENS

So here's another crunch question that you will rarely, if ever, hear asked: even if enlightened companies were not just filling the space available to them for more sustainable behaviour, but keen for government to expand that space so that they could go even further, as in the example of the Corporate Leaders Group of the Prince of Wales's Business and the Environment Programme (see Chapter 14), and even if governments were responding to today's ever stronger signals of impending breakdown with real purpose and consistent leadership, *would consumers and voters be prepared to go along with it?* Would they be rewarding those companies through the preferential use of their purchasing power, and rewarding those politicians through the use of their votes?

Having acknowledged right up front that any reform agenda for contemporary capitalism has to be mediated through fair and efficient markets *and* through healthy, functioning democracies, there's no avoiding that question. And the harsh, unpalatable truth *as of now* is not particularly supportive of a reform agenda of this kind. Survey after survey tells us that the majority of people are broadly content with our greed-driven consumer society (even if it doesn't make them any happier), and election after election tells us that only a minority of people are prepared to vote for the only political party (the Greens) that has, as yet, honestly confronted those macro-trends.

But is this so surprising? If the vast majority of people continue to live lives that depend upon systematic denial, and if all our political leaders (and the media that feed off them and on them) are strenuously promoting such denial, it seems to me to be something of a miracle that such large minorities have so steadfastly resisted co-option until now. Whether we are talking votes or profits, a healthy interest in the 'what's in it for me/my party/my company?' is hardly surprising, and for the vast majority of politicians and business leaders, it appears that there is just not enough in it for them. The risks are too high, the potential benefits too speculative. Denial is an infinitely easier choice than commercial or political damnation.

This makes consumer behaviour the most problematic of all today's potential drivers for change. It is true, of course, that there are many inspiring examples of consumer power mobilizing in defence of both the environment and oppressed people, going right back to hugely successful campaigns in the 1980s focusing on the elimination of chlorofluorocarbons (CFCs) from aerosols, all the way through to current campaigns to promote fair trade or resist the introduction of genetically modified (GM) crops. Historically, such successes work best when it's a question of *stopping* bad things from happening rather than making good things happen. Far larger numbers of consumers can be mobilized for the former than for the latter.

Beyond that minority of concerned consumers (to which I will return in a moment), many environmentally destructive activities and products seem to remain deeply attractive to the majority of consumers. At the glamorous end of 'conspicuous consumption', which does so much to fuel mass consumer aspirations, environmentally friendly technologies are not going to find it easy to deliver the ever-expanding 'choice set' involving speed, fashion, change, variety and luxury which the globalized affluent middle classes increasingly expect. At the more mundane level of mass consumption, there is, as yet, minimal consumer willingness to trade off the conventional consumer values of comfort, convenience and low prices against enhanced environmental or social performance. Even if it is technically possible to combine environmental sustainability and economic growth, it is by no means apparent that consumers are yet prepared to choose the kind of economic growth that this implies.

It seems likely that an environmentally sustainable form of capitalism will need to have both very large numbers of consumers who want green products enough for them to rate their sustainability value as highly as other non-price considerations, and a significant minority of consumers who are willing and able to pay more for green products on a regular basis. It will also need to have found ways of reliably informing consumers about 'sustainability best buys' and of overcoming market failures where these exist. Achieving these conditions is likely to be among the most challenging tasks involved in moving a capitalist, market-driven economy towards biophysical sustainability and simultaneously ensuring that future economic activity remains compatible with it – especially if it means that people can't have their £15 flights to Malaga, 'trophy kitchens', patio heaters or garden hot tubs. Even more challengingly, we have to be much more realistic about the so-called 'rebound effect'. As we have seen, more efficient resource use usually reduces costs in a way that makes it naturally attractive to companies. But the responses of consumers may be rather different in that any personal efficiency savings they make may even stimulate *increased* consumption. The 'rebound effect', as this latter phenomenon is sometimes called, is well established in the field of domestic energy efficiency improvements, in which the beneficiaries regularly choose greater comfort (higher room temperature) in preference to reduced fuel use. Where the beneficiaries are less well-off, and room temperatures are excessively low, no one would grudge this extra comfort. Indeed, the efficiency gain may be justified in these social and quality of life terms alone. But rebound effects apply in other contexts as well, and can sometimes ensure that efficiency improvements of themselves actually do little to improve the environment.

One such area is electronic and electrical goods. When asked about energy-efficient products, the vast majority of UK consumers will unfailingly indicate a readiness to buy more such products, and around 50 per cent are even prepared to pay quite a lot more for them. But there's little awareness that the huge projected growth both in the sheer number of appliances in each household, and in their increased energy consumption (a plasma TV screen can use up to four times as much energy as a normal TV), will completely swamp savings made on marginally more efficient products. The Energy Saving Trust calculates that energy consumption from domestic appliances doubled between 1972 and 2002, and will double again by 2010 - hence the Trust's campaign to completely revamp energy efficiency standards by 2008, and to set a rigorous new standard for all stand-by functions in *any* appliance – astonishingly, somewhere between 5 per cent and 10 per cent of household energy is wasted through appliances left on standby!

In the end, it's just simpler for governments to regulate for reduced environmental footprints than it is to leave it up to individual consumers to find their own way there. The best example of this is energy-efficient light bulbs. These have been widely available in Organisation for Economic Co-operation and Development (OECD) countries for years, yet their market share has increased only very slowly, with surveys demonstrating that too many people just couldn't get beyond the price tag at the point of purchase. Even though compact fluorescent lamps (CFLs) use no more than 20 per cent of the energy that incandescent light bulbs do, and last on average ten times as long, the higher price of the point of purchase remains a huge barrier. Given that lighting accounts for around one fifth of the electricity OECD countries consume, this 'consumer confusion' over the last decade has resulted in tens of millions of tonnes of CO_2 being released into the atmosphere that could so easily have been avoided.

Improbably, given its appalling record on anything to do with climate change, it is Australia that has moved first to escape this impasse, with the Federal Government agreeing in February 2007 to phase out all incandescents by 2012. California followed suit, and the UK Government made a similar announcement in March. Politicians often pluck up courage from seeing others take a bit of a risk and survive to tell the tale, so by the time you read this, I can pretty much guarantee that many more governments will have realized just how quick a 'quick win' this one is. Unfortunately, the US is unlikely to be among them, notwithstanding the fact that if the US made sure it was a CFL plugged into every one of its 4 billion or so sockets, rather than an incandescent, it would reduce CO_2 emissions by 158 million tonnes and reduce total expenditure on electricity by $18 billion.

This kind of shift represents just a tiny fraction of the reductions in our environmental footprint that could now be achieved. In *Natural Capitalism*, Paul Hawken and his co-authors set the bar just about as high as you can get: '90 per cent to 95 per cent reductions in material and energy flows are possible in developed nations without diminishing the quality of the services people want' (Hawken et al, 2000). Companies that have been adept in 'design for the environment', or even the kind of 'cradle-to-cradle' thinking touched on in Chapter 10, are just beginning to demonstrate what this might look like in practice. Tough new standards in both the EU and Japan now mandate much more ambitious targets for disassembly and re-use of components in electrical and electronic products, and some believe that the current wave of interest in environmental issues will usher in a new age of what was referred to in Chapter 10 as 'emotionally durable design':

> There's likely to be a move away from mass production and towards tailor-made articles, and products designed and manufactured with greater craftsmanship. Companies will replace profit from bulk sales by servicing and repairing products chosen because we want them to last – just like Grandma used to do. (Douglas, 2007)

The idea of 'wanting things to last' again is important because that's one of the few ways one can overcome the problems associated with the so-called 'rebound effect'. If everything is simply 'sorted' for the individual, either by governments progressively ratcheting up ever tougher standards or by companies improving their own performance by 'editing out' environmentally and socially irresponsible products, the end result could be consumers with a marginally lower personal 'footprint' who still have no idea about the scale of the transformation required, and may therefore be inclined to deploy any savings they have made in other areas of consumption. I prefer to call this the 'Schwarzenegger effect'. The Governor of California now prides himself on having converted two of his Hummers, one to use biofuels, the other to use hydrogen. Thousands of Americans are now trading in their standard SUVs for bigger, more powerful hybrid SUVs, persuaded perhaps by the Schwarzenegger school of 'muscular environmentalism'. Here he is speaking at a conference in Washington in April 2007:

> *Weightlifting was once considered a pursuit for weirdoes, carried out in dungeon-like gyms by people embarrassed to admit to doing it. Then it became mainstream, sexy, attractive, and that is exactly what has to happen with the environment movement. We don't really want to take away the 'muscle cars', the Hummers and the SUVs, because that's a formula for failure: what we have to do is to make these cars more environmentally muscular.*

By contrast, the school of 'emotionally durable design' gets a lot of support from those who are seeking to relocate the debate about consumerism in a much more explicit moral framework. Each act of consumption, however small, impacts both up and down the particular value chain in which it is transacted, with inevitable moral consequences that remain for the most part entirely invisible. In July 2006, Richard Chartres, the Bishop of London, broke ranks with many of today's church leaders when he made a direct comparison between certain aspects of consumerism and sinfulness:

> *Given that we have an overriding imperative to walk more lightly upon the Earth, making selfish choices such as flying on holiday or buying a large car are symptoms of sin. Sin is not just a restricted list of moral mistakes, it is living a life turned in on itself where people ignore the consequences of their actions.*

This unleashed a splendid round of invective from motoring organizations and various affronted airlines. Michael O'Leary, Chief Executive of Ryan Air and a man not known for verbal temperance, offered the following:

> *God bless the Bishop. The Bishops have got their own crosses to bear, including empty churches, and presumably if no-one went on holiday, perhaps they might turn up and listen to his sermons. But God knows what he would know about greenhouse gases anyway.*

This (of course) is to ignore what Richard Chartres was really pointing out: that the potential sinfulness of any action is proportionate to the knowledge we may have about the consequences on others of that action. Acting *knowingly* in ways that harm other people, as most of us do today, is clearly different morally from acting in ignorance – but ignorance is less and less available to us today as an excuse for not confronting the moral implications of our actions.

That said, I have to admit to more than a little disquiet at the new school of eco-puritanism that seems to be flexing its muscles. In some quarters, even to contemplate the possibility of flying anywhere is seen as eco-thought-crime of the most heinous kind. Three years ago, aviation barely featured in the pantheon of unacceptable behaviour: now it's public enemy number one. This hardly seems sensible given that aviation is still a relatively small net contributor to total global emissions (though growing very fast). By adopting a position of 'no flying on any terms' as the 'morally correct' position, rather than 'fly as little as you need to and offset all the emissions that your flights may cause' today's eco-zealots risk alienating an awful lot of people who are just beginning to think through their personal carbon footprint with a lot more information available to them than they have ever had before.

SUSTAINABLE CONSUMPTION

Such complexities, both morally and practically, are extremely difficult for govern-ments to wrestle with from a public policy point of view. In 2006, the UK Government warmly welcomed a new report from the Sustainable Development Commission and the National Consumer Council, the title of which, *I Will if You Will*, provides an important insight into the kind of strategic approach governments now need to adopt – not dumping all the responsibility for rescuing the planet onto the weary shoulders of confused and often disempowered consumers, but working with them to make it easier, step by step, to reduce the negative impacts of their everyday consumption. Consume differently (as in more responsibly, ethically, sustainably and so on), but not, as yet, consume *less*.

Nowhere is this clearer than in the area of mobility. In 1950, UK citizens travelled an average of 5 miles a day. In 2000, that had risen to an average of 30 miles a day. It is still rising, and the Department for Transport sees no reason why it shouldn't go on rising, notwithstanding its theoretical commitment to helping other government departments secure key policy outcomes on climate change, reduced pollution, healthier lifestyles, more stable, vibrant communities and so on. As Simon Jenkins has written:

> *Hyper-mobility erodes the bonds that hold family and society together.*
> *It is the enemy of civic pride, good neighbourliness and clean air. The*
> *yearning for the holiday cottage, air miles and the fly-drive weekend*

> *break denudes home communities of their vigour and disrupts destinat-*
> *ion communities. It uses quantities of energy, while creating migratory*
> *hordes in perpetual and polluting transit.* (Jenkins, 2006)

But woe betide the government minister who dares give voice to the obvious conclusion that the UK would be a much better place if that average mobility figure was falling not rising.

One begins to wonder, in such circumstances, whether consumer-driven materialism is a beast that can ever be tamed. Might it not be more sensible for politicians explicitly to espouse a wholly different approach, based explicitly on low consumption, sufficiency, simplicity and *real* quality of life? Paul Ekins has written at length about the benefits of sufficiency as a key policy driver of this kind:

> *In a society devoted to ever-greater consumption, it is hard not to identify*
> *sufficiency with notions of sacrifice, of 'doing without' or 'giving things*
> *up'. Such identifications are, however, misplaced. Certainly, sufficiency*
> *implies relatively modest consumption and simplicity in personal lifestyle.*
> *But these are not motivated by abstract aestheticism or self-denial, but*
> *arise from a perception that sufficiency in consumption permits a greater*
> *emphasis to be placed on other aspects of human experience, which are*
> *actually more personally rewarding and fulfilling than consumption.*
> *Far from entailing self-denial, sufficiency in this reading is a means of*
> *liberation. An all-absorbing concern with consumption is replaced by*
> *the pursuit of other values that yield more happiness.* (Ekins, 1998)

This overall orientation has led many environmentalists to argue that the only route to sustainability is for people not just to consume more responsibly, but to consume *less*. To bring that about, the hypothesis is advanced that people who have reached a certain level of material comfort and security can (and should) be persuaded that their future quality of life resides in freeing themselves of the trappings of consumerism and in opting, instead, for low-maintenance, low-throughput, low-stress patterns of work, recreation and home life.

One extreme manifestation of this can be seen in the campaigning in the US of the Reverend Billy and his supporting Choir of the Church of Stop Shopping. Using theatre, non-violent direct action and protests of every kind, Bill Talen (the real name of the Reverend Billy) has become a cult figure of various video-clip websites for his constant disruption of Starbucks stores and other star performers on the global high street. Behind the fun and games, there are some extremely serious messages inviting US citizens (and particularly social conservatives) to wake up to the appalling personal and social costs entailed in converting America into one unending shopping mall – to wake up to the 'institutionalized hypnosis' that is being practised across the country, and particularly on young people.

The number of anti-consumerism activists of that kind is still very small, both in the US and in Europe. But the numbers of people increasingly disaffected with the high-earning, high-spending lifestyles that have become so commonplace in the last 20 years are growing all the time. This phenomenon is often described as 'downshifting', evidenced by a growing number of people quietly reconfiguring their work to spend more time at home, with their children, doing other things entailing a lower income but a higher quality of life. The fact that this is a predominantly middle-class phenomenon does not invalidate its significance; but it inevitably raises questions about its usefulness in policy-making terms. With levels of poverty as high as they still are in many developed nations, let alone in the developing world, alternatives to economic growth are non-starters unless underpinned by an equally strong commitment to eliminate poverty (particularly among the young and the old) as espoused by more conventional political paradigms.

It also has to be acknowledged that there are significant macro-economic implications in any low-consumption economic model. Lower levels of economic growth (the inevitable consequence of large numbers of people opting for lower levels of economic activity) would mean lower tax revenues, which, in turn, would necessitate lower levels of public expenditure on key public services such as health and education, as well as lower levels of capital expenditure on things such as transport. The negative impact of this upon society and people's individual quality of life is as much of concern to advocates of genuine sustainable development as the negative impacts upon the environment of current levels of economic growth.

While it's fair to say, therefore, that the concept of 'voluntary simplicity' may well have considerable resonance with a relatively small number of people in rich Northern countries, it is less likely to have much purchase either with OECD governments intent on addressing residual poverty within their own borders or, in global terms, where the principal challenge resides in the fate of the world's poorest 2 billion people who live on less than $2 a day. Such a crude generalization cannot, however, do justice to the rich debate about the meaning of poverty. Average income is widely and conveniently used as a proxy for human wellbeing or happiness, notwithstanding the evidence that many people in developing countries who are leading secure and dignified lives in rural areas, but on very low incomes, are often a great deal 'happier' than those on higher incomes in hellish urban slums.

From a demand-side perspective, there would appear to be very little public support for 'consume less' political alternatives. Green parties the world over have succeeded in attracting significant minorities of voters, but have rarely seen that percentage move above 10 per cent even in the world's richest countries, which one might reasonably assume to be more open to the concept of reaching some kind of 'affluence threshold' beyond which further increases in consumption or material standard of living are perceived to bring diminishing utility. With regard to the developing world, there is very little, if any, evidence that those countries are prepared in any way to forego the notional delights of Western consumerism which they see paraded in front of them through a constant battery of mass media programming and advertising that reaches into the poorest corners of the poorest countries.

Such concerns provide a formidable set of impediments to engaging in the 'consume less' debate. The concept of deferred gratification seems unlikely to make any kind of comeback in the foreseeable future. After 50 years of aspirational, growth-at-all-costs, no-holds-barred individualism, the harsh reality is that the available psychological terrain for politicians currently to operate within in pursuit of sustainable development is severely constrained. Rather than 'consume less', the thrust of any new debate here is likely to be 'consume wisely' for the foreseeable future. That may not be sufficient, but it's all that would appear to be manageable right now in terms of mainstream political responses in capitalist economies. As Marcel Wissenburg concluded in his analysis of the compatibility between sustainability and market-based economic liberalism: 'Economic liberalism contains many elements that impede sustainability, but none of these threats seems invincible – assuming the right kind of preferences' (Wissenburg, 1998). The 'right kind of preferences' in this context are those that help move us faster and further down the road towards a sustainable world. But until now, those preferences simply haven't been emerging fast enough.

One of the major problems about sustainable consumption is that mainstream business people and politicians are extremely reluctant to confront one of the most pernicious of all myths in this particular area: that in markets geared towards meeting consumer needs and aspirations, the consumer is assumed to be 'sovereign'. As Clive Hamilton points out, this assumption can be disturbingly disingenuous:

> *It is perverse to characterize the market as a want-satisfying mechanism when we are exposed every day to attempts by the market to influence what we want. Consumers' preferences do not develop 'outside the system'; they are created and reinforced by the system so that consumer sovereignty is a myth. The question is not one of personal consumer choice versus elitist social engineering; it is one of corporate manipulation of consumer behaviour versus individuals in a society understanding what is in their real interests. Instead of society being populated by free agents rationally maximizing their welfare through their consumption choices, it is people as complex beings whose taste, priorities and value systems are, to a large degree, manipulated by the very 'markets' that are supposed to serve them.* (Hamilton, 2003)

Such a view is fiercely denied by most leading companies and retailers, who hate to be portrayed as anything other than needs-meeting enterprises, and certainly not as needs-creating enterprises. Either way, consumption must be seen as a much more complex phenomenon than the conventional model would still have us believe. As many commentators have pointed out, there has been a slow but steady shift over the last few decades away from the phenomenon of people identifying themselves by reference to what they *do* in life, to people identifying themselves by reference to what they *consume*. This has hugely expanded the opportunities for marketeers to pitch their wares to consumers in terms of the identity they would like to project, rather than the needs they would like to have met for a better life.

One can conclude from all this that working the 'sustainable consumption' end of policy-making is never going to be easy. But policy-makers in most OECD countries seem to have lapsed into a pudding-like state of inertia in which sustainable consumption is deemed to be relevant to only a tiny minority of citizens (the socially responsible niche), and where doing anything about it implies 'bucking the market' or, worse yet, limiting the range of choices available to the consumers – 'increased choice' being as sacrosanct a *desideratum* in the canon of contemporary capitalism as increased growth. Although there is much discussion in these countries on how best to decouple higher levels of economic activity from any environmental externalities, little effort is made to explore an equally important 'decoupling' issue: how to decouple unsustainable levels of consumption from real improvements in people's quality of life. As we have already seen, contemporary research clearly demonstrates that increased personal consumption does not necessarily improve people's sense of wellbeing, and may often cause severe domestic problems by accelerating unsustainable levels of debt.

One obvious way out of this dilemma is for governments to lead by example in those areas over which they do have complete control – particularly with public expenditure. If governments deployed their tax revenues in such a way as to promote sustainable consumption across the whole economy, the knock-on impacts could be enormous. The UK Government, for instance, buys £13 billion worth of goods and services each year, and directly or indirectly controls £150 billion worth of expenditure in the public sector.

But the UK debate about sustainable consumption is further confused by the Government's fixation with increasing the amount of choice available to citizens, particularly in terms of its efforts to modernize public services such as education and health. Opinion polls indicate quite clearly that the idea of increased consumer choice in the context of improving public services just doesn't 'do it' for most people. 'Parental choice' often means very little for parents whose notional choice of schools is strictly limited in geographical terms. What most parents want is for *every* school to be resourced in such a way as to meet most of their reasonable expectations, rather than to end up with a situation in which some schools excel and others sink without trace. Anna Coote of the UK Sustainable Development Commission has highlighted a similar problem with the UK Government's almost obsessive pursuit of increased choice in the National Health Service:

> *'Choice' is the 'big idea' in the Government's Public Health Strategy. This is mainly devoted not to tackling the social, economic and environmental causes of illness, but to encouraging individuals to 'choose' healthy lifestyles (covering smoking, diet, exercise, alcohol and sex). Yet, health policies that focus on choice – whether it's choosing health services or healthy living – usually favour the better off. They don't have the same effect on people who are poor, disadvantaged, socially excluded – the very people whose health is most at risk. Choice may be highly desirable in theory; but individual choice as a policy driver, unless firmly rooted in policies to promote shared responsibility and equal capacity to choose, is likely to widen health inequalities and so undermine the purpose of sustainable development.* (Coote, 2005)

This is also a key theme in the Fabian Society's report *A Better Choice of Choice* (Levett et al, 2003), commissioned by the UK Sustainable Development Commission as part of its ongoing work on sustainable consumption. It, too, questions the desirability of politicians becoming fixated on the idea that since choice is good, more choice must necessarily be better. Yet the privilege of increased choice still features high in the pantheon of capitalism's many benefits: some economists indeed look on the whole process of economic development as anything that increases people's options. To espouse political positions that appear to limit choice (as the green parties in Europe often do) is a high-risk and politically unpopular strategy. For the vast majority of people, it is certainly counter-intuitive to suggest that improvements in our quality of life might come about as a consequence of restricting rather than expanding choice.

For all that, it is clear that increasing individual choice does not automatically make us better off. There are several reasons for this. First, there is no such thing as a completely 'free' choice. Every choice we make is conditioned and constrained by the choices others have already made; this, in turn, conditions future choices. Individually rational choices to travel by car, for example, lead cumulatively to traffic-clogged, degraded inner cities, car-dependent suburbs and amenities accessible only by car – a mess nobody wanted or intended, in which nobody can access what they want reliably and easily, those without cars are further disadvantaged, and the unnecessary use of fossil fuel waste is structured into our lifestyles. Claiming that a policy or decision 'increases choice' should be the beginning not the end of debate. Are the kinds of choice being increased the ones that really matter? What other choices do they curtail or foreclose? Can we be certain the gains are worth the losses?

Such insights make me wonder what would happen if the media really began to open themselves up to some of these questions, or if the government really began to think seriously about working these issues into their engagement strategies with voters.

Addressing the Governance Gap

As we have seen, one of the most profound consequences of our 25-year love affair with economic neo-liberalism is that more and more of the management of people's lives in most OECD countries has been consigned to the marketplace, with politicians across the entire political spectrum increasingly disinclined to intervene through discredited 'command and control' measures. Governance as such would appear to have become more about individual consumer choice than about decisions taken through the ballot box. This worldview has, of course, always been popular with the right, but is now promoted with equal vigour by today's progressive 'centre-left' think-tanks, such as Demos in the UK:

> *Command and control is a framework unsuited to the complex, unpredictable demands of contemporary organizational life. The challenge is to recreate public institutions and governance regimes as open, porous and decentred systems which can thrive on diversity, adapt to radical innovation and still maintain coherent purpose and progress [...] in seeking to stimulate and influence such change, the underlying goal of political intervention should be seen as developing or supporting systems of self-governance in a complex and fluid environment, rather than simply establishing institutional control or imposing a simplified set of priorities on existing systems.* (Bentley, 2002)

But what the devil does that mean in practice? From a sustainability perspective, how does 'self-governance' play out in a world where (as we have seen) short-term personal gratification and corporate profit maximization remain utterly dominant? Where many people's favourite 'coping strategy' is simply to deny the reality of what is happening around them and cheer themselves up by doing some serious shopping? Where the global media are managing and manipulating coverage of the 'state of the world' explicitly to protect the interests of a tiny elite of the unelected super-rich – described by some as a 'corporatocracy' or 'global monetocracy'? Where politicians themselves seem disinclined even to participate in a more intelligent discourse about the viability of today's model of progress? In such a world, talk of authentic self-governance, let alone 'open, porous and decentred systems', is clearly vulnerable to a charge of extreme naivety.

This may explain why the different approaches to governance adopted by many of the international NGOs at the heart of these issues remain rather more *dirigiste* and open to the possibility of 'command and control' still having an important role to play. This balance is pragmatically captured in the Real World Coalition's *From Here to Sustainability* (Christie and Warburton, 2001), which identifies the four critical linkages between sustainable development and better governance:

1   *Movement away from unsustainable 'business as usual' can only be based on consent, democratically given. We need a system that promotes rich debate about the state we're in. This means a thorough renewal of the institutions that have seen public trust and enthusiasm leak away over the years in order to re-engage citizens with politics. It also means devising better systems for civic and moral education so that everyone is equipped with the 'moral fluency' to participate in debate and make informed choices.*

2   *We need a renewal of trust between citizens and government simply because sustainable development cannot be delivered solely through individual choices, business innovation and voluntary action. It requires a huge and complex long-term negotiation of change; tradeoffs between private choices and public goods; changes to market frameworks; and strategic investment in public services and new technologies. All this requires an effective, legitimate and trusted state.*

3   *Sustainable development demands a renewal of local democracy. We know that national and global frameworks can only sketch the direction and principles for action. As the Agenda 21 statement from the 1992 Earth Summit underlined, effective measures for sustainable development must, to a large extent, be devised and implemented through democratic local government and partnerships at the local level between communities, public agencies and business.*

4   *The nature of the present phase of globalization emphasizes the need for democratic accountability and deliberation to be extended to the international level, and for global institutions and corporations to be more open, democratic and accountable. The greatest challenge for democratic governments is to find ways to foster a global democratic culture and process so that international agencies that shape strategies on development work better, more accountably, and in the interests of environmental sustainability and wellbeing for all.*
    (Christie and Warburton, 2001)

That particular wording in the third paragraph ('a renewal of local democracy') somewhat undersells what has historically been one of the mainstays of the green movement – a passionate commitment to decentralization. Much of this text has concentrated unapologetically on a 'reform' agenda – albeit a fairly radical reform agenda – but for many, the idea of seeking to temper the destructive storms of globalization is extremely naïve, in that the global institutions and global elites that preside over this process clearly have little interest in a 'globalization for all' alternative. Today's globalization is just 'centralization beyond reason'. In their eyes, it is a system dedicated to the further enrichment of very small numbers of people at the expense of the vast majority. More positively, proponents of 'localization' and the idea of refocusing the global economy around local markets make a strong case for the knock-on benefits this would have in terms of improving people's quality of life and wellbeing:

> *The alternative is that everything that could be produced within a nation or region should be. Long-distance trade is then reduced to supplying what could not come from within one country or geographical grouping of countries. This would allow an increase in local control of the economy, and the potential for it being shared out more fairly, locally. Technology and information would be encouraged to flow, when and where they could strengthen local economies. Under these circumstances, beggar-your-neighbour globalization gives way to the potentially more cooperative better-your-neighbour localization.* (Hines, 2000)

However, the policies required to get us from 'beggar-your-neighbour globalization' to 'better-your-neighbour localization' are definitely not for the faint-hearted! It's difficult to imagine mainstream politicians finding much room in their manifestos for the sort of proposals that inform today's localization agenda:

- Safeguarding national and regional economies against imports of goods and services that can be produced locally;
- 'Site-here-to-sell-here' rules for industry and all multinational companies;
- Localizing money flows to rebuild the economy of communities, minimizing 'leakage' from the local to the national and global;
- Local competition policies to ensure high-quality goods and services;
- The introduction of resource and other green taxes to help pay for the transition;
- Fostering democratic involvement in both the local economic and political systems; and
- A redirection of trade and aid, so that it is geared to focus on the rebuilding of local economies rather than on international competitiveness.

As you can imagine, the explicit advocacy of protectionist policies of this kind draws virulent condemnation from the advocates of international competitiveness at all costs. However, these ideas are now being given new impetus through the combination of climate change and the peak oil controversy – as explored in Chapter 3. As I've explained, nobody can be certain when we'll reach that 'half gone' tipping point in terms of oil (the point at which oil does not run out, but at which demand for oil permanently exceeds supply), but even if the optimists are correct in indicating 2030 as the peak oil moment rather than 2010, that's still just around the corner in terms of preparing our oil-intensive societies for an oil-scarce world. And if we don't start preparing now, the shock will be traumatic, and the dislocation intense. Add into the mix the projected impacts of climate change, and the challenge to politicians to engineer tolerant and equitable responses to those 'system shocks' will be enormous.

Which brings us back to Thomas Homer-Dixon's ideas about breakdown leading either to breakthrough or cataclysmic collapse. The governance aspects of this are as compelling as the physical aspects: how can we future-proof our political and economic systems so that they are capable of withstanding those shocks? How do we nurture the capacity of *resilience* in our communities and in society at large so that we are not taken completely by surprise when the inevitable breakdowns start coming at us thick and fast? This has prompted some experts to start talking about an inevitable 'energy descent', as we learn to get by with less and less energy in re-localized economies, with more and more people contributing directly to meeting the needs of their local communities, particularly in terms of food production, energy supply, infrastructure maintenance and so on. This vision of communities based on low-energy and local food remains so disturbingly different from the way most people see the future that it is usually just waved away as an incoherent brainstorm on the part of people who hate contemporary progress.

There are two further layers of complexity in advocating any wholesale reform of existing governance systems. The first is the astonishing collapse in levels of trust between the governed and their governments. In 2002, the World Economic Forum asked 36,000 people to rate their 'level of trust' for 17 different institutions involved in protecting the interests of society. Two-thirds of them did not believe that their country was 'governed by the will of the people'. Across the world, the principal democratic institution in each country (for example, parliament or congress) is the least trusted of the 17 institutions tested. Global companies and large domestic companies are equally distrusted, ranking next to national legislative bodies at the bottom of the trust ratings.

Second, there remains a serious tension for anyone involved in promoting an accelerated move to a more sustainable world: how is this to be done in ways that strengthen rather than erode democracy? Simon Dresner painfully exposes this dilemma:

> *The paradox is that sustainability is a philosophy firmly based on the notion that attempts to transform Nature are likely to be self-defeating, but is itself committed to attempting to transform society and control its future direction. The Green movement attempts to get round this problem by advocating radical decentralization of decision-making so that sustainability can be implemented from the grassroots upwards. One difficulty with that answer is that sustainability is a global problem requiring global coordination of action. Leaving all decisions to local communities is not very different from the neo-liberal solution of leaving everything to the market to decide; there is every possibility for free-riding and the tragedy of the commons.* (Dresner, 2002)

I know of no easy way of resolving that paradox. But I do know that the best starting point is for people to make a rather better job of articulating what a sustainable society would actually look like, both in aspirational and in operational terms.

REFERENCES

Bentley, T. (2002) 'Letting go: Complexity, individualism and the left', *Renewal*, vol 10
Christie, I. and Warburton, D. (2001) *From Here to Sustainability*, Real World Coalition/ Earthscan, London
Coote, A. (2005) *Sustainable Development and Public Health*, UK Sustainable Development Commission, London
Douglas, E. (2007) 'Better by design', *New Scientist*, 6 January
Dresner, S. (2002) *The Principles of Sustainability*, Earthscan, London
Ekins, P. (1998) 'Can humanity go beyond consumerism?', in *1998 Development Report*, Society for International Development, Rome
Hamilton, C. (2003) *Growth Fetish*, Allen and Unwin, Sydney
Hawken, P., Lovins, A. B. and Lovins, L. H. (2000) *Natural Capitalism: The Next Industrial Revolution*, Earthscan, London
Hines, C. (2000) *Localization: A Global Manifesto*, Earthscan, London
Jenkins, S. (2006) 'The curse of hypermobility', *Guardian*, 16 August
Levett, R., with Christie, I., Jacobs, M. and Therivel, R. (2003) *A Better Choice of Choice*, Fabian Society, London
Sustainable Development Commission (2006) *I Will if You Will: Towards Sustainable Consumption*, available at www.sd-commission.org.uk
Wissenburg, M. (1998) *Green Liberalism*, UCL Press, London

Visions and Values

INTRODUCTION

Utopias have been out of fashion for a long time now, and the nearest thing to a sustainability Utopia (Ernest Callenbach's *Ecotopia*) is now 30 years old. That leaves sustainable development advocates struggling to explain what life would really be like if we did, indeed, get on top of today's sustainability challenges. Is it really possible to retain the best of the dynamism and efficiency of capitalism while simultaneously learning to abide by the laws of nature? This chapter seeks to address that conundrum by looking at the kind of values upon which the attaining of a sustainable society depends (interdependence, empathy, equity, personal responsibility and intergenerational justice), and explores the degree to which it is possible to be optimistic about such values 'winning out' in a world such as ours. It also examines how it is that the religious right in the US has been able to 'see off' environmentalism and every other progressive cause by making such strong play on the American dream and core American values.

DEFINING THE UNIVERSAL DREAM

There was a time in the affairs of humankind when the only vision on offer was a vision of life after death – for the virtuous, of an eternity in the company of angels somewhere in the celestial beyond; for the wicked, of an eternity in hell. Throughout most of human history, notwithstanding literary gems such as Thomas More's *Utopia*, published in 1518, there wasn't much point in offering people any vision of a better life on Earth. For the vast majority of people, such a vision would have been neither conceivable nor deliverable. In modern times, from the 18th century onwards, Earth-bound visions of a better world have taken on an increasingly important role as part and parcel of various secular models of progress. The sheer dynamism of the capitalist economy, as it gradually extended its reach to embrace most of the world, has ensured that those secular visions of a better world have become all but synonymous with personal visions of being better off (for oneself or for one's children) or more secure in material terms.

The American dream is well on the way to becoming today's universal dream, even if the ways in which different nations pursue it remain sharply differentiated, as explored in the context of the debate about globalization in Chapter 5. A powerful combination of economic and psychological drivers keeps that dream alive and well. Some of those drivers are largely altruistic, inspired by a commitment to social justice, and to the elimination of poverty in the rich world and of the increasingly grotesque disparities in wealth between the rich and the poor world – the solutions to which are understandably assumed to depend upon the generation of yet more wealth rather than the more effective distribution of the wealth that has already been amassed. Other drivers are largely, if not entirely, venal and self-interested, underpinned by some sense of 'rightful entitlement', however spurious, or by insecurity, greed or envy. But for most, those who are neither ultra-rich nor desperately poor, the principal drivers are material independence, to secure one's old age, to look after one's children, and to have something set aside against disaster or tragedy. One way or another, personal visions of a better world usually entail some constant improvement in one's own financial situation.

This poses a rarely acknowledged dilemma for advocates of sustainable capitalism: is it possible to offer people a vision of a better world in which each and every individual in that world will not necessarily be seeing their material standard of living improving year on year, and in which the imperative of 9 billion people learning to live sustainably within the Earth's biophysical limits will demand that missing ingredient so dangerously absent from today's universal dream – namely, the *truth*? For the truth of it is that if 9 billion people wanted to live like the richest 1 billion live right now (and we don't seem to be particularly satisfied with what we've already got anyway), we would need the resources and natural services of at least five – and probably seven – more planet Earth look-alikes. At the risk of over-egging the message, just the one planet Earth is all we've got.

And that's the dilemma. Is this fragile, seemingly preposterous, notion of sustainable capitalism all but dead in the water not just (as many orthodox economists would have us believe) because it can't be made to work anyway, but because the vision of what such an economy might mean for people and their communities is inherently 'unsellable', constantly overwhelmed by a materialistic 'universal dream' and its promise of ever greater wealth forever for everyone – however dishonest and *truly* preposterous such a promise might really be? And if it's *not* possible, in today's mature, well-educated and largely well-fed democracies, to win serious support for a vision of a better world secured by virtue of the global economy evolving its way towards something resembling sustainable capitalism, then we are inevitably stuck with business as usual – that is to say, utterly unsustainable capitalism, all but guaranteeing the acceleration of every one of the destructive trends identified in Chapters 1 and 12.

It might help to be a little bit more explicit about what exactly this 'vision of a better world' might look like. In 1975, Ernest Callenbach published his hugely stimulating novel *Ecotopia*, set in California in 1999 – that is to say, looking forward over a quarter of a century. *Ecotopia* is made up of California, Oregon and Washington State, which seceded from the US in 1980 after threatening to detonate nuclear mines in New York and Washington, DC, unless they were allowed to go their independent way! Twenty years on, after total isolation, a leading US journalist is allowed to visit to see the ways in which Ecotopia has evolved in the meantime. Many of the developments are not that surprising now: organic food; balanced diets; everyone involved in food production in one way or another; hyper-efficient public transport, walking and cycling, and very few cars; 100 per cent recycling and incredibly strict pollution controls; small-scale, close-knit communities with access to work shared much more equitably – with a return to the Protestant work ethic; a free and easy approach to sexuality – it is California, after all; a dynamic population reduction programme; all buildings made of renewable and biodegradable materials, and 100 per cent renewable energy.

Nothing too outrageous – but this just shows the degree to which a huge number of green ideas that were considered to be totally outlandish back in the mid-1970s have now entered the political mainstream. Nevertheless, *Ecotopia* still has the potential to surprise with some of its more radical ideas: no advertising whatsoever and a hugely reduced use of the TV; ritual war games to 'manage' inherent violent tendencies, predominantly in men; political parties dominated almost entirely by women (who make up a substantial majority of the population of Ecotopia); no income tax, sales tax or property tax – with all tax revenues based upon a turnover tax on productive enterprise; schools that are more like farms or outward-bound centres; and so on.

Ever since then, green theorists and activists have spent countless person years drafting and redrafting an almost limitless multiplicity of visions. Off-the-shelf hand-me-downs just don't cut it; every organization and every newcomer to the embrace of sustainable development seems to be seized with the need to work out for themselves what a sustainable future might actually look like – even though there has always been an intense, ongoing debate about whether the very process of 'visioning a sustainable society' has any real legitimacy or usefulness. Some 'vision critics' believe all such ecotopias to be either childish or, much more seriously, an opening of the door to lurking totalitarian tendencies in the green movement: 'we know what's good for you, and this really will make you a lot happier'.

Others find such visions predictable, formulaic or stultifyingly monolithic, a real turn-off for today's pragmatic politicians, unappealingly presenting the sustainable development project as a take-it-or-leave-it blockbuster in which organics, fair trade, beards, human rights, photovoltaics, bicycles, animal welfare and an end to global poverty are all inextricably woven together. Michael Jacobs, the former director general of the Fabian Society and now a political adviser to UK Prime Minister Gordon Brown, captured this sentiment perfectly in his 1999 pamphlet *Environmental Modernisation* (Jacobs, 1999), in which he advocated a series of ideology-free, vision-lite and resolutely pragmatic campaigns to overcome the deep instinctive antipathy of most Labour politicians (new or old) to the environment movement, let alone to the sustainable development cause. He highlighted five key aspects that would make an environmental modernization agenda 'acceptable' to mainstream Labour politicians:

> *First, it is intended to 'go with the grain' of globalization. Second, it acknowledges the trend towards individualization and understands the role of consumption in modern life, but seeks to encourage consumption towards environmentally benign forms. Third, environmental modernization gives a central place to the perception of risk and scientific uncertainty, and makes risk management a key policy field. Fourth, it seeks to counter the trend towards greater environmental inequality or exclusion. Fifth, it is firmly a modernist project, accepting the central role of science and technology in tackling as well as contributing to environmental problems. It sees the future as essentially optimistic and environmental problems as soluble.* (Jacobs, 1999)

By implication, therefore, there are no 'limits to growth' ideas, no suggestions of any *structural* problems within the conventional model of progress, and nothing that might scare the horses about consuming less, demand management through radical tax reform and so on. Everything must be 100 per cent compatible with mainstream ideas about globalization, free markets, constant economic growth and technocratic progress.

I for one find it hard to accept that this is likely to be the best way of getting real traction for the uncompromisingly radical ideas that lie behind sustainable development – a theme to which I will return in Chapter 17. But it has to be acknowledged that there *is* a genuine problem in contemplating a vision of a sustainable society. If sustainability is, indeed, the 'end goal' – the 'stable state' which we need to arrive at to ensure compatibility with the life-support systems upon which we depend – how do we then avoid stagnation? More specifically, in the context of trying to define what sustainable capitalism might look like, how do we retain capitalism's dynamism, creativity, innovation and hunger for change and 'progress' that has made it one of the most powerful forces in the history of humankind, and yet still stay within those biophysical limits? Apart from resorting to slightly pretentious analogies – 'Think of Shakespeare's sonnets: do you suppose for a moment that his creativity was stifled by the fact that he had to stick to a given number of lines, each containing a given number of syllables?' – this tension between the imperative of a biophysical 'steady state' (albeit with some room for manoeuvre around what science determines as the limits) and the life blood of capitalism at its best remains hugely problematic.

It's a dilemma that goes back to J. S. Mill's exploration during the 1860s of the notion of the 'stationary state'. Unlike most of his contemporaries, Mill felt that it was critical to keep interrogating the fundamental *objectives* of industrialism at that time – where was it all headed and what would happen when society actually got there? Would people be better or worse off? Although his articulation of this sometimes makes him sound somewhat old-fashioned ('I confess I'm not charmed with the ideal of life held out by those who think that the normal state of human beings is that of struggling to get on; that the trampling, crushing, elbowing and treading on each other's heels, which forms the existing type of social life, are the most desirable lot of humankind'), his understanding of the trade-offs involved in the pursuit of constant expansion and growth ring as true today as they did then:

> *If the Earth must lose that great portion of its pleasantness which it owes to things that the unlimited increase of wealth and population would extirpate from it, for the mere purpose of enabling it to support a larger but not a better or happier population, I sincerely hope, for the sake of posterity, that they will be content to be stationary long before necessity compels them to it.* (Mill, 1861)

Orthodox economists have never been happy with the notion of the stationary state, and there is, indeed, something both absurd and deeply unappealing about the idea of aiming at a future state of equilibrium which from that point on would remain constant – especially in an age where the only thing that seems to be constant is change itself. But it would be wrong to dismiss J. S. Mill's anxieties too quickly. What do we really gain if, in the process of gaining it, we lose both 'the art of living' and that indispensable harmony between ourselves and the natural world? Jay Griffiths offers her own lyrical riposte to the idea that sustainability is incompatible with any true sense of progress:

> *'Sustainability' seems to weigh in with the burden of a heavy stasis. A life half-lived and a death half-died, all the dirgey effort of a worthy cause and none of the dynamite of 'progress'. But the opposite is true. Progress, along the trajectory Euro-American culture is now on, is a one-word lie; it is neither the travel nor the arrival, but the ultimate ending; not the flame of thought, but a bonfire of humanity: the vaunted 'progress' of cars and unlimited plane travel leading to global warming and millions of environmental refugees – this so-called progress is a politics which tends towards death. Sustainability, on the other hand, is where the life lies, where time touches eternity, the time of the natural world, of ice and melt, of the seas' times and tides. Both sustainability and progress need to be redefined and reclaimed. In order to do this, Western culture needs to listen to indigenous peoples because in their ideas of cyclical time, time is constantly restored, nature sustained and*

sustaining. These are the very ideas the world needs most. (Griffiths, 2005)

Finding an elegant way out of this impasse (how to be visionary about a sustainable future without coming up with completely unworldly or static visions) is not easy. Some resort to finely honed *principles* intended to speak to such a vision, but framed as contemporaneously as possible. Others prefer to rely upon defining the kind of *values* that will inform a sustainable society without necessarily going to the extent of defining what that society would look like. There is, after all, a very powerful *moral* case for sustainable development – notwithstanding the fact that these days we tend to hear far more about the *business* case for sustainable development rather than we do about the moral case. As we saw in Part I, that moral case rests on a fundamental commitment both to greater equity and social justice (within and between different generations, and within and between different countries), and on the recognition that we have a moral obligation to secure the wellbeing of other creatures regardless of whether or not they bring any benefit to humankind. The concept of 'stewardship', of taking responsibility in so far as we can for the whole of life on Earth, is a powerful source of moral inspiration for hundreds of millions of people and an important element in all the world's major religions and faith systems.

SUSTAINABILITY VALUES

Within that kind of moral framework, is it possible to advocate a set of generic values (regardless of cultural diversity, different norms and lifestyles) that would be conducive to establishing a genuinely sustainable way of life? Promoting equity and social justice requires awareness of the difficulties of others and compassion for the disadvantaged; recognition of the value of difference, tolerance and freedom is critical; living within environmental limits calls for a much deeper understanding of nature; intergenerational equity rests on the simple notion that no one generation should promote its own material interests at the expense of succeeding generations. Putting these together, we come up with a list of values that might look something like this:

- recognition of interdependence;
- self-determination;
- diversity and tolerance;
- compassion for others;
- upholding the principle of equity;
- recognition of the rights and interests of non-humans;
- respect for the integrity of natural systems; and
- respect for the interests of future generations.

Some of those values overlap substantively with the core values of most progressive organizations and individuals broadly seeking to make the world a better place. But some are very different – intergenerational justice (justice between different generations), concern for the non-human world of natural systems, and a desire to see the rights of the individual to determine as much as possible of his or her own life properly balanced with the recognition of our dependence upon everyone else and everything else. The *Declaration of Interdependence* developed by the Canadian environmental activist David Suzuki takes us one stage further in terms of unpacking that notion of interdependence, widening the circle of relationships not just to embrace all human beings within the meaning of 'one world' but all living creatures (see Box 16.1).

Values can be thought of as a system of implicitly agreed norms that enable the smooth running of society; they are not agreed by committee or imposed upon societies from above. They emerge from the collective behaviour of individuals and respond to the needs of society as a whole. For this system to function, a feedback mechanism needs to be in place; people need to be able to see the effects of their actions on others. In a small community, this is a straightforward process. But sustainable development is a global problem and the effects of our actions are often indirect, taking place thousands of miles away. For values to develop that are aligned to sustainable development, adequate feedback mechanisms are required – mechanisms that nurture empathy, and that allow us to witness global problems and connect them to their cause.

For those who want them, there are many visions of a sustainable society to inform and inspire. And there are literally dozens of books mapping out in varying degrees of detail how a sustainable economy might work; how sustainable lifestyles would transform current living patterns; and how radical policy change in different areas would rise to the challenge of providing health services, education, transportation, planning, food, leisure and so on – all on a genuinely sustainable basis. Although many in the green movement perceive themselves to have been in the political wilderness over the last 30 years, a huge amount of creative and intellectually rigorous endeavour has been invested in preparing the policy seedbeds for a more sustainable future.

Much of this has just started to emerge in some of the new thinking about sustainable cities. However improbable it may sound, we have no alternative but to re-conceptualize (and eventually re-engineer) our cities so that they cease to be today's resource-intensive and highly polluting environmental disaster areas, and play instead a central role in delivering a sustainable world. The simple reason for this is that more people now live in cities than in rural areas, and that percentage is increasing every year. Cities occupy just 2 per cent of the land surface of the Earth, but consume more than 75 per cent of resources used every year; a city like London needs 125 times its own surface area to provide the resources it consumes – and London (with just 7.5 million people) is now one of the smaller mega-cities

---

Box 16.1 Declaration of interdependence

This we know

We are the Earth, through the plants and animals that nourish us. We are the rains and the oceans that flow through our veins. We are the breath of the forests of the land, and the plants of the sea. We are human animals, related to all other life as descendants of the firstborn cell.

We share with these kin a common history, written in our genes. We share a common present, filled with uncertainty. And we share a common future, as yet untold.

We humans are but one of 30 million species weaving the thin layer of life enveloping the world. The stability of communities of living things depends upon this diversity. Linked in that web, we are interconnected – using, cleansing, sharing and replenishing the fundamental elements of life. Our home, planet Earth, is finite; all life shares its resources and the energy from the sun and therefore has limits to growth. For the first time, we have touched those limits.

When we compromise the air, the water, the soil and the variety of life, we steal from the endless future to serve the fleeting present.

This we believe

Humans have become so numerous and our tools so powerful that we have driven fellow creatures to extinction, dammed the great rivers, torn down ancient forests, poisoned the Earth, rain and wind, and ripped holes in the sky. Our science has brought pain as well as joy; our comfort is paid for by the suffering of millions. We are learning from our mistakes, we are mourning our vanished kin and we now build a new politics of hope. We respect and uphold the absolute need for clean air, water and soil. We see that economic activities that benefit the few while shrinking the inheritance of many are wrong. And since environmental degradation erodes biological capital forever, full ecological and social cost must enter all equations of development. We are one brief generation in the long march of time; the future is not ours to erase. So where knowledge is limited, we will remember all those who will walk after us and err on the side of caution.

This we resolve

All this that we know and believe must now become the foundation of the way we live. At this turning point in our relationship with Earth, we work for an evolution: from dominance to partnership; from fragmentation to connection; from insecurity to interdependence.

Source: Suzuki (1997)

---

of the world. There are now more than 20 cities with populations in excess of 10 million.

Given that there's little likelihood of any major move back to rural areas, city planners and urban experts are devoting serious thought to the 'core constituents' of what makes for a sustainable city. The biggest factor by far is that cities will have to be designed around people not around cars – not even hyper-efficient 'green cars' running on hydrogen or biofuels. The sheer amount of land required to service any car-bound transportation system entirely rules out what has been the principal design feature of almost all 20th century cities. Other new features include much higher densities in terms of dwellings per hectare (but not so dense that cities are turned into unmanageable 'heat islands'), a focus on green spaces, tree-lined streets (a single city tree can evaporate up to 400 litres of water a day – a major cooling impact on average temperatures), and small-scale food production in gardens and allotments to help recycle waste, cut down on freight transport and prevent soil erosion.

This is a hugely exciting area for design innovation and new thinking. Proposals to create the world's first eco-city at a place called Dongtan on the fringes of Shanghai have created a huge stir of interest across the world. China already has around 100 cities with more than a million people, and estimates indicate that another 400 million people could move from the countryside to urban areas over the next 25 years – raising huge questions about China's ability to cope with this unprecedented process of urbanization. Dongtan will eventually cater for around half a million people, and if the plans currently being masterminded by the engineering firm Arup come to fruition, it will blaze a sustainable urban trail that many others will soon be following.

But for hundreds of millions of people, the urban reality is not some kind of sustainable, high-tech high rise, but a precarious existence in countless shanty towns that have sprung up around so many big cities in the developing world. As Fred Pearce points out, we shouldn't ignore the contribution they can make to a sustainable urban future:

> From a purely ecological perspective, shanties and their inhabitants are a good example of the new, green urban metabolism. Despite their sanitary and security failings, they often have a social vibrancy and ecological systems that get lost in most planned urban environments. They are high-density but low-rise; their lanes and alleys are largely pedestrianized; and many of their inhabitants recycle waste materials from the wider city. So perhaps something can be taken from the chaos and decentralized spontaneity embodied in shanties, and combined with the planned infrastructure of a designed eco-city. (Pearce, 2006)

This may seem a very long way away from the ecotopian idealism referred to earlier in this chapter. But visions with too much 'blue sky' in them tend to leave one with little more than a big 'if only' in one's mind. Like most future-oriented organizations, Forum for the Future suffers from its own 'vision itch', partly because so many of our partners (in all different sectors) tend to end up asking us what this elusive 'sustainable society' would actually look like, and partly because of what we are – an organization made up of 70 people single-mindedly intent on helping others to deliver solutions to today's environmental, social and economic problems. Here is the latest version – as of 2007 – offered very much as 'work in progress':

> *In a sustainable society, everyone's human rights and basic needs are met. Everyone has access to good food, water, shelter and sustainable sources of energy at reasonable cost. People's health is protected by creating safe, clean and pleasant environments, as well as health services that prioritize the prevention of illness while providing proper care for the sick. People live without fear of personal violence from crime or persecution on account of their personal beliefs, race, gender or sexuality.*
>
> *The economic system serves people and the environment. It is market based to ensure innovation and efficiency, but rigorously regulated to secure social and environmental benefits as well as economic benefits. Where practical, local needs are met locally. The ambition of politicians and community leaders is to ensure the highest possible quality of life within the operating limits of the natural world. Everyone has access to the skills, knowledge and information needed to enable them to play a full part in society, and everyone has the opportunity to undertake satisfying work in a diverse economy. The value of unpaid work is recognized, while payments for work are fair and fairly distributed.*
>
> *Society is founded on democracy, tolerance and diversity. All sections of the community are empowered to participate in decision-making. Opportunities for culture, leisure and recreation are readily available to all, and places, spaces and objects combine meaning and beauty with utility. Settlements are 'human' in scale and form. Ethnic and cultural diversity and local distinctiveness are valued and protected.*
>
> *The Earth is nurtured as a single community, bound together with interdependent relationships. Our life-support systems are afforded the highest political priority. Resources are used ultra-efficiently, waste is minimized by closing cycles, and pollution is limited to levels which natural systems can cope with without damage. The diversity of nature is valued and protected, regardless of its usefulness to humankind.*
> (Forum for the Future, 2007)

It is important not to pass too quickly over the role that compelling visions can play in transforming people's views and even their voting habits. Adam Werbach's speech 'Is environmentalism dead?' (2004) homes in on the way in which the neo-conservatives in the US gradually built a vision that played so effectively to core American values that it eventually won out over every progressive cause it came up against, including environmentalism. Throughout the 1970s and 1980s, the

US environment movement stuck to its narrow, regulatory guns ('polluter pays', 'command-and-control regulation', detailed inventories of toxic substances, etc), much of it working against the kind of 'frontier values' and aspirational culture of the typical American. Meanwhile, the conservative right went broad rather than narrow, appealing directly to those aspirational values (based on individual liberty, limited government, free enterprise and the right to own and use property), persuading Americans that a free market was pretty much ordained by God and that it was both 'un-American' and morally wrong to regulate the hell out of God-fearing Americans intent on building responsible businesses here on Earth.

That kind of alignment with core American values eventually enabled the neo-conservatives to take control of all three branches of the federal government – and the state governorships and the school boards. From these commanding heights, the neo-conservatives have set about systematically dismantling all of the key institutions – the taxation system, the United Nations, federal research budgets, the public schools, core environmental legislation – upon which any resolution to today's interlocking sustainability crises depends.

In asserting that environmentalism is dead in no small part because it could never match the right wing's power to narrate a compelling vision of America's future, Werbach's real challenge to a substantially weakened environment movement in the US is to step outside the confines of the standard environmental discourse that it has relied upon for 40 years in order 'to articulate a more expansive, more inclusive and more compelling vision for the future'.

This is controversial stuff and is fiercely resisted by many mainstream American environmentalists who point to the fact that, paradoxically, both membership and income have been on the rise in the US over the last four or five years, not least because of the role that President Bush and his Administration play as 'recruiting sergeants'. And such a transformation would exact a heavy price: it would mean all the big environmental organizations downplaying their environmental or conservation labels and identifying themselves more as 'American progressives'. This is not too hard, perhaps, for the likes of the Sierra Club or Greenpeace, but is a bit of a stretch for Conservation International (CI) or even the World Wide Fund for Nature (WWF). Nonetheless, Werbach believes this is the price that has to be paid for having wasted so many years addressing 'the environment' as a compendium of scientific and technical issues, rather than the territory upon which to engage with American citizens about core values and aspirations. Whether the same strictures can be levelled against UK environmentalists is a controversy to which I will return in the final chapter.

CONFRONTING THE SCEPTICS

For some, however, this is all just so much moonshine – as are all the transitional strategies for government, business and civil society sketched out in Part III.

However much sense they might make, however desirable and even preferable they might be, there is one overwhelmingly powerful reason why they are seen to be doomed to failure: human nature.

There are a very large number of people whose view of human nature is so gloomy that no amount of well-meaning endeavour to reform or even transform contemporary capitalism warrants any credibility whatsoever. According to this worldview, we've got the economic system that we've got (triumphalist, all pervading, hugely resilient and creative, on the one hand, hugely destructive and inequitable, on the other) because it's the one that most powerfully reflects our *true* human nature: greedy, aggressive, self-interested, short-termist, irresponsible and cruel. It is the job of politicians and social institutions to 'manage' those characteristics and to mitigate their most destructive impacts; but that's the way we are because evolution made us that way and those characteristics are unalterably encoded in our genes. So, set aside unworldly dreams of some kind of sustainable capitalism and let rip the red-in-tooth-and-claw version that we've ended up with today until its destructive force is spent and something else (about which there is little point speculating) arises from its ashes.

We have all met those who subscribe to such a worldview. A steely, contempt-uous look comes into their eye in the presence even of tentative optimism. Look around you, it says. Check out your *own* analysis of the state of the world and its people. What further proof could you possibly require to demonstrate that the 'perfectibility of the human spirit' is and always will be an utterly forlorn notion?

There are many personal attributes that one needs to be a sustainable develop-ment activist or a campaigner for human rights, the environment and social justice – but perhaps the most important of all is a lack of fatalism about human nature! One has to have faith in humankind's capacity for good ultimately winning out over humankind's capacity for evil – both at a societal and an individual level. It doesn't matter how marginal that faith may be, how attenuated it may have become in the face of 'man's inhumanity to man' (let alone to the rest of life on Earth), or how hard one has to work to keep it alive: one has to be able to take on those steely-eyed fatalists lest one's vision of a better world gets smothered under their cynical negativity.

Realistically, it is only in the last 30 years or so (if you go back to the first United Nations Conference on the Environment and Human Development in Stockholm in 1972) that we have woken up to today's sustainability crisis. There were a few voices in the wilderness before then, but no concerted movement for change. In the intervening 30 years, a huge amount of scientific data has been generated, providing us with an extraordinary wealth of knowledge and practical know-how about learning to live more sustainably on planet Earth. The fact that we don't yet take advantage of that science (the gap between what we know about the state of the Earth and what we are doing about it remains as large as ever) is massively regrettable; but this vast store of intellectual capital is not going to disappear just because we don't value it properly today. Indeed, it is growing all the time.

And that, in turn, drives a powerful process of technological innovation. Notwithstanding the worst prognostications of Sir Martin Rees (2003) and Bill Joy (2000) (see Chapter 12), only the most churlish of fatalists would deny the potential for benign change through the next generation of sustainable technologies. The fact that it is possible, for instance, even now, to map out a 30-year transition from a world powered predominantly by fossil fuels to one powered predominantly by renewable energy is extraordinary. There are, of course, huge structural and institutional hurdles to be overcome (not least the fact that the current power-brokers in the world of renewables are the self-same multinational companies whose short-term commercial fortunes depend utterly upon maximizing the value of their hydrocarbon assets); but the renewables revolution is at last under way.

For others, the source of their optimism is much more cultural than techno-logical. It often rests upon the hypothesis that underneath all the hurly-burly of crass consumerism there is, in all Organisation for Economic Co-operation and Development (OECD) countries, a nation of caring 'inner-directeds' struggling to get out. During the 1950s, the sociologist David Riesman divided consumers into three categories: sustenance driven – insecure and driven primarily by where the next meal would come from; outer-directeds – in control of their insecurity, but busy consuming as conspicuously as possible; and inner-directeds. This category has been defined as follows:

> [...]people whose prime motivation is no longer conspicuous consumption or keeping up with their neighbours, but autonomy, self-expression, health and independence. These are people who are suspicious of mass production, who want things customized or tailor made, who may or may not be excited by information technology and computers, but who are definitely part of the world of self-actualization and may be self-employed. (Boyle, 2004)

By some calculations, up to 50 per cent of people in a country such as the UK can now be categorized as *potentially* inner-directed. The same kind of analysis in the US shows something like 25 per cent of people who can be classified as 'cultural creatives', to use Paul Ray's terminology, interested in health and spirituality, and searching for integrity and quality in everything they buy.

But to what extent can one really claim (as I have tried to do in this book) that significant elements in the modern business world are now part of the solution rather than still being part of the problem? If our knowledge base has been growing for the last 30 years, it is only during the last 10 or so that some of the world's most powerful multinationals have begun to internalize that knowledge about the state of the world and to change their ways. The changes to date are modest, slow, inadequate and inconsistent. There are still *very* few companies that have really got to grips with sustainable development; for most, the business model remains largely unchanged. But it *is* happening, and it's not all for show and public relations glory, as so many campaigners would still have you believe. For whatever reason, this is an upward curve moving in the right direction – and, even more astonishingly, doing so at a time when the utterly aberrant pressures of short-term profit maximization to boost shareholder value have been at their most intense and most destructive.

Raising our spirits

Looking beyond the world of Mammon, many other commentators believe that religious and spiritual perspectives will play a key role in the pursuit of a more authentic and more sustainable way of life. Fritjof Capra, for instance, has written:

> *Ultimately, deep ecological awareness is spiritual or religious awareness. When the concept of the human spirit is understood as the mode of consciousness in which the individual feels a sense of belonging, of connectedness, to the cosmos as a whole, it becomes clear that ecological awareness is spiritual in its deepest essence.* (Capra, 2002)

There's a more worldly aspect to this which merits much greater attention. The geopolitics of climate change are currently being fought out through the time-honoured frameworks of science, economics and geography. The US won't play ball with Kyoto until China and India accept mandatory emission reductions; China and India refuse even to discuss such reductions until the US, Europe and Japan begin to deliver on some of their targeted reductions. The debate is viciously and nonsensically circular. Politicians seem permanently trapped in a game of tit-for-tat blame-laying, so much so that the *moral* implications of this time-wasting folly are rarely considered.

Until now, religious leaders in these countries have either had little influence on the debate (as in India, South America, Europe and so on), or a damaging influence, as in the interventions of certain evangelical churches in the US. But as the horror of failing to address climate change becomes more and more present in people's lives, it seems legitimate to speculate that the kind of leadership that will be needed to avoid dangerous and even irreversible climate change is just as likely to come from religious and spiritual leaders as from today's political leaders. On all three of the great challenges involved in addressing climate change (stewardship of the Earth and all its life-forms; living modestly and responsibly; and demonstrating compassion for all other people), the world's great religions and spiritual traditions have at least as much if not more to teach than contemporary political ideologies. As the former President of Czechoslovakia so tellingly put it:

In today's multicultural world, the truly reliable path to coexistence, to peaceful coexistence and creative cooperation, must start from what is at the root of all cultures and what lies infinitely deeper in human hearts and minds than political opinion, convictions, antipathies or sympathies. It must be rooted in self-transcendence. Transcendence as a hand reached out to those close to us, to foreigners, to the human community, to all living creatures, to nature, to the universe; transcendence as a deeply and joyously experienced need to be in harmony even with what we ourselves are not, what we do not understand, what seems distant from us in time and space, but with which we are nevertheless mysteriously linked because, together with us, all this constitutes a single world; transcendence as the only real alternative to extinction. (Havel, 1994)

Interestingly, such views command much less support than might be supposed in the wider green movement. As covered in Chapter 3, there is often hostility to those who promote a spiritually-inspired perspective on today's sustainable development challenges, the roots of which tell us a lot about some of the barriers that will need to be overcome if we are to fashion a genuinely sustainable future for the whole of humankind. For some, that hostility is simply part and parcel of a completely consistent antagonism to anything non-rational or 'unscientific', as they would see it. For others, it goes deeper than that. They are hugely suspicious of anything with a whiff of 'New Age' mysticism about it, seeing such perspectives as both intellectually defective and prejudicial to their constant, ongoing efforts to mainstream environmental and social justice issues on the basis of scientific credibility. One might be amused by this defensive secularism were it not such an impediment to accelerating the uptake of more sustainable behaviours and mindsets. As I have pointed out before, we are unlikely to counter the all-but-universal seduction of consumerism or to meet the need for people to go beyond 'detached respect' for the natural systems upon which we depend by developing a much more humble, reverential ethos without some kind of spiritual support. There are few voices of authority (let alone wisdom) in addressing these two challenges that are not derived from religious or spiritual sources. Commenting upon the life of St Francis of Assisi, Richard Chartres (the Bishop of London) concluded quite simply that 'we move towards God by subtraction rather than accumulation'. In his 'Reflection on the Reith Lectures' in 2000, HRH The Prince of Wales staked out the ground for a more spiritual perspective:

The idea that there is a sacred trust between mankind and our Creator, under which we accept a duty of stewardship for the Earth, has been an important feature of most religious and spiritual thought throughout the ages. Even those whose beliefs have not included the existence of a Creator have, nevertheless, adopted a similar position on moral and ethical grounds. I believe that if we are to achieve genuinely sustainable development we will first have to rediscover, or re-acknowledge, a sense of the sacred in our dealings with the natural world and with each other. If literally nothing is held sacred any more – because it is considered to be synonymous with superstition or in some other way 'irrational' – what is there to prevent us treating our entire world as some 'great laboratory of life', with potentially disastrous long-term consequences? (HRH Prince of Wales, 2000, cited in Lorimer, 2003)

My own feeling is that we constantly underestimate this hunger for transcendence, just as we underestimate our extraordinary capacity for the deepest feelings of empathy and compassion for other people and for the living world. Too much is made of the highly visible manifestations of self-interest and apparent indifference; the less visible (and often completely invisible) outpouring of acts of altruism and selflessness are rarely factored into the rather crude generalizations that those steely-eyed fatalists tend to make about human nature. One has only to take account of the countless millions of people in most developed countries involved in volunteering or charity work of one kind or another to realize how misleading this can be.

This, of course, is standard fare for humanitarian idealists of every description, whatever the cause of their optimism. It has taken on an added dimension in the green movement, where the natural world itself is still held to have some influence over the behaviour and, indeed, the aspirations of humankind. That sense of interdependence referred to above (regardless of whether it is intuited in a secular or spiritual way) connects many environmentalists into a richer perception of their evolutionary origins. For many years, a number of so-called 'eco-psychologists' have argued that one of the principal reasons why so many people in the developed world are unhappy, unfulfilled and generally out of sorts is that they are 'alienated from the rest of life on Earth' and clearly suffering from many different varieties of Nature Deficit Disorder. Theodore Roszak articulates this most powerfully in his book *The Voice of the Earth*:

A culture that can do so much to damage the planetary fabric that sustains it, and yet continues along its course unimpeded, is mad with the madness of a deadly compulsion that reaches beyond our own kind to all the brute innocence about us. We are pressing forward to create a monocultural world society in which whatever survives must do so as the adjunct of urban-industrial civilization. And the loss that comes of that crime falls upon us as much as on any species of plant or animal we annihilate; for the planet will, of course, endure, perhaps to generate new adventures in life in the aeons to come. But we are being diminished by our destructive insensitivity in ways that cripple our ability to enjoy, grow, create. By becoming so aggressively and masterfully 'human', we lose our essential humanity. (Roszak, 1993)

Our 'essential humanity' is necessarily Earth-bound, contextualized both physically and cosmologically by the evolution of life on Earth and our part in it. Despite our every effort, we cannot disconnect from that context. The great biologist E. O. Wilson suggests in *Biophilia* (1984) that 'the urge to affiliate with other forms of life is to some degree innate', and ascribes all sorts of basic behaviours (gardening, keeping pets, rambling, watching natural history programmes on television and even golf!) to a genetic, Earth-loving inheritance that we can temporarily ignore but never entirely suppress.

For many, however, all of these upbeat 'reasons to be cheerful' look very frail indeed when set against the massively powerful onward momentum of the particular model of capitalism that has dominated the world for at least the last 30 years. For them, uncompromising resistance and opposition is the only course of action which provides any cause for optimism. I will return to that theme in Chapter 17, as it goes right to the heart of whether or not some kind of accommodation with this particular model of capitalism is feasible. But one thing is for sure: those forces of opposition and resistance are still growing, all around the world, in all sorts of different ways. Nowhere has this been made more compelling (and more personal, in terms of the individual stories that it tells) than in Paul Kingsnorth's powerful book *One No, Many Yeses*:

> *I can't help being optimistic, and my optimism comes from the answers I find to a few simple questions. Has a movement this big ever existed before? Has such a diversity of forces, uncontrolled, decentralized, egalitarian, ever existed on a global scale? Has a movement led by the poor, the disenfranchised, the South, ever existed at all, without being hijacked by intellectual demagogues or party politicians in a way that this movement looks unlikely, because of both its principles and its organizing methods, ever to do? How have we achieved so much in such a short time? Do the world's people want to listen? Are we going in the right direction? Are we gaining in momentum? I get the right answer to every one of those questions, and every one of those answers helps to answer another: can the world afford to ignore this any more?* (Kingsnorth, 2003)

It isn't just the anger and passion at today's environmental destruction and global injustice that keeps campaigners going. They know from their own experiences, at the local and community level, that the vast majority of people are far more hungry for change than you would ever guess if you are stuck with our lamentably biased mainstream media for insights into the world around you. For instance, when Local Agenda 21 was at its most influential in the UK, during 1999 and 2000, literally thousands of 'visioning exercises' across the country asked people what they hoped the future would look like. They may not have been familiar with the concept of sustainable development and all the jargon that goes with it;

but time after time they identified the key social, environmental and economic foundations of sustainable development as central to their own personal visions. Many had come to those conclusions not just because of anxieties about the present, but because they were already seeing the future through the eyes of their children and grandchildren. And that's often when sustainable development really begins to bite.

References

Boyle, D. (2004) *Authenticity: Brands, Fakes, Spin and the Lust for Real Life*, HarperCollins, London
Callenbach, E. (1975) *Ecotopia*, Banyan Tree Books, Berkeley, CA
Capra, F. (2002) *The Hidden Connections*, HarperCollins, London
Forum for the Future (2007) 'A vision of a sustainable future', internal paper
Griffiths, J. (2005) 'Living time', *Green Futures*, no 51
Havel, V. (1994) 'The path to co-existence', speech on receiving the Philadelphia Liberty Medal, Philadelphia, PA, 4 July
Jacobs, M. (1999) *Environmental Modernisation: The New Labour Agenda*, Fabian Society, London
Joy, B. (2000) 'Why the future doesn't need us', *Wired*, April
Kingsnorth, P. (2003) *One No, Many Yeses*, Free Press, London
Lorimer, D. (2003) *Radical Prince*, Floris Books, Edinburgh
Mill, J. S. (1861) *Utilitarianism*, first published in three issues of *Fraser's Magazine*, first book publication by Parker, Son and Bourn, London (1863)
Pearce, F. (2006) 'Ecopolis now', *New Scientist*, 17 June
Rees, M. (2003) *Our Final Century*, William Heinemann, London
Roszak, T. (1993) *The Voice of the Earth*, Bantam Press, London
Suzuki, D. (1997) *Declaration of Interdependence*, David Suzuki Foundation, Vancouver, Canada
Werbach, A. (2004) 'Is environmentalism dead?', speech at The Commonwealth Club, San Francisco, 8 December. Text available at www.grist.org/news/maindish/2005/01/13/werbach-reprint
Wilson, E. O. (1984) *Biophilia*, Harvard University Press, Cambridge, MA

Converging Imperatives

INTRODUCTION

So, does it all come down to how we interpret human nature? Are we genetically predisposed, as Richard Dawkins (2002) argues, to raise up the short term and the selfish over the long term and the altruistic? Sustainable development activists have to resist such genetic determinism, not least in terms of the influence they can bring to bear on both formal and informal educational systems. But a lot more needs to be done to persuade people that a more sustainable system of wealth creation would not only enhance security in such a troubled world, but would enable them to enjoy a higher quality of life, and to be *happier* in themselves, in their work and their communities. Unfortunately, sustainable development activists are unlikely to get much support in this either from the progressive left (which has been largely co-opted by the myth of permanent economic growth as the answer to everything), or from mainstream environmentalists, who are now so depoliticized as to be unable to confront today's ideological reality. Until sustainable development is embraced as the genuinely 'big idea' that it really is, then things are likely to get a very great deal worse before they start to get any better. And it is only a transformation towards a very different kind of capitalism – as if the world really matters – that offers any kind of prospect of a sustainable future.

PROGRAMMED FOR SUSTAINABILITY?

As will by now be abundantly clear, sustainability and capitalism do not make natural bedfellows. Sustainability is all about the long term, about working within limits, about making more from less, about accommodation with others to secure equilibrium – and it demands a deep and often disconcerting re-engagement with the natural world. Contemporary capitalism responds to the shortest of short terms, abominates the very notion of limits, celebrates excess, accepts that its 'invisible hand' will fashion as many losers as winners – and has no connectedness with the natural world other than as a dumping ground and a store of raw materials.

In this regard, regrettably, defenders of contemporary capitalism can justifiably claim that it would appear to be aligned a great deal more closely with human nature (as we understand human nature today) than the precepts of sustainability. And that's a tough call for the emerging sustainable development movement. In a fascinating lecture given at the Royal Institution in London in 2002, Richard Dawkins rubbed our sensitive little noses in this particular aspect of Darwinian *realpolitik*:

> *There is something profoundly anti-Darwinian about the very idea of sustainability. Sustainability is all about long-term benefits of the world at the expense of short-term benefits. But short-term genetic benefit is all that matters in a Darwinian world. Superficially, the values that will have been built into us will have been short-term values, not long-term ones. If it were left to Darwinism alone, there would be no hope. Short-term greed is bound to win.* (Dawkins, 2002)

And frankly, it's hard to come to any other conclusion at the moment. In all sorts of ways, consumerism has more or less established itself as the new religion in the rich world. In rallying US citizens after the 11 September 2001 terrorist attacks, President Bush was quick to exhort them to get out there and go shopping, as proof positive that the American way of life was untouched by such a trauma. Every year, the story of Christmas is the story of just how much consumption people can pack in to the festive season, with what impact on the national economy. And year on year, a few more tens of millions of people are conscripted into a global 'consumertariat' – the sole task of which is to keep on shopping, and throwing away, and shopping some more.

Yet Richard Dawkins went on to suggest that we should not despair:

> *If any species in the history of life has the possibility of breaking away from short-term Darwinian selfishness, and of planning for the distant future, it is our species. Although we are products of Darwinism, we are not slaves to it. Using the large brains that Darwinian natural selection has given us, it is possible to fashion new values that contradict Darwinian values. What it does mean is that we must work all the harder for the long-term future, in spite of getting no help from nature, precisely because nature is not on our side.* (Dawkins, 2002)

That's an intriguing way of articulating the sustainability challenge for humankind: to overcome our natural tendencies, encoded ineluctably in our selfish genes, to enable us to put long-term species survival and the prospect of a better life ahead of instantaneous, selfish gratification. A tough call! But this may represent a rather gloomier understanding of our evolutionary destiny than may be warranted. It all depends upon how one reads the relative importance of 'competition versus collaboration' in our evolutionary history – and in this regard the work of Herbert Spencer may have had a more influential role even than that of Charles Darwin himself.

It was Spencer who seized hold of Darwin's ideas about natural selection and sought to apply them in every particular to the human species. If competition and 'survival of the fittest' were the laws that drove natural selection for all other organisms, then these had to be the laws for human beings since we were no more than very smart animals in evolutionary terms. So, shed no tears for those who fall by the wayside. Social Darwinism was born, in its crudest, cruellest form, allowing no room for any other human instinct or impulse other than all-out self-interest and power-hungry aggression.

As already explored in Chapter 4, we now know that this kind of 'red-in-tooth-and-claw' interpretation of evolution is a grotesque distortion of a much more subtle balance of competitive and collaborative behaviours among organisms sharing the same ecosystem. And these rival interpretations of evolution have had a big impact upon different variations of capitalism. In *Moral Capitalism*, Stephen Young holds up Enron as an archetypal manifestation of 'brute capitalism', descended (via various pathways) from the social Darwinism of Herbert Spencer – and he reminds us in no uncertain terms of just how dangerous it is to raise up Herbert Spencer over Adam Smith:

> *Spencer did not see any value in symbiosis. To analogize people to animals in every important sense, as Spencer did, is a mistake. Perhaps in the excitement of his conceptual breakthrough, Spencer overlooked just how inconsistent his theory was with the insights of Adam Smith. Where Smith had seen specialization and accelerating divisions of labour producing more and more cross-dependencies and interdependencies as capitalist economic growth expanded, Spencer only saw more and more autonomy, independence and conflict to get one's way in the world.*
> (Young, 2003)

So perhaps Adam Smith was one of the first of many individuals intent on using 'the large brains that Darwinian natural selection has given us' to fashion the kind of values that will dig us out of our Darwinian heritage! Darwin himself would have acknowledged the feasibility of such a shift, with his pertinent reminder that 'it is not the strongest or most intelligent that survive, but the ones that are most responsive to change' (Darwin, 1859).

But one can take little succour here when one looks out at a world seemingly bereft of any serious sustainability leadership in this respect or, indeed, of any applied readiness to respond to the scientific knowledge which is now available to our decision-makers. The idea that we now live in an age of evidence-based policy-making is preposterous. Although it's true that the unfolding empirical reality of a changing climate is forcing politicians to accept that it is their responsibility in their *own* term of office to do something about it, this for the most part is the only bit of the evidence base they seem prepared to address. Talk of the cumulative and seemingly inexorable build-up of toxic chemicals in the environment, and that's a different story. Talk of the incremental but seemingly inexorable loss of land to new development, and that's a different story again. Talk of a whole host of natural limits to economic growth as presented in the Millennium Ecosystem Assessment report (MA, 2005), and that's a *completely* different story. You're suddenly, in their eyes, a radical subversive operating beyond the pale of intelligent discourse.

Looking back on 20 years as an 'economic hit man' serving the interests of today's American imperium, John Perkins expresses his anger at the continuing act of collective denial on the part of so many people in that political and business elite:

> *We prefer to believe the myth that thousands of years of human social evolution has finally perfected the ideal economic system, rather than to face the fact that we have merely bought into a false concept and accepted it as gospel. We have convinced ourselves that all economic growth benefits humankind, and that the greater the growth, the more widespread the benefits. Finally, we have persuaded one another that the corollary to this concept is valid and morally just: that people who excel at stoking the fires of economic growth should be exalted, and rewarded, while those born at the fringes are available for exploitation. The real story is that we are living a lie.* (Perkins, 2004)

To observe how the so-called 'progressive left' here in the UK, or the recovering Democrats in the US, find it so easy to go on living that lie, continuing to shy away from the incontrovertible physical reality of the continuing damage we are doing both to the Earth and to a very large number of its people on the grounds that sustainability is an 'unsellable concept', demonstrates a degree of co-option that is sometimes hard to believe. Deep down, they know that to embrace sustainable development as the 'big idea' that it indisputably is would call into question the deeply compromised accommodation they have come to with today's neo-conservative, globalized 'growthism'. It's just that they are a great deal less open about their fear of sustainable development (at this more ideological level) than the American Policy Center, which was quoted earlier on describing sustainable development as 'the enemy' of all self-respecting Americans fighting to keep their guns, property, children and God!

But as Perkins says, it's all too easy to blame such a regrettable state of affairs on anybody but ourselves: on the 'corporatocracy' that has taken so much power and such undeserved wealth unto itself; on our largely corrupted media that live so clearly (and, these days, unapologetically) in the pockets of the corporatocracy without whose advertising revenue they could no longer survive; on some surreal conspiracy of fundamentalist Christians and neo-conservative imperialists who would appear to have taken over the White House; or on a generation of economists who have perpetuated the impossibilism of exponential economic growth, forever, on a finite planet.

This is one of the reasons why I feel increasingly disinclined to give an inch to those who complain about the inadequacy of sustainable development as a mobilizing concept in such a troubled world. Behind all their slick protestations about its un-sellability, there lurks an extraordinarily persistent reluctance to confront the limits to growth head on, to explore what today's chronic lack of biophysical headroom means in practice, right now, for a Spencerian model of brute capitalism that could never in a million years accommodate itself to anything as irrelevant to it as the laws of nature. As Richard Reeves puts it:

> *But the penny hasn't dropped yet. Our cultures, political systems, yardsticks of success have utterly failed to adapt to the new world – one in which economics does not equal or even equate to progress. Governments remain as obsessed as ever with economic productivity and growth. No serious challenge has yet been mounted to the Enlightenment model of rationalist economic growth – a model that served us so well for so long, but is now past its sell-by date.* (Reeves, 2002)

From that perspective, the tactics of environmental and development NGOs around the world must be called into question. The argument developed in this book – that sustainable development provides the only intellectually coherent basis upon which to transform contemporary capitalism – is still not one that commands a huge groundswell of support among the NGO community at large. Indeed, the acute reluctance on the part of tens of millions of activists around the world who are happy to be described as 'environmentalists' even to acknowledge the ideological heartland of what they call 'environmentalism' has become a major problem. If the future of humankind depends upon transforming this particular model of capitalism into one that has a rather better chance of embracing both equity and sustainability (as sketched out in Part II of this book), then it is a massive problem if the vast majority of environmentalists choose to remain semi-detached and so depoliticized that any mention of the bigger picture (namely, a root-and-branch transformation of today's capitalism) sends them running off back to their bird-boxes and gently simmering organic lentils.

I hope it is clear that I am *not* talking about some revolutionary taking to the barricades. The notion of 'capitalism as if the world matters' demands a *reform* agenda, however radical it may appear to some, not a *revolutionary* agenda. But it does require a different level of engagement, both as citizens and as consumers, and a much greater readiness to confront denial at every point, to challenge the slow, soul-destroying descent into displacement consumerism, and to take on today's all too dominant 'I consume therefore I am' mindsets and lifestyles.

EDUCATION FOR SUSTAINABLE DEVELOPMENT

Whichever way one looks at this, education is absolutely at the heart of the transformation process – starting in our own homes, workplaces, leisure centres, professional bodies or institutions, clubs, trade unions and so on. And it's as much a re-education of the heart that we are talking about here as the continuing education of the mind. Janine Benyus is lucky enough to live in one of the most beautiful valleys of one of the most beautiful states of the US (Montana), but her guidance here should have some resonance with all of us, however gritty our suburban or urban confines may be:

> We need to put down our books about nature and actually get into a rain storm, be startled by the deer we startle, climb a tree like a chameleon. It's good for the soul to go where humans do not have a great say about what happens. Between these trips to 'the big outside', we need only open our hearts to the smaller encounters: the smell of old sunlight in a leaf pile, the chrysalis of a butterfly inside our mailbox, the glimpse of that earthworm that helps us grow tomatoes. This literal immersion in nature prepares us for the figurative immersion. This is where we take our reasoned minds and stuff them back into our bodies, realizing that there is no membrane separating us from the natural world. (Benyus, 1997)

In terms of more formal educational systems in our schools, colleges and universities, the battle is already well and truly joined in most Organisation for Economic Co-operative Development (OECD) countries. Two priorities emerge as regards 'education for sustainable development' (ESD) on the formal curriculum: competing for space and funds to find creative and intelligent ways of enabling young people to learn and experience what it means, in practice, to be a citizen of our living Earth; and making sure that *all* places of learning embody that heightened awareness about responsibility to the world and its people in their design, construction, management and engagement with their surrounding communities. If one subscribes to the inspirational rallying cry of the annual World Social Forum in Porto Alegre that 'another world *is* possible', then we have to start to make it possible first and foremost for young people. From the relatively privileged position of the UK, the signs here are hopeful, with a lot of smart NGOs working away at both the curriculum end of things (with a fantastic array of ESD materials now available to schools and colleges) and the practical end of things around the broad concepts of eco-schools, playground regeneration and so on. A lot of schools, colleges and individual teachers are intent on finding the time and resources to make these things happen, and are now doing so within a political system that has finally woken up to the urgency of getting our own educational house in order.

It's hard not to compare that reasonably encouraging outlook with that which confronts ESD activists in the US. Tim Kasser reminds us of the way in which American educational systems have been comprehensively co-opted into promoting crude consumerist values:

> *Society works through various means to indoctrinate children, including the school system, behaviour of parents, mass media and the internet. As the world has become increasingly materialistic, so have our children. Since the mid-1960s, Alexander Astin and his colleagues have been asking over 200,000 first-year college students in the US what is important to them in life. The percentage of students who believe that it is very important or essential to 'develop a meaningful philosophy of life' decreased from over 80 per cent in the late 1960s to around 40 per cent in the late 1990s. At the same time, the percentage who believe that it is very important or essential to be 'very well off financially' has risen from just over 40 per cent to over 70 per cent. Society's value-making machine is an effective one.* (Kasser, 2002)

As we saw in Chapter 12, a major battle in the US right now is to hold the line on teaching some of the scientific building blocks that underpin any real understanding of sustainability, with up to half of all Americans finding creationism a more convincing way of explaining the origins of life on Earth than Darwin's theory of evolution through natural selection. Again, it's easy for Europeans to snicker away about these outlandish intellectual eccentricities notwithstanding the growth of creationist support in the UK and elsewhere. One might justifiably point out that the majority of Christians in the US still see no profound clash between religion and science – and with the theory of evolution in particular, but Suzanne Goldenberg offers a corrective to that kind of complacency:

> *For the conservative forces engaged in the struggle for America's soul, the true battleground is public education, the laboratory of the next generation and an opportunity for the religious Right to effect lasting change on popular culture. Science teachers believe that the genteel questioning of the Intelligent Design movement masks a larger project to discredit an entire body of rational thought.* (Goldenberg, 2005)

Some may feel that I am setting too much store on what is happening in the US in terms of the gradual annexation of the 'commanding heights' of that country (Capitol Hill, government agencies, the educational system and so on) by the religious right. If I am, it is only to challenge the often unspoken assumption on the part of most reasonable, decent people that we are slowly but surely getting these big picture environmental and social justice challenges under control. So let's just keep pushing things along in the same old dogged, incrementalist way that we all feel so comfortable with.

But who knows what kind of backlash we might witness in our own, apparently more reasonable European backyards when some of the worst effects of extreme weather events and climate change converge with the already severe impacts of chronic poverty in Africa and elsewhere? In most European countries, there is already a powerful political backlash against the EU's 'open borders' philosophy, with a growing number of political parties (and not just on the extreme or centre right) calling for much stricter controls on immigration and on the movement of people between countries. Facing up to this threat to political stability in advance, rather than waiting for it to catch us 'unawares', would seem to make a lot of sense.

What is currently happening in The Netherlands may turn out to be the most interesting of these European test cases. The resurgence of a much less tolerant anti-immigration political creed, under the leadership of Pim Fortuyn's party (*Lijst Pim Fortuyn*) until his murder in May 2002, has shocked many people both within and outside this traditionally welcoming and consensus-seeking country. Interestingly, there is a widely accepted school of thought among Dutch people that this historical readiness to play down conflicting social and political interests has much to do with the country's uniquely vulnerable geography. One fifth of the total land mass of The Netherlands is below sea level, some of it by as much as 6 metres, reclaimed from the sea over the centuries. These reclaimed lands are called 'polders' and are protected from the sea by an extraordinarily complex system of dykes, ditches and pumping operations. One of their favourite catchphrases is 'God created the Earth, but we Dutch created The Netherlands' – though they would be unwise to give voice to such a blasphemy in the US!

In *Collapse*, Jared Diamond (2005) was so taken with the effect of this engineering triumph on the populace ('We feel that we're all down in the polders together – it's not the case that rich people live safely up on the tops of the dykes while poor people live down in the polder bottoms below sea level: if the dykes and pumps fail, we'll all drown together, so we've learned through our history that we're all living in the same polder, and that our survival depends on each other's survival') that he used it for the title of his book's final chapter – 'The world as a polder' (Diamond, 2005). In a wonderful expression of 'against the odds' optimism, many people subscribe to that kind of 'polder mindset'. As the threat of ecological meltdown seems to become greater year by year, so, too, does our awareness of our interdependence and the need for unprecedented solidarity if we are to secure any kind of sustainable future. There is no other planet to which we can turn for help or to which we can export our problems.

Or will it go the other way? Take an extreme but not impossible scenario: if the Greenland ice sheet starts to melt at an accelerated rate (as many scientists believe is all but inevitable), and sea level rises of a metre or more become a reality within the next 30 years, the consequences will be more severe for The Netherlands than for any other country in the northern hemisphere. Will that threat inspire a recasting of their traditional solidarity and interdependence, maintaining that special Dutch balance of mutuality and individualism, or usher in a new dark age of intolerance, xenophobia and isolationism?

This goes to the heart of just how resilient our societies are likely to be in the event not just of the occasional discontinuity but of cataclysmic shocks. Very sensibly, there is now growing interest in planning for and funding a wide range of what are called 'adaptation strategies' regarding some of the likely impacts of climate change. But the adaptations pursued are almost invariably *physical*: higher flood defences or levees, 'climate-proofed' buildings, transport infrastructure built to higher engineering specifications, and so on. There would appear to be little interest in what might be described as 'psychological adaptation' either at the level of the individual or of whole communities.

Yet Hurricane Katrina in 2005 offered a deeply disturbing insight into how people might behave in the event of similar disasters. The outbreak of widespread looting, violence and something resembling general anarchy can, on the one hand, be interpreted as a phenomenon specific to New Orleans, a city fractured for many years both by institutionalized racism and by some of the highest levels of murder, gun crime and drug abuse anywhere in the US. On the other hand, it can be seen as a more chilling reflection of how the majority of people are likely to behave in circumstances where law and order have so clearly broken down. Raising the nightmarish prospect of 'decivilization', Timothy Garton Ash (2005) draws precisely that conclusion:

> *Katrina's big lesson is that the crust of civilization on which we tread is always wafer thin. One tremor, and you've fallen through, scratching and gouging for your life like a wild dog. Remove the elementary staples of organized, civilized life – food, shelter, drinkable water, minimal security – and we go back within hours to a Hobbesian state of nature, a war of all against all. Some people, for a time, behave with heroic solidarity; most people, most of the time, engage in a ruthless fight for individual and genetic survival. A few become temporary angels, most revert to being apes.* (Ash, 2005)

MAKING SUSTAINABLE DEVELOPMENT DESIRABLE

I suspect we will come to look back on Hurricane Katrina and subsequent events in New Orleans as one of those defining 'foreshocks' of a much greater climate-induced shock still to come. As a curious aside, Lee Scott (Chief Executive of Wal-Mart) has revealed that it was the horror of Hurricane Katrina and its aftermath that caused him to reflect on the massive damage that Wal-Mart's operations were doing to the environment – and to launch the transformation programme referred to in Chapter 14. Having come to the conclusion that today's unfolding environmental disaster is, in effect, 'Hurricane Katrina in slow motion', he persuaded Wal-Mart's most powerful investors that Wal-Mart would need to move on from being one of the worst performing companies in the world to one of the very best. However, it's too early to judge how effective the Wal-Mart revolution will be – and campaigners have been quick to point out that it isn't really a revolution at all. The basic business model remains intact, and all the social issues (to do with wages, healthcare, working conditions, unionization, impact on local communities and so on) have as yet been ignored.

In a world so profoundly damaged and corrupted by the impacts of 'capital run amok', it's hardly surprising that so many people have come to the conclusion that *any* transformation agenda is misguided, and even self-indulgent; for them, there can be no accommodation with a system that is clearly exacerbating so many of today's symptoms of stress and potential collapse. But the idea that we might transition, abruptly yet peacefully, from where we are now to some non-capitalist system in the near future (it has to be soon, after all, or not at all) seems fantastical. Far more probable is a grim descent into the kind of Hobbesian nightmare that dominated the global coverage of Hurricane Katrina.

For all that it's a compromise, radical and urgent transformation of the worst dysfunctionalities of contemporary capitalism, based on the kind of principles and practice of sustainable capitalism outlined in Parts II and III of this book, must therefore constitute a more realistic strategy than urging people to take to some anti-capitalist barricade. This side of a precipitate descent into a new 'barbarism' (a real possibility, even in Europe, according to Timothy Garton Ash, let alone in much more troubled parts of the world), we still have a time-limited opportunity to make the necessary changes democratically and through effective international consensus.

It's not as if we don't know that these dilemmas will be upon us anyway in the not so distant future. Much of this book has emphasized the *inevitability* of change (indeed, the inevitability of some kind of breakdown), and the *necessity* of adapting our political and economic systems to cope with that change. Even if politicians have not yet internalized the degree to which things must change on account of this broader limits-to-growth analysis (looking at the relationship between humankind and the natural world from a systems perspective), most have now started to internalize the implications of having to cope with climate change – treated in this case as a symptom of the inherent unsustainability of the broader system. But the degree of internalization remains remarkably shallow.

My explanation for this (sketched out in earlier chapters) is that proof of the necessity of change, however incontrovertible it may be, is a necessary but not sufficient condition for change actually to happen. It is not sufficient because at the moment it doesn't come with any compelling explanation of how to make that necessary change *desirable* to the people who are going to have to make the changes! In this respect, our contemporary model of consumer capitalism sets a very stiff challenge indeed. Ideas have to be *sold*; our citizenry (or 'consumertariat', as I think more accurately defines the body politic today) has to be *seduced* into seeing the world in a different way; and increased choice, increased private benefits, and increased material wellbeing would all appear to have to be part of that kind of offer. Is it any wonder that politicians are struggling to find either the language or the incentives to start bringing people into a shared sense of the need for radical change?

It's not that people haven't tried to come up with one or two bridging devices to achieve this 'desirability element'. From time to time, for instance, there are great flurries of excitement about the potential for 'green consumerism' to become a sufficiently significant force to bring about substantial market shifts. And as we saw in Chapter 15, this remains an important element in the mix and continues to grow from year to year. But as a genuinely transformative influence, this kind of approach has always been constrained by the rather dowdy niche psychology that seems to go with it. Efforts to convert that niche into a dynamic, mainstream consumer movement have had very limited success.

Interestingly, that very traditional approach to green consumerism has over the last two or three years been complemented (and, in some cases, overtaken) by what one might describe as 'aspirational green consumerism'. This is exemplified by such phenomena as American Express's 'Red' credit card marketed to the world's rich as a small way of 'offsetting' some of the damage done through mass consumption; by Arnie Schwarzenegger's 'muscular environmentalism', referred to in Chapter 15 ('Successful movements are not built on guilt, they are built on passion; environmentalists have got to stop sounding like prohibitionists at a fraternity party!'); by up-market fashion designers sourcing more of their ephemeral creations from ethical suppliers and donating more of the proceeds to right-on causes; and even by Honda's decision in 2007 to brand its Formula One (F1) racing car as the 'Earth Car', dispensing with all commercial logos and branding to replace them with images of the Earth, with the idea that this should become the focus of a major fundraising drive to raise money for green causes.

Honda probably has as much right as any other car manufacturer to lay claim to some kind of green credibility. The Honda Civic Hybrid recently won the 'Greenest Car of the Year' award, and the company has the most ambitious plans for reducing emissions of CO_2 from both its manufacturing plants and the cars themselves. But as Friends of the Earth was quick to point out, it's not quite as simple as that. Honda's racing cars emit around 1500 grammes of CO_2 per kilometre (almost 9 times as much as an ordinary new car today), which will mount up to a whacking 17 tonnes of CO_2 by the end of this season. Add on all the air miles that Jenson Button and Rubens Barrichello will be totting up on behalf of Honda, and the total rises to 54 tonnes of CO_2 for each driver – *before* taking into account the emissions associated with moving all the rest of the team all around the planet! By any standards, F1 racing will remain a hugely polluting and carbon-intensive sport.

As Kermit the Frog said, 'It ain't easy being green!' But at least Honda is trying, as are the organizers of F1. They're already committed to being 'carbon neutral', and have recently set new targets for the adoption of biofuels by 2008, with a view to achieving 100 per cent biofuels by 2011. The potential for using F1 as 'an innovation laboratory' for research into new engine design and fuel development is enormous. Indeed, many more innovators are now out there cranking away at a much more technocratic approach to demonstrating desirability, emphasizing the potential for a 'green industrial revolution' in terms of massive efficiency gains, reduced material throughput, strict carbon neutrality, industrial symbiosis and so on. This is very much part of the 'opportunity agenda' that I've emphasized time after time throughout this book.

It's also what gets many individual business leaders really fired up, positioning sustainable development in the zone of innovation, creativity and making money rather than as a constraint or regulated burden. It's easy to sneer at Arnie Schwarzenegger's muscular environmentalism, but if cars are the problem, and people (particularly men) show little sign of emancipating themselves from the weird idea that your car is the most powerful expression of your aspirational personality, then sorting out the car's environmental impacts rather than campaigning for a world without cars makes *some* transitional sense. That's what seems to be behind the Lotus Tesla, an electric vehicle that accelerates more quickly than a Ferrari, has a top speed of 130 mph, and boasts twice the fuel efficiency of a Toyota Prius – as telling a riposte as car-lovers could possibly want to the idea that all electric cars look like golf carts and run out of juice by the time you get to the end of your drive.

Despite such heroic design endeavours, however, even this approach has proved to have a limited appeal so far; beyond the geeks and the techies, most people are not interested in the technologies per se, but primarily in the value, service or functionality that any particular technology may give them. That may have something to do with the way in which we articulate that particular technocratic vision. In the US, the campaign behind the New Apollo Project for Energy Independence and Good Jobs (which was set up in 2003) succeeded in getting out of the technocratic, environmental box by appealing directly to US workers whose principal concern is the loss of jobs in manufacturing, particularly to new economies such as India and China. The campaign wasn't billed as an 'environmental' or 'green' project, and tried hard not to present climate change as a problem of pollution to be sorted out by getting after the polluters or making everybody pay more for their oil and gas. The purpose was to stop trying to shock people with horrific scenarios about climate change (the only consequence of which, in the US, is to persuade people to go out and buy an even bigger SUV so that they're properly prepared for the coming meltdown!) and to inspire them, instead, with a vision of economic opportunity, new jobs and energy security. The New Apollo Project would have been paid for by a new $30 billion investment fund, and 'sold' to US voters on the basis that this represented much better value for money than trying to secure energy independence by annexing Iraq or any other oil-rich country. Unfortunately, John Kerry's advisers baulked at the price, and the New Apollo Project remains little more than an ambitious dream.

A third group of seekers after the missing aspect of desirability (apart from the 'green consumers' and the 'eco-technocrats') have been the 'down-shifters' and the advocates of 'voluntary simplicity'. Again, as we saw in Chapter 15, although a surprisingly large number of people sympathize with the ideals and some of the practicalities of leading a simpler, less materialistic lifestyle, there is still too much of the 'giving up' about it, and too much about sacrifice and self-denial – however unfair a representation of the art of living a simpler life that may really be.

For me, all three of those directional trends have enormous importance; they clearly constitute a very significant part of what might be described as 'our sustainable world in waiting'. Many of the details of the new thinking will come through one of these three strands, though *not* in isolation from each other. But over the years, it's been sobering to see how disparaging and dismissive mainstream politicians, commentators and business people can be about these trends, seeing them as marginal to the core tasks of meeting mass consumer demand, or making markets deliver more efficiently, or providing an ever higher material standard of living.

This brings me back to Figures 3.2 and 3.3 in Chapter 3, comparing constantly rising economic growth with levels of perceived happiness or contentment. If anything is ever going to make sustainable development genuinely desirable to very large numbers of people in such a compelling way that they come to embrace the necessity of change, it must surely be the possibility that sustainable development could change their lives by putting personal wellbeing and happiness at the very heart of its 'offer' to citizens. For all sorts of reasons, that is *not* the principal objective of today's economies. Macro-economic goals might include financial stability, fair taxation, low inflation, high levels of employment, a reliable and cost-effective welfare system and, of course, year-on-year increases in exponential economic growth – but absolutely *not* making more people feel happier about themselves and their lives. If happiness has any political salience at all, it is as the assumed by-product of achieving all those other 'grown-up goals'.

THE HIGH PRICE OF MATERIALISM

The conclusions from more than 20 years of psychological and social research are crystal clear. Those people who are driven predominantly by *extrinsic goals* (money, relative status, exhibitionistic affluence and so on) are far more likely to experience a lower quality of life than those driven by *intrinsic goals* (such as good relationships, personal growth, a meaningful job, and being 'at home' in the community and useful to others). By far the most elegant exposition of this research (and its implications) can be found in a helpfully slim book *The*

High Price of Materialism, by Tim Kasser (2002). For me, it turned out to be one of those books that transformed an intuitive gut feeling (in this instance, astonishment that such an important reflection on the relative success or failure of contemporary capitalism was being so comprehensively ignored) into a much better informed realization that this issue lies as much at the heart of sustainable development as the limits-to-growth thesis.

What makes the book so special is that it is very dry, very understated and very cautious in the inferences that the author draws from an extraordinary wealth of empirical and perceptual data – largely drawn from studies in the US. In elaborating upon the familiar but still controversial view that all people have psychological needs just as they have physical needs, Kasser advances the hypothesis that at least four sets of needs are basic to the motivation, functioning and wellbeing of all humans. These are the needs for safety, security and sustenance; for basic competency and self-esteem; for connectedness; and for autonomy and authenticity. Substantial research suggests that people are highly motivated to feel safe and secure, competent, connected to others, and autonomous and authentically engaged in the way that they lead their lives. 'This literature proposes that wellbeing and quality of life increases when these four sets of needs are satisfied, and decreases when they are not', is Kasser's overall conclusion. Yet, it seems to me that the sum of the book's modestly stated conclusions is the equivalent of political dynamite:

- *People who are highly focused on materialistic values have lower personal wellbeing and psychological health than those who believe that materialistic pursuits are relatively unimportant.*
- *When needs for security, safety and sustenance are not fully satisfied, people place a strong focus on materialistic values and desires. Insecurity also makes it likely that people will pursue materialistic aims, as both inner predispositions and external consumer culture suggest that resources can purchase security.*
- *Children who feel insecure about themselves may be likely to look for approval from other people in order to feel better about themselves. Because they are exposed to frequent messages in society glorifying image, fame and wealth, they may strongly pursue materialistic aspirations as a way to obtain that approval.*
- *When women have less opportunity to become educated or to control their reproduction, they are likely to feel less secure about their abilities to fend for themselves and, thus, are more materialistic in the desires they have for mates.*
- *Beyond the point of providing for food, shelter and safety, increases in wealth do little to improve people's wellbeing and happiness.*
- *People with a strong materialistic orientation are likely to watch a lot of television, compare themselves unfavourably with people*

whom they see on television, be dissatisfied with their standard of living, and have low life satisfaction.

- *People who hold materialistic aims as central to their values have shorter, more conflicting relationships with friends and lovers, and feel alienated and disconnected from others in society.*
- *Materialistic values of wealth, status and image work against close interpersonal relationships and connection to others – thus, materialistic values lead people to 'invest' less in their relationships and in their communities.*
- *Materialistic values are associated with making more anti-social and self-centred decisions involving getting ahead rather than cooperating.*
- *Materialistic values are associated with low interest in environmental and ecological issues.*
- *People believe in materialism because society is so materialistic, and society is so materialistic because many people believe that materialistic pursuits are a path to happiness.* (Kasser, 2002)

How else can we interpret findings of this kind (which are backed by literally dozens of studies in many different countries going back over many years) than to conclude quite simply that the kind of materialism driven on by our contemporary consumer capitalism is leaving people unfulfilled and is killing the human spirit even as it degrades and despoils the natural world? This is, indeed, the dark side of the American dream, as the richest nation on Earth is traumatized by an epidemic of psychological disorders and dysfunctionalities. And there is little reason to suppose that European countries will be far behind.

It must, in part, have been this realization that persuaded Richard Layard to leave behind the safe but often irrelevant confines of conventional economics, and recommend a wholesale transformation in the way in which economists set about their trade. In *Happiness* (Layard, 2005), he exhorts his professional colleagues to reconnect with the real world by looking at how and why people really behave the way they do, and to be far more open to the insights of psychology, neuroscience, sociology and philosophy – 'to learn the lessons of a new science'. In that regard, he still believes that Jeremy Bentham has more to teach us about a new definition of progress for the 21st century than any other contemporary thinker:

> *Create all the happiness you are able to create: remove all the misery you are able to remove. Every day will allow you to add something to the pleasure of others or to diminish something of their pains. And for every grain of enjoyment you sow in the bosom of another, you shall find a harvest in your own bosom; while every sorrow which you pluck out from the thoughts and feelings of a fellow creature shall be replaced by beautiful peace and joy in the sanctuary of your soul.* (Bentham, An

Introduction to the Principles of Morals and Legislation, 1789, cited in Layard, 2005)

Many economists have sought to interpret those insights for their own age, but since economic growth became the undisputed (though entirely inappropriate) proxy for all other measures of social progress, it's been increasingly difficult to bring forward compelling alternatives to such a stultifying orthodoxy. As we saw in Chapter 4, the Chilean economist Manfred Max Neef has devoted his entire life to demonstrating to politicians four simple truths: first, that *all* individuals, regardless of their social status, culture, religion or expectations, have the same *fundamental* human needs, which he defines as subsistence, protection, understanding, affection, participation, leisure, creativeness, identity and freedom; second, that those fundamental needs can be satisfied in different, culturally-specific ways at different times, and it is the task of governments to work with its wealth creators and citizens to develop the optimal policy framework to fashion the most appropriate 'satisfiers' for meeting those needs at any time; third, that increases in per capita consumption do not, *of themselves*, act as a genuine satisfier of those needs, in that the satisfaction derived from any act of consumption can often be very shallow and short-lived; and fourth, that any economy geared exclusively to promoting increases in per capita consumption as a way of meeting those needs (however forlorn an endeavour that may be) may well end up undermining the very conditions which *would* permit those needs to be met – social cohesion, for example, or personal integrity, secure communities, high levels of participation in civic processes and so on.

In policy terms, that throws up some interesting challenges for our politicians. If we are to rededicate our society to the pursuit of happiness rather than the goals of growth, efficiency and competitiveness, then we will need to be monitoring people's wellbeing and happiness just as closely as we measure income and Gross Domestic Product. We should be focusing far more on the problems of mental health; we should be actively investing in activities that promote community life and build social capital; we should eliminate high unemployment altogether; we should rethink our education system – 'we should teach the systematic practice of empathy and the desire to serve others', in Layard's words – and be less coy about the importance of moral education; we should get real about family-friendly practices at work; and we should ban all advertising to children!

As I made clear in Chapter 2, one of the principal differences between sustainable development and conventional environmentalism is that sustainable development is as much about the wellbeing of the human species as about the wellbeing of the natural world. The idea of an environmental organization devoting as much time and effort to prevent the erosion of the human spirit as it does to prevent the erosion of our physical life-support systems is all but unthinkable. For sustainable development activists, on the other hand, not to be as concerned about the impacts of unsustainable capitalism upon the individual, the community and society at large as about those upon the natural world would represent a betrayal of what sustainable development really stands for.

THE POLITICS OF INTERDEPENDENCE

So, is this where the progressive politics of the 21st century will begin to redefine itself: at the interface between the non-negotiable *necessity* of profound and radical change in the face of climate change and environmental collapse, and the *desirability* of putting the physical, psychological and spiritual wellbeing of people absolutely at the heart of our political and economic systems? And will the gradual realization of total interdependence (upon each other and upon the Earth's life-support systems) lead to a reconfiguring of the progressive forces in society to reshape that political landscape? Will it transform the way in which we use capitalism to help meet our *real* needs for security, happiness, self-esteem and connectedness, rather than remain enslaved to today's abhorrent, neo-conservative travesty of capitalism that brings misery for the majority of humankind and mayhem for the planet?

This awareness of *interdependence* (between ourselves and the natural world) is undoubtedly the most powerful driver of psychological change available to us today – the necessary stimulus to engage those big brains of ours (to return to the challenge of Richard Dawkins) to overcome our selfish genes. It remains the deepest disappointment of my life as a political activist to see how alien an insight this still is to those on the progressive or centre left in the UK or in the Democratic Party in the US. How is it that they have become so alienated from the natural world that there is just no deeper connection within them at all?

Reluctantly, I've come to the conclusion that the progressive left – as it chooses to define itself today – has simply run out of relevance on two or three counts. First, so preoccupied has it been with the challenges of material poverty and inequity that it simply hasn't noticed the simultaneous impoverishment of the human spirit. Its sole prescription for any social ill is to press down ever harder on the pedal of economic growth to generate enough tax revenues to chuck yet more money at the problems caused by the economic model itself. You have only to look at the inherent irrationality (let alone unsustainability) of most healthcare systems in the developed world, with demand for illness services of every conceivable kind increasing every year, even as the macro-economic policies that provide the cash to pay for those services contribute *directly* and massively to worsening patterns of physical and mental ill health. And what does the progressive left offer here in the UK in response to that structural absurdity? Yet more money to hurl into the black hole, and increased consumer choice in the range of illness services available to us!

Second, as we saw in Chapter 12, governments that may still claim to represent something akin to social democracy (as ours does here in the UK) have been so fundamentally co-opted by private sector interests as to invalidate their ability to judge what 'public value' really means. New Labour has lost this particular plot on so many occasions that even the latest and perhaps most egregious example of co-option (in the shape of the decision to encourage the growth of new casinos across the UK) is no longer seen as the startling betrayal of public interest that it really is. Between 2001 and 2005, turnover from all forms of gambling in the UK increased from £2 billion to £50 billion, much of it on-line. But this 'economic success story', which the gambling industry has been keen to press home on government ministers, has another, darker side. Charities dealing with the social fall-out from gambling reckon that there are at least 375,000 gambling addicts in the UK at the moment. This impacts on all social classes, but poorer families often suffer most severely, especially in terms of the impacts on children. New casinos will exacerbate all these problems. Ministers know this, and know that the Government's commitment to eliminating child poverty will therefore be materially affected by this. But still the decision stands, with a few pathetic words from the Culture Minister about enforcing 'high standards of social responsibility in all casinos', and the Chancellor introducing a tax of 50 per cent on casino takings and 15 per cent on on-line gambling – paving the way for the inevitable 'fiscal dependency' this will create as the Government itself becomes addicted to the addiction of hundreds of thousands of gamblers.

Third, the progressive left has largely failed to understand the environmental agenda, and continues to see it as a second-order priority of little direct interest to them or the people whom they claim to represent. This is a more complicated charge, as I suspect that the responsibility for this lies as much with today's environmental movements as with the progressive left. By sticking to their single issues, their narrow protectionist agenda, their nay-saying tactics, and their (explicit or implicit) prioritizing of the interests of the natural world over those of the disenfranchised and disadvantaged, many environmentalists have hardly endeared themselves to those whose principal concerns are social justice and increased equity. One area where environmentalists and the progressive left are 'as one', as we saw in Chapter 5, is in their out-and-out refusal even to discuss the importance of population. While recognizing the political and religious sensitivities associated with population issues, it's hard to explain this continuing conspiracy of silence. Whichever way you look at it, managing climate change, declining resources and collapsing ecosystem services is going to be a great deal harder for 9 billion people than it would be for 8 billion, 7 billion or even 6 billion. While many environmentalists wax eloquent about the impending horrors of global oil production peaking within the next decade, or about runaway climate change, the next logical step (in terms of thinking through the demographic implications) is constantly shied away from. But just try answering this one question: how are we going to feed 9 billion people, in the middle of this century, when the agricultural systems on which most nations depend are no longer underpinned by cheap and easily available fossil fuels?

This silence is all the more strange given that the evidence demonstrates incontrovertibly that investment in enlightened family planning (with the focus on education and better healthcare for girls and women, combined with easy access to safe and reliable contraception) is not just *the* most effective way of reducing average fertility, but supportive of every other economic and social aspiration that developing countries may have. Bizarrely, by turning their back on this available synergy, environmentalists and the progressive left have chosen to align themselves in practice with the Bush Administration which has so disastrously cut back on almost all funding for family planning – even in those countries that are crying out for financial support.

Nor should this focus on population be restricted to the developing world. It's important that OECD countries should be seeking actively to manage down their own populations, as has already been happening in several European countries. But not in the UK. Figures from the Office of National Statistics earlier this year show that there are now more than 60 million people in the UK, with forecasts showing continuing growth for several decades to come. And there is still significant growth, year on year, in the population of the US, though this critical issue is nowhere to be seen on the mainstream environmental agenda in the US today.

In 'Is environmentalism dead?', a speech given at The Commonwealth Club in San Francisco, Adam Werbach (2004) calls for a total overhaul of traditional environmentalism in the US, a stepping away from the single-issue 'problem categories' that have characterized environmental campaigning in the US for more than 30 years – as embodied, for example, in the Clean Air Act and the Endangered Species Act. He exhorts US environmentalists to throw in their lot with a broader coalition of progressive causes, all of which have been as comprehensively routed by the religious right and the neo-conservatives as environmentalism has been. 'I'm done calling myself an environmentalist', he declares:

> *For 30 years, American liberals have defined themselves according to a set of problem-categories that divide us, whether they be racial, gender, economic or environmental. We have spent far less time defining ourselves according to the values that unite us, such as shared prosperity, progress, interdependence, fairness, ecological restoration and equality. We can no longer afford the laundry list of 'isms' to define and divide our world and ourselves.* (Werbach, 2004)

From this side of the Atlantic, it's interesting that Werbach's stirring polemic makes not one single mention of either sustainable development or capitalism itself – in its current or any other manifestation. Sustainable development just doesn't do it for most people in the US, and it plays little part in the current debate about reconfiguring progressive politics. Nonetheless, the 'coalition of progressive causes' that Werbach talks about (unavoidably triggering a nostalgic resonance with

Jesse Jackson's erstwhile 'Rainbow Coalition') would bring together a combination of environmental, fair trade, development, social justice and human rights organizations that looks pretty much like sustainable development to me. The lack of any reference to capitalism is also not that surprising. US politics does not yet allow for much subtlety about different expressions of capitalism; if you criticize capitalism, you're a communist. It's pretty much as simple as that. The suggestion of some kind of 'root-and-branch transformation of contemporary capitalism' would condemn one to political oblivion.

This is not the case in Europe, where there is already a lively debate about the most appropriate way of harnessing the dynamism of capitalist systems to help secure central social and economic objectives – and substantial disagreement among EU members, old and new. However, it is a debate that most environmentalists have been slow to engage in substantively for fear of undermining their credibility as technical and policy experts, as well as their lobbying access to the EU Commission and the EU Parliament. There are, indeed, significant risks entailed in taking on such politicized tasks, and given that European environmentalists do not currently see themselves as having quite the endangered status that their US counterparts would appear to see themselves as having, I suspect there will be little appetite for setting out to 'fix something' that isn't actually perceived to be broken.

Yet you have to wonder about this. Those who are pushing the EU's Lisbon Agenda on competitiveness and liberalization are not that different from the less rabid wing of the neo-conservatives in the US. European environmentalists might have been more successful than their US counterparts in holding their ground on core environmental regulations and standards; but this has demanded a growing investment in defensive campaigning and lobbying to prevent the constantly threatened erosion of that ground. Public support is both shallow and fickle. In real terms, it can hardly be claimed that environmentalists are having much success in addressing new environmental challenges – on aviation or other transport issues, for instance, or on the build-up of toxins in the environment. The measures taken, to date, to address climate change are almost universally acknowledged to be hopelessly inadequate.

So, while we bang on about the burning *necessity* of urgent and comprehensive change, electorates remain unmoved by this rhetoric and apprehensive about the implications of any such change for their own quality of life. Although they know our current system of capitalism is seriously flawed, there is little recognition that it is completely unsustainable. There's little deep awareness of what interdependence really means – even down in the Dutch polders. John Muir's observation that 'when we try to pick out anything by itself, we find it hitched to everything else in the universe' means little if anything in today's culture of instant gratification and atomized self-indulgence. Meanwhile, as catalogued at length in this final chapter, few people in the rich world seem to be getting any happier – and neither the environmental movement nor the progressive left have anything much to say about that extraordinary state of affairs. The new European Constitution fails to find space either for any wording that reflects real awareness of the biophysical limits to future growth, or any equivalent to those stirring words in the US Declaration of Independence: 'We hold these truths to be self-evident, that all men are created equal, that they are endowed by their Creator with certain unalienable Rights, that among these are Life, Liberty and the pursuit of Happiness.'

I have set out in this book to demonstrate that the bipolar challenges of, on the one hand, the biophysical limits to growth and, on the other, of the terrible damage being done to the human spirit through the pursuit of unbridled materialism, will compel a profound transformation of contemporary capitalism – and sooner rather than later if we want to avoid dramatic social and economic disruption. Hence this book has advocated the idea of capitalism as if the world matters: an evolved, intelligent and elegant form of capitalism that puts the Earth at its very centre (as our one and only world) and ensures that all people are its beneficiaries in recognition of our unavoidable interdependence.

And I have argued, perhaps more controversially, that it is only sustainable development that can provide both the intellectual foundations and the operational pragmatism upon which to base such a transformation. This is why sustainable development remains for me the only seriously 'big idea' that can bear the weight of that challenge, and why the core values that underpin sustainable development – interdependence, empathy, equity, personal responsibility and intergenerational justice – are the only foundation upon which any viable vision of a better world can possibly be constructed.

REFERENCES

Ash, T. G. (2005) 'It always lies below', *Guardian*, 8 September

Benyus, J. (1997) *Biomimicry: Innovation Inspired by Nature*, Quill, William Morrow, New York

Darwin, C. (1859) *On the Origin of Species by Means of Natural Selection, or the Preservation of Favoured Races in the Struggle for Life*, John Murray, London

Dawkins, R. (2002) 'Our big brains can overcome our selfish genes', *Independent*, 2 September

Diamond, J. (2005) *Collapse: How Societies Choose to Fail or Succeed*, Allen Lane, London

Goldenberg, S. (2005) 'Religious right fights science for the heart of America', *Guardian*, 7 February

Kasser, T. (2002) *The High Price of Materialism*, MIT Press, Cambridge, MA

Layard, R. (2005) *Happiness*, Allen Lane, London

MA (2005) *Ecosystems and Human Well-being: Opportunities and Challenges for Business and Industry*, the fourth Millennium Ecosystem Assessment report, available at www.millenniumassessment.org

Perkins, J. (2004) *Confessions of an Economic Hit Man*, Berrett-Koehler, San Francisco, CA

Reeves, R. (2002) 'The sun sets on the enlightenment', *RSA Journal*, December

Werbach, A. (2004) 'Is environmentalism dead?', speech at The Commonwealth Club, San Francisco, 8 December. Text available at www.grist.org/news/maindish/2005/01/13/werbach-reprint

Young, S. (2003) *Moral Capitalism: Reconciling Private Interest with the Public Good*, Berrett-Koehler, San Francisco, CA

Index